Stories of Change and Sustainability in the Arctic Regions

This book presents stories of sustainability from communities in circumpolar regions as they grapple with environmental, economic and societal changes and challenges.

Polar regions are changing rapidly. These changes will dramatically effect ecosystems, economy, people, communities and their interdependencies. Given this, the stories being told about lives and livelihood development are changing also. This book is the first of its kind to curate stories about opportunity and responsibility, tensions and contradictions, un/ethical action, resilience, adaptability and sustainability, all within the shifting geopolitics of the north. The book looks at change and sustainability through multidisciplinary and empirically based work, drawing on case studies from Norway, Sweden, Alaska, Canada, Finland and Northwest Russia, with a notable focus on indigenous peoples. Chapters touch on topics as wide ranging as reindeer herding, mental health, climate change, land-use conflicts and sustainable business. The volume asks whose voices are being heard, who benefits, how particular changes affect people's sense of community and longstanding and cherished values plus livelihood practices and what are the environmental, economic and social impacts of contemporary and future oriented changes with regard to issues of sustainability?

This volume will be of great interest to students and scholars of sustainability studies, sustainable development, environmental sociology, indigenous studies and environmental anthropology.

Rita Sørly is an Associate Professor in Social Work at UiT The Arctic University of Norway and a Senior Researcher at the Norwegian Research Centre (NORCE), Norway.

Tony Ghaye is a Professor at Loughborough University in London, UK.

Bård Kårtveit is a Senior Researcher in the Department for Regional Development at the Norwegian Research Centre (NORCE), Norway.

Routledge Studies in Sustainability

Sustainability Governance and Hierarchy
Philippe Hamman

Energy, Environmental and Economic Sustainability in East Asia
Policies and Institutional Reforms
Edited by Soocheol Lee, Hector Pollitt and Kiyoshi Fujikawa

Green Skills Research in South Africa
Models, Cases and Methods
Eureta Rosenberg, Presha Ramsarup and Heila Lotz-Sisitka

Sustainability and the Automobile Industry in Asia
Policy and Governance
Edited by Aki Suwa and Masahiko Iguchi

Smart Green World?
Making Digitalization Work for Sustainability
Steffen Lange and Tilman Santarius

Contesting Hydropower in the Brazilian Amazon
Ed Atkins

Circular Cities
A Revolution in Urban Sustainability
Jo Williams

Stories of Change and Sustainability in the Arctic Regions
The Interdependence of Local and Global
Edited by Rita Sørly, Tony Ghaye and Bård Kårtveit

For more information on this series, please visit: www.routledge.com/Routledge-Studies-in-Sustainability/book-series/RSSTY

Stories of Change and Sustainability in the Arctic Regions
The Interdependence of Local and Global

Edited by Rita Sørly, Tony Ghaye and
Bård Kårtveit

LONDON AND NEW YORK

First published 2022
by Routledge
2 Park Square, Milton Park, Abingdon, Oxon OX14 4RN

and by Routledge
605 Third Avenue, New York, NY 10158

Routledge is an imprint of the Taylor & Francis Group, an informa business

© 2022 selection and editorial matter, Rita Sørly, Tony Ghaye and Bård Kårtveit; individual chapters, the contributors

The right of Rita Sørly, Tony Ghaye and Bård Kårtveit to be identified as the authors of the editorial material, and of the authors for their individual chapters, has been asserted in accordance with sections 77 and 78 of the Copyright, Designs and Patents Act 1988.

All rights reserved. No part of this book may be reprinted or reproduced or utilized in any form or by any electronic, mechanical, or other means, now known or hereafter invented, including photocopying and recording, or in any information storage or retrieval system, without permission in writing from the publishers.

Trademark notice: Product or corporate names may be trademarks or registered trademarks, and are used only for identification and explanation without intent to infringe.

British Library Cataloguing-in-Publication Data
A catalogue record for this book is available from the British Library

Library of Congress Cataloging-in-Publication Data
Names: Sørly, Rita, editor. | Ghaye, Tony, editor. | Kårtveit, Bård Helge, editor.
Title: Stories of change and sustainability in the Arctic regions : the interdependence of local and global / edited by Rita Sørly, Tony Ghaye and Bård Kårtveit.
Description: Abingdon, Oxon ; New York, NY : Routledge, 2022. | Series: Routledge studies in sustainability | Includes bibliographical references and index.
Identifiers: LCCN 2021024298 (print) | LCCN 2021024299 (ebook) | ISBN 9780367632847 (hardback) | ISBN 9780367632854 (paperback) | ISBN 9781003118633 (ebook)
Subjects: LCSH: Sustainable development–Arctic regions. | Economic development–Arctic regions. | Arctic regions–Economic conditions.
Classification: LCC HC740.E5 S76 2022 (print) | LCC HC740.E5 (ebook) | DDC 338.9/2709113–dc23
LC record available at https://lccn.loc.gov/2021024298
LC ebook record available at https://lccn.loc.gov/2021024299

ISBN: 978-0-367-63284-7 (hbk)
ISBN: 978-0-367-63285-4 (pbk)
ISBN: 978-1-003-11863-3 (ebk)

DOI: 10.4324/9781003118633

Typeset in Goudy
by KnowledgeWorks Global Ltd.

Contents

List of figures	vii
List of tables	ix
List of contributors	x

Introduction: Being in-between stories   1
TONY GHAYE, RITA SØRLY, AND BÅRD KÅRTVEIT

1 **Concerned Arctic peoples: Characteristics of conversations-that-matter**   16
TONY GHAYE

2 **Disappearing flexibility: The story of Gielas reindeer herding district**   41
JAN ÅGE RISETH

3 **Stories transmitted through art for the revitalization and decolonization of the Arctic**   57
TIMO JOKELA AND MARIA HUHMARNIEMI

4 **Mental health research in an Arctic Indigenous context: The presence of silent dominant narratives**   72
RITA SØRLY, VÅR MATHISEN, AND VIGDIS NYGAARD

5 **Stories of empowerment, resilience and healing: A participatory research project with two Indigenous communities in Québec**   88
LILIANA GOMEZ CARDONA, KRISTYN BROWN, MARY MCCOMBER, ECHO PARENT-RACINE, OUTI LINNARANTA

vi *Contents*

6 **Learning through lived experiences: A structural narrative analysis of one person's journey of recovery and implications for peer support services** 111
RITA SØRLY, TONY GHAYE, AND WIBECKE ÅRST

7 **The decline and changes in the tundra today: The nature of state systems and services as a critical factor in the condition of minority indigenous peoples in Russia** 126
ZOIA VYLKA RAVNA

8 **Overcoming isolation in the Arctic during COVID-19 times through new ways of co-writing research** 143
RITA SØRLY, BÅRD KÅRTVEIT, VIGDIS NYGAARD, ANNE KATRINE NORMANN, LUDMILA IVANOVA, SVETLANA BRITVINA & LARISSA RIABOVA

9 **Green colonialism: The story of wind power in Sápmi** 157
BÅRD KÅRTVEIT

10 **Transforming Arctic municipalities: The winding road to low-emission communities** 178
NILS AARSÆTHER AND HEGE WESTSKOG

11 **The quest for fresh vegetables: Stories about the future of Arctic farming** 193
DORIS FRIEDRICH

12 **Greening discourses of the Nordic Arctic region: The region as vulnerable, late bloomer or the arena of possibilities?** 218
TROND NILSEN AND JUKKA TERÄS

Reflections: What can we create together? 232
TONY GHAYE, RITA SØRLY, BÅRD KÅRTVEIT

Index 235

Figures

0.1	Three generic lenses (frames) through which change and sustainability in the Arctic may be viewed.	2
0.2	The book's generative questions.	4
0.3	Longyear river, Svalbard – a 'braided' Arctic river.	6
0.4	The 'braided' metaphor of change and sustainability in the Arctic.	7
1.1	The relationships between "mattering"' and four conceptions of sustainability.	24
1.2	Situating doubt alongside the characteristics of sustainability conversations-that-matter.	28
1.3	Wibecke a story-teller. Photo: Marie Louise Somby	35
2.1	Gielas. Spring pastures, collecting and migration zones (adapted from Riseth et al., 2021).	48
2.2	Gielas. Season pastures. Summer to winter (adapted from Riseth et al., 2021).	49
2.3	Screenshot of MySheep GPS plot of the movements of a female reindeer 11–19.01.2020. By permission of Gielas reindeer pasture district.	50
3.1	Mapping the visual references for community-based art using museums archives, place-specific investigations, narratives and sketching. Collage and photos: Timo Jokela.	61
3.2	a and b. Working with community to build up a memorial The Story of Kirkkokuusikko. Photos: Timo Jokela.	63
3.3	Celebration of the monument was designed as a performative and communal event. Photo: Timo Jokela.	64
4.1	The herd. Photo: Rita Sørly.	73
4.2	The girl by the reindeer fences. Photo: Rita Sørly.	77
4.3	Food supply for the coming year. Photo: Rita Sørly.	79
6.1	Wibecke having a coffee. Photo: Marie Louise Somby.	113
6.2	Wibecke at work. Photo: Marie Louise Somby.	119
7.1	Pedavane and her friend. Photo: Zoia Ravna.	129
7.2	Map of the Nenets territories.	130

viii *Figures*

7.3   The caravan of reindeer http://lelang.ru/english/films/forrest-gamp-na-anglijskom-yazyke-s-subtitrami/appears in the following order: Nerdena (in front), Muzandana (leading), Pudana (the last). (Interview 17). Photo: Zoia Ravna.   135

7.4   Women are walking back to the camp with firewood they have gathered. Photo: Zoia Vylka Ravna.   137

8.1   The Arctic. Source: Arctic centre, University of Lapland.   145

8.2   Meeting on Zoom. Photo: Vigdis Nygaard.   147

9.1   Imagined view of Davvi Wind Farm as seen from Rásttigáisá.   162

9.2   View to Rásttigáisá (1066 m above sea level), regarded by many Sámi as a sacred mountain.   169

10.1   Parking in front of the main grocery store in Lyngen.   188

10.2   Skjervøy.   189

11.1   View of one of Calypso Farm's fields, 2020. Photo: Calypso Farm.   198

11.2   Addie Willsrud harvesting beets during the 2020 season. Photo: Calypso Farm.   201

11.3   Research in the greenhouse centred on what fertilizer could best enhance locally inert soil and which plants were most productive. Each bed contained a different soil mixture, but the same type of plants. Photo: Aqqiumavvik society.   207

11.4   Plants were tended daily by a team of youth researchers. They also monitored aspects of heat, humidity and soil moisture. Photo: Aqqiumavvik society.   208

11.5   Growth in each bed was monitored, measured and logged to help determine the most effective soil combinations and the types of seeds that resulted in the biggest yield. Photo: Aqqiumavvik society.   209

Tables

1.1	Different kinds of space for sustainability conversations.	31
2.1	Summary of cause–impact–effect chains in Gielas RPD	49
5.1	Phases of the thematic analysis	95
5.2	Stories of healing, resilience and empowerment among Kanien'kehá:ka and Inuit	99

Contributors

Nils Aarsæther, Dr. philos. (political science/sociology). Senior researcher 2018–2020 at Norce Research, Regional Development Research Group and CASS. Research interests: Local democracy, municipal innovation activities and municipal planning in the face of climate policy. During 1993–2017, professor in Community Planning at the University of Tromsø.

Wibecke Årst is a peer recovery worker and the manager of "Brukerbasen". This is a user-driven rehabilitation service for people struggling with mental health and/or substance abuse. The service is situated in Tromsø, Norway.

Svetlana Britvina is a Senior researcher at the Luzin Institute for Economic Studies of the Kola Science Centre of the Russian Academy of Sciences in Apatity, Murmansk region, Russia. She holds a PhD in Economics. Her research interests are social sustainability, well-being and community studies in the Arctic.

Kristyn Kawennano:ron Brown is a Kanien'kehá:ka from Kahnawake Mohawk Territory. She has been a registered nurse for several years working within her community hospital. She has broad experience in the treatment of addictions, detox and mental health among Indigenous people from different nations in Quebec. She worked as a research assistant for the project of cultural adaptation of a mental health assessment and support tool with Douglas research team.

Liliana Gomez Cardona, PhD, in anthropology, and I am currently a Postdoctoral Candidate and researcher at the Douglas Mental Health Center, affiliated to McGill University. During my Postdoctoral Fellowship, I am focusing on the development and adaptation of culturally appropriate and safe tools for Indigenous populations in Quebec. These tools include mental health assessments and interventions that aim to empower and promote individual, community and culture-based resilience resources.

Doris Friedrich is a Senior Fellow at the Arctic Institute and a PhD student at the Department of Social and Cultural Anthropology of the University of Vienna. Her research interests include human-environment relations and environmental issues, with a focus on the Arctic. She holds a master's degree

(Mag.) in international business from the Vienna University of Economics and Business (WU) and a M.Sc. in global politics from the London School of Economics and Political Science (LSE). Friedrich is the secretary of the Vienna-based Working Group Arctic and Subarctic and co-editor of the volume More Than "Nature".

Tony Ghaye is a community-based researcher, deep into sustainable action for positive social change, human rights elevation & wellbeing. He works to promote social justice, lessen disadvantage and challenge prejudice. In 2021, he was formally honored by the GLOBAL PEACE organization for his work which contributed to 100 Global Peace Inter-Generational Dialogues (IGDs).

Tony is regarded as the world's top Participatory & Appreciative Action Researcher (PAAR), as a world class facilitator & a global leader in strength-based leadership development. He has written or edited 15 academic books and 135 scientific papers, many exploring how our "best self" is a blend of achievement, growth, support and continuous learning. Currently, Tony leads the Global Human Rights and Wellbeing project called U MATTER project.

Dr. Maria Huhmarniemi is an artist and a teacher in the University of Lapland, Faculty of Art and Design. In her work as a visual artist, she engages with questions concerning the North and environmental issues such as the relationship between people and nature and environmental responsibility. She does socially and environmentally engaged art. As a researcher, she is interested in political contemporary art and education for sustainability through art.

Ludmila Ivanova, Senior researcher at the Luzin Institute for Economic Studies of the Kola Science Centre of the Russian Academy of Sciences in Apatity, Murmansk region, Russia. She holds a PhD in Economics. Her research interest is nature resource management in the North and the Arctic.

Timo Jokela is a Professor of Art Education in the University of Lapland in Finland. He is former dean of the Faculty of Art and Design (2009–2017). Currently, he is a lead of University of Arctic's thematic network on Arctic Sustainable Arts and Design (ASAD). Jokela has been responsible for several international and regional development and research projects in the field of art and design. His theoretical studies, artistic activities and art-based action research development projects focuses on relationship between northern cultures, art and nature.

Bård Kårtveit, is a Senior Researcher at NORCE. He holds a PhD in Social Anthropology, and has worked extensively on minority-majority relations in the Middle East, with a focus on history, religion, identity and conflict over land narratives and resources in Palestine and in Egypt.

Since early 2018 he has worked as a researcher at NORCE with a focus on Arctic Norway but following up on themes he worked on in other parts of the world. In particular, he has focused on challenges facing indigenous

xii *Contributors*

Sami communities and on conflicts over natural resources, land use and historical narratives in Arctic Norway. Tension between conflicting notions of sustainability is a central concern in his research.

Larissa Riabova is Research Director at the Luzin Institute for Economic Studies of the Kola Science Centre of the Russian Academy of Sciences in Apatity, Murmansk region, Russia. She holds a PhD in Economics. Her research interests are social sustainability, social policy, well-being and life quality and community studies in the Arctic. She studies mining, forestry and fishery-based Arctic communities, and impacts of globalization and neoliberal policies on these communities. Riabova is a member of editorial board of the Russian academic journal The North and the Market, and she is a co-editor of the international academic journal "Barents Studies: Peoples, Economies and Politics".

Outi Linnaranta is an adjunct professor of psychiatry at the McGill University, QC, Canada, and medical director at the Finnish Institute for Health and Welfare, Mental Health Unit, Finland. During the five years she spent in Canada as an associate professor of psychiatry, she became the director of a project to improve quality of psychiatric care and soon realized the importance of participatory work. During the past years, she has sought innovative, often technology-assisted solutions to improve access to treatment. After returning to Finland in 2021, she has been leading implementation of a National Mental Health Policy Program in Finland.

Vår Mathisen, PhD, in mental health work, associate professor at the Faculty of Health Sciences, Department of Health and Care Sciences, UiT Norway's Arctic University. The research area is substance abuse and mental health protection, user participation and co-research. I have worked for many years in the field of mental health care and substance abuse with young people, adults and families as an occupational therapist.

Mary Kawennarò:oks McComber is Tsi Niionkwarihò:ten Program Coordinator at the Kahnawake Shakotiia'takehnhas Community Services

Trond Nilsen, PhD, work as an associate professor at the Inland Norway University of Applied Science and a Senior Researcher at NORCE. Nilsens publish international papers within the field of regional development, innovation in services and global production networks.

Anne Katrine Normann (Dr. polit, political geography, NORCE) is a project manager at Center for the Ocean and the Arctic, based in Tromsø, Norway. Dr Normann has worked in several research project in collaboration with Russian researchers, with a special focus on risk perception and risk communication related to environmental hazardous substances, Arctic shipping and marine plastic littering in the Arctic. Normann has worked with the research team from Kola Research Center on several project.

Contributors xiii

Vigdis Nygaard is a political scientist at NORCE in Alta, Norway. Her research interests are regional development in the North and how local and Sami communities are affected by global policies and resource extraction industries. Nygaard has long experiences in cross-border cooperation between Norway and Russia in the fields of health and wellbeing, business cooperation, forestry management and mining industry.

Echo Parent-Racine is a licensed clinical social worker practicing in the territory of Tiohtià:ke/Montréal and is of mixed background of Kanien'kehá:ka Nation and Quebecois ancestry. She possesses a graduate and undergraduate degree in social work from McGill University. She has been involved with research projects affiliated with the Douglas Institute and McGill University to support Inuit, First Nations and Métis peoples living in an urban setting. She takes a special interest in gender and colonialization, federally unrecognized indigenous communities of urban status and non-status Métis, Inuit and First Nations Identities.

Jan Åge Riseth holds an MSc in Nature Management and a PhD in resource economics. He is a Research Professor at NORCE and a Judge at Finnmark Land Tribunal. His main research interest is the natural and societal conditions for sustainability in Sámi reindeer husbandry including management, resource use, modernization, climate change, traditional knowledge, impact analyses and planning.

Zoia Vylka Ravna is a Nenets-born anthropologist and educator. She has a PhD in cultural studies from the Arctic University of Norway, Visual Cultural Studies, Norway and a bachelor's degree in History and Culture, The Herzen State Pedagogical University of Russia, St. Petersburg, Russian Federation. She was born and raised in a nomadic Nenets family of reindeer herders in Ngarka Ya, in the Arctic tundra, and attended a boarding school for nomadic children in Krasnoye, a small village in Northern Russia. As a student and researcher, she has worked on topic connected to indigenous peoples around the world.

Rita Sørly is an Associate Professor in Social Work at The Arctic University of Norway, senior researcher at NORCE, Tromsø and editor of a Nordic Journal in mental health care. She is also the leader of Network for Participatory Research in Mental Health and Substance Abuse in northern Norway. Research interests are narrative theory and method, community mental health, mental health and substance abuse, user involvement and indigenous health research.

Jukka Teräs is senior researcher at NORCE, Tromso, Norway/Senior Research Fellow at Nordregio in Stockholm, Sweden. Academic qualifications: D.Sc. (Tech), MBA. Post-doc studies in Pisa, Italy & Turku, Finland (economic geography).

Jukka holds a Doctor of Science (Technology) degree from University of Oulu in Finland and an MBA from the Helsinki School of Economics. Jukka has

xiv *Contributors*

more than 20 years of experience on innovation promotion and regional development from both public and private sectors. He has major research interests and special expertise on regional clusters, innovation environments, smart specialization and issues related to the Arctic regions. The current tasks at NORCE include assignments related to green transition of industries and smart specialization in the Arctic. Jukka has contributed to smart specialization strategy and implementation, e.g. in the Finnish Lapland.

Hege Westskog is senior researcher at Center for Development and the Environment at the University of Oslo. She holds a PhD in economics from the University of Oslo. Her work is solution oriented with a focus on co-production of knowledge and addresses policies and measures to transform to a low-emission society. She is part of Include – a research centre on socially inclusive energy transition, where she leads the work on municipalities as change agents. She has served as research director at CICERO (Center for International Climate Research) for more than ten years.

Introduction
Being in-between stories

Tony Ghaye, Rita Sørly, and Bård Kårtveit

> It's all a question of story. We are in trouble just now because we do not have a good story. We are in-between stories.
>
> (Berry, 1988, p. 123).

Stories are important. The famous poet Muriel Rukeyser once wrote *"the universe is made of stories, not atoms"* (Rukeyser, 1968). Telling stories represents a process of ongoing meaning-making (Miller & Taylor, 2006). They tell of situated experience and how this shapes our relationships towards others and the local and global community we are a part of (Klausen, Haugsgjerd, & Lorem, 2013; Langellier & Peterson, 2006). As written by Kirmayer (2019), our brain is "a story machine, weaving webs of meaning through language, imagery and performance" (p.31). Stories help focus attention beyond ourselves as individuals and outwards to our interactions with others, both local and global. Story-making is a knowledge generation process (Czarniawska, 2004). For some, the terms "narrative" and "story" have their own identity but are also related ideas. (Blix & Sørly, 2017; Riessman, 1993). Stories and narratives can take many forms and have different meanings (Frank, 2010.) However, in this book, we have been guided by Denning's (2000) rationale and use the terms interchangeably.

We feel that through using different kinds of stories we give ourselves the chance to engage with a potentially wide and pluralistic readership. So we hope complex stories of Arctic change and sustainability are communicated in a way that (first) actually gets the reader's attention and (second) serves to enable the readership to reflect on what they really care about? (see Chapter 1). Stories have the power to do this. They not only capture and (re)tell what has happened, they also shape the life we choose to move toward and the world we wish to create. They have this capability to help us name what we have and are living through. They help us give meaning and purpose to what is to come. They play an important role in helping to bring us to a better place. This might be a better tomorrow. A better next year, or a better next living, in a changing Arctic.

DOI: 10.4324/9781003118633-1

The book's three generic lenses (frames) through which change and sustainability in the Arctic may be viewed.

Across the chapters in this book, there is no single unifying consensus about the lenses, or "frames", that could/should be used to help make sense of the challenges, uncertainties and doubts associated with Arctic change and sustainability. This reflects the different perspectives of the authors and offers a flavour of the debate about what matters most and for whom. However, all contributors, from different standpoints and across diverse fields feel that in general, the three lenses shown in Figure 0.1. have the potential for increasing our ability to interpret events, form views, values, make judgements and, for some, act as a rationale for action. There is no intention to try and prescribe which lens to use and for what purpose, or that one is more superior to others. On the contrary, the position we argue here is that they do different and complementary jobs. They open-up different Arctic vistas. If we can also imagine them to have permeable boundaries, we can begin to benefit from a process of ideas flowing back and forth, constantly being redefined, redesigned and reimagined until they may be regarded as fit-for-purpose. So a key reflective question emerges namely, *through which lens/es are we viewing the Arctic region?* The meanings we assign to events unfolding in the Arctic, are a consequence of the lens/ses through which we see the region. Figure 0.1 carries

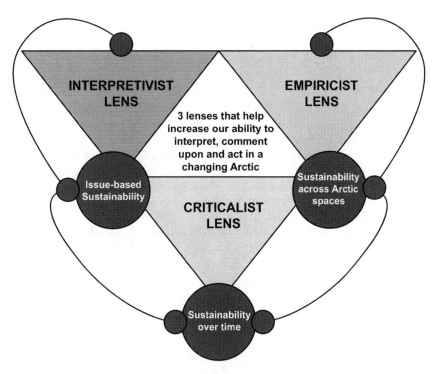

Figure 0.1 Three generic lenses (frames) through which change and sustainability in the Arctic may be viewed.

Being in-between stories   3

a hope we wish to convey, that creating and sustaining a flourishing Arctic will require at least interpretation, creative data and knowledge management, collaboration and criticality. This also embraces a view that changes in the Arctic can be regarded as uncertain and doubted. These lenses offer the possibility that they can be used to reveal what 'we' don't yet know and to use this as a means to challenge what 'we' feel we do know and what we plan to do with this knowing!

The interpretivist, empiricist and criticalist lenses in Figure 0.1 are well documented in the research literature so we don't go into each one in any length in this book. What we do say however, is that we offer the empiricist lens to reflect a general focus on Arctic work (research and practice) as data driven and where evidence is also derived from experiences of social realities, collected and represented in many forms, (see for example Chapter 3 by Jokela & Huhmarniemi, *Stories Transmitted through Art for the Revitalization and Decolonization of the Arctic*, Chapter 10 Aarsæther & Westskog, *Transforming Arctic Municipalities: The winding road to low-emission communities*, Chapter 11 by Friedrich, *The Quest for Fresh Vegetables: Stories about the Future of Arctic Farming*). We offer the interpretivist lens as a general way of challenging the dualistic notion of objective and subjective Arctic realities and foregrounding the central role of Arctic experiences that are lived and felt, reconstructed, reinterpreted and understood. In other words meanings are made, rather than found, (see for example Chapter 2 by Riseth, *Disappearing flexibility: The story of Gielas reindeer herding district*, Chapter 4 by Sørly, Mathisen & Nygaard, *Mental Health research in an Arctic Indigenous context: The presence of silent dominant narratives*, Chapter 5 by Cardona Gomez, Brown, McComber, Parent-Racine & Linnaranta, *Stories of Empowerment, Resilience and Healing: A participatory research project with two Indigenous communities in Québec*). Finally, the broad purpose of the criticalist lens is to celebrate the need for a critical eye that can break apart the interactions between agency and structure/s that both suffocate and constrain, alienate and emancipate, celebrate and enlighten, and in so doing, reveal the stories of marginalized, minority and silenced groups, omitted from (or worse) denied access to, decision-making processes that affect their lives in the Arctic region, (see for example Chapter 9 by Kårtveit, *Green Colonialism: The story of wind power in Sápmi*, Chapter 12 by Nilsen and Teräs, *Greening discourses of the Nordic Arctic region: The region as vulnerable, late bloomer or the arena of possibilities?* Chapter 7 by Ravna, *The decline and changes in the tundra today: The nature of state systems and services as a critical factor in the condition of minority indigenous peoples in Russia*).

The book's generative questions

So how can those involved in Arctic work accelerate the most desirable future for the region? What we can postulate is that efforts at *eradicating* something, like trying to fix, or get rid of, biophysical collapse due to runaway climate change, biodiversity loss through species extinction, human population growth beyond supportable levels, the alienation of indigenous Arctic values and peoples, skewed and mal-governance, national agrandissement and so on, is not the

4 Tony Ghaye, Rita Sørly, and Bård Kårtveit

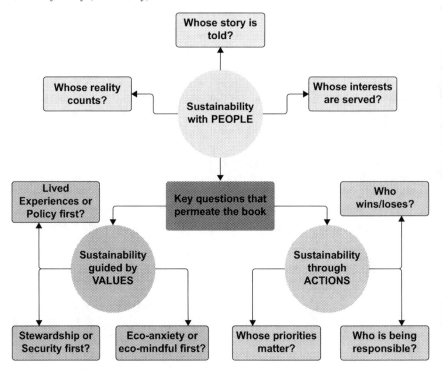

Figure 0.2 The book's generative questions.

same as *enabling* something such as the achievement of a flourishing Arctic. We need to be clear about our priorities for action! The 3 lenses described above can help us with this as they enable us to frame significant Arctic-relevant questions (see Figure 0.2). How-to questions are not the only significant ones to formulate. There are also questions about why, what and who is implicated in and impacted by these questions. We grow in the direction in which we ask questions (Cooperrider, Whitney, & Stavros, 2008), so it's important we try to frame them in the most appropriate way.

We make a distinction in this book between generic and generative questions. Examples of the former might be:

- How do we build shared values about the prosperity and future of the Arctic region?
- How do we build sustainable economies across the Arctic region?
- How do we collectively protect Arctic environments?
- How can we effectively share knowledge and wisdom across the Arctic that impacts positively on human progress there?

However, Figure 0.2 shows examples of the book's *generative* questions. We have drawn our inspiration for this from Bushe (2013) who defines generativity as something which acts as a catalyst to help create new images, metaphors, physical representations and so on, that have two qualities; (1) they change how people think so that new options for decisions and/or actions become available to them, and (2) they are compelling catalysts or images that people want to act on.

As a general marker, the term sustainability was popularized by the 1987 UN-report Our Common Future, which stated that sustainable development should meet the needs of the generations of today, without reducing the chances of future generations having their needs met. The core idea, was that our concern for future generations, constrains our consumption and the actions of today (WCED, 1987). At the same time, what was stressed was the notion of a balancing between environmental, social and economic concerns in our aspirations for a sustainable future (Holden, Linnerud, & Banister, 2017). Arguably the notion of balance is untenable in a post-pandemic and VUCA (volatile, uncertain, chaotic and ambiguous) world? In this book, we open up a broader understanding of the term, where sustainability, for example, can refer to forms of conduct, lifestyles and management of resources, that allows for the healthy continuation of one's life and personal health, the preservation of a way of life, or a set of finite natural resources. A sustainable Arctic region might therefore be generally thought about as one that; (a) meets the needs of the present generation; (b) does not compromise the ability of future generations to meet their own needs; As evidenced in chapters in this book, we can regard sustainability as a political concept, if only because it defines and shapes different discourses and stories about future developments; that is, competing visions of the future. (Petrov et al, 2016). Identity, space and places in the Arctic are all potentially reconfigured by processes of change and sustainability. So we need to be specific and ask, "what exactly is to be sustained and how is the best way to do this"?

The book's metaphor of a 'braid'

In the spirit of generativity, we also offer readers the metaphor of a "braid" to help capture some of the fluidity and dynamic complexity of Arctic change and sustainability issues set out in the book. Figure 0.3 visualizes what we wish to convey. It's a braided arctic river course.

The most relevant features of Figure 0.3 we suggest, are the river's infolding and unfurling, wholeness but also separateness, the seeming disentanglement but then the reconnection with something bigger (the river's main course), with parts always moving into new spaces, always changing. We have stylized the notion of a braid in Figure 0.4 and show some of the more significant issues alluded to in the book. We have drawn upon the artistic thinking and transcognitive practices of Sullivan (2002) to do this.

The chapters in the book discuss, in their own ways, those influences which we might usefully think of as "behavioural enablers and blockers". Conventionally and in general, many have thought about sustainability as having three pillars referring to economic viability, environmental protection and social equity. But due to developments in our knowledge bases and particularly in systems thinking,

Figure 0.3 Longyear river, Svalbard – a 'braided' Arctic river.

Source: Tom Andreas Østrem

other dimensions are becoming significant and more identifiable such as for example "technical feasibility", "political legitimacy" and "governance" of the Arctic. The latter is beginning to express itself in the notion of ES&G sustainability (environmental, social and corporate governance).

We feel the 'G' dimension is a critical, arguably even an essential (McKeown, 2014) one. For example Chapter 1 by Ghaye, *Concerned Arctic Peoples: Characteristics of conversations-that-matter*, Chapter 9 by Kårtveit, *Green Colonialism: The story of wind power in Sápmi* and Chapter 11 Friedrich, *The Quest for Fresh Vegetables - Stories about the Future of Arctic Farming* all explore, amongst other things, governance and corporate issues. When we use the expression "behavioural enables and blockers" we are referring to those agency-structure ("structuration") issues that help, or get in the way, of positive change in the Arctic.

In Figure 0.4 we also lift up the processes of "activism, advocacy and allyship" as these are also essential aspects of change and sustainability. When we think

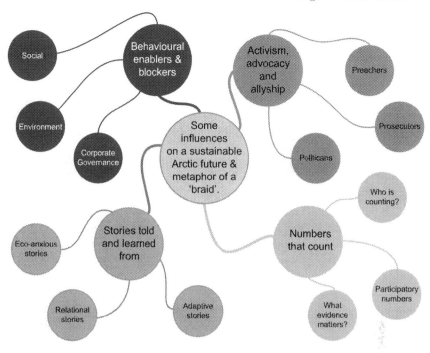

Figure 0.4 The 'braided' metaphor of change and sustainability in the Arctic.

about these three things as practices, the work of Mondros and Wilson (1994) becomes relevant as they articulate ways through which groups can seek to accumulate and wield power (or not) in the face of larger (global) power structures and influences. Their work also opens up the experiences of disempowerment that are often felt by particular groups (see for example, Chapter 6 by Sørly, Ghaye and Årst, *Learning through lived experiences: A structural narrative analysis of one person's journey of recovery and implications for peer support services* and Chapter 5 by Cardona Gomez, Brown, McComber, Parent-Racine & Linnaranta, *Stories of Empowerment, Resilience and Healing: A participatory research project with two Indigenous communities in Québec*). In brief, Mondros and Wilson's 3 models are; (1) grassroots (2) lobbying (3) mobilizing. The first emphasizes the differences in thinking and doing between elites and the powerful and those who are marginalized, silenced and peripheralized. Lobbying is all about how we create spaces and places for everyone affected by Arctic change to influence those things that affect their lives and livelihoods. Mobilizing takes us into general social movement thinking and approaches. It can be about protest, disruption, deviance and having one's voice heard and acted upon. The book is full of signs of all three issues. Additionally, in this particular part of the braided metaphor, we borrow from the work of Grant (2021) and offer his typology of actors as a heuristic as readers progress through the book. Although none of the contributors explicitly refer to Grant's preacher, prosecutor and politician typology, all these characters

8   *Tony Ghaye, Rita Sørly, and Bård Kårtveit*

certainly make their appearance and presence felt. Preachers are those who are already convinced that they have found the 'truth' and they way, in this case with regard to creating a flourishing Arctic, but maybe one that only serves their interests! They are deaf to alternative voices from the margins and from those who may regard themselves (and be regarded as) being the 'last' (Chambers, 1997). They don't question their values, don't self-reflect. Don't consider that they might even be wrong! Prosecutors are all about people who are trying to win and avoid losing. This means others miss out, others are wrong while they are right. There is no room for compromise. They are often very articulate and have strong political acuity. Finally we see politicians at work throughout the book. These are people who are sensitive to the needs and wishes of their audiences, campaign, in different ways, for their approval, can do a little flexing and are open to some re-thinking as long as they get their way in the end.

The third aspect of the braided metaphor is about data and evidence. We have called it *numbers that count*. By this we mean that change and sustainability is inextricably linked to knowledge generation, its analysis, use and dissemination. Chambers (2017) poses the helpful question, *'Can we know better?'* What he is expressing is a concern for how can we know better in order to positively confront an uncertain future? When Arctic change and sustainability are linked to the word 'development', we need to be aware that this term, like change and sustainability, is also continuously evolving and diversifying. So what would be regarded as 'good' development and 'good' change? Also, what is 'good' sustainability? These are epistemological as well as moral, ethical and pragmatic questions. Maybe they invite us to think about practical realism? When we use the phrase numbers that count, we are inviting readers of this book to critically reflect on what the word 'numbers' might be taken to mean, (exploring its full bandwidth), what numbers are worth gathering, by whom, how participatory this process can be and who counts! In reading through the book we wish to open up opportunities to think about the best ways to move beyond conventional qual-quant complementarities. By this we mean qualitative research and the value of 'precision in meaning' that it brings, together with the value of quantitative research and its 'accuracy in measurement'. And finally here we suggest the whole sustainability debate requires the adoption of a benefit mindset, because a critical question in conversations and actions about change and sustainability is, 'who benefits?' Very little can be regarded as objective and neutral. All is open to doubt and interpretation. Data and how this is turned into evidence cannot be ignored. But what evidence matters? To do better we need to know more about, and be open-minded and courageous enough, to let the evidence speak. If we can achieve this disposition, multiple options for action in a changing Arctic, rather than just single, narrow 'solutions' might be revealed.

And finally we turn to that part of the braid we have called *stories told and learned from*. This is the heart of the book and reflects our position that we need to generate, listen to and learn from stories of Arctic change and sustainability. We say this because we believe that we live storied lives (Whitney et al, 2019) and inhabit storied landscapes that stimulates our imagination, guides and influences

Being in-between stories 9

our behaviour, shapes our ideas of what is possible and governs our actions for change (Göpel, 2016). Stories also offer a basis for achieving mutual understanding. What constitutes change and sustainability is subject to continuous debate, which gets endlessly reignited in an uncertain and ambiguous world and one transitioning through a pandemic. For many, the magnitude, nature and pace of change in the Arctic, together with previously presumed certainties and conventional ways of thinking and working, are all being challenged. Although change and sustainability elude easy captivity, what this book illustrates is that the Arctic can be viewed as a repository of complex, dynamic, sacred, wicked, wondrous and also deeply conflicted stories.

This book is not what some might regard, as a 'normal' way of reporting on science, because we have chosen to report through different kinds of stories and with these being a means to an end. The end is that they are a way of understanding change and sustainability issues. A way of understanding complex realities. Understanding tensions between continuity and change. Between resistance and progress (Riedy, 2020). A way of conveying feelings, thoughts and actions. Many 'actors' above and below the Arctic Circle in the business of change and sustainability, argue that an effective response to these challenges will require not only the positive transformation of technologies (Geels, 2019), economies and institutions (Scoones, 2020), but also a 'psycho-cultural transformation' (Berzonsky & Moser, 2017) of the values and stories that shape our individual and collective consciousness (Narayanan & Adams, 2017; Pesch, 2015; Waddock, 2016). Hendersson and Wamsler (2020), open up the interesting notion of being in-between stories in this moment in history. "Sustainability philosophers claim that we are at an impasse of stories, finding ourselves in a blank chapter between the old and the new. The old story, characterized by separation, technological dominance and human superiority over nature, is unfolding in an ecological crisis giving space for a new narrative defined by inter-being, cooperation and balance" (p. 345). This book hopes to start to fill in the words of this 'blank chapter'.

In this book, three core stories (all with 'chapters' and sub-plots therein) emerge. They are that the practices of change and sustainability, regardless of scale, are stories that might generally be regarded as eco-anxious, relational and/ or adaptive (see Figure 0.4). By this we mean that, foundationally, the stories depict the interplay between the oft used notion of the triple bottom line of people (social), planet (environmental) and profit (economy). But when we add issues of stewardship, ethical governance, moral courage and organizational purpose to this for example, then Arctic change and sustainability issues become both complex and complicated. Working through them requires wisdom from the physical sciences, social research and from the direct experience and knowledge of people who live and have lived in the Arctic regions. Where indigenous peoples are on the frontlines of Arctic environmental challenges such as climate change, biodiversity loss and numerous other forms of critical planetary deterioration, their indigenous experiences, responses and cultural practices should not be underestimated (Figueres & Carnac, 2020). This book looks forward through the lens of stories. Provocatively Leinaweaver (2015) and Hendersson and Wamsler (2020)

10 Tony Ghaye, Rita Sørly, and Bård Kårtveit

assert that there is a growing realization, within the sustainability debate, that it is increasingly less important to claim and portray data and facts. It should be more about owning and conveying "stories and languages of value, culture and ideology", (Leinaweaver, 2015, p. 66).

Arguably, a stereotypical sustainability story contains a person, or several persons, responding to a challenge, regarding different concerns, developing skills and knowledge and perhaps to become a sustainability change agent (Bernier, 2020). Sustainability stories characterized in this way are often meant to show how and why we do what we do. A dominant storyline within these stories is one of sustainability or collapse, or both. They can also be apocalyptic in kind. But of course, there are alternative stories that can be found which are more about transition and transformation involving resilience, hope and ways to overcome subjugation, assimilation, oppression and even extinction. (Strunz, Marselle, & Schröter, 2019). The stories in this book are framed in different ways. Some arguably are more 'political' in nature and especially when they are about who gets what, where and how and who is denied! There are stories of possibility and transition (see Chapter 12 for example by Nilsen and Teräs, *Greening narratives of the Nordic Arctic: The region as vulnerable, late bloomer or the arena of possibilities?*), of tensions, conflict and contradiction (for example see Chapter 2 by Riseth, *Disappearing flexibility: The story of Gielas reindeer herding district*). Sustainability stories like this are related to indigenous knowledge, focusing on in-depth understandings of ecosystems and people-environment inter-connectedness (Edwards, 2010). A Sámi reindeer herder explains the world view of his people thus. *Just to be able to manage outside in nature and treat it in a good way. To understand how everything relates to each other – that's important no matter what you do. There has been enough people who do not understand nature and look at what the world is becoming. I think you need an understanding of nature. We belong to nature. [...] Sámi values are very sustainable. I want to bring this further [to the next generation]* (Sørly, Mathisen, & Kvernmo, 2020, pp. 10–11).

There are also stories in the book which capture the flavour of serious artic paradoxes. The Arctic can be seen as a region of myths and resources defined by large stretches of wild, dramatic landscapes and a challenging climate. A region that has historically been settled by an array of indigenous communities that have lived as hunters and gatherers, as fishermen, and as nomadic pastoralists, primarily in small communities characterized with basic technologies and living lives closely adapted the rhythm and resources of their natural surroundings. These indigenous communities are still there, but in many places, their languages, their social structures, and their ways of living have disintegrated or weakened through their encounters with state-based, industrialized communities. It is also a region settled by non-indigenous communities that have been established both in tension and collaboration with indigenous communities and that tend to self-identify as highly adaptive and resilient in response to economic hardship and great versatility in their utilization of available natural resources. The Arctic can also be viewed as a region rich in minerals, oil reserves, and other resources that have been open to extraction, attracting the attention of industrial forces from other parts of the world.

Being in-between stories   11

While international industries amass vast profits from extracting resources in the Arctic region, its people rarely get to benefit from these resources. Overall, local communities in the Arctic have been characterized by economic marginalization, lack of employment opportunities and population decline (BIN-report 2020) This is often regarded as the Arctic resource paradox (Holm, 2020; Olsen, 2018). For example the Arctic is at the center of a growing tension between the imperative to reduce global carbon emissions and the opportunities for further oil and gas extractions opened up by global warming. This represents an Arctic extractive paradox which can be described as the faster we use fossil fuels, the sooner we get access to new oil and gas resources (Palosaari, 2019). There is also an Arctic climate paradox. Pushed by an assertive wind power industry and that climate change mitigation depends on clean energy production arguably this requires the building of large-scale wind farms with potentially devastating environmental consequences (Rehbein et al., 2020). These paradoxes come together in the latest initiative from Norwegian authorities and the petroleum industry.

As of Spring 2021, Equinor, Norway's partly state-owned oil company highlights the following story on its website:

> Several of Norway's largest oil fields are now going to be powered with renewable energy. How? By providing electricity from land-based hydropower plants directly to the platforms. This way, both new and existing platforms can be electrified – dramatically cutting emissions from production
> (Equinor website: We energize the lives of 170 million people. Every day. - equinor.com, March 2021).

As a part of this plan, natural gas that has been used to power offshore platforms will be exported for consumption to other parts of the world. It is argued this will enable Norway to reach its 2030 climate goal of reducing carbon emissions by 50%. However, critics fear that this will demand the building of new large-scale wind parks, on land as well as off-shore, as well as an expansion of hydro power plants, causing large-scale environmental destruction throughout the country (Motvind, 2021). While initially a response to global calls for lower carbon emissions, the "greening" of Norway's oil fields may have dramatic impacts on local communities and livelihoods in the Arctic (see Chapter 9 by Kårtveit, *Green Colonialism: The Story of wind power in Sápmi*). Industrial extraction of resources, both renewable and non-renewable, can complicate the lives of local inhabitants throughout the Arctic region. Several chapters explore the hardships facing local communities, partly as a result of these encounters.

As editors, we made some decisions related to what kind of stories we wanted to use to explore change and sustainability in the Arctic regions. We wanted stories that demonstrated knowledge needed to make 'good' changes in local communities, that were empowering and motivating to those whose lives are being touched by change and to inspire active sustainability agents (Meisner, 2014). However there is a back 'story', which is sometimes more hidden, sometimes more visible and explicit throughout the book. As a reader you may feel 'us versus them'

12   *Tony Ghaye, Rita Sørly, and Bård Kårtveit*

tensions, that there are heroes and villains, (also see they 'actor' typology above), one moral code pitted against another moral code. Change and sustainability is a conflicted space and the book reflects this.

After this Introduction, Ghaye reflects upon conversations-that-matter, regarding the causes, influences and behaviours that give rise to a changing Arctic. In his chapter, Ghaye underlines the need for a shift of focus, 'away from a preoccupation with trying to achieve less un-sustainable activities in the Arctic. Away from Arctic peoples seeing themselves as victims of inevitable and unstoppable global processes. Away from trying to reduce, or even reverse the harms associated with un-sustainability and with fate control! So much is committed to solving what's wrong. What might happen if we focused more on what's right' (p.xx). The following contributions can be read as attempts towards telling different stories about the Arctic. Riseth describes the disappearing flexibility in Gielas reindeer district in Finnmark and Troms county, Northern Norway. Riseth's chapter shows how Norwegian state and local authorities fail to protect the livelihood of the Gielas herders, by allowing for step-by step territorial incursions that threaten the sustainability of reindeer herding in Gielas district. Jokela and Huhmarniemi give us a narrative description and theoretical conceptualization of the premises, processes, execution and results of a place-specific public art project. The artwork *The Story of Kirkkokuusikko* is a memorial to the first Christian church in the Kittilä region in Finnish Lapland. Sørly, Mathisen and Nygaard look at narratives while working with Indigenous mental health research, a topic related to social sustainability. They give an in- depth analysis of prominent dominant narratives, or big stories, in an interview with a Swedish reindeer herder. Gomez Cardona, Brown, McComber, Parent, Racine and Linnaranta describe a participatory research project related to empowerment, resilience and healing among two Indigenous communities in Québec, Canada. Wibecke's story, a chapter written by Sørly, Ghaye and Årst, provides a structural narrative analysis of one person's journey of recovery from substance abuse, and implications for peer support services". Who's voice and who's knowledge counts? How can we have conversations where all voices are heard and what we come to know, is appreciated, and acted upon? Ravna offers a unique ethnographic based insight into the nomadic Nenets' everyday life on the Russian tundra. The progressive development of a culture and economy in a nomadic Nenets way of life has ended. Ravna's chapter explores how the Nenet herder's social structure and way of life is threatened by external forces as well as internal changes. Still, the Nenets's dependency on reindeer herding on the tundra is still such that any Nenets will tell you that "reindeer is life". While working on this book, the world has gone through a global pandemic. Sørly, Nygaard, Kårtveit, Normann, Ivanova, Riabova and Britvina give us an impression on how isolation became a part of the new "Covid reality", and how this affected their everyday lives, and their ongoing research project. Kårtveit offers a perspective related to greening narratives. He writes about the emergence of green colonialism as a narrative informing Sámi experiences of, and resistance to, wind power incursions on Sámi herding land. Aarsæther and Westskog give an insight into local efforts to implement the ISG in three small communities in the Arctic,

Being in-between stories 13

detecting greater commitment to climate action in local businesses than in municipal authorities. Friedrich presents stories about the future of Arctic farming, from Calypso Farm in Ester, Alaska (US), Arviat's community gardens and greenhouses in Nunavut, Canada, and Polar Permaculture in Svalbard, Norway. Both chapters have growth as a topic, but in very different framings. Greening narratives of the North is in focus, when Nilsen and Teräs describe green transition in the Nordic North innovation system. The green transition, a global megatrend, is highly complicated in the region. Nilsen and Teräs present three dominant narratives related to the task. Ghaye, Sørly and Kårtveit then conclude the book with the question, what can we create together?

References

Bernier, A., (2020). Sustainability storytelling is not just telling stories about sustainability. In: Goldstein, M.I., DellaSala, D.A. (Eds.). *Encyclopedia of the World's biomes* (vol. 5, pp. 430–437). Elsevier. ISBN:9780128160961

Berry, T. (1988). *The dream of the earth*. San Francisco: Sierra Club Books, University of California Press.

Berzonsky, C., & Moser, S. (2017). Becoming homo sapiens sapiens: Mapping the psycho-cultural transformation in the anthropocene. *Anthropocene, 20*, 15–23.

Blix, B., & Sørly, R. (2017). Introduksjon. In R. Sørly, & B. Blix (Eds.), *Fortelling og forskning. narrativ teori i tverrfaglig forskning*. Stamsund: Orkana akademisk Forlag.

Bushe, G., (2013). Generative process, generative outcome: The transformational potential of appreciative inquiry, in Cooperrider, D., Zandee, D., Godwin, L., et al (eds.) *Organizational generativity: The appreciative inquiry summit and a scholarship of transformation* (Advances in Appreciative Inquiry, Volume 4) (pp. 89–113). Bingley: Emerald Group Publishing Limited.

Chambers, R. (1997). *Whose reality counts? Putting the last first*. London: Intermediate Technology Publications.

Chambers, R. (2017). *Can we know better? Reflections for development*. Rugby: Practical Action Publishing.

Cooperrider, D., Whitney, D., & Stavros, J. (2008). *Appreciative inquiry handbook for leaders of change*. San Francisco, CA: Berrett-Koehler Publishers.

Czarniawska, B. (2004). *Narratives in social science research*. London: Sage

Denning, S. (2000). *The springboard: How storytelling ignites action in knowledge-era organizations*. Boston, London: Butterworth Heinemann.

Edwards, E. (2010). *Thriving beyond sustainability*. Gabriola Island, BC, Canada: New Society.

Equinor website, We energize the lives of 170 million people. Every day. - equinor.com

Figueres, C. & Rivett-Carnac, T. (2020). Surviving the climate crisis. New York, NY: Alfred A. Knopf.

Frank, A. (2010). *Letting stories breathe. A socio- narratology*. Chicago, IL: University of Chicago Press.

Geels, F. W. (2019). Socio-technical transitions to sustainability: A review of criticisms and elaborations of the multi-level perspective. *Current Opinion in Environmental Sustainability, 39*, 187–201.

Göpel (2016). M. *the great mindshift. How a new economic paradigm and sustainability transformations to hand in hand*. New York, NY, USA: Springer Nature, 2016.

14 *Tony Ghaye, Rita Sørly, and Bård Kårtveit*

Grant, A. (2021). *Think again*. London: W.H. Allen.

Hendersson, H., & Wamsler, C. (2020). New stories for a more conscious, sustainable society: Claiming authorship of the climate story. *Climatic Change*, 158, 345–359.

Holden, E., Linnerud, K., & Banister, D., (2017). The sustainable development area: Satisfying basic needs and safeguarding ecological sustainability. *Sustainable Development*, 15 (3), 174–187.

Holm, A. O. (2020). The arctic paradox. Op-ed. *High North News*, May 22. 2020, available from: https://www.highnorthnews.com/en/arctic-paradox

Kirmayer, L. J. (2019). Toward an ecosocial psychiatry. *World Social Psychiatry*, 1(1), 30.

Klausen, R. K., Haugsgjerd, S., & Lorem, G. F. (2013). "The lady in the coffin"–Delusions and hearing voices: A narrative performance of insight. *Qualitative Inquiry*, 19(6), 431–440.

Langellier, K., & Peterson, E. (2006). Shifting contexts in personal narrative performance. In D. S. Madison, & J. Hamera (Eds.), *The sage handbook of performance studies* (pp. 151–168). Thousand Oaks, CA: SAGE.

Leinaweaver, J. (2015). *Storytelling for sustainability: Deepening the case for change.*. London, UK: Routledge.

McKeown, G. (2014). *Essentialism: The disciplined pursuit of less*. Elbury, UK: Virgin Books.

Meisner, M., (2014). *Consciousness raising. Achieving sustainability: Visions, principles, and practices*. Debra Rowe (Ed.), Detroit: Macmillan Reference USA.

Miller, L. C., & Taylor, J. (2006). The constructed self: Strategic and aesthetic choices in autobiographic performance. In D. S. Madison & J. Hamera (Eds.), The Sage handbook of performance studies (pp. 169–187). Thousand Oaks, CA: Sage

Mondros, J., & Wilson, S. (1994). *Organizing for power and empowerment*. New York: Columbia University Press.

Motvind. (2021). Stans videre elektrifisering av sokkelen! Statement retrieved from Motvind's website: https://motvind.org/stans-videre-elektrifisering-av-sokkelen/

Narayanan, N., & Adams, C. (2017). Transformative change towards sustainability: The interaction between organisational discourses and organisational practices. *Acc Bus Res*, 47, 344–368.

Olsen, B. (2018) *Op-Ed: Barriers and opportunities for Arctic growth – Arctic paradoxes and solutions*. High North News, 24.08.2018, available from: https://www.highnorthnews.com/en/newsletter-arctic-paradise-or-paradox

Palosaari, T. (2019). The arctic paradox (and how to solve it). Oil, gas and climate ethics in the arctic. In M. Finger, & L. Heininen (Eds.), *The global arctic handbook*. Cham: Springer.

Pesch, U. (2015). Tracing discursive space: Agency and change in sustainability transitions. *Technol Forecast Soc Change*, 90, 379–388.

Petrov, A. N., BurnSilver, S., Stuart Chapin III, F., Fondahl, G., Graybill, J., Keil, K. … Schweitzer, P. (2016) Arctic sustainability research: toward a new agenda. *Polar geography*, 39(3), 165–178, DOI: 10.1080/1088937X.2016.1217095Riessman, C. (1993). *Narrative analysis*. Newbury Park, CA: Sage.

Rehbein, J. A., Watson, J. E., Lane, J. L., Sonter, L. J., Venter, O., Atkinson, S. C., & Allan, J. R. (2020). Renewable energy development threatens many globally important biodiversity areas. *Global change biology*, 26(5), 3040–3051.

Riedy, C. (2020). Discourse coalitions for sustainability transformations: Common ground and conflict beyond neoliberalism. *Current Opinion in Environmental Sustainability*, 45, 100–112.

Rukeyser, M. (1968). *The speed of darkness*. New York: Random House.

Being in-between stories 15

Sørly, R., Mathisen, V., & Kvernmo, S. (2020). "We belong to nature": Communicating mental health in an indigenous context. *Qualitative Social Work,* 1–17. doi: 10.1177/1473325020932374

Scoones, I. (2020). Transformations to sustainability: Combining structural, systemic and enabling. *Current Opinion in Environmental Sustainability, 42,* 65–75.

Strunz, S., Marselle, M., & Schröter, M. (2019). Leaving the "sustainability or collapse" narrative behind. *Sustainability Science, 14*(6), 1717–1728.

Sullivan, G. (2002). Artistic thinking and trans cognitive practice: A reconciliation of the process-product dichotomy. *Visual Arts Research, 2*(1), 2–12.

Whitney, D., Miller, C. A., Teller, T. C., Ogawa, M., Cocciolone, J., Leon de la Barra, A., … Britton, K. (2019). *Thriving women, thriving world.* Chagrin Falls, OH: Taos Institute Publication.

Waddock, S. (2016). Foundational memes for a new narrative about the role of business in society. *Humanist Management Journal, 1,* 91–105.

World Commission on Environment and Development (WCED) (1987). *Our common future.* Oxford: Oxford University Press.

1 Concerned Arctic peoples

Characteristics of conversations-that-matter

Tony Ghaye

Introduction

Stories that are told

> When I was young, I remember a quiet stillness about Fort Yukon. There were no street lights, yet our eyes adjusted to the dark outlines of night. In the winter, stars, northern lights, and the moon reflected brightly off the snow. Sometimes the night seems brighter than the days because our sun is below the horizon during the winters. My Aunt Nina used to tell us about how the children of her days loved this type of moonlit night, when they could frolic just like the rabbits that they could see jumping to and from. I have had such nights. We almost never wanted to come back inside, and my mother had to scold us as we reluctantly came into the house, throwing a wistful look over our shoulders. You always hear people of my generation telling these kinds of stories. To the young, I am sure we are like old, senile people who remember a time and world gone by. But for people my age, it seems like just yesterday.
>
> (Bannergee, 2012, p. 486)

I have four major reasons for writing this chapter. First, I believe positive change is possible. When I use it together with the word sustainability, I use it to mean "good change" that applies universally to those impacted by it (Cooperrider, Whitney, & Stavros, 2008). Additionally, and because sustainable changes at all scales for human benefit are also possible, I have come to believe it is a responsibility for everyone to be part of that change. There should be no one left behind, nobody left out. And more to the point, I suggest we need to listen carefully to the stories that are told. The past is not irrelevant. In this chapter I will, where appropriate, illuminate some of the major issues of "concerned peoples", by drawing on and adapting the psychological notion of "thin slice" methodology. This is the way we can convey meaning through narrow windows of experience, very short stories, fragments of and significant moments in life (Gladwell, 2006).

A second reason is the proposition that our language is holding us back and that the time has come to advance beyond the language of unsustainability and less harm, to that of focusing more on the language of thriving and flourishing (Redclift, 2005; Spaiser, Ranganathan, Swain, & Sumpter, 2016). The limits of language set

DOI: 10.4324/9781003118633-2

Concerned Arctic peoples   17

the boundaries for the limits of our worlds. As Cooperrider, Barrett, and Srivastva (1995) say, "words enable worlds". Through the notion of *conversations-that-matter*, I try to illustrate how we might improve the ways we converse with each other, balancing "sustainability-as-surviving" with "sustainability-as-flourishing". This opens up the possibility to think about human connection rather than consumerism, about purpose rather than profit, feelings of place and community rather than placelessness and on human thriving rather than selfishness. These are just some of the critical lenses through which to examine the notion of "concerned arctic peoples". Arguably happiness, health, respect for the land and others, the security of productive and meaningful work, dignity and a sense of belonging are the things that matter most to our experience as human beings. But all of these things are enmeshed in complex and delicate politico-economic, social and biophysical "systems" which give rise to tough problems (Kahane, 2004). This invites all involved to think through how we might transform the way we talk, think and act together, in order to address pressing Arctic problems of the moment. Sometimes when sustainability issues are on the table, we are unable to talk productively about the complex issues that arise because we are unable to listen. Listening requires, at least, an ability to open ourselves up to and appreciate alternative views that differ from our own. If we listen to others speak about sustainability issues with tactical, rather than relational ears, then all we do is listen for what we want or expect to hear. We sift through what others say, others who hold different values to us and have different lived experiences, only for what we can use to reinforce our own position on issues. Success in these kinds of conversation is measured by how effective we have been in securing advantage for our preferred position. This is what psychologists often call seizing and freezing. In other words, we favour the comfort of conviction over the discomfort of doubt. We listen to views that make us, and those to whom we feel accountable to, feel good, instead of ideas that make us think hard or differently (Grant, 2021). For local community leaders, through to those representing the views and wants of non-local peoples and multi-national corporations, listening to the insights and opinions of others is a critical part of strategic decision making, not only during unprecedented crises like the COVID-19 pandemic but also in more "normal" times. But the ability to listen requires deliberate cultivation. Ferrari (2012) proposed three principles for better listening: respect other people, keep quiet and let others speak, and open yourself up to their ideas by challenging your own assumptions.

A third reason is that I believe that in making positive and sustainable change, there are no shortcuts. I want to illustrate that it's often very hard and conflicted work if it is to be done ethically, with moral courage and with strategies that respect all the voices that have shaped the world (or the region) gone before. It's complex work if we wish to hold onto the best of what was, whilst contributing to the building of a just, fair, productive and peaceful future world. Perhaps there is some truth in Albert Einstein's view that great spirits always encounter violent opposition from mediocre minds? Taking this on further and if we use a socio-psychological mind, for example, we could argue that behaviour seems largely dependent on perceived threats. Sometimes these require new and better ways of perceiving the world with both rule makers and rule breakers

18   *Tony Ghaye*

(Buckingham & Coffman, 1999) needing to find a way (Wheatley, 2007) to work together. Without doubt we are all living through a pivotal moment in history.

My fourth and last reason for writing this chapter is to acknowledge some "new kids on the block!" A new generation and world-changing human resource that is rising. One that is conscious of how they live, what they buy, what they contribute to and how they work. This so-called Generation Z is the source of many voices who express their unwillingness to work for companies who are not committed to various forms of sustainability. Some may see them as positive deviants (Pascale, Sternin, & Sternin, 2010), stepping away from and arguing against values and practices that are exploitative, marginalizing and ecologically disruptive. But there are other voices to be heard also. Ones that believe we need a shift towards benefit and abundance mindsets which ask questions of the kind, who benefits through the proposed change and how, and in what ways does this build a better world? There are others who argue with passion that the past needs to be cherished and respected. It is not irrelevant. Learning from our experiences, good and bad, and turning this learning into positively sustainable and appropriate future action requires all involved to reflect together publicly and in an evidence-based way (Ghaye, 2011).

What do you really care about?

Conversations-that-matter, with regard to the causes, influences and behaviours that give rise to a changing Arctic, relate to the fundamental epistemological issue of *what we believe*. Or put in a more nuanced way, *what we allow ourselves to believe*. In turn this is related to *how we behave*. If we take these two suggestions together it leads us to another question namely, *so what do I/we care about?* (Wheatley, 2017). Finally I suggest, it leads us on to the fundamental question of, "whose reality counts?" (Chambers, 1997). There are significant connections between what Arctic peoples care about and what they did in the past, do now and may do in the future. When we care about something or someone, we become invested in it/them. And of course, anything people actually do will make *some* impact, environmentally, economically or socially. But there is another dimension to this which is associated with the how Arctic peoples approach the challenges they are facing. It's something developed between the 1970s and 1980s by Bowlby (1969, 1980) called attachment theory. This has been brought up-to-date by the research of Kohlrieser, Goldsworthy, and Coombe (2012) and re-framed in terms of people having a secure base and being a secure base. In essence this work relates to those experiences in life which give rise to, or impair, lasting socio-psychological connection between human beings and between people and places. So, it's highly relevant to our understandings, I suggest, to those living in a changing Arctic. A secure base can be defined thus: "A person, place, goal or object that provides a sense of protection, safety and caring and offers a source of inspiration and energy for daring, exploration, risk taking and seeking challenge" (Kohlrieser et al., 2012, p. 8). In the context of this book, it is worth stressing that a secure base is someone and/or something that is inspiring, that we care about and which gives us energy and a sense of purpose and meaning with which to

Concerned Arctic peoples   19

take responsible action. Change forces in the Arctic can both strengthen and erode people's secure base. Strengthening is linked with a sense of safety, bonding, attunement, knowing that peoples' feelings and thoughts matter. But as we know, both bonds and attachments are far from permanent! Erosion is linked with peoples and communities feeling at risk, alienated, marginalized, forgotten, colonized and silenced.

All this gives rise to other generic sustainability issues. Framed as questions for example, "what are the interests and objectives, stakes and goals of non-local, non-indigenous actors in the Arctic? What does sustainability in the Arctic mean to them? What is their potential impact and means of influence on the region? How do these nations and businesses see the future development of the Arctic?" The heightened connectivity between the Arctic nations and others that are playing a part in a changing region suggests that the voices of actors from well below the line of the Arctic Circle need to be taken seriously. So, understanding these actors' visions of and actions for sustainability of the Arctic is of high relevance to conversations on its future. Globalization, economic and political transformations, changing cultural landscapes, often driven from afar but experienced in the North, are all requiring constant adaptations, and the re-imagining of accountabilities and responsibilities.

I concur with the position taken by Novogratz (2020) that whatever community we come from, what is needed is the *moral imagination* to ensure that our future solutions are inclusive and pursue just and sustainable outcomes for all involved. She goes on to suggest that this takes certain kinds of capability, all of which are relevant to a changing Arctic. They are actions driven by empathy and connection, an appreciation of what a sense of belonging really means and an acceptance of socially just ways of resolving the dilemmas of ethical living. It's time to think again (Grant, 2021).

Other people coming

> ...... And in ten years when we look back on this and we're still breathing clean air and we're still drinking clean water, you know, you can take pride in the fact that you were involved in defeating these (conflicts). And you can tell your grandchildren that we had to fight for this, and that it's their duty then to continue fighting for this, because there will be other people coming.
>
> (Bannergee, 2012, p. 452).

The global–local interdependence story

To truly understand sustainability issues in the Arctic region, it's important to use a wide-angle lens through which to appreciate how global and local are interdependent. By this I mean positioning Arctic sustainability issues in relation to general issues in the rest of the world. This is a big story requiring the use of a global lens. The recently published Dasgupta Review sets the scene and the tone: "Now we are plundering every corner of the world, apparently neither knowing

20 *Tony Ghaye*

or caring what the consequences might be" (Dasgupta, 2021, p. 1). This places sustainability in a role of survivorship, of doing less harm to things and people and reducing the impact of unsustainable actions.

In essence, sustainability is a human-centred concept and process, concerning what we believe matters to our survival. It's about what the future might look like from a projection of the present. The future is extrapolated from what we know of the past (data, trends) and present interests and values. How we orient ourselves to this future world and determine what we might do is part of what some call "progress narratives". But herein lies a central sustainability challenge. It's concerned with the way we resolve tough choices (Kidder, 1995). It's the way we navigate our way through ethical (Howard & Korver, 2008), moral, legal and quasi-legal conflicts and dilemmas. Conflicts characterized by decisions about right versus wrong. Dilemmas characterized by the ethics of right versus right. Tough choices between loyalties, principles and relationships with nature and each other. A commitment to sustainable development, together with an ability to operationalize and implement the multi-dimensional United Nation's Sustainable Development Goals, brings with it an inherent conflict between politico-economic development, the socio-cultural realm and ecological sustainability. Together this makes it challenging to determine the most effective strategy to create sustainable development for global and local benefit.

As the Dasgupta Review (2021) suggests with its use of the term "plundering", progress narratives can take on an apocalyptic form, employing prophetic language bolstered by scientific data on potential destructive trajectories of socio-economic, cultural and biophysical change. We hear *apocalyptic narratives* with regard to, for example, biophysical collapse due to runaway climate change, biodiversity loss through species extinction, human population growth beyond supportable levels and other worst-case scenarios. "Whether as farmers or fishers, foresters or miners, households or businesses, governments or communities, we manage the assets to which we have access, in line with our motivations as best as we can. But the best each of us is able to achieve with our portfolios may nevertheless result in a massive collective failure to manage the global portfolio of all our assets" (Dasgupta, 2021, abridged. P11). Furthermore, there are often two other central aspects of apocalyptic narratives to bear in mind, that of judgement as well as revelation (Northcott, 2013).

Having said this, it's also important to say that we should be open to telling and listening to stories that matter. By this I mean that make a meaningful difference to thinking, conversations and actions. For example, the kind of stories where we are not able to talk about food security without talking about human health, green energy or the blue economy. Stories where we are not able talk about access to quality and appropriate education for all, without talking about gender, equality and access. Where we are not able to talk about the fragility of some ecosystems without talking about financing resilience or infrastructural improvements. Where stories about indigenous knowledge and ritual cannot be told without listening beyond the words to appreciate how they help us understand identity, connection and how individual and collective wholeness is necessarily enmeshed.

The 17 Sustainable Development Goals apply everywhere (Bali Swain & Yang-Wallentin, 2020). They are for everyone, everywhere who are wishing to, "… contribute to the goals and what they stand for, and to achieve justice, equality, sustainability, security and a better life for all, now and in the future" (Chambers, 2017, p. xi). Such is the nature of interdependence.

In the UK Government's Report, "Beyond the Ice – UK's Policy towards the Arctic" (2018), the notion of interdependence is clearly stated. "We have all heard how greenhouse gases produced elsewhere on the planet are causing Arctic temperatures to increase, which are in turn causing sea ice to melt and sea levels to rise. This is just one example of the interdependence between the Arctic and the rest of the world. This mutual influence means that what happens in the Arctic matters to Arctic and non-Arctic states alike" (p.3). Interdependence can give rise to conflicts and dilemmas around what is valued and how those involved express their cherished and valued beliefs in action.

> Since at least 1972, the Arctic has been the dominant source of global sea level rise, most of which is due to meltwater from Greenland. The white surface of snow and ice in the Arctic reflects the sun's radiation. Less sea-ice results in more of the sun's radiation being absorbed by the sea creating a self-reinforcing loop of warmer water and less sea ice. Similarly, thawing permafrost leads to more warming and emissions of methane and $CO2$ increase as soil microbial activity increases as well as potential damage to infrastructure built on it. These processes, known as 'Arctic amplification', may create profound implications for the regional and global climate, as well as for the people who live in and around the Arctic. Thawing permafrost changes the landscape, creating warmer, wetter and more densely vegetated land mass, which in turn caused difficulties for humans and animals orienting areas once so familiar.
>
> (UK Govt Arctic Report, p. 15)

A dilemmas and conflicts story

From the winter of 2021, in Northern Russia, emerges the story of an ice lens which formed in parts of the Yamal peninsula and negatively impacted on an estimated 60–80,000 reindeer and their herder communities. The impact of an ice lens makes it impossible for the reindeer to access the lichen that sustains them throughout the winter. The food is there, but the reindeer can't reach it under the snow and ice. Reindeer normally manage to dig through the snow to access its favourite food, but during the winter of 2020–2021, the ground was covered by unbreakable ice. A rescue operation, dependent on local oil companies' infrastructure and the bringing in of food, was seen as a solution. So here we have the ingredients of a conflicted and tensioned relationship between the development of sustainable, local herding economies and the phenomenon of growing extractive ones. Sixty percent of reindeer stocks in the Yamal are owned by family-based herder communities.

On one side of the issue are some Russian researcher voices who claim that ice lenses are naturally occurring in permafrost regions and may be affected by

22 *Tony Ghaye*

climate change. On the other side are some herder voices claiming the ice lens was formed as a result of steam generated by waters kept ice-free by increased shipping associated with oil and gas development. Russia's Yamal gas project is so far inside the Arctic Circle that purpose-built ships have been built to plough through 2 metre ice to reach it.

"The reindeer are not able to get food, and the weak animals quickly die while the remaining parts of the herds lose their strength", local herder and politician Eiko Serotetto told newspaper Neft. "If this continues, 300 families in the Seyakha village will be completely without livestock – all animals will die", Serotetto stated. Several herders believe the expansive oil and gas industry is to blame for the situation. Through the whole 2020–2021 winter, icebreakers have criss-crossed the Gulf of Ob as part of the development of new major industrial projects in the region. Among them is the Arctic LNG 2, the major natural gas project currently under development on the eastern shore of the Ob. The open waters generate steam that drifts over the tundra and subsequently crystalizes on the snow, the herders argue. However, the theory is rebuffed by Russian researchers. They argue that the ice layer is a natural phenomenon and likely connected with climate change saying, "the icebreakers are definitely not the reason for the ice formation. But the climate is changing globally, the temperatures are increasing". Temperatures in Yamal and surrounding Arctic areas have, over the past years, seen a dramatic increase. The year 2020, for example, was the warmest on record, and parts of Yamal, Taymyr and other Russian Arctic territories had average temperatures up to 7 degrees Celsius above normal.

Companies such as Gazprom and Novatek operate several major gas projects in the Yamal Peninsula, among them the Bovanenkovo field and the Yamal LNG. The projects all include major developments of infrastructure such as roads, airports, railway and pipelines. And more is being planned with regard to offshore oil, liquified natural gas and the petrochemical industry all likely to benefit from big tax cuts for new Russian Arctic projects. It is therefore not surprising that much of it may be in conflict with the reindeer herders. According to the herder Serotetto, representatives of the reindeer herders themselves must be involved in the development of a strategy for the indigenous industry. "Unless we make a full-fledged support strategy for the herders, nothing will change", he underlines. "Today, we are temporarily helped by the oil companies, and they are eager to tell the world about that. So, today they helped us and feed us, but tomorrow – what will the reindeer herder have to eat then? He will be left with nothing", Serotetto argues.

The mattering story

As I have already sketched out in this chapter, sustainable actions for human benefit are not just a matter of knowing what to do but rather about knowing the right thing to do and taking coordinated, responsible and value-based action, often at scale, to face the challenges of building a better future, head-on. This is not just a question of can we know better, in order to do better, (Chambers, 2017). It's deeper than this. I suggest it's about how we create knowledge, practices and

Concerned Arctic peoples 23

theory that gives all actors involved, a better chance to explore what's possible and what's desirable (Wheatley, 2006). And as we re-define sustainability (see later in this chapter) how this might relate to a kind of sustainability defined in terms of thriving and flourishing.

The past is not irrelevant

> I grew up with traditional people and spiritual people. I listened to them. I understand their language. Even though they've all passed on, I'm still living in Arctic Village. I try to speak for my people about the land all the time. I try to protect my traditional value and protect the land and water. I don't worry about myself, but I worry about the next generation. We have to stand together and fight for this land we have.
>
> (Bannergee, 2012, p. 269)

What is front and central here is the idea of who and what matters most, why and where? I would suggest that the principles and processes of mattering are at the core of all sustainability conversations because they serve to frame the powerful impact changes in the Arctic have on individuals and communities. It reflects how Arctic peoples are strongly influenced by their beliefs, their histories, how they matter to each other, to the land and are seen by others from "outside" and from below the Arctic Circle.

Warrior cries

> It feels as if the government and industry want us to forget who we are, what we have a right to, and what we deserve. They repeatedly overwhelm us with information, requests, and deadlines, and it seems as if they hope that we will either give up or die fighting. We are not giving up. We must fight.
>
> (Cannon in Bannergee, 2012, p. 286)

The idea of mattering leads all those involved in sustainability conversations to ask the fundamental question namely, "who really cares about me/us?" We should not forget that feeling you matter, or not, is central to many people's sense of identity (Flett, 2018; Ghaye, 2021; Rosenberg, 1985; Rosenberg & McCullough, 1981).

Figure 1.1 illuminates some of the critical relationships between feeling you matter and conversations about four conceptions of sustainability. The question, "what and who matters here and why?" is at the heart building a better history and central to Figure 1.1.

1 *Living from*: This captures the interdependencies of the biophysical, economic and social worlds. It can be thought about in terms of how we benefit from each other's work and lives and also thought of as the earth as a resource, supporting and sustaining livelihoods. It also engages us with issues related to biophysical and human resilience.

24 Tony Ghaye

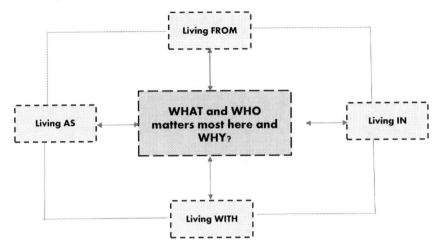

Figure 1.1 The relationships between "mattering'" and four conceptions of sustainability.

2 *Living in*: This refers to the spaces and places we inhabit where life is enacted. From an environmental psychology perspective, it is related to important people-place concepts such as topophilia and topophobia (Tuan, 1974) and a sense of place and of placelessness (Relph, 1976).
3 *Living with*: This is how we co-exist with other peoples and our environment. We live and thrive in relationship (Whitney et al., 2019). Living with embraces both conflict and human thriving and flourishing as we navigate our way through sustainability challenges.
4 *Living as*: This is about living as responsible citizens, acting with an ethical compass and with moral courage. It is people cognizant of the fact that sustainability issues mean that we have to, "address complex, wicked problems, where facts are uncertain, stakes are high, and decisions are urgent …. Here, the choices about what and how we research are inherently normative, because all problem descriptions partially result from the value lenses through which issues are viewed. Different lenses give rise to competing knowledge claims, which can be addressed through deliberative processes of knowledge co-production that extend peer review from expert-only, to a transdisciplinary community also involving practitioners, and policy makers" (Kenter et al., 2019, p. 1440).

Letting the future have a future story

I wish to explore the idea of letting the future have a future, by relating it to the ways we think about and create spaces and places for responsible engagement and action (Stavros & Torres, 2018). To do this I need to open up the nature and role of a virus (not COVID-19!) but something called the *responsibility virus*

Concerned Arctic peoples   25

(Martin, 2003). This can impact conversations-that-matter about sustainability issues in significant ways. In essence, understanding this virus takes us to the heart of actions for sustainability because it helps us with the question, "did I/we make the right decision/choice?"

Imagine a scenario where we broadcast to others that our favourite ice hockey team will win the weekend match. If our team wins, it's no real problem taking responsibility for our prediction. But if they lose, we might blame chance because our prediction has turned out wrong. It's human nature for people to take credit when things go well and avoid blame when they go badly. It's the same when thinking about sustainable development work and especially about those that lead it. "The virus propels the heroic leader to a failure generated by taking on more responsibility than any one person can carry. But then, as over-responsible leaders approach the point of failure, they do an abrupt turnaround, flipping to an under-responsible stance in order to insulate themselves from the pain and responsibility they see looming" (Martin, 2003, p. 8). This vacillation between over- and under-responsibility feeds dysfunctionality and frustration in development groups and a loss of confidence from others involved in the development process. The combination of such vacillation together with failure to learn from failure can cause sustainability conversations to get stuck.

This leads us to another key question I suggest. How, as part of our conceptual construction of responsibilities and of political action, do we acknowledge (pay heed to, take care of, represent, recognize, etc.) the otherness of nature and of the future? The link between our concerns for the future and concerns for the earth is at the heart of sustainability thinking. With such thinking, a sense that the future matters takes on a specific weight because it raises the issue of understanding the dynamics of responsibility. More specifically, as illustrated above, who is responsible for what, how and why? Also, who's interests are being served and whose are not? Problematically and stated as a challenge, "It would seem then that, ultimately, we each have to serve as judge and jury for our own actions" (Dasgupta, 2021, abridged p. 5). This is a complex undertaking and one that requires an understanding of responsible action.

So what might be construed as responsible action? What follows, I suggest could be a legitimate example and one which interestingly illustrates the use of the "precautionary principle", its role in responsible action and in the debate about fishing in the Central Arctic Ocean (CAO). The case is eloquently set out by Vylegzhanin, Young, and Berkman (2020). They say that the signing of the "Agreement to Prevent Unregulated High Seas Fisheries in the Central Arctic Ocean", in 2018, by representatives of the five Arctic coastal states together with representatives of four other states (China, Iceland, Japan and Korea) and the European Union produced a kind of legal euphoria. For the first time, Canada, Denmark/Greenland, Norway, Russia and the United States – the Arctic 5 – joined together with a group of non-Arctic states to forge a legally binding agreement dealing with an Arctic-specific issue.

26 *Tony Ghaye*

The CAO has recently attracted increased attention because of the 2018 Agreement. Some argue that it constitutes a progressive contribution to the evolving governance process for the Arctic Ocean. Eye-catching features of the Agreement are (i) its reliance on a precautionary approach put in place and designed to ensure sustainability and (ii) the inclusion of non-Arctic states and the European Union as signatories. Arguably the Central Arctic Ocean Fisheries Agreement may emerge as an important precedent with significant implications for the governance of the CAO as an area beyond national jurisdiction and for Arctic Ocean governance more generally. Taking into account the dramatic biophysical changes now occurring in the region, the agreement prohibits the initiation of unregulated fishing in the CAO. It provides for a Joint Program of Scientific Research and Monitoring to assess prospects for the development of commercially significant fish stocks in the future and calls for regular meetings of the parties to determine whether to take steps towards the establishment of one or more fisheries management organizations in the event that commercial fishing does become an attractive prospect.

> The link between the use of the "precautionary principle" and responsible action can be stated thus. ....calls on nations to take preventive measures whenever an action may cause damage to ecosystems, even when there is no conclusive evidence of a causal relationship between the action and its alleged effects. Simply put, the legal obligations embedded in the precautionary principle specify that relevant states should not use the lack of scientific certainty as a reason for postponing measures to prevent environmental degradation
>
> (Vylegzhanin et al., 2020, p. 6).

The CAO and the statement "...that relevant states should not use the lack of scientific certainty as a reason for postponing measures to prevent environmental degradation", leads us into a consideration of the central role that doubt (or lack of) can play as a generative process in seeking sustainable solutions for positive impact.

The role of doubt in sustainability conversations-that-matter

Here are some familiar clarion cries that we hear in the field of sustainability. For example, "we should protect people and environments". Another is, "the Arctic is a place where economic and commercial development needs to occur in a sustainable and responsible manner. Where the people of the region benefit from the prosperity that a changing Arctic may bring". And a further example, "the Government will respect the views, interests, culture and traditions of the Arctic indigenous people. Hearing directly from the people whose lives are most impacted by changes in the Arctic is a powerful motivation to support sustainable development there". The language of "should-isms" of "there" not here, of respect, commitment, personal and collective accountability and responsibility, as well as of complaint and blame for example, start to open-up issues of what matters most, to whom and why? In the context of responsible sustainable Arctic action, it seems advisable to develop our appreciation of the following:

- Those responsible for initiating, or leading change processes in the Arctic, might usefully be fully aware of the human and biophysical "significance" of the proposed change/s.
- That it can be very hard to bring about significant change in people and/or environments if all concerned get trapped in win/lose conversations because this gives rise to participants not really wanting to listen to each other. If they lose out or become convinced that their views of Arctic change are wrong, this can be construed as a loss!
- That's it's very hard to have sustainability conversations-that-matter unless all involved reflect on the issue of control. Who is controlling what, how and for what reasons? If one group, who are at the sustainability table, wish to maintain control, it means that they may not wish to employ doubt, or engage in open-ended brainstorming, as this might lead in unanticipated and uncomfortable directions.

A central problem here is the human tendency to "commodify" the contents of sustainability conversations. For example, we treat what is said as if they were possessions, that we might keep or lose, as we try to generate, or maintain, illusions of victory, control, respect, dignity and so on. I am suggesting that it might be useful to increase our understanding of how we might positively transform sustainability conversations by foregrounding the role of doubt and seeing this as a generative process in seeking sustainable solutions for positive impact. Although doubt might immediately conjure up feelings of nervousness or risk, when used appropriately, it can be a powerful antidote to the "governing values" of many sustainability dialogues of win, don't lose, maintain control, avoid embarrassment and loss of face, don't relinquish cherished beliefs and habits, I'm right/they're wrong and my sole purpose is to convince and confirm what I believe to be right!

So how might doubt be seen as a positively generative process in such conversations? Doubt is not a weakness. Used appropriately it's a strength and an important element in helping everyone involved think again and more clearly as to what actions are to be supported (or not) and in what ways. Often, we don't just hesitate to rethink our answers to complex biophysical, socio-cultural and economic problems. We hesitate at the very idea of rethinking. This is not just cognitive laziness, even though some involved in sustainability work prefer the ease of hanging onto their old views, or the views of dominant and more powerful groups, over the difficulty and discomfort of grappling with new ones. Questioning ourselves, our value position and our actions make everything more unpredictable. And in a VUCA world (volatile, uncertain, chaotic, ambiguous) and one transitioning through a global COVID-19 pandemic, who wants to positively embrace more unpredictability? From a psychological perspective this is called seizing and freezing. Both can get in the way of generating sustainable

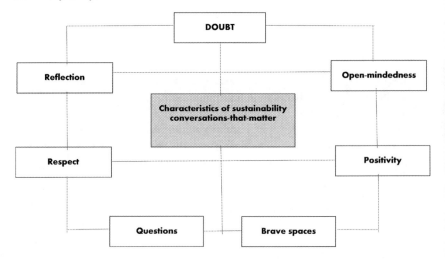

Figure 1.2 Situating doubt alongside the characteristics of sustainability conversations-that-matter.

and responsible conversations-that-matter (Ghaye, 2021). I suggest we have to ask ourselves how far, and when, do we favour the comfort of our convictions over the discomfort of doubt? Additionally, when engaging in sustainable conversations, how far, and when, do we listen and align ourselves with views that make us feel good, right and "on top", instead of ideas that make us think hard and again? Figure 1.2 is a way of describing some of the important elements of conversations-that-matter and how we might position doubt therein.

Doubt

Certainty needs to be complemented with doubt. If we are extremely evangelical in our sustainability conversations, it's often hard for us to see gaps in our knowledge and to consider options and appreciate alternative viewpoints. Often what is known and by whom can limit the possibility of discovering what is not known. I am therefore an advocate of "doubting narratives" and practices when trying to come to sustainable solutions. "What we want to attain is confident humility: having faith in our capability while appreciating that we may not have the right solution or even be addressing the right problem. That gives us enough doubt to re-examine our old knowledge and enough confidence to pursue new insights" (Grant, 2021, p. 47).

Open-Mindedness

Typically open-mindedness is not at the top of many lists of virtues required for sustainability conversations. To be open-minded is to be aware of one's fallibility and to acknowledge the possibility that anytime we believe in someone or something, we

Concerned Arctic peoples   29

could be wrong. There is an interesting relationship between doubt and open-mindedness. Doubt needs a good portion of open-mindedness to be effective. The more closed-minded we are, the more difficult it is to have sustainability conversations because nobody is open to the joys of being wrong! And they are prone to being enslaved by confirmation and conviction biases. Also, these conversations can suffer from what is called the "backfire effect". Conversations about fisheries, oil and mineral extraction strategies, arctic farming policies, the benefits of distance-spanning healthcare, the need to engage seriously and meaningfully with all those whose livelihoods and traditions are being threatened by peoples and policies from "elsewhere", for example, potentially can all backfire. The causes of backfire effects are conflicts between parties over espoused values and values-in-action (Argyris & Schon, 1992). This can be brutal when our closely held values that we are invested in are not just contested but overpowered by other values, more dominant voices or more convincing and relevant evidence. In this situation, conversations can get stuck. In conversations where values conflict, problems about sustainability either don't get solved at all, or they get solved by force!

Positivity

In every chapter in this book, moral, ethical and legal issues jump off the page. In every chapter, we can find examples of how (arguably) good people try to make tough decisions to resolve complex sustainability issues (Kidder, 1995). Therefore, I am suggesting that a critical characteristic of productive conversations-that-matter is positivity (Fredrickson, 2003, 2009) along with many others, all talk about the power of positivity and the need to draw upon the benefits that the acknowledgement and use of positive emotions can bring in trying to find a way through complex and complicated sustainability issues. Positive emotions such as love, pride, significance, harmony, hope, interest, inspiration and awe, for example, in relation to cherished Arctic lives and livelihoods.

I suggest we also need to talk about empowerment, participation and sustainability, for example, in Arctic change conversations as mutually reinforcing concepts and processes. Empowering conversations can provide the fuel for change. This can't, in my view, happen without participation. The more individuals, families and communities feel empowered to participate in decisions that affect their lives, the more likely it is that the outcomes will be received positively and be able to be sustained. The danger, of course, is when seemingly productive conversations get infected with *toxic positivity*. We can define this as the excessive and inappropriate use of positive and overly optimistic comments when conducting sustainability conversations. This can lead to accusations that we are "out of touch", "in a bubble", "wear rose-tinted glasses" and should "get real"!

Brave spaces

"Rapid change, both physical and social, challenge Arctic communities. While climate change is perhaps the most obvious and widely acknowledged influence on the

30   *Tony Ghaye*

future of circumpolar societies, other factors play a more immediate role in the lives of Arctic residents in many areas. Globalization, economic and political transformations, changing cultural landscapes, often driven from afar but experienced in the North, are all requiring adaptations" (Nymand Larsen, Fondahl & Schweitzer, 2010, p. 11). With the Arctic affected by both global environmental change and globalization processes, I would argue that the time has come to think about how sustainability conversations require not just safe spaces but brave spaces in order to be fit for purpose (Ali, 2017; Arao & Clemens, 2013). This chapter is being written at a time when we are living through a period of extraordinary uncertainty caused by COVID-19. Uncertainty about our physical health and safety, our economic security, daily living conditions, between change and stability and collective futures. The Arctic is no different. It's just a question of degree. So, creating appropriate places and spaces for conversations-that-matter is important. Table 1.1 illustrates how different kinds of space serve to liberate or constrain what is enacted there. This is a critical element in understanding how context affects actions.

The nature of the psycho-physical spaces and places we create for sustainability conversations are more decisive in generating appropriate conversational climates than many appreciate. Most meeting places are designed for control, negotiation and persuasion. When moving from left to right in Table 1.1 we are increasing the potential for building communal consciousness and communal intimacy, which I feel are critical characteristics of conversations-that-matter. These two qualities, I suggest, are positive behavioural enablers that affect the nature and level of connectedness, openness and curiosity of the group gathered in that space.

Questions

"Questions that have the power to make a difference are ones that engage people in an intimate way, confront them with their freedom and invite them to co-create a future possibility .... Powerful questions are the ones that cause you to become an actor as soon as you answer them. You no longer have the luxury to be a spectator of whatever it is you are concerned about" (Block, 2008, p. 168). On the other hand, questions with little power are those that don't help us create an alternative and better future.

Often when discussing issues about sustainable development, we find ourselves trapped in asking a particular kind of powerful question. A deficit-based one. Put another way, these are questions to solve a problem, fix or mend something. They can also be targeted at getting rid of things we don't want in our lives. They are important questions to ask, but of course, not the only ones that help us build better futures for Arctic people's. For example, a problem-based question might be, "how can new satellite monitoring of the Arctic be developed that could have global benefits?" Due to the slow rotation of the earth near the poles, satellites are unable to operate in "geostationary orbit" – that is, travelling at the same speed as the rotation of the earth – above 81°3' latitude. The problem is uniquely tricky. Another example would be with regard to better understanding

Table 1.1 Different kinds of space for sustainability conversations.

Closed	Invited	Claimed	Safe	Brave
This space is closed when decisions about Arctic people's lives and livelihoods are made without them being present. These spaces do not provide opportunities for inclusion and no participation by those who are affected by changes the most.	This space can only be occupied by invitation. However, this doesn't necessarily mean Arctic peoples actually have their voices heard, or their arguments acted upon. In these kinds of space manipulative and passive participation can prevail. In other words, people are there but they are being told what to say or told about what has already been decided.	This space is created and claimed by those most invested and affected by proposed Arctic changes. It's where Arctic people are able to gain more control of their future. It's more authentic participation as people who may have less power set their own agendas for change or stability. They see participation as a right and self-mobilize.	This space tends to develop over time. It's where participants (especially marginalized or oppressed community members) feel able to say what they truly feel and think without punishment, rejection, exclusion and shame. In safe spaces, Arctic peoples can feel sufficiently secure to be able to exercise doubt, open-mindedness and positivity. This is supportive of efforts to change themselves and their communities, if necessary. But feeling safe is a very personal construct. It can also be a place to hide.	This space is a step on from an emphasis on psychological safety. It's where there can be controversy with civility, where varying opinions are accepted. It's where Arctic peoples can openly own their beliefs and intentions. It's a space where people can challenge by choice. In other words, where people have the option to step in and out of challenging conversations. Being respectful of one another's personhood is also another characteristic.

32 Tony Ghaye

permafrost thaw and it being one of the world's most pressing climate problems that is already disrupting lifestyles, livelihoods, economies and ecosystems in the Arctic north and threatening to spill beyond the boundaries of the Arctic as our planet continues to warm. "Drunken forests" are a tricky problem. A further example of questions of this kind can be illustrated from the field of defence and security and the problem of the increased militarization of the Arctic. The region is becoming more accessible due to rapidly melting ice, giving rise to intensified maritime traffic and resource exploitation. As a result, the circumpolar states are gaining more national assets that they need to protect in the Arctic. One consequence of this is the deployment of armed forces in the region. This shifting regional security environment, which potentially heightens the risk of a conflict, is another tricky problem. And finally an illustration of a problem-based question with regard to First Nations culture in Canada. In summary Carvill (2020) puts it this way. The suicide rate among First Nations people in Canada was three times higher than in non-indigenous populations between 2011 and 2016, according to Statistics Canada. Suicide rates were highest for youth and young adults aged 15–24 years old among First Nations men and Inuit men and women. She argues that traditional values and practices are fundamental to physical, mental, emotional and spiritual wellbeing and reliance on them make a significant contribution to maintaining mental wellbeing and responding to mental health issues. The importance of drawing on the cultural traditions as First Nations people in addressing contemporary challenges in local communities cannot be overstated. Carvill says that the problem which emerges is again complex. In 2020, she states that mental health issues were a serious challenge to the wellbeing of First Nation families and community. The problems that arise are in the form of addictions, depression, stress, post-traumatic stress, breakdowns in families, dysfunctional behaviour including crimes and rising suicide rates. The solution to this problem, she argues, is the invigoration of traditional values and practices.

So let's step back for a moment. We grow in the direction in which we ask questions. Deficit-based (problem) questions lead to deficit-based conversations and actions. However, if we change the question, we have a chance to change to conversation, change that and we change the action (Ghaye, 2011; Kegan & Lahey, 2001; Stone, Patton, & Heen, 1999). Sustainability conversations, I suggest, need to feature another kind of powerful question. A strength-based one. These focus not on what we wish to alleviate or get rid of, but what we wish to have more of, or amplify. This opens the door for re-considering what positive strategic sustainability actions really mean. Additionally and ideally, we need to be armed with an abundance mindset. One that offers us a view that we live in a universe of strengths and that there are no limits to the growth of constructive cooperation. So, two central challenges in conversations about sustainability are, "where would you like to start?" and "what question ignites the most productive conversation you might have and one that we've never had before?" Talk across the Arctic of sustainable development, coupled with social responsibility, does not even come close to what I suggest is needed, even though (re-)designing for more sustainable business practices and socially responsible organizations who act respectfully with regard to indigenous peoples, seems like progress today. While this is certainly a big subject, too large to tackle all at once and in this chapter, I am strongly suggesting that in this pivotal moment of an on-going story of Arctic change, we might usefully think about "sustainability-as-flourishing".

Respect

A traditional story, from the Canadian north (reported by Carvill, 2020) and based on First Nation member Keish, nicknamed Skookum Jim, offers an important window into issues of respect when engaging with issues of sustainability.

Skookum Jim's frog helper story

Skookum Jim saves the life of a frog who had been trapped in a deep hole by providing a board for the frog to crawl out on, to be carried to the safety of a creek. About a year later, because he was a natural peacemaker and attempted to make peace between two men he had never met, Skookum Jim was kicked in the stomach by one of the men. The kick developed a large wound that threatened his life. His aunt, who was tending to him during his illness, found a frog licking his wounds. The frog would not leave him until his wound was healed. It was the same frog that he had saved a year prior! Once back to full health, Keish travelled home. During his journey he had a dream about finding gold; in the dream the frog is thanking him and says he will find gold. Keish did in fact find gold, the most important gold discovery in North America, the discovery that triggered the Gold Rush of 1898. The teachings of this story are about respecting mother earth's creatures, the relationships between life and land, about trust, the wellbeing of nature and of caring for others only because it is "the right thing to do.

(Carvill, 2020, p. 7)

But there is another important aspect of respect that needs to characterize sustainability conversations-that-matter. It is a relational one (Chambers, 2017; Wheatley, 2002). This is what truly gives life to these conversations. And because many conversations about sustainability issues require skilful navigation through value-laden issues, moral courage is also needed. Kidder (2005) asks the question, "*what does moral mean?*" and suggests that it relates to three values, namely honesty, responsibility and respect. If we add two more values, those of fairness and compassion, Kidder suggests we have a five-fingered hand that appears to constitute humanity's common moral framework. Can there be such a thing as this in sustainability conversations? A moral framework? As I've alluded to earlier, the toughest sustainability issues are not always right versus wrong, but right versus right ones. Determining which party, group or community has the higher claim to rightness, requires deep ethical reasoning. And implementing the conclusion we come to, which is standing up for what our reasoning tells us, requires the enactment of respectful relationships, where both issues of conscience and

34 *Tony Ghaye*

consequence can be put on the table. Respect allows for the discovery of what is, and also what is to be done. It also helps us move from impasse to reciprocity. And finally when respect is part of sustainability conversations, sometimes almost without knowing, everyone involved is learning to practice the "principle of accompaniment". This has its roots in a Jesuit idea meaning to live and walk alongside. "It is a willingness to encounter another, to make someone feel valued and seen, bettered for knowing you, never belittled.......This kind of accompaniment requires the patience to listen to others' stories without judgement, to offer skills and solutions without imposition" (Novogratz, 2020, p. 187).

Reflection

To create new and better realities for those who live in the Arctic, I suggest we have to learn the skill of listening reflectively. Conversations of the kind I am proposing in this chapter are not simply ones where we are able to hear the chorus of other voices at the table. I am proposing that we must also learn to hear the contribution of our own voice. "It is not enough to be able to see others in the picture of what is going on; we must also see what we ourselves are doing. It is not enough to be observers of the problem situation; we must also recognise ourselves as actors who influence the outcome" (Kahane, 2004, p. 83).

But reflectiveness in sustainability conversations-that-matter is problematic for at least three reasons. If we wish to change the systems we are part of, our communities and governing organizations, for example, we must also see and be open to the possibility that we need to change ourselves. This requires our ability to be self-reflective. This is not as easy as it sounds because it requires skills of self-awareness, self-confidence, belief and disclosure. Secondly, as I have mentioned earlier, problems of sustainability are enmeshed in complex biophysical, economic and psycho-social systems. Therefore, they often entail conflicts of conscience and solutions that can be rife with unforeseeable or unintended consequences. In situations like this, problems often need to be reframed and often unfrozen. To achieve this, reflection needs to move from "I" to "we". From a personal disposition and skill, to a collective and more public one. Thirdly, sustainable solutions require a willingness from those both inside the Arctic and from other places, to sustain connections with each other around the promises they make to each other. This requires an understanding of the difference and roles of "reflective-but-retributive conversations" (a problem to be solved) and "reflective-and-restorative conversations" (acceptable possibilities to be lived into).

Subjective wellbeing

One important back-story to the notion of concerned Arctic peoples is that of subjective wellbeing (SWB). Over the last decade, sustainability scholarship in the Arctic has made substantial progress in respect to theoretical development, empirical knowledge base and methodological advancement. More specifically and with regard to wellbeing as a sustainability issue, several international

Figure 1.3 Wibecke a story-teller. Photo: Marie Louise Somby

organizations promote this across Arctic countries and regions. The International Union of Circumpolar Health and the Circumpolar Health Research Network are two examples. But arguably, there are still considerable knowledge gaps, two of which are the lack of both cross-sectional and longitudinal Pan-Arctic SWB research. SWB can be considered as having two interacting parts to it, feeling good in life and functioning well. There is a paucity of research and especially work drawing on participatory and appreciative action-based research (PAAR) principles and processes (see Ghaye et al., 2008) and illustrated, for example, in an Arctic context in the work of Ghaye and Sørly (2019). In this work, we find the story of Wibecke (see also Chapter 6 in this book). Wibecke lives in the high north of Norway. She is in her forties and comes from Tromsø. She is a recovering drug addict and has a grown-up daughter called Christina (Figure 1.3).

What does your mum do story

> I grew up as a military child. So I didn't come to Tromsø until I was twelve. I didn't have any problems making friends. Sport helped a lot. But obviously … then it started. I had a child (Christina) when I was sixteen with someone who did drugs. I had this rebellious side. I started experimenting when I was pretty young. I was just really curious. When I stopped doing sport – THEN. Then I really quickly started … if I had the weekend off I used to hit the town. I didn't just drink; I took amphetamines and cocaine as well … those weekends were one long party.

36   *Tony Ghaye*

My family didn't notice anything. You become good at hiding what you're doing. I left home when I turned eighteen. Things got out of control. In due course I started taking opiates, and heroin dominated my life from the age of around nineteen or twenty. There's more shame attached to being a girl and doing drugs, particularly if you're a mum. Being a mum who does drugs – there's almost nothing worse than that. Society sees it as an aggravating factor that a mother is putting drugs ahead of her child, because that's what many people think you're doing. That's because they don't understand the forces at work. I don't feel that I ever put drugs ahead of Christina. It was just a problem that I wasn't able to handle. That's more how I see it. Of course, you can say that I had a choice at one point. When I started partying at weekends … but when you're seventeen or eighteen you're not able to see the consequences of what you're doing. I thought that I could choose to take drugs occasionally. I didn't see the consequences of my actions. We're so bad at talking about when it turns into an addiction ….

I wanted to stop for the sake of my daughter. She was my main motivation. And it had gone so far that I was tired of taking drugs. I felt like I couldn't go on…. I had been arrested a few times and social services had got involved. But you get so good at fooling and tricking people and at lying and cheating. …… The disease blinds you. Obviously, it hasn't been good for Christina, growing up with a mum who was a heroin addict. You wouldn't wish that on your worst enemy, let alone your own child. But you don't see that when you're sick. You don't see the harm you're causing until you recover. …. But when I started with methadone-assisted rehab, I became a team leader as part of a job-training scheme run by an organisation that works with addicts. As a team leader, you were supposed to help and instruct people taking methadone. They worked four hours a day. We were given jobs by the municipality and other organisations …… That was incredibly important for me. And for Christina. Before that she'd never had an answer when people asked "What does your mum do?".

Ghaye and Sørly (2019)

The quest for a flourishing Arctic

One telling of the Arctic story is of a region experiencing accelerating change. One that is unfolding in many ways all of which are having dramatic impacts on the region's peoples and ecosystems. Climate change is a major issue, while other environmental changes are also occurring, along with rapid economic development and social transformation. This is creating new realities and involving new players in the Arctic which, in turn, is situated in a world that is increasingly connected, interdependent and competitive. Additionally, and gripped by COVID-19, it is a pivotal moment to re-imagine sustainability work and its Arctic impact.

As stated at the outset, one reason for this chapter focusing on sustainability conversations-that-matter is the proposition that our language is holding us back and that the time has come to advance beyond the language of sustainability to

Concerned Arctic peoples 37

reduce harm, to that of focusing on the language of human thriving and flourishing (Cooperrider & Fry, 2021; Pyles, 2021; Seligman, 2011; Werder, 2014). The limits of language are the limits of our worlds. As Cooperrider et al. (1995) say, "words enable worlds".

I wonder how many Arctic peoples have an ever-expanding dream of a future where economy and ecology flourish together whilst being respectful of indigenous knowledge and customs? Maybe the moment has come to shift our thinking and conversations away from "sustainability-as-surviving" to "sustainability-as-flourishing"? (Ehrenfeld & Hoffman, 2013). Could a focus on flourishing create significant action flows through families, communities, organizations, networks, nations and across the Arctic region, just as a positive virus might? Would this inspire, excite and encourage conversations-that-REALLY-matter? Would these conversations help to bring the sustainability domain and human flourishing one together?

I feel there is an urgency about needing to, at least consider, a shift of focus, away from a preoccupation with trying to achieve less unsustainable activities in the Arctic. Away from Arctic peoples seeing themselves as victims of inevitable and unstoppable global processes. Away from trying to reduce, or even reverse the harms associated with unsustainability and with fate control! So much is committed to solving what's wrong. What might happen if we focused more on what's right?

Sustainability as "surviving" or "doing less harm" to Arctic biophysical and socio-cultural systems over time becomes draining. Those involved become depleted (Byrne et al., 2014; McArthur-Blair & Cockell, 2018). The notion of sustainable conversations-that-matter articulated here are those that might constitute a new conversational arena for exploring what we want more of, rather than less of. Arenas where we talk about thriving not just surviving. Flourishing not just floundering. Does the quest for a flourishing Arctic inspire? If yes, what do we want tomorrow in the Arctic to look like and how can we co-create it for human benefit?

References

Ali, D. (2017). Safe spaces and brave spaces historical context and recommendations for student affairs professionals. *NASPA Policy and Practice Series*, Issue 2, 1–13.

Arao, B., & Clemens, K. (2013). From safe spaces to brave spaces: A new way to frame dialogue around diversity and social justice. In L. Landreman (Ed.), *The art of effective facilitation: Reflections from social justice educators* (pp. 135–150). Sterling, VA: Stylus.

Argyris, C., & Schon, D. (1992). *Theory in practice: Increasing professional effectiveness*. San Francisco, CA: Jossey-Bass.

Bali Swain, R., & Yang-Wallentin, F. (2020) Achieving sustainable development goals: predicaments and strategies. *International Journal of Sustainable Development & World Ecology, 27*(2), 96–106. DOI: 10.1080/13504509.2019.1692316

Bannergee, S. (Ed.) (2012). *Arctic voices at the tipping point*. New York, NY: Seven Stories Press.

Block, P. (2008). *Community – The structure of belonging*. San Francisco, CA: Berrett-Koehler Publishers.

38 Tony Ghaye

Bowlby, J. (1969). Attachment and loss. *Attachment* (Vol. 1). New York, NY: Basic Books.

Bowlby, J. (1980). Attachment and Loss. *Loss, sadness and depression* (Vol. 3). New York, NY: Basic Books.

Buckingham, M., & Coffman, C. (1999). *First break all the rules.* London: Simon & Schuster.

Byrne, A. C., Dionisi, A., Barling, J., Akers, A., Robertson, J., Lys, R. ... Dupré, K. (2014). The depleted leader: The influence of leaders' diminished psychological resources on leadership behaviors. *The Leadership Quarterly, 25*(2), 344–357.

Carvill, A. (2020). *Turning to traditional processes for supporting mental health.* Toronto, Canada: The Gordon Foundation.

Chambers, R. (1997). *Whose reality counts? Putting the last first.* London: Intermediate Technology Publications.

Chambers, R. (2017). *Can we know better? Reflections for development.* Rugby: Practical Action Publishing.

Cooperrider, D. L., Barrett, F. J., & Srivastva, S. (1995). Social construction and apprecia-tive inquiry: A journey in organizational theory. In D. M. E., Hosking, H., Dachler, & K. J, Gergen. (1995). Management and organization: Relational alternatives to individ-ualism (157–200). Avebury: Ashgate Publishing Co.

Cooperrider, D. L., & Fry, R. E. (2021). Mirror flourishing and the positive psychology of sustainability. *Journal of Corporate Citizenship, 46,* 3–12.

Cooperrider, D. L., Whitney, D., & Stavros, J. M. (2008), *Appreciative inquiry handbook for leaders of change,* (2nd ed.). Brunswick, OH: Crown Custom Publishing Inc..

Dasgupta, P. (2021). The economics of biodiversity: *The Dasgupta review. Abridged version.* London: HM Treasury.

Ehrenfeld, J. R., & Hoffman, A. J. (2013). *Flourishing: A frank conversation about sustaina-bility.* Redwood City, CA: Stanford University Press.

Ferrari, B. (2012). *Power listening: Mastering the most critical business skill of all.* New York, NY: Penguin.

Flett, G. L. (2018). *The psychology of mattering: Understanding the human need to be signifi-cant.* London: Academic Press.

Fredrickson, B. L. (2003). The value of positive emotions. *American Scientist, 91,* 330–335.

Fredrickson, B. (2009). *Positivity -groundbreaking research to release your inner optimist and thrive.* Oxford: One World Publications.

Ghaye, T. et al (2008) Participatory and appreciative action and reflection (PAAR) – Democratizing reflective practices. *Reflective Practice – International and Multidisciplinary Journal, 9*(4), 361–397.

Ghaye, T. (2011). *Teaching and learning through reflective practice – A practical guide for pos-itive action.* Abingdon, Oxon: Routledge.

Ghaye, T. (2022). *The contours of feeling you matter – Issues for a flourishing life,* London: Sequoia Books (forthcoming).

Ghaye, T., & Sørly, R. (2019). Participatory and appreciative action research in mental health and substance abuse in Norway's high North. *AI Practitioner, 21*(3), 35–41.

Gladwell, M. (2006). *Blink – The power of thinking without thinking.* London: Penguin Books.

Grant, A. (2021). *Think again.* London: W.H. Allen.

H.M Government (2018). *Beyond the ice UK policy towards the arctic.* King Charles Street, London: Foreign and Commonwealth Office.

Howard, R., & Korver, C. (2008). *Ethics for the real world.* Boston, MA: Harvard Business Press.

Kahane, A. (2004). *Solving tough problems.* San Francisco, CA: Berrett-Koehler Publishers.

Kegan, R., & Lahey, K. (2001). *How the way we talk can change the way we work*. San Francisco, CA: Jossey-Bass.

Kenter, J., et al. (2019). Loving the mess: Navigating diversity and conflict in social values for sustainability. *Sustainability Science, 14*, 1439–1461

Kidder, R. M. (1995). *How good people make tough choices*. New York, NY: William Morrow & Company.

Kidder, R. M. (2005). *Moral courage*. New York, NY: HarperCollins Publishers.

Kohlrieser, G., Goldsworthy, S., & Coombe, D. (2012). *Care to Dare: Unleashing astonishing potential through secure-base leadership*. San Francisco, CA: Jossey-bass.

Martin, R. L. (2003). *The responsibility virus*. Edinburgh: Pearson Education Ltd.

McArthur-Blair, J., & Cockell, J. (2018). *Building resilience with appreciative inquiry: A leadership journey through Hope, despair and forgiveness*. San Francisco, CA: Berrett-Koehler Publishers.

Northcott, M. S. (2013). *A political theology of climate change*. Grand Rapids, MI: William B. Eerdmans Publishing Company.

Novogratz, J. (2020). *Manifesto for a moral revolution: Practices to build a better world*. New York, NY: Henry Holt & Company.

Nymand Larsen, J., Fondahl, G., & Schweitzer, P. (2010). Arctic social indicators: a follow-up to the Arctic Human Development Report. Copenhagen: Nordic Council of Ministers Publication.

Pascale, R., Sternin, J., & Sternin, M. (2010). *The power of positive deviance*. Boston, MA: Harvard Business Press.

Pyles, L. (2021). *Progressive community organizing: Transformative practice in a globalizing world*. (3rd ed.). New York, NY: Routledge.

Redclift, M. (2005). Sustainable development (1987–2005): An oxymoron comes of age. *Sustainable Development, 13*, 212–227.

Relph, E. (1976). *Place and placelessness*. London: Pion.

Rosenberg, M. (1985). Self-concept and psychological well-being in adolescence. In R. L. Leahy (Ed.), The development of self (pp. 205–246). Orlando, FL: Academic Press.

Rosenberg, M., & McCullough, B. C. (1981). Mattering: Inferred significance and mental health among adolescents, research. *Community and Mental Health, 2*, 163–182.

Seligman, M. P. (2011). *Flourish*. New York, NY: Simon & Schuster Inc.

Spaiser, V., Ranganathan, S., Swain, R. B., & Sumpter, D. (2016). The sustainable development oxymoron: Quantifying and modelling the incompatibility of sustainable development goals. *International Journal of Sustainable Development & World Ecology, 24*, 457–470. doi:10.1080/13504509.2016.1235624

Stavros, J., & Torres, C. (2018). *Conversations worth having*. Oakland, CA: Berrett-Koehler Publishers.

Stone, D., Patton, B., & Heen, S. (1999). *Difficult conversations: How to discuss what matters most*. London: Penguin Book.

Tuan, Y.-F. (1974). *Topophilia: A study of environmental perceptions, attitudes, and values*. Englewood Cliffs, NJ: Prentice-Hall.

Vylegzhanin, A. N., Young, O. R., & Berkman, P. A. (2020). The Central arctic ocean fisheries agreement as an element in the evolving arctic ocean governance complex. *Marine Policy, 118*, 104001.

Werder, P. (2014). *Flourishing enterprise: The new spirit of business*. CA: Stanford Business Books.

Wheatley, M. J. (2002). *Turning to one another – Simple conversations to restore: Hope for the future*. San Francisco, CA: Berrett-Koehler Publishers.

40 Tony Ghaye

Wheatley, M. (2006). Leadership and the new science: discovering order in a chaotic world, San Francisco, CA: Berrett-Koehler.

Wheatley, M. (2007). *Finding our way: leadership for uncertain times*. San Francisco, CA: Berrett-Koehler.

Wheatley, M. J. (2017). *Who do we choose to be? Facing reality, claiming leadership*. San Francisco, CA: Berrett-Koehler Publishers.

Whitney, D., et al. (2019). *Thriving women-thriving world*. Chagrin Falls, OH: A Taos Institute Publication.

2 Disappearing flexibility

The story of Gielas reindeer herding district

Jan Åge Riseth

Introduction

Ever since the last glaciation reindeer (Eurasia) and caribou (America) have been basic resources for around 30 small Indigenous peoples around the whole circumpolar Arctic and Subarctic tundra and taiga. The Sámi with their traditional homeland (Sápmi) in northern and middle Fennoscandia and Kola Peninsula in Russia are one of these peoples. Reindeer herding is a core traditional livelihood for the Sámi and as such a basic pillar in their culture. Though this culture and livelihood is based on change, and plasticity is as an inherent part of its character, the accumulated load of external impact currently challenges its sustainability. The background for this is colonialism. Though there are decolonial trends in Norway's current policy, neo-colonialism is still dominant. Evolving tensions and contradictions are extensive, and the Sámi quite often is powerless in decision-making confronted with majority economical, social and even environmental considerations. In spite of this, significant locals also think that Sámi influence is too high.

Personally I have a four decade long working life story of learning herders and herder life to know. Gradually my mind was opened for their rich traditional knowledge. This has nuanced my attitudes and increased my understanding and respect for the challenges of herder life. The example narrative of this chapter is based on data from a commissioned work for Troms County. The narrative of Gielas reindeer herding district, which is considered representative, is the outcome of a rich herder interview, though assisted by other sources; Sámi Reindeer Husbandry (SRH) as a livelihood is dependent on specific types of landscapes during subsequent seasons. Variation between years requires flexibility to adapt to changing conditions. Climate change effects reinforce this need. However, the current trend is quite opposite. As the story of the chosen Gielas shows, the cumulative effects of encroachments and disturbance from competing land-use result in that the herders struggle to perform the annual cycle, leading to inferior use of landscapes and pastures, decreased income as well as increased costs and management that are felt culturally improper by the herders. This is a part of a national trend, but it is largely overlooked by the majority of politicians. The ongoing development is not sustainable either for SRH, Norway or the

DOI: 10.4324/9781003118633-3

42 *Jan Åge Riseth*

international community. Moreover, new alliances are built in Norway, and new strategies may be possible.

Sámi reindeer herding

The Sámi are an Indigenous people who practice reindeer herding across Sápmi. The traditional Sámi homelands were split by national borders of colonial expansion northwards in Finland, Norway, Sweden and the Kola Peninsula in Russia. According to the recent population estimates, there are 50–65,000 Sámi in Norway, including 3,329 individuals recognized as reindeer herders (Landbruksdirektoratet, 2020). The animals are herbivores living in dynamic settings with pastures, climate and predators. The core institution of Sámi reindeer herding is the siida (the band), which is a group of herding partners usually with family bonds. In Norway, reindeer husbandry is formally organized in reindeer pasture districts (RPDs).

Norway has a long history of marginalizing the Sámi people through assimilation of children in the majority language educational system, undermining property rights and restricting traditional land-use (Pedersen, 2015; Ravna, 2019). Thus, as other Indigenous peoples, Sámi people have been subject to a history of colonialism, i.e., dispossession of their lands, marginalization, racism and discrimination (Reimerson, 2015). The Sámi's experiences of colonization mainly depart with the geographical intrusion by the nation states without their consent, against their resistance and sometimes also by force. The nation states have subjected the Sámi people to political control, cultural domination, economic exploitation and undermining their own social, cultural and economic structures (Kuokkanen, 2011). In this respect, the territorial rights to land are at core, i.e., the nation states want control over natural resources in Sápmi, while the Sámi people has their livelihood and cultural survival at stake. While SRH is a core livelihood for the Indigenous Sámi people and major land-use form in middle and northern Fennoscandia, it is just a minor industry for society at large and may be seen as even a nuisance by competing land-users.

The purpose of this chapter is primarily to create an understanding for how externally imposed changes gradually, and at an increasing pace, are approaching tolerance levels where the accumulated burden of external impacts threatens its sustainability. To achieve this, I will provide the narrative of the adaptation challenges for a single RPD as presented by herder representatives. However, the concrete study of the specific example district should be seen in context with an overarching narrative of general and long-lasting changes affecting the natural and societal frames of SRH. Though modernized, the needs of the reindeer define the basics of the SRH land-use pattern. The animals use different types of pastures in various seasons. Accordingly, different RPDs with unique combinations of geology, precipitation and temperature patterns can provide these needs dissimilarly. Consequently, each RPD will have its individual pattern of reindeer movements. Such patterns are on different scales, both horizontally and vertically, creating an optimal annual cycle (Skarin & Åhman, 2014; Svonni, 1983).

Disappearing flexibility 43

Reindeer herders are familiar with variable weather patterns. *Jahki ii leat jagi viellja* (one year is not the other year's brother) is a Sámi saying highlighting their familiarity with this uncertainty. The implication of this variation is that there is a clear need of *flexibility*, i.e., possibilities for varying the pasture use according to the actual situation (Beach, 1981; Riseth, 2006; Riseth et al., 2011, Löf, 2014). However, political and societal long-term changes have heavily influenced the room of flexibility at hand.

Colonization and control

Global policies have shaped nationalism and colonialism on the Top of Europe. In a half millennium before the mid-19th century, the geopolitical situation in northern Fennoscandia was ambiguous. The national borders were partly unclear or not strictly enforced (Sandberg, 2008). Conflicts and wars between the states were often about the Sámi as objects for taxation (Hansen & Olsen, 2004). The nomadic Sámi reindeer herders could then follow old patterns and move relatively freely between the territories claimed by the separate nation states in a de facto Sápmi. The first change was formal colonization. The national border between Denmark–Norway and Sweden–Finland was set up in 1751. The so-called "Lapp Codicil", an addendum to the border treaty, codified that national borders should not obstruct Sámi migration from time immemorial, though one-state citizenship was required. The relative freedom of Sámi herders lasted for about a century after the border establishment. In the wake of the Napoleonic Wars, the national state map of Europe underwent several changes, which later led to international events that undermined the treaty.

Moreover, the Nordic states' internal colonization processes got momentum from the late 19th century. Legislation both closed national borders for transnational reindeer herding and restricted Sámi rights and adopted a top-down control of SRH (Riseth, Tømmervik, & Bjerke, 2016). The main motivation was promotion of non-Sámi farming settlers in Sámi areas. It was justified by Social-Darwinistic and nationalistic ideologies (Pedersen, 2015; Riseth et al., 2016). The first Norwegian Swedish reindeer pasture convention (1919) had particular extensive effects in Troms County. In general, the extent of cross-border reindeer husbandry was dramatically reduced both in area and number of reindeer and families. This has been aggravated by new conventions and gradually led to pushing Swedish citizen Sámi herders back towards the national border (Prestbakmo, 2007; Riseth et al., 2016). The last agreed reindeer pasture convention went out in 2005. Since then the governments of Norway and Sweden have not managed to unite upon a renewed convention. Norway has adopted a unilateral prolongation of the last convention (Ravna, 2019), but the legal situation is unclear making SRH land-use challenging for herders at both sides of the border, including pending lawsuits for Norwegian courts about grazing rights.

The group worse affected was about 70 herder families with their summer land on the large Troms islands such as Senja, Kvaløya, Ringvassøya and some mainland districts too. From 1923 around 350–400 persons with at least

44 Jan Åge Riseth

20–25,000 reindeer were completely denied access to Norwegian territory. They lost their homes and land both in Norway and Sweden and was forcibly relocated up to 300–500 km southwards in Sweden to the lands of other Sámi with repercussions for several generations of Sámi herders in Northern and Middle Fennoscandia. This is a story of eviction of an Indigenous group because of citizenship which after a century still live as an open wound in the memory of the families, with living conflicts between groups in the herder society and pending lawsuits for Swedish courts. It is dark story of assaults by the governments of two countries. Still no government has recognized that this was massive infringes, but now the story is told in a prize-winning narrative by one of the descendants (Labba, 2020).

Modernization and encroachments

From the late 19th century and throughout the 20th century, the internal colonization of Sápmi also included infrastructure and industry development with roads, railways, mines, hydropower regulations and industrial forestry (dominant in Sweden and Finland). The major effect on SRH is loss and fragmentation of habitats (Fahrig, 2019), i.e., a process where large and contiguous habitats divided into smaller and isolated patches of habitats.

> The more the land is cut up and crisscrossed by the railway and road networks, and the more grazing lands are cut up into an uneven patchwork by the timber industry, the more difficult it becomes to stabilize the reindeer's movement.
>
> (Beach, 1981, p. 52).

During the latest half century this situation is gradually aggravated by addition of new types of competing land-use and disturbance to this; other energy facilities including wind turbine plants and major power transmission lines, climate change (CC), predation, recreation facilities and activities as well as other types of human disturbance (Hovelsrud et al., 2020).

CC has a number of *direct* impacts for SRH, such as uncertain winter pastures, movement challenges on shoulder seasons, and shrubification and rising treelines (Riseth & Tømmervik, 2017). Moreover, in the short run the *secondary* impacts of CC with a new generation encroachment seem to have even larger impact on SRH than CC itself. Concretely, measures such as wind turbines and high voltage power transmission lines, mines for provision of rare metals needed in lithium batteries are examples of high effect encroachments often coined as *green colonialism* (Retter, 2021). In sum, SRH is generally under severe pressure due to the multiple stressor effects of encroachment and human disturbance. The severity varies but impact analyses and evaluation reports provide strong indications that the accumulated effects of encroachments over time approaches the limits of tolerability in many RPDs (Kløcker-Larsen et al., 2017; Riseth & Johansen, 2019, Risvoll et al., submitted).

Decolonization

The Sámi Reindeer Herders Association (NRL) was established already in 1948. From the 1960s political tides started slowly to change and a broader ethnopolitical Sámi movement developed. In the late 1970s, SRH was recognized as an industry by a double reform establishing both an industrial agreement between NRL and the Ministry of Agriculture (1976) and a new Reindeer Husbandry Act (1978) with positive and development-oriented goals. The political movement received extra momentum through the strong Sámi resistance against the hydropower regulation of a major river (Alta-Kautokeino) in Sámi core areas. Two hunger strikes by young Sámi and large civil disobedience actions (the Alta action) blocking the construction work grew to a political crisis that was solved by appointment of the first Sámi Rights Commission (SRC) in 1980. The SRC produced a series of reports over nearly three decades. Based on their first report the government of Norway passed laws recognizing the Sámi as Indigenous people and passed a Constitutional Amendment (1988) and established a national Sámi Parliament (1987) as a representative body for all Sámi in Norway. An important legal source for the SRC was the *International Covenant on Civil and Political Rights* (ICCPR), article 27 that reads:

> In those States in which ethnic, religious or linguistic minorities exist, persons belonging to such minorities shall not be denied the right, in community with the other members of their group, to enjoy their own culture, to profess and practice their own religion, or to use their own language.

The SRC interpreted article 27 that culture also includes the material foundation, i.e., the economical and physical basis of a culture. Accordingly, for an Indigenous minority the right to culture also includes the right to natural resources as Indigenous peoples have a special tie to nature. The Parliament's Justice Committee agreed that this view should be regarded as Norway's perception of international law. The Constitutional Amendment made it the duty of the state to "enable the Sámi to develop their language, culture and community life". The wording mirrors the referred interpretation of article 27. In 1990 Norway ratified ILO convention 169. Later this ratification became important in a large land reform that was an outcome of SRC's work (the Finnmark Act) which in 2005 transferred alleged state land in Finnmark County to a new body, the Finnmark Estate, as the inhabitants' collective property. The creation process of the Finnmark Act initiated a constitutional reform as the government bill was treated through an extensive process of direct consultations between the Justice Committee of the Norwegian Parliament and the Sámi Parliament. The new practice was expanded and formalized through a comprehensive 2005 consultation agreement between the Government and Sámi Parliament (Smith, 2007).

In the wake of this agreement, several relevant acts received purpose clauses that reflected the Constitutional Amendment. The planning part of the Plan and Building Act (PBA) of 2008 has one of its purpose clauses: "to ensure the natural basis for Sámi culture, businesses and community life" (Section 3-1c). Since then

46   *Jan Åge Riseth*

a series of cabinets have passed the document "National Expectations" as an order to regional, and local authorities, including:

> The county and municipal authorities attach importance to preserving the natural resource base for Sámi culture and economic development. Planning safeguards reindeer husbandry areas, while ensuring the needs of reindeer husbandry are balanced against other societal interests.
>
> (KMD, 2019, p. 19).

Personal engagement with reindeer husbandry

Personally I have a near to lifelong history of engagement with reindeer husbandry, as I was raised in a small farmer household in Snåsa, Mid-Norway, used to practical work. Reindeer herders were part of our rural community, we went to the same school, but they were not close to my daily life. As a student of nature conservancy, I became familiar with SRH as an academic subject. After graduation (1979) two issues turned my attention northwards; military service and the ongoing Alta action. Before long, reindeer herding and its position in society became my main professional interest. My career started with a job in the national reindeer herding bureaucracy located in Alta, Finnmark. As a bureaucrat I sometimes experienced frustrating challenges as herders' firm opinions could deviate from our professional analyses. Later I went into research. My working life through four decades has consisted not only of theoretical studies but also of more important following herders in the field with on-spot dialogues (cf. Riseth et al., 2011). This have gradually opened my mind for their rich traditional knowledge (Riseth, 2020) and made me reflect upon ways of knowing (cf. Agrawal, 1995), and my own position. Clearly, it has nuanced my attitudes and increased my understanding and respect for the challenges of herder life.

The concrete basis for this contribution is an encroachment analysis (Riseth & Johansen 2019), a commissioned work for Troms County. The focus of the analysis was the cumulative effects of encroachments on reindeer herding. We used multiple sources and methods, but the main source was a questionnaire to and interviews with RPD leaders. I chose to use the narrative of Gielas RPD as the backbone of this chapter since its leader provided a rich and representative description of the encroachment situation in Gielas. I also consider the district to be representative for many other districts. Moreover, I live near the area and have relevant personal observations. As an alternative to a thick description (Geertz, 1973) I have aimed to write a more condensed story (cf. Bain, Nagrani, Brown, & Zisserman, 2020). The background material of this contribution is developed in near dialogue with the herders involved, and I have their full consent for publication. The material is also utilized in local/regional media and national publications.

Land-use, encroachments and disturbances

The current Gielas RPD was established in 1965 with two herder families moving in from Finnmark (Reinbeitekommisjonen, 2001). To depict the land-use

Disappearing flexibility 47

narrative of Gielas, a good basis will be the same platform as reindeer herders that have not met for a while (cf. Åhrén, 2007) will use. After greetings and necessary queries, the main conversation often starts with "How has last year been?" Therefore, our Gielas narrative follows the reindeer year, i.e., the annual cycle of reindeer land-use.

Calves are born in May. The best calving pastures in the North East unfortunately became a military shooting and training field (Rørholt, 2009). Though, the military is by legal judgement imposed a month's activity stop, so the area is still used for calving but fixed dates are difficult as spring time varies between years. Therefore, the second best areas in the North West also are used for calving. However, the calving areas are in the transition zone between birch forest and low mountain plateaus, which are also very attractive sites for recreation homes. Spring weekends means skiing and human disturbance implying that animals drift out of the area and need to be moved back in week days. Disturbance by dogs and skiers may scare female reindeer to leave its progeny which will then be more exposed to predators, eagles in particular.

Figure 2.1 shows an overview map. Note the core natural infrastructure of collecting and migration zones. The district includes some areas in Sweden (lower right corner) starting with the spring pasture that are depicted on the first map, up north.

Figure 2.2 depicts the land-use for the remainder of the year. The figure on the left depicts summer and autumn pastures while the one right late autumn and winter pastures. Due to the disturbance from human activity, the animals have a tendency to drift early to the East side that have more predators.

From spring towards summer reindeer naturally follow the greening upwards in the landscape. Thus, the summer pastures are around the highest mountains. They are mostly located in the middle part of the district; the best and most used areas are towards the East. During summer main challenges are disturbance from hikers and anglers.

From high summer towards autumn the animals lower themselves in the landscape. During autumn they follow low valleys with mires and watercourses. In early fall, on move southwards, the animals encounter a new 420 kV powerline established parallel and close to the E6 main road. In September, 2016, the powerline stressed the herd under collection to the corral site for early autumn slaughter. The bottom line was that the whole process failed, and this corral site has been abandoned.

Core autumn pastures are in the southern part of the district. Late autumn and winter pastures are the southernmost. The Ofoten railway for transportation of iron ore from the mining town Kiruna to the shipment in Narvik was opened in 1902. This initiated a long series of encroachments. Cumulative effects appear as an outcome of cause – effect chains caused by different interventions and disturbances interacting within each of the seasonal pastures. This adds up and affects reindeer husbandry throughout the annual cycle. Table 2.1 provides a summary.

For Gielas the accumulated effect is a *gradual development of a barrier for the natural movement between the seasonal pastures*. Already disturbed by buildings,

48 Jan Åge Riseth

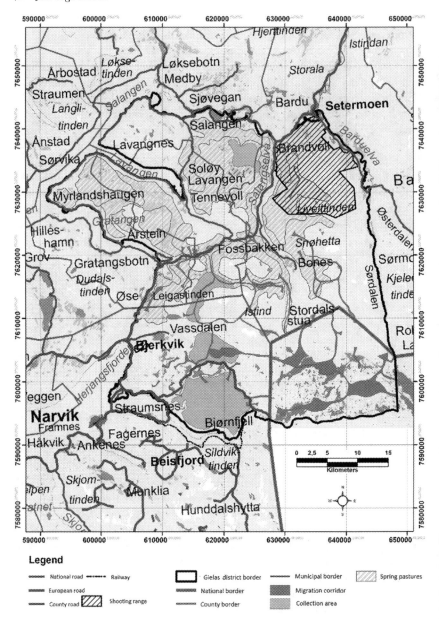

Figure 2.1 Gielas. Spring pastures, collecting and migration zones (adapted from Riseth et al., 2021).

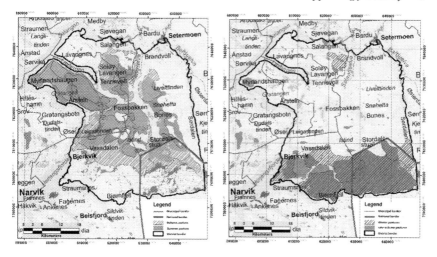

Figure 2.2 Gielas. Season pastures. Summer to winter (adapted from Riseth et al., 2021).

Table 2.1 Summary of cause–impact–effect chains in Gielas RPD

		Cause	Impact	Effect
1	a	Shooting range (East side)	Substantial calving area reduction	Increased use of western area
	b	New recreation cabin areas (West side)	Reduced and disturbed grazing	Animals stray East. More predation. Enter summer area too early
2	a	E6 Gratangsfjellet	Challenging barrier	Strict control of moving
	b	420 kV powerline	Impossible barrier	No early autumn slaughter
3		Iron ore findings (Sweden)	Kiruna mines	Need of ice-free harbour
	a	Railway & Narvik town	Recreation/cottage area Bjørnfjell	Passage narrowed step by step
	b		Hydro-power regulation of lakes	
	c	Border-crossing road (E10)	More recreation cottage areas	
	d	Wind turbine industry	Stop in free migration. Animals move in wrong directions	No autumn slaughter. Very difficult to control animals. Too early into Sweden
4		No border convention since 2005		No access to late winter areas. Pellets feeding required

humans and roads, animals now become scared when facing wind turbines on their migration route (Skarin, Nellemann, Rönnegård, Sandström, & Lundqvist, 2015) and try to escape in other directions making it very difficult for the herders to steer the animals in the right direction.

Recently, I witnessed some indications of the effects, and I got them contextualized and explained by the district leader. I present this story as a side-narrative:

First, visiting our recreation cabin a couple of kilometers from the nearest wind turbines, my wife and I on Thursday, November 26, 2020, observed a small herd of reindeer passing over the new ice of Sierggaljávri moving East towards Ruovdejávri and Haugfjell (late autumn pasture). Second, on Sunday, January 17, 2021, on a E10 parking lot near Sierggaljávri we observed an adult single reindeer coming running very fast (perhaps 40 km/h) along the road. We never saw something like it.

A few days later the district leader on request confirmed my suspicion: While the main herd had moved up to Haugfjell as it should and later continued East into Sweden, a minor herd that passed Sierggaljávri in late November had stopped in front of the wind turbines and spread north and westwards. The tracking of a GPS-collared reindeer indicates the movements of this subherd over 9 days in January, 2021 (cf. Figure 2.3).

The figure shows that this reindeer has passed over the ice of Sierggaljávri moving straight East and suddenly directly back in the opposite direction. The running reindeer accordingly seem to have been scared by the wind turbines. This little story adds to the documentation of wind turbine effects on SRH.

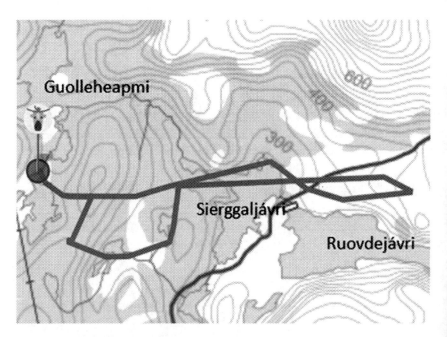

Figure 2.3 Screenshot of MySheep GPS plot of the movements of a female reindeer 11–19.01.2020. By permission of Gielas reindeer pasture district.

The general picture of Gielas pasture use challenges can be summed like this: *The reindeer do not get rest during any of the seasons.* The stay within each of the seasonal pastures is shortened. The direct consequence is that grazing is shifted and comes out of phase with both vegetation development and reindeer's needs. Climate change and increased exposure to predators amplify the negative effects of this. *Overall, this leads to as well poor resource utilization, extra work, increased costs as reduced revenues.*

Moreover, it may become even worse. Plans for a new cottage field, if realized, can block the Haugfjell autumn pastures. The most serious is that plans of several wind farms may both destroy calving grounds and autumn pastures. *The worst case scenario is that only summer pastures are left untouched. This may be the end of reindeer herding in Gielas.*

Reflections

This narrative is not unique. Many RPDs are not far from the tolerance level for accumulated encroachments. Typically, series of subsequent technical infrastructure interventions have laid the basis for recreational communities to become dominant users of large reindeer herding areas over the course of a few decades (Riseth & Johansen, 2019; Riseth, Eilertsen, & Johansen, 2021). New opportunities for the larger society, means a strong national trend of a general loss of nature and habitats for many species, including necessary reindeer herding area (Hanssen et al., 2018, IPBES). Moreover, that the most significant impacts of any single encroachments for Gielas are secondary CC impacts, is not random. The most controversial encroachment cases in Norwegian Sápmi currently are of the same type (e.g., Nussir, Fosen, Øyfjellet).

In general, SRH is *plastic*, i.e., as part of a changing nature it has an inherent flexibility and can adapt by reorganizing, also to external impacts (Rørholt, 2009). However, adaptations usually have costs (direct or indirect), and each change means that the potential room of flexibility is reduced (Beach, 1981). Some challenges are solved with extra work or by technology, such as fences, helicopter use, drones, trailer transport, etc., others will demand reorganization of seasonal pasture use. Anyhow, reducing the room of flexibility implies reduction of total pasture capacity, and accordingly the extent of SRH. In the long run, some household(s) tend to be forced out of business, against international law requirements (NOU, 2007:13A, 203).

For the most part, local people and their political representatives cannot fathom how serious this is for reindeer husbandry. In general, slow and gradual development is difficult to notice. Man's memory does not stretch far back in time. Some changes in question have developed within a time span of two to three generations. Moreover, changes often becomes part of the normal rather fast. When it also affects a small minority and an outlying industry most people in Norway have little knowledge of and lack relationships with, it is demanding to establish institutions that can help counter such effects (Bjärstig, Nygaard, Riseth, & Sandström, 2020; Riseth & Nygaard, 2018). So far, what really happens is often exactly what the PBA section 3-1c intends to prevent.

52 Jan Åge Riseth

To understand why this takes place, we need to take a step back to ontological level and be conscious about ways of seeing. Accordingly, the SRH narrative as presented here, is not all dominant, rather it is dominated by the narratives about the *recreation landscape* or *natural resources* that should be exploited for profitable ends. Comparative case study analysis of municipal-level planning processes in Norway and Sweden showed that local politicians in both case study areas *highlighted the minority position of the Sámi as a justification of failure to prioritize reindeer husbandry in relation to other economic sectors* (Bjärstig et al., 2020).

Thus, the politicians are not only making trade-offs between competing interests, which is a major element of the inherent nature and point of politics, but also denying the Sámi's specific rights to land and water as an Indigenous people that are enshrined in legislation and international obligations. One could additionally ask what is at stake in cases like these? For the Sámi it is all about the sustenance of a culturally based livelihood that lives under the threat of marginalization (Riseth, Tømmervik, & Forbes, 2018). For the Governments, it more seems that the main issue is to continue "business as usual". Reindeer herding is often merely seen as an industry among others by the politicians, without the recognition to Sámi rights and cultural survival.

The general picture in both countries is that interests of the Sámi minority often lose out to those of stronger actors (cf. Inga, 2014; Skum & Henrik, 2017). This indicates an important limitation with the planning systems. Porter and Barry (2014) conceptualize this as *bounded recognition*; "where a dominant power takes an emergent discourse or practice and recontextualizes it to construct and reinforce preestablished power relations" (Porter & Barry, 2014, p. 16). This can be seen as a form of co-optation where planning power is *an ability to not hear what is being said*. We can see this as a problem of equity; colonization and historical marginalization of the Sámi interest can explain some of the problems of integrating current Sámi needs in the planning process, as well as in Indigenous planning internationally (cf. Bouvier & Walker, 2018; Porter & Barry, 2014; Prusak, Walker, & Innes, 2016).

The political implication of this can be illustrated by quoting the President of the Sámi Parliament in Norway, Aili Keskitalo. In her New Year Speech on TV she worded how demanding it is to acquire support for Sámi land rights:

> ...to acknowledge our traditional knowledge of what reindeer can stand of disturbance. It is more demanding to recognize that Sámi legal certainty is more than access to legal services. It is all about being understood and respected when coming there.
>
> (Ságat, 2021: 5).

The president continued:

> If we should live and raise our children in trust to each other and the authorities, we cannot accept that the trust is broken through unfair regulations, decisions and judgements. It should not be like that in a society like Norway where human rights and dignity should be basic values
>
> (Ságat, 2021: 5).

In other words, the President gave a warning from the Sámi side. The general trust towards big society Norway is threatened.

Conclusion

This chapter has sketched general challenges for SRH and placed them in a historical context of step-by-step encroachment on reindeer herding areas. The example of Gielas RPD, which is not unique, and the serious message from President Keskitalo indicate that the accumulated effects of historical and contemporary infringement and disturbance threaten sustainability for SRH. Nevertheless, the herders of Gielas are robust and optimistic in spite of the serious situation. Moreover, the current development does not seem to be sustainable from a national nor a global position. Due to the complex challenges of both climate change and loss of intact nature Norway is in a clear need of a new industrial strategy (cf. Kattel, Mazzucato, & Mikheeva, 2021), and an alliance between environmentalists and industry trade unions has emerged.[1] What this will mean with reference to industrial incursions in Arctic areas, and how this will affect SRHs such as Gielas – whose livelihoods and way of life depend on these areas – remains to be seen.

Acknowledgements

I am very grateful to the Sámi reindeer herders I have met for receiving parts of their extensive knowledge. I also thank the editors and my wife Randi for useful comments to earlier versions of my text.

References

Agrawal, A. (1995). Dismantling the divide between indigenous and scientific knowledge. *Development and Change*, 26(1995), 413–439.

Åhrén, I. M. E. (2007). Samisk eldreomsorg; Hva er det og er det forbeholdt den samiske kvinnen? In B. I. G. Stenfjell (Ed.), *Åarjel-saemieh samer i sør Årbok*, (Vol. 9, pp. 53–55). Snåsa, Norge: Saemien Sijte,

Bain, M., Nagrani, A., Brown, A., & Zisserman, A. (2020). Condensed movies: Story based retrieval with contextual embeddings. *Asian Conference on Computer Vision.* Retrieved from Condensed Movies: Story Based Retrieval with Contextual Embeddings (thecvf.com)

Beach, H. (1981). *Reindeer-Herd management in transition: The case of Tuorpon Saameby in Northern Sweden.* Uppsala studies in cultural anthropology, 3, Ph. D. dissertation, Acta Universitas Uppsalensis, Uppsala.

Bjärstig, T., Nygaard, V., Riseth, J. Å., & Sandström, C. (2020). The institutionalisation of Sámi interest in municipal comprehensive planning – A comparison between Norway and Sweden. *International Indigenous Policy Journal*, 11(2), 1–26. https://doi.org/10.18584/iipj.2020.11.2.10574

Bouvier, N., & Walker, R. (2018). Indigenous planning and municipal governance: Lessons from the transformative frontier. *Canadian Public Administration*, 61(1), 130–135. https://doi.org/10.1111/capa.12249

54   Jan Åge Riseth

Fahrig, L. (2019). Habitat fragmentation: A long and tangled tale. *Global Ecology and Biogeography, 28*(1), 33–41. https://doi.org/10.1111/geb.12839.

Geertz, C. (1973). *The interpretation of cultures.* New York, NY: Basic Books.

Hansen, L. I., & Olsen, B. (2004). *Samenes historie fram til 1750.* Oslo: Cappelen.

Hanssen, G. S., Aarsæther, N., Hofstad, H., Anker, H. T., Kalbro, T., Buanes, A., ... Winge, N. (2018). En operativ lov? Spenningen mellom lovens intensjoner og planpraksis – Behov for forbedring? In G. S. Hanssen & N. Aarsæther (Eds.), *Plan- og bygningsloven 2008 - en lov for vår tid* (pp. 481–521). Oslo: Universitetsforlaget.

Hovelsrud, G. K., Risvoll, C., Riseth, J. Å., Tømmervik, H., Omazic, A., & Albihn, A. (2020). Reindeer herding and coastal pastures: Adaptation to multiple stressors and cumulative effects. In D. C. Nord (Ed.), *Nordic perspectives on the responsible development of the arctic: Pathways to action* (pp. 113–134). Springer, Cham: Springer Polar Sciences. Retrieved from: https://doi.org/10.1007/978-3-030-52324-4_6

Inga, K. M. (2014). *Hvor går vegen videre? En studie av Kanstadfjord/Vestre Hinnøy reinbeitedistrikts møte med vegutbyggingene Lofast og panoramavegen (Masteroppgave i samfunnsplanlegging og kulturforståelse).* Tromsø: UiT.

Kattel, R., Mazzucato, M. A., & Mikheeva, J. M. (2021). *The green giant: New industrial strategy for Norway.* London: University College London, Institute for Innovation and Public Purpose.

Kløcker-Larsen, R. (2017). Sami-state collaboration in the governance of cumulative effects assessment: A critical action research approach. *Environmental Impact Assessment Review, 64,* 67–76.

KMD. (2019). *National expectations regarding regional and municipal planning 2019–2023.* Established by Royal Decree of 14 May 2019. Ministry of Local Government and Modernisation. Retrieved from: https://www.regjeringen.no/contentassets/cc2c53c65af-24b8ea560c0156d885703/nasjonale-forventninger-2019-engelsk.pdf

Kuokkanen, R. (2011). Indigenous economies, theories of subsistence, and women: Exploring the social economy model for indigenous governance. *American Indian Quarterly, 35*(2), 215–240. https://doi.org/10.5250/amerindiquar.35.2.0215

Labba, E. I. (2020). *Herrarna satte oss hit. Om tvångsförflyttningarna i Sverige.* Stockholm: Nordstedts.

Landbruksdirektoratet. (2020). *Ressursregnskap for reindriftsnæringen. Reindriftsåret 1. april 2019 - 31. mars 2020.* Rapport nr. 43/2020 10.12.2020.

Löf, A. (2014). *Challenging adaptability. Analysing the governance of reindeer husbandry in Sweden.* Ph.D. dissertation, Umeå University, Department of Political Science, Sweden.

NOU. (2007:13A). *Den nye sameretten. Samerettsutvalget II.* Bind A. Norwegian Ministry of Justice.

Pedersen, S. (2015). Samenes historie; Fra undertrykking til kulturelt likeverd. In A. Holt-Jensen & S. Dyrvik (Eds.), *Likeverd. Grunnlaget for demokrati* (pp. 173–192). Oslo: Res Publica.

Persen, L. B. (2021). Sametingspresidentens aller siste nyttårstale. *Ságat,* January 5.

Porter, L., & Barry, J. (2014). Bounded recognition: Urban planning and the textual mediation of indigenous rights in Canada and USA. *Critical Policy Studies, 9*(1), 22–40. https://doi.org/10.1080/19460171.2014.912960

Prestbakmo, H. (2007). *Bardu og Målselv-"østlappenes" land?* Skånland: Skániid girje.

Prusak, S. Y., Walker, R., & Innes, R. (2016). Toward indigenous planning? First nation community planning in Saskatchewan, Canada. *Journal of Planning Education and Research, 36*(4), 440–450. https://doi.org/10.1177/0739456X15621147

Ravna, Ø (2019). *Same- Og reindriftsrett.* Oslo: Gyldendal.

Reimerson, E. (2015). *Nature, culture, rights: Exploring space for Indigenous agency in protected area discourses*. Doctoral dissertation, Umeå University. Retrieved from: http://www.divaportal.org/smash/record.jsf?pid=diva2%3A865188&dswid=586

Reinbeitekommisjonen. (2001). *Innstilling. Norsk-svensk reinbeitekommisjon av 1997*. Helsingfors. Retrived from Reindrift Evttohus Samisk (regjeringen.no)

Retter, G.-B. (2021, January 15–21). Vi kaller det for grønn kolonisering. *Morgenbladet*, 24–27. Retrieved from Vi kaller det for grønn kolonisering – Morgenbladet

Riseth, J. Å. (2006). Sámi reindeer herd managers: Why do they stay in a low-profit business? *The British Food Journal*, 108(7), 541–559.

Riseth, J. Å. (2020). Hvilken status har reindriftssamisk kunnskap? Hvordan kan samfunnet anvende den bedre? In Birgitta Fossum (Ed.), *Åarjel-saemieh. Samer i sør* (pp. 95–109). Årbok nr. 13. Snåsa: Saemien Sijte.

Riseth, J. Å., Eilertsen, S. M., & Johansen, B. (2021). Accepted. reindriftas sårbarhet. In F. Flemsæter & B. E. Flø (Eds.), *Utmark i endring-frå beitemark til rekreativ koloni*. Oslo: Cappelen.

Riseth, J. Å., & Johansen, B. (2019). Inngrepskartlegging for reindrifta i Troms fylke (23/2018). Rapport nr. 23/2018 ISSN: 2535-3004. Norway: Norut (NORCE).

Riseth, J. Å., & Nygaard, V. (2018). Samiske hensyn i planleggingen. In G. S. Hanssen & N. Aarsæther (Eds.), *Plan- og bygningsloven 2008 - en lov for vår tid?* (pp. 307–324). Oslo: Universitetsforlaget.

Riseth, J. Å., & Tømmervik, H. (2017). *Klimautfordringer og arealforvaltning for reindrifta i Norge. Kunnskapsstatus og forslag til tiltak – Eksempler fra troms* (Rapport 6/2017). Tromsø: Norut.

Riseth, J. Å., Tømmervik, H., & Bjerke, J. W. (2016). 175 years of adaptation: North Scandinavian Sámi reindeer herding between government policies and winter climate variability (1835–2010). *Journal of Forest Economics*, 24(2016), 186–204. http://dx.doi.org/10.1016/j.jfe.2016.05.002

Riseth, J. Å., Tømmervik, H., & Forbes, B. C. (2018). Sustainable and resilient reindeer herding. In M. Tryland & S. J. Kutz (Eds.), *Reindeer and caribou: Health and disease* (pp. 23–43). Boca Raton, FL: CRC Press.

Riseth, J. Å., Tømmervik, H., Helander-Renvall, E., Labba, N., Johansson, C., Malnes, E., … Callaghan, T. V. (2011). Sámi traditional ecological knowledge as a guide to science: Snow, ice and reindeer pasture facing climate change. *Polar Record*, 47, 202–217. https://doi.org/10.1017/S0032247410000434

Risvoll, Haavelsrud, C., & Riseth, G. K., J. Å. (forthcoming). Falling between the cracks of the governing system: Present realities of risk and uncertainty in pastoralism in northern Norway. Special collection: Weather, climate and society.

Rørholt, A. C. (2009). *Encroachments as a problem for sami reindeer husbandry*. Master of Philosophy in Indigenous Studies, Universitetet i Tromsø.

Sandberg, A. (2008). Collective rights in a modernizing North – On institutionalizing sámi and local rights to land and water in Northern Norway. *International Journal of the Commons*, 2, 269–287.

Skarin, A., & Åhman, B. (2014). Do human activity and infrastructure disturb domesticated reindeer? The need for the reindeer's perspective. *Polar Biology*, 37, 1041–1054.

Skarin, A., Nellemann, C., Rönnegård, L., Sandström, P., & Lundqvist, H. (2015). Wind farm construction impacts reindeer migration and movement corridors. *Landscape Ecology*, 30, 1527–1540. https://doi.org/10.1007/s10980-015-0210-8

Skum, N., & Henrik, J. (2017). *Arealplanlegging og reindriftsinteresser. En casestudie av planprosesser i Røros kommune*. Masteroppgave i fysisk planlegging. Trondheim: NTNU.

56 Jan Åge Riseth

Smith, C. (2007). The development of sámi rights in Norway from 1980 to 2007. In G. Minnerup & P. Solberg (Eds.), *First world, first nations. Internal colonialism and indigenous self-determination in Northern Europe and Australia* (pp. 22–30). Brighton, Portland, Toronto: Sussex Academic Press.

Svonni, L. (1983). Fjällrenskötselns årscykel sett ur en helhetsbedömning av markebehovet og hur ulika orsakskedjor styr detta behov (bilaga 1 i SOU 1983: 67) rennäringens ekonomi. Betänkande av Rennäringskomittén, 251–266.

3 Stories transmitted through art for the revitalization and decolonization of the Arctic

Timo Jokela and Maria Huhmarniemi

A story of a Church in a forest

This story began when Pekka Niva from the Kittilä municipality in Finnish Lapland challenged the locals to build a memorial for a vanished church. Niva was born in 1931 and raised near the presumed location of the forgotten church. He told the story as follows:

> I remember at the end of the 1930s, or maybe it was the summer of 1940, when I was with my grandfather, my mother's father that is, and my aunts Mallu and Eevi, picking cloudberries. I remember the duckboards and my old grandfather saying that this was Kirkkokuusikko (Spruce Forest with the Church). Kirkkokuusikko was the core of the story for that generation; they told it as though it was all true, and they believed it completely. They didn't mention the exact place of the church, though, just that it had been there.

Timo Jokela, the environmental artist and the author of this article, accepted the challenge to make the memorial, following Professor of Cultural History Marja Tuominen's (2005) notion of Northern peoples' right and obligation to "constantly evoke from the past those whose dreams were not realized, who fell over the edge of history, whose story was left untold".

The memorial project had the following two aims: to strengthen the village community and to create a local symbol of belonging to a place and a time in a location affected by rapid changes caused by the nearby Suurikuusikko gold mine, the Porsche winter-testing track and the growing Levi skiing centre and Kittilä Airport. The Parish of Kittilä and Metsähallitus (Finnish state enterprise for forest industry), which owned the land of the planned memorial, supported the project. When the art project was commissioned, Jokela needed to decide whose version of the story the artwork would tell. He did not know whether the stories of the church were true, and nobody even knew when the church was supposed to have been built. While some doubted the story, other locals were eager to share the memory and participate in the collective heritage-making process. It was evident that the story was important for the cultural and regional identity of the locals. Jokela listened to the stories and started designing the memorial in a

DOI: 10.4324/9781003118633-4

58 Timo Jokela and Maria Huhmarniemi

participatory manner with the local village community by following Tuominen's (2005) argument:

> Each story told of the past is a reconstruction, which can never be identical to its target, or fully recapture its authentic meanings ... Every historical study is an interpretation, which is restricted by and imbued with the conditions imposed by our current understanding. But finally, a historical study is just one of the many forums in which history is interpreted and images of the past conveyed. The arts, many sciences, and journalism all participate in this.

Historical knowledge: Truth or narrative?

Jokela investigated archival sources and connected them with multidisciplinary research literature (Enbuske, 2003; Joona, 2006, 2013; Kehusmaa & Onnela, 1995; Massa, 1994; Tegengren, 1952; Vahtola, 1985a, 1985b; Virrankoski, 1973) to find evidence regarding the truth and historical background of the Kirkkokuusikko story told by the villagers. There is unquestionable proof that the Kemi-Lapland church was built in Kittilä. In 1620, the vicar of the Kajaani (Paltamo) parish, Mansuetes Jacobi Fellman, wrote to his friend Johannes Messenius that "a church had been built in the village of Kittilä in Kemi-Lapland in the time of Karl IX, where a priest visited once a year immediately after New Year's Day" (Virrankoski, 1973, pp. 717–719). Therefore, sources indicated that the local story of the church was based on a historical event with a date. The Church was erected, by the order of the Swedish King Karl IX, sometime between 1607 and 1611. The church survived at least until 1620, after which it was evidently destroyed. The precise location of the church could not be determined with certainty, but the villagers strongly believed that the location was the Kirkkokuusikko forest hill. In the early 1600s, church construction and Evangelical Lutheran proselytizing were part of Sweden's policy for Lapland and the Arctic Ocean. His policy was meant to counter the efforts of Russia and the Orthodox Church in the White Sea and the Kola Peninsula as well Denmark-Norway's expansion to the shores of the Arctic Ocean and from there to the interior and the area that is now Kautokeino. In order to strengthen the link between Kemi-Lapland and his kingdom, Karl IX ordered the construction of churches in Lapland. According to the king's orders, Lapland residents had to gather to the church twice a year and stay there two weeks from St Thomas's Day to Candlemas and around Mary's Day. Around St Thomas Day the Forest Sámi of ancient Kemi-Lapland, the indigenous minority of the Sámi people, gathered in their winter villages to share the year's catch and to spend time together. On those occasions, tax collectors and traders also visited the Sámi villages. The presumed purpose of the church was to strengthen the settlement in the area, even though settling within the borders of Lapland had not yet been authorized. Together with the tax collectors and the authorities, the church enabled the gradual alteration of the Forest Sámi way of life.

However, just as the Forest Sámi embraced the settlers' way of life, so the settlers assimilated the way of life of the Forest Sámi, resulting in the village's multi-ethnic background. The lifestyle and culture of the Forest Sámi did not vanish completely, even though their language was lost and lives on only in place names and terms related to fishing, hunting and reindeer herding. However, neither Jokela nor the village community wanted to design a monument only to the "Northern policy" of the Swedish king. Instead, they wanted to know who used to attend this church that was established on the lands of their ancestors.

In whose voice does the story speak

Jokela wanted to bring the voices of Kittilä's Forest Sámi into the artwork. The background survey for the monument raised ethnic and cultural questions. However, he did not want to involve *The Story of Kirkkokuusikko* in the highly political and emotional debate regarding relations of indigenous people and other people in Lapland; rather, Jokela wanted the artwork to resonate with the worldview and lifestyle of the Forest Sámi who lived in the days of the old church. He wanted to understand the core of the story and to find its meaning for the region. Jokela designed the memorial to resonate with the past while preserving the aspect of art that creates new current and future meanings.

The shamanistic worldview gave birth to a narrative tradition that was typical of the native peoples in the northern hemisphere, but said narrative also contained local ingredients. The narrative tradition conveyed the local memories of the worldview of the Forest Sámi, their social system and the arrival of the Finnish settlers and Christianity in the region. At the centre of the stories are the shamans, who in Lapland were and are regarded as communicating with ancestors and nature spirits and who defended their communities from other Sami villages or intruders. It is likely that the shamans functioned as "village elders" and leaders of their communities (Helander-Renvall, 2009, 2016; Joy, 2018; Kylli, 2012; Pentikäinen, 1995). One storyline was more prominent than the rest.

The construction of the church took place during the presumed lifetime of Päiviö, the leading figure or the so-called chief shaman of the Kittilä Sami village. Scholars have discovered many stories related to Päiviö in Kittilä area (Andersson, 1914; Paulaharju, 1934, 1977). Päiviö converted to Christianity, perhaps against his will, and at the same time lost his abilities as a shaman. The story goes that this event is related to his visit to Stockholm. The representatives of the Sami villages from Lapland did indeed visit Stockholm, where they complained about the incursions of Birkarls (traders/tax collectors) and peasants into their territory. In 1602, Duke Karl (crowned Karl IX) provided the Sami of Kemi-Lapland with a letter of protection, which guaranteed to the Forest Sámi the usufruct of their territory (Joona, 2006). Perhaps the price of this letter of protection was Päiviö's baptism and conversion to Christianity.

The stories about Päiviö reflect the encounter between the two eras and the two perceptions of the world. The Sámi people were, perhaps, opposed to the construction of churches, but Päiviö appears to have adopted the new culture and

60   Timo Jokela and Maria Huhmarniemi

to have considered it a better defence for his village community. Päiviö became a representative the new culture, even though he mourned his lost powers. A preserved incantation states the following:

> In my youth a shaman
> Without a hanging cross
> Without a priestly ribbon
> I knew the spells full well
> And sang the Lappish charms
>   (Andersson, 1914, p. 122)

The essence of Kirkkokuusikko's story lies in this meeting of two eras, two different world views and two different social systems (a centralized state and the self-governing community of the Forest Sámi). Therefore, the subject matter of the memorial is not merely the church as a building but a question of larger ideas, meanings, values and consequences: the end of one era and the beginning of another in Lapland. As an artist, Jokela simplified the content of the artwork so that it would simultaneously depict the coming of the king's church and the beginning of the gradual disappearance of Päiviö's Sami village.

Visually crafted language from the past

Jokela emphasized the importance of subject matter in *The Story of Kirkkokuusikko* memorial and wanted it to have a form that would resonate with the content (Figure 3.1). To achieve such a fit, he first wanted to get an idea of what the church may have looked like. Of course, there were examples of the size and style of other churches from the same period. The size of the church could also be inferred from the king's building order: "For the church, every Lapp owner of at least ten reindeer and every Birkarl had to pull five lengths of timber to the spot …" (Andersson, 1914, pp. 107–108; Virrankoski, 1973, pp. 717–719). Knowing that only a few families lived in Kittilä at the time, the church was really just a modest sermon room. In terms of style and construction, it would hardly have differed from the other buildings in the area, although to the residents of the region it must have seemed big and representative of power.

Several sources reference Forest Sámi buildings. Historical sources for the year 1740 provide a description of the Forest Sámi living in rectangular houses with four to six layers of logs (Joona, 2006, pp. 199–200). Illustrations of log buildings, such as shelters, *nili* storehouses, ground shelters and the like, have been recovered from the Russian and Swedish Lapland, where the lifestyle of the Forest Sámi survived longer and could be documented and examined. Jokela assumed that it was possible to infer the buildings' technical solutions and shapes from these sources and that the local men still had the skills for constructing such buildings.

In addition to buildings, Jokela also looked for other objects that could serve as visual starting points for the monument. Few objects from the age of the Church, have survived, but the objects in the Sámi Museum of Swedish Lapland supply

Stories transmitted through art 61

Figure 3.1 Mapping the visual references for community-based art using museums archives, place-specific investigations, narratives and sketching. Collage and photos: Timo Jokela.

62 Timo Jokela and Maria Huhmarniemi

hints regarding the visual idiom. Images of the time are also available. In the 1660s, Johannes Schefferus, who was one of the most important Swedish humanists of 17th century, recorded illustrations of the objects and shaman drums of the Kemi Lapps. The drumskins provided not only an understanding of the cosmological nature of the world typical of the period but also sources of livelihood at the time (Manker, 1965). A Kemi Sami drum sent to Stockholm by Tuderus, a fiercely evangelical Christian priest, contained references to the arrival of Christianity and its churches and possibly even a picture of the Kirkkokuusikko church. More visual material on the meeting between the shamanistic world and Christianity in Lapland can be found in the Tanhua "shaman grave" dated 1595–1635: wrought iron crosses, bear teeth and other charms are in perfect harmony, telling of the meeting of two religions, cultures and eras.

The memorial comes alive

A survey of the visual material provided a wealth of details for the design of the artwork, but the form remained open. Jokela was determined that the material for the memorial should be massive wood, the material of the original church (Figure 3.2). The artist wanted to treat the surface of the artwork with agents resistant to fire and mould and to give it a dark patina in reference to the past. He included details related to the Christian faith as well as the living conditions in the area, such as wild forest deer, fish and the grain brought by settlers. Some local elders helped Jokela with the carving using their knives and chisels.

Jokela decided on the structure and form of *The Story of Kirkkokuusikko* monument when, in the Saltdal Museum, he saw a guardhouse on tall poles, designed to protect cattle from wild animals and a Sámi storehouse on skis. As the location of the church is uncertain, Jokela decided to build the monument on skis. Therefore, the monument continues to search for its place and, perhaps, also for its meaning. It can be moved should new studies be conducted. The visual form and building method for the monument on columns and mounted on skis specifically reference the construction of storehouses (*nili*), dwellings and even the first buildings of the settlers as well as the church. However, Jokela wished that the monument should not convey a strong interpretation, but would rather be closed and quiet, yet at the same time suggestive. Its nature must imitate the secrecy of the stories told in the area, but it must also provide enough information for people to discover what the monument refers to. Therefore, the artwork is closed, but it can be opened.

The shape of a relic cabinet, coming from the Middle Ages, with its opening and pictured doors, offered an iconostasis-like solution to present the double meaning of the monument to the viewer. Jokela decided to build the work in such a way that opening the double doors would lead, on one side, to the church and the story of the king, and, on the other side, to Päiviö and the ancient village of Kittilä.

Jokela planned the implementation of the artwork in such a manner that he would be able to build it in his studio, dismantle it, transport the parts to the site and re-erect it at Kirkkokuusikko. The site was located in the middle of a swamp,

Stories transmitted through art 63

Figure 3.2 a and b. Working with community to build up a memorial *The Story of Kirkkokuusikko*. Photos: Timo Jokela.

several kilometres from the nearest road, meaning that transportation required the assistance of local reindeer herders. The transportation, assembly and celebration of the monument were designed as a performative and communal event (Figure 3.3). During the event, the bishop blessed the monument, and Jokela described its background and dual meaning to a large audience. A video documentary of the project made it possible to share the story with a much wider audience.

Art-based action research

Methodologically, the Kirkkokuusikko project was a case of art-based action research (ABAR). More a research strategy than a complete method, ABAR

Figure 3.3 Celebration of the monument was designed as a performative and communal event. Photo: Timo Jokela.

has been developed at the University of Lapland to combine artistic practices with regional development and community empowerment (Jokela, 2019; Jokela, Hiltunen, & Härkönen, 2015). ABAR aims to develop the professional methods and working approaches of the artist-teacher-researcher and the artist-researcher. The strategy shares some common features with international arts-based research, artistic research and action research. In all of these research approaches, practical and theoretical forms of research are conducted simultaneously, and research topics are situated in the middle ground between art and other academic fields, such as the social sciences, education studies and regional development.

For *The Story of Kirkkokuusikko*, one of the main challenges – typical to ABAR – was to achieve enough multidisciplinary knowledge and merge the aims of social improvement that are common in action research with individual artistic creativity and art-based research. In this case, ABAR also meant engaging with culturally sustainable, decolonizing activities and respecting Northern knowledge when designing research on art initiatives and interventions in place- and community-specific ways.

Jokela started his ABAR by using the research methods of history and visual ethnography (Jokela, 2018) to establish the basis for the place-specific public artwork. Visual mapping and the analysis of the village's appearance, livelihood, traditions and stories interested the locals and helped to engage them in the research. The participatory manner of the realization and the evocative celebration of the

Stories transmitted through art 65

memorial further strengthened the artwork's impact in the local community. The ABAR methodology combines social activity, evocative art and critical and analytical research.

Northern knowledge transmitted via place-specific public art

The Kirkkokuusikko memorial's roots can be found in environmental art, an independent form of art created in the 1960s and the 1970s, when land and performance artists began to create artwork outside galleries and art museums. According to Malcolm Andrews (1999, p. 204), a researcher of environmental aesthetics, such environmental artworks are representations of the relationships between the untouched environment and the environment touched by the artist. In environmental art, meaning is created in relation to the space and nature that surround the artworks. The artwork is not just an artistic object that has been placed outdoors; instead, its significance is derived from its environment. Moreover, the artwork creates the nature of the environment itself – in this case, the monument re-created the forest hill in Kirkkokuusikko.

Besides the essence of environmental art, Jokela followed the approach to public art described by Suzanne Lacy (1995, 2008) as "new genre public art" and the principles of place-specific community art presented by Lucy Lippard (1997). Using these approaches, artists refer to the social challenges of a certain community or location in their artwork while involving local operators in the artistic processes. Such art is always place-specific, and being situation-specific, it is also defined as community art. Interaction and communication were key goals in *The Story of Kirkkokuusikko*; to achieve these goals, Jokela combined traditional forms of art and craft with participatory methods. The locals participated in the creating process, and Jokela worked as a motivator and facilitator, often employing a culture-sensitive approach. Thus, *The Story of Kirkkokuusikko* monument is place-specific public art rather than environmental art, even though the artwork is located in an inaccessible spot in the middle of a forest.

Knowing that Northern knowledge played a role in *The Story of Kirkkokuusikko* creation process, it is important to clarify this concept of Northern knowledge. Many scholars have argued that in the North, the *indigenous knowledge system* has much to offer as a basis for indigenous research, particularly in the areas of art, design and culture (Guttorm, 2015). The concept of *Northern knowledge systems*, based on the indigenous knowledge system, consists of shared traditions, a historic understanding of nature and the use of natural materials and has been a key principle in Arctic art (Jokela, 2018; Huhmarniemi & Jokela, 2020a, 2020b).

The term Northern knowledge system (Huhmarniemi & Jokela, 2020b) refers to interlinked ecological and cultural knowledge applied to the process of art creation. Northern knowledge emphasizes that stories are not always told verbally but can also be conveyed through visual signs, symbols, the choice of material and building techniques. This visually crafted language has communicative significance both inside and outside of the communities that use such a language. The language of crafts is important for sharing traditions, beliefs and worldviews (e.g.,

66 Timo Jokela and Maria Huhmarniemi

Minnakhmetova, Usenyuk-Kravchuk, & Konkova, 2019; Schilar & Keskitalo, 2018). While the material culture of the locals can carry spiritual and religious content (Helander-Renvall, 2009; Joy, 2018), *The Story of Kirkkokuusikko* memorial was designed to transmit Northern knowledge and renew cultural heritage. Northern knowledge was seen as a performative process that is valued, built and constantly renewed, which involved merging the Northern knowledge system and its traditional and sustainable methods of creating with contemporary art. Therefore, the Kirkkokuusikko project could be seen as a place-based regional strategy described by Daniels, Baldacchino, and Vodden (2015) and Jokela (2018).

The Story of Kirkkokuusikko can also be discussed using the concept of Arctic art, which is central to addressing contemporary Northern and Arctic themes (Huhmarniemi & Jokela, 2020a). This relatively new concept views art, design and crafts as interwoven and as an integrated part of the eco-social culture of the North. Besides art, design and craft, Arctic art includes indigenous forms of creation and promotes a dynamic relationship across traditional disciplines and processes. It promotes the best contemporary art practices and design thinking in their application to contemporary sociocultural problems and contexts. According to Huhmarniemi and Jokela (2020a), Arctic art offers an alternative way of seeing art, design and crafts as mutually beneficial and integrated instead of following the dualistic Western culture of separating art, design and crafts into disciplines of their own. The essential aim of Arctic art is to seek appropriate ways of sensitively addressing environmental and sociocultural issues by using art and art education methodologies whilst promoting sustainable development and recognizing cultural diversity of the North and the Arctic (Huhmarniemi & Jokela, 2020a). The sustainability dimensions in the context of *The Story of Kirkkokuusikko* memorial included cultural and social sustainability, while the production of the artwork respected cultural diversity and heritage and was carried out in collaboration with local inhabitants, valuing their skills, knowledge and stories.

Revitalization and decolonization through art

Jokela's ABAR approach in the realization of the Kirkkokuusikko memorial could be understood as an effort in decolonization. By bringing up the colonial past of the region for discussion, he followed Smith's (1999) vision of decolonization as a process that requires dismantling the power of administrative, cultural, linguistic and psychological colonialism. This means that the locals must understand history from their multi-ethnic perspective and build on who they are culturally. Decolonization is a further step towards collective wellness and self-determination.

Besides decolonization (Smith, 1999), which has become important in the context of indigenous studies and cultural activism, revitalization is a key method to restore the value of traditions in a socio-cultural situation that is no longer traditional but contemporary. Revitalization does not mean recovering a historical culture and identity that would be authentic or unmixed. Just as in *The Story of*

Stories transmitted through art   67

Kirkkokuusikko memorial, revitalization demands an interpretation of history that changes according to the sources of historical knowledge, personal and communal perceptions, judgements and values.

In the North and the Arctic, both decolonization and revitalization are discussed mainly in the context of indigenous cultures. According to Huhmarniemi and Jokela (2020a), the discussions regarding decolonization and revitalization show that similar processes should also be implemented in Arctic art activities in multi-ethnic communities and non-indigenous communities. This is what happened when the memorial was designed in a place-specific manner. Revitalization, based on the philosophy of contemporary Arctic art and conducted by the means of place-specific public art, does not refer exclusively to cultural practices but also to places, villages and whole regions based on their local and regional identity and potential vitality. The process of creating the memorial showed that revitalization can be intergenerational, transmitting traditional knowledge, artistry and cultural practices to new generations and new community members. In our case of *The Story of Kirkkokuusikko*, revitalization was also intercultural, with the aim of sharing heritage with newcomers in the village. Symbols, rituals and crafting methods were studied as part of contemporary creation and were imbued with new meanings.

The Story of Kirkkokuusikko memorial is an example of the growing interest in new forms of culture inspired by local or regional heritage in the North and the Arctic. Using the methods of revitalization and place-specific art, many artists and art educators have been renewing heritage as art (Härkönen, Huhmarniemi, & Jokela, 2018; Stöckell, 2018), as community-based art education (Hiltunen, 2010; Hiltunen & Zemtsova, 2014) and as art-based creative tourism (Huhmarniemi et al., forthcoming). In fact, today's contemporary art and cultural practices, whether created through education or as cultural services, may eventually become traditions. Also, contemporary political art in the Arctic reveals one way of drawing inspiration from the past that is relevant to contemporary interests and value production (see, e.g., Guttorm, 2015; Horsberg Hansen, 2016; Igloliorte, 2019).

Both revitalization and decolonization relate to issues and conceptions of sustainability, especially cultural and social sustainability. In the case of *The Story of Kirkkokuusikko* some elements of narrative heritage were sustained for current and future locals in the village. Social and cultural aspects of sustainability have a reciprocal relationship in which culture constructs society and society shapes culture. To remember the stories of the past strengthens cultural identities and can enhance well-being which enables cultural and social sustainability in a community.

Resources for place-conscious art education

We argue that ABAR research projects, such as *The Story of Kirkkokuusikko* memorial, can be understood as forms of place-based education meant to increase the understanding of a place as an educational tool for sustainability and revitalization of regional identity. Place-conscious education contributes to sustainability

68 *Timo Jokela and Maria Huhmarniemi*

by strengthening the connections between people and the worlds they inhabit as well as by initiating discussions of communities' hopes for and trust in the future (Dessein, Soini, Fairclough, & Horlings, 2015).

While both authors of this chapter are working in the field of art education at the University of Lapland, place-specific art projects, such as *The Story of Kirkkokuusikko*, are constantly renewing art-education practices in higher education. Concurrent with the rapid changes taking place in the North, the paradigm of contemporary art practice has shifted from an artist's self-expression and individualism to a more community-focused and dialogical approach. We argue that, when adopting the models of relational and dialogical contemporary art (Gablik, 1995; Kwon, 2002; Lacy, 1995, 2008; Lippard, 1997) and celebrating its processes and results – as was the case with *The Story of Kirkkokuusikko* memorial – art education rejects the modernist ideology of art education as having universal cultural values and thus enhances decolonization efforts. The best methods for art education and artist training in higher education are not the same everywhere. Bringing the methods and processes of contemporary art into Northern contexts and combining them with the aim of sustainable education requires rethinking art education and discussing Arctic art and the development of ABAR methodologies. Even when Arctic art is a local and place-specific activity in the North, Arctic art operates in the age of global sociocultural change.

Conclusion

The Story of Kirkkokuusikko is a memorial, based on the principles of place-specific public art, to the first Christian church in the Kittilä region in Finnish Lapland. In the process of designing and making the memorial, Jokela combined contemporary artistic approaches with traditional wood-construction techniques, local oral heritage and a study of cultural history. He revealed local content and meanings that had been almost forgotten in the contemporary geographical and mental triangle of new economies: the nearby Suurikuusikko gold mine, the Porsche winter-testing track and the growing Levi ski resort. The design and making of *The Story of Kirkkokuusikko* memorial involved the principles of sensitivity and decolonization in a multi-ethnic community in order to strengthen regional vitality and identity through art. Jokela revealed the heritage of the Kemi-Lapland Forest Sámi, already half-forgotten in Kittilä, which is relevant for the current and politicized debates on identities.

The ABAR approach supported the combination of contemporary art and place-specific design of public art. Visual mapping and the analysis of the village's appearance, way of life, livelihoods, traditions and stories helped create art activities that engaged the people and the entire village community. The project brought together people of different ages and generations, helping to understand, convey and renew the significance of the history and life of places through art. In Northern place-specific outdoor activities, power lies in the creation of cultural continuation and intergenerational knowledge, in the reconstruction of traditional skills and in the support for local cultural identities. The creation process

Stories transmitted through art 69

of the memorial reconstructed elders' and ancestors' skills and enhanced local cultural identities. Also, the project provided a model for implementing Northern knowledge for the purposes of decolonization, revitalization and art education.

Jokela and the local participants hoped that the Kirkkokuusikko memorial would result in a debate about who and what is remembered or forgotten, what is worth remembering and who can remember the history of Lapland. According to Professor of Cultural History Tuominen (2010, p. 135), northern cultural history is needed to dissolve the mental and social structures that, for centuries, have defined the periphery and the centre, the object and the subject and what is worth remembering and what deserves only oblivion. In the Kirkkokuusikko memorial project, the community and the place where art creation took place were not marginal; instead, the presented approaches treated remote, rural and peripheral places as centres for their inhabitants. ABAR and placemaking are regional development strategies that support ecocultural resilience and involve using places and a community's capacities to improve the sustainability and well-being of the inhabitants. Revitalization and decolonization are not only about people but also about places and entire regions.

References

Andersson, G. A. (1914). *Tietoja sodankylän ja kittilän pitäjän aikaisemmista ja myöhemmistä vaiheista.* Kemi. Finland: Lapin Kansa.

Andrews, M. (1999). *Landscape and Western art.* Oxford, UK: Oxford University Press.

Daniels, J., Baldacchino, G., & Vodden, R. (2015). Matters of place: The making of place and identity. In K. Vodden, R. Gibson, & G. Baldacchino (Eds.), *Place peripheral: Place-based development in rural, island, and remote regions* (pp. 23–40). St. John's: ISER Books.

Dessein, J., Soini, K., Fairclough, G., & Horlings, L. (Eds.). (2015). *Culture in, for and as sustainable development. Conclusions from the COST action IS1007 investigating cultural sustainability.* Jyväskylä, Finland: University of Jyväskylä.

Enbuske, M. (2003). Lapin asuttamisen historia. In I. Massa & H. Snellman (Eds.), *Lappi – Maa, kansat, kulttuurit* (pp. 39–63). Helsinki, Finland: Suomalaisen Kirjallisuuden Seura.

Gablik, S. (1995). Connective aesthetics: Art after individualism. In S. Lacy (Ed.), *Mapping the terrain: New genre public art* (pp. 74–87). Seattle, WA: Bay Press.

Guttorm, G. (2015). Contemporary duodji: A personal experience in understanding traditions. In T. Jokela & G. Coutts (Eds.), *Relate North: Art, heritage and identity* (pp. 60–77). Rovaniemi, Finland: Lapland University Press.

Härkönen, E., Huhmarniemi, M., & Jokela, T. (2018) Crafting sustainability: Handcraft in contemporary art and cultural sustainability in Lapland. *Sustainability, 10*(6), 1907. https://doi.org/10.3390/su10061907

Helander-Renvall, E. (2009). Animism, personhood and the nature of reality: Sami perspectives. *Polar Record, 46*(1). https://doi.org/10.1017/S0032247409990040

Helander-Renvall, E. (2016). *Sámi society matters.* Rovaniemi, Finland: Lapland University Press.

Hiltunen, M. (2010). Slow activism: Art in progress in the North. In A. Linjakumpu & S. Wallenius-Korkalo (Eds.), *Progress or perish: Northern Perspectives on social change* (pp. 119–138). Farnham, UK: Ashgate.

70   Timo Jokela and Maria Huhmarniemi

Hiltunen, M., & Zemtsova, I. (2014). Northern Places: Tracking the finno-ugric traces through place-specific art. In T. Jokela & G. Coutts (Eds.), *Relate North 2014: Engagement, art and representation* (pp. 60–81). Rovaniemi, Finland: Lapland University Press.

Horsberg Hansen, H. (2016). Constructing Sami national heritage: Encounters between tradition and modernity in Sami art. *Konsthistorisk tidskrif/Journal of Art History*, 85(3), 240–255. https://doi.org/10.1080/00233609.2016.1207701

Huhmarniemi, M., & Jokela, T. (2020a). Arctic arts with pride: Discourses on arctic arts, culture and sustainability. *Sustainability*, 12(2), 604. https://doi.org/10.3390/su12020604

Huhmarniemi, M., & Jokela, T. (2020b). Arctic art and material culture: Northern Knowledge and cultural resilience in the northernmost Europe. In L. Heininen, H. Exner-Pirot, & J. Barnes (Eds.), *Arctic yearbook 2020: Climate change and the arctic: Global origins, regional responsibilities?* Akureyri, Iceland: Arctic Portal. Retrieved from: https://arcticyearbook.com/

Huhmarniemi, M., Kugapi, O., Miettinen, S., & Laivamaa, L. (Forthcoming) Sustainable future for creative tourism in Lapland. In N. Duxbury, S. Albino, & C. Pato Carvalho (Eds.), *Creative tourism: Activating cultural resources and engaging creative travellers.* Oxfordshire, UK: Cabi International.

Igloliorte, H. (2019). Hooked forever on primitive peoples: James Houston and the transformation of 'Eskimo Handicrafts' to Inuit art. In E. Harney & R. Phillips (Eds.), *Mapping modernisms: Art, indigeneity, colonialism* (pp. 62–90). Durham, UK: Duke University Press.

Jokela, T. (2018). Culture sensitive participatory art as visual ethnography in the North. *Visual Ethnography*, 6(2), 89–112.

Jokela, T. (2019). Arts-based action research in the North. In G. Noblit (Ed.), *Oxford research encyclopedia of education.* Oxford, UK: Oxford University.

Jokela, T., Hiltunen, M., & Härkönen, E. (2015). Art-based action research–participatory art for the north. *International Journal of Education through Art*, 11(3), 433–448.

Joona, J. (2006). *Entisiin tornion ja Kemin lapinmaihin kuuluneiden alueiden maa- ja vesioike-uksista.* Rovaniemi, Finland: Lapin yliopisto.

Joona, J. (2013). Suomen metsäsaamelaisten historiasta [history of the Finnish forest sámi]. In E. Sarivaara, K. Määttä, & S. Uusiautti (Eds.), *Kuka on saamelainen ja mitä on saamelaisuus – Identiteetin juurilla* (pp. 9–31). Rovaniemi, Finland: Lapland University Press.

Joy, F. (2018). *Sami shamanism, cosmology and art: As systems of embedded knowledge.* PhD thesis, University of Lapland, Rovaniemi, Finland.

Kehusmaa, A., & Onnela, S. (1995). Suur-Sodankylän historia. Suur-Sodankylän historiatoimikunta.

Kwon, M. (2002). *One place after another: Site-specific art and locational identity.* London, UK: The MIT Press.

Kylli, R. (2012). *Saamelaisten kaksi kääntymystä. Uskonnon muuttuminen utsjoen ja enontekiön lapinmailla 1602–1905.* Helsinki, Finland: SKS.

Lacy, S. (1995). Debated territory: Towards a critical language for public art. In S. Lacy (Ed.), *Mapping the terrain. New genre public art* (pp. 171–185). Seattle, WA: Bay Press.

Lacy, S. (2008). Time in place: New genre public art a decade later. In C. Cameron & S. Willis (Eds.), *The practice of public art* (pp. 18–32). New York, NY: Routledge.

Lippard, L. (1997). *The lure of the local: Senses of place in a multicentered society.* New York, NY: New Press.

Manker, E. (1965). *Nåidkonst. Trolltrummans bilvärd.* Stockholm, Sweden: LT.

Stories transmitted through art   71

Massa, I. (1994). *Pohjoinen luonnonvalloitus. Suunnistus ympäristöhistoriaan lapissa ja suomessa.* Helsink, Finland: Gaudeamus.

Minnakhmetova, R., Usenyuk-Kravchuk, S., & Konkova, Y. (2019) A context-sensitive approach to the use of traditional ornament in contemporary design practice. *Synnyt/ origins, Special Issue on Arctic Arts Summit, 1,* 49–62. Retrieved from: https://wiki.aalto. fi/pages/viewpage.action?pageId=151504259 [Accessed 26 June 2019].

Paulaharju, S. (1934) Kittilän kiveliöiden tarinaa. In *Suomen matkailuyhdistyksen vuosikirja 1934* (pp. 63–74). Helsinki, Finland: Mectorin kirjapaino osakeyhtiö.

Paulaharju, S. (1977 [1922]). *Lapin muisteluksia.* Helsinki, Finland: WSOY.

Pentikäinen, J. (1995). *Saamelaiset. Pohjoisen kansan mytologia.* Helsinki, Finland: SKS.

Schilar, H., & Keskitalo, E. C. H. (2018). Ethnic boundaries and boundary-making in handicrafts: Examples from northern Norway, Sweden and Finland. *Acta Borealia, 35*(1), 29–48. https://doi.org/10.1080/08003831.2018.1456073

Smith, L. T. (1999). *Decolonizing methodologies: Research and indigenous peoples.* London, UK: Zed Books.

Stöckell, A. (2018). Making wooden spoons around the campfire: Dialogue, hand-craft-based art and sustainability. In T. Jokela & G. Coutts (Eds.), *Relate North: Art and design for education and sustainability* (pp. 80–97). Rovaniemi, Finland: Lapland University Press.

Tegengren, H. (1952). *En utdöd lappkultur i Kemi lappmark.* Åbo, Finland: Acta Academia Åboensis.

Tuominen, M. (2005). "Me kutsumme menneisyyttä nykyisyytemme tueksi." Näkökulmia aikoihin ja niiden kokemiseen. Inaugural presentation at the University of Lapland on 28 February 2005. Retrieved from: http://www.ulapland.fi/?deptid=4824

Tuominen, M. (2010). Missä maanpiiri päättyy? Pohjoisen kulttuurihistorian paikat ja haasteet. In H. Rantala & S. Ollitervo (Eds.), *Kulttuurihistoriallinen katse* (pp. 338–359). Turku, Finland: Turun yliopisto.

Vahtola, J. (1985a). Lapin historiaa keskiajalta 1600-luvun alkupuolelle. Teoksessa lappi 4. Saamelaisten ja suomalaisten maa. In A. Arvi (Ed.), *Lappi 4. Saamelaisten ja suomalaisten maa* (pp. 331–358). Hämeenlinna, Finland: Karisto Oy.

Vahtola, J. (1985b). Suomalaisen asutuksen synty ja kehitys lapissa. In A. Arvi (Ed.), *Lappi 4. Saamelaisten ja s. Uomalaisten maa* (pp. 209–234). Hämeenlinna, Finland: Karisto Oy.

Virrankoski, P. (1973). *Pohjois-pohjanmaa ja lappi 1600-luvulla. Pohjois-pohjanmaan ja lapin historia III.* Oulu, Finland: ainuun Ja Lapin maakuntaliittojen yhteinen historiatoimikunta.

4 Mental health research in an Arctic Indigenous context

The presence of silent dominant narratives

Rita Sørly, Vår Mathisen and Vigdis Nygaard

About stories

As human beings, we are the stories we tell about ourselves (Fivush, 2010). There is a complex relation between culture and identity and identifying is an ongoing process that continues throughout life (Blix, 2016). In this study we are concerned with the interaction of social and personal constructions, namely narratives, drawing from cultural beliefs and practice to further a specific project of self-presentation or social positioning (Kirmayer, 2000) within Sámi contexts. People organize their storytelling according to culturally available narratives and plots (Sørly, Mathisen, & Kvernmo, 2020). We agree with Fivush (2010) that people, through narratives, enrichened with explanatory and evaluative frameworks that weave people, places and events together, create stories that define who we are in time and place and in relation to others. Through multiple storytellings, narratives become accepted or contested as evaluative versions of the past. Stories take on moral perspectives, explaining not only what happened and what it means, but also what it should mean (Fivush, 2010). Different groups have different dominant narratives they relate to and define as "the truth of the matter".

The Norwegian society is a society living in a post-conflict after years of harsh assimilation policy and oppression from the state against the Sámi population. Despite the country's national self-image as a peacebuilding, inherently good and humble country that is innocent of imperialism and colonialism (Eidsvik, 2016; Gullestad, 2006), the wounds from the Norwegianization era is still creating pain in the Sámi population (Nergård, 2011). Is this articulated in our participants' narratives? If yes, how is it told? How are dominant narratives visible in the participants' stories? How do Sámi people living with mental distress navigate in their storytelling? Are there differences from how any others tell their stories to researchers? How are we as researchers affected by our expectations related to the storytelling? These were questions we wanted to explore when working with Niilas' story.

We want to investigate how we as Norwegian researchers understand, interpret, analyze and discuss cultural stories of our Sámi participants, based on the dominant narratives we bring with us into the empirical field and data.

In the following, we introduce the Sámi as Indigenous people. We will give a brief insight of Sámi mental health and the current situation in Norway/Sápmi.

DOI: 10.4324/9781003118633-5

Figure 4.1 The herd. Photo: Rita Sørly.

We present data and method, the context of the study and the participants. Further, we introduce the chosen narrative approach, before we meet Niilas, through an excerpt from the interview with him. We analyze the interview in relation to the following dominant narratives in context: (1) The mainstream Western school of narrative, (2) The Norwegianization narrative of assimilation policy and oppression, (3) The reindeer herder narrative and finally (4) The Norwegian researcher narrative. Based on this analysis we emphasize how the notion of ongoing dominant narratives in mental health research context with Indigenous people can make us more aware of how surrounding stories affect our work (Figure 4.1). In the end, we reflect upon narratives as social justice and practice in an Indigenous mental health context.

The Sámi

The Sámi are Indigenous people living in Norway, Sweden, Finland and the Kola Peninsula in Russia (Sørly et al., 2020). The Sámi population is estimated to be approximately 100,000 people (Dagsvold, Mollersen, & Stordahl, 2015). The estimated Sámi population in Norway is approximately 55,000 (Statistics Norway, 2019), and approximately 25,000 members of this population speak a Sámi language (Ministry of Labor and Social Affairs, 2000–2001). Beginning in the mid-19th century, the Sámi people in Norway experienced about a 150-year long period

74 Rita Sørly, Vår Mathisen and Vigdis Nygaard

of linguistic and cultural oppression and harsh assimilation policy (Minde, 2005) defined as the era of the "Norwegianization" of the Sámi people. This period of colonization led to the loss of the Sámi language, stigmatization and discrimination (Blix et al., 2013). From being an assimilation ideology, the Norwegian Sámi policy has gradually shifted, and currently, Sámi society is being revitalized (Dagsvold, Møllersen, & Stordahl, 2016). According to Minde (2005), the purposeful, systematic and long-lasting assimilation policy distinguishes Norway from other Scandinavian countries. This policy exposed Sámi to forced assimilation, discrimination and prejudice from the Norwegian society, including its mental health system (Turi, Bals, Skre, & Kvernmo, 2009). For many Sámi people, the historical legacy of the policy of ignorance is still politically inflamed (Minde, 2005). For example, users of mental health services who have been exposed to the Norwegianization policy may have limited confidence in the Norwegian authorities. Many Sámi people still experience the decolonization process as extremely painful and ongoing (Nergård, 2011). The mechanisms of colonization and colonial power still live in the Sámi people (Mikkelsen, 2013). However, the collective identity narrative based on cultural traits, such as language, traditional clothing, traditional music, handicrafts and reindeer herding, has enabled individuals to develop their own identity narratives within an Indigenous context (Sørly et al., 2020).

Health services for the Sámi are integrated into the public welfare state system in Norway. As Norwegian citizens, the Sámi are legally entitled to public health services, and as an ethnic minority and Indigenous population, to culturally and linguistically adapted health services. In reality, standardized services in Norwegian mental health care are tailored to the needs of the majority population which overshadows approaches that understands, values and emphasizes Sámi storytelling and everyday life (Sørly et al., 2020). This entails dilemmas, and a need for reflexivity when working within these contexts.

Sámi mental health and current situation

The Sámi have status as Indigenous peoples with its own language and administrative area and its own parliament, which gives the Sámi a strong, legal status in Norway. As Indigenous people, the Sámi have special rights, as outlined by the UN Indigenous Declaration. The declaration addresses *Indigenous* peoples' rights to be involved and influence one's own health situation (Stoor, Haetta, & Javo, 2017), to which mental health belong. However, the legal status of Indigenous peoples does not in itself prevent incidence of discrimination. Present research shows the opposite; the Sámi population in Norway have experience with discrimination as a result of their Sámi background (Midtbøen, 2015). This complicates mental health services for the Sámi population.

There is little research on Sámi people and mental health (Mathisen & Sørly, 2020). The existing research focuses to a large extent on risk factors in connection with mental health, and to a small extent highlights the positive aspects of growing up in a Sámi environment (Nystad, Spein, & Ingstad, 2014). A culturally relevant definition of mental distress is missing in the circumpolar context

Mental health research in an Arctic Indigenous context   75

(Willox et al., 2015). Bongo (2012) find the Sámi approach towards health and illness as addressing it in silent and indirect ways. The standards for caring for oneself are strongly rooted in the culture. Care is provided by the nearest family members and relatives without the need of professional healthcare. Speaking openly about diseases is considered inappropriate (ibid.), and diagnostic terms are rejected as belonging to the majority population. Nymo's (2011) study showed that interaction within stable collectives, such as families and neighborhood communities, provided security and opportunities to combine traditions and innovation. The findings in both Bongo's (2012) and Nymo's (2011) research might indicate a skepticism among Sámi people towards the health care system of the majority population.

The current situation of Sámi people in Norway is complicated; some Sámi areas have strong and ethnic support and a high density of Sámi; different languages have equal status and several Sámi institutions reside there. In other regions, the Sámi are a minority, and there is less support of their culture (Sørly, Mathisen, & Kvernmo, 2020). Conflicts regarding land rights and Sámi language are a part of everyday life (Bals, Turi, Skre, & Kvernmo, 2010). Sámi people understand suicide among themselves as related to historical and ongoing oppression, negative treatment of Sámi by other Sámi, shortage of culturally adapted mental health care, issues within Sámi networks and traditional cultural values (Stoor, Berntsen, Hjelmeland, & Silviken, 2019). Related to this complex context, Sámi patients within the Norwegian mental health system require a different approach to mental distress (Minde, 2005).

Data and methods

The study from which this interview emerged included 18 in depth interviews. The study was approved by the Norwegian Center for Research Data. All professionals, patients and relatives received information about the study and gave written consent to participate. They were able to withdraw from the study at any time, without having to give a reason. We have maintained the anonymity of the participants. The study aimed to contribute to our knowledge of what can promote increased user involvement in mental health care for Sámi users with complex needs and strengthen knowledge about involvement for service providers working within these contexts. The participants were recruited from Sámi core areas, through a local manager at each community mental health center. Information letters were distributed, and individuals who were interested in participating signed letters of consent. The participants could bring a companion if they wished.

A thematic interview guide was used, and all the participants preferred to speak Norwegian/Swedish. Most of the interviews were approximately 1–2 hours long. Interviews were digitally recorded, and the sound files were transcribed verbatim.

The context

The context of the study was mental health services for Sámi patients with complex needs and mental distress, and their relatives. The services are provided by

76 Rita Sørly, Vår Mathisen and Vigdis Nygaard

the *Sámi Norwegian National Advisory Unit on Mental Health and Substance Use* (SANKS) and cover a wide range of diagnosis. SANKS is located in many municipalities in Norway, covering the Northern, Southern and Lule Sámi areas. In addition, they also have services in Oslo (the capital), and Jæmtland Härjedalen Region in Sweden. In other words, they cover large parts of the area known as Sápmi. SANKS has an outpatient service for children and young people, adults and people struggling with substance abuse. They also have a 24-hour offer in family treatment, adolescent and adult mental health services. SANKS has a nationwide function and has Sámi -speaking professionals employed. Many Sámi patients who live outside SANKS office locations are receiving their services.

The participants

We interviewed nine health professionals working with Sámi mental health patients and nine Sámi patients and relatives who are, or have been, in contact with mental health services. The professionals and the patients come from northern, southern and Lule Sámi areas. This means that all the participants were in contact with a health service is culturally adapted, and that understands the Sámi language, Sámi traditions and understanding of illness.

Among the patients and relatives, there were five active reindeer herders. The other four often had a connection to reindeer husbandry through family and relatives. Two men and seven women were interviewed, aged 20–75 years. While all the interviews with patients and relatives were conducted at physical meetings, the interviews with professionals were conducted in different ways. Three interviews were conducted via Skype, two interviews per. telephone, and four interviews were conducted face to face. The employees work at various departments for children and young people, families, and adults. Both at the outpatient clinic and bed posts. Occupational groups they represent are, for example, nurses, family therapists, social workers and psychologists. In various ways, everyone has a close connection to Sámi culture, either as a Sámi themselves, and/or that they are related to Sámi, or have lived in Sámi culture for a long time.

In this chapter, we will take a closer look on the interview with Niilas, a Sámi reindeer herder in his mid-60s. First, we will present the narrative approach we have chosen in the study.

Narrative approach

This study employed a narrative approach. Stories are produced, distributed, and circulated in society (Gubrium, 2005; Klausen, 2017). How the stories we tell relate to particular social contexts requires an understanding of what those contexts do with words. The social consequences of stories must be understood in relation of what is at stake in the everyday storytelling context (ibid.). Contexts are of great importance in storytelling. In line with Ahmed and Rogers (2017) our epistemological approach to narrative analysis focus on the significance and influence of context, and hence, knowledge can be understood to be temporally, culturally

Figure 4.2 The girl by the reindeer fences. Photo: Rita Sørly.

and spatially specific (Figure 4.2). As researchers we wanted to explore Indigenous storytelling in this study. We expected the Sámi storytelling to be grounded in a unique history and trajectory, revealing Sámi value-systems and ways of knowing. Inspired by Caxaj (2015), we thought of Indigenous storytelling as practices of nurturing and teaching and acts of resistance that communicate colonial injustices.

Niilas story of the reindeer year

Niilas was a reindeer herder in his mid-60s. He had spent his whole life within reindeer herding. He had drove for many hours to come to the interview and was waiting for us to show up at the SANKS' office the afternoon we met him. There is a tradition among reindeer herders that you must get a reindeer landmark from your father to be able to start as a herder. Niilas' father did not have a reindeer landmark, so he got it from his mother. But there were no reindeer there, and he had to build up the herd himself. It was hard work. He had to work as a teacher, as a carpenter and a waiter for many years to get enough money. He also worked for other reindeer herders, both in Norway and Sweden. But he never gave up; he always knew what his dream was. He had been living away from his parents as a boy, going to different residential schools for 12 years. These were Norwegian and Swedish residential schools, where the Sámi children were not allowed to speak their own language, and they experienced many traumas in early childhood. Niilas was bullied by the other children, and he had a difficult childhood.

78   *Rita Sørly, Vår Mathisen and Vigdis Nygaard*

He was the only child in his family, and he spent his holidays together with his grandmother. His mother was working in the mountains, and he seldom saw her. Niilas did not mention his father in the interview. He told us he struggled with periods of depression and use of alcohol.

We have been talking quite a while, when one of us ask Niilas: Can you give us an insight into a reindeer herder's everyday life? What do you do from morning to evening?

Yes, in the past you were more dependent on how the weather was. But nowadays there are helicopters and scooters and everything. And it is – yes – NOW we have had reindeer herding then … in four winter groups in our city … Because they have made a group, so that you do not have the whole herd in ONE place, so you relieve the pasture a little. Because it's nice to … – that you are in a small group. And it can often be relatives … So now we monitor the reindeer [pause]. And then you have this natural operation, that then you go up the mountain where they [the reindeer] have become… [pause], and there they will calve. So [pause]if there is a lot of snow in the mountains, that you do not [pause], then you have to [pause] stop [silence]… In the end it is not possible to stop them [the reindeer]. They carry on. And you try to pull in a gathering squad then. Then they [the reindeer] come towards the Norwegian border and into there too, and then … we take care of them, so they do not go into Norway, towards other neighboring towns and … And there they calve at the beginning of May and through May … So – when the snow melts and it becomes – yes, large rivers and lakes [pause] and the calves are small, then it is calm for a while then … Until the middle of June. Then we start to guard and starts collecting them, because then there will be calf marking in July …. Then we gather the whole reindeer herd and have them in a place we call [pause]. Before, then we had a fence a little here and there, where you had the reindeer herd … Not everything – Now we have the whole reindeer herd in a large [silence]… And there we are about 10–12 days, calves are being marked. So we have to finish by the middle of July, because since then it is not possible to collect them anymore, because then they spread out.

And then it's calm then … in August then … And then after – BEFORE, then we could slaughter the reindeers ourselves (Figure 4.3). When you slaughtered – we collected the big bulls before they went … – before they came into heat – Do you understand when I say that?

And then you always had – then we had [pause]. around September 12 … Too often they [the reindeer] gathered together even then, on the mountain. If it's cold nights and hot days then … But now there are new regulations there. All slaughterhouses in Sweden …. there were new regulations, with a slaughter bus. And it became an expensive slaughter, that. And then it could be bad weather, and then it was a bad result then, to collect the reindeer … Plus we had a helicopter and [pause]. So it was over, more or less, with … slaughtering the animals ourselves. But [pause] rather in October. The beginning of October then … And then there will be more calf slaughter, you slaughter … [pause] calf then … And when we – yes, that's it – the snow comes fast, then there will be full speed on the reindeer then. Then they [the reindeer] will go down to the forest land.

Figure 4.3 Food supply for the coming year. Photo: Rita Sørly.

Dominant narratives in context

In the following we present dominant narratives we experienced as present in the interview context with Niilas. These were not outspoken, but rather present as normative and prescriptive silent big stories, co- existing within the frames of our research. These dominant narratives can be understood as expressions of canonical stories, and the ways in which specific experiences conform or deviate from these stories create space for voice and silence in the interview context (Fivush, 2010). As the interview progressed, these narratives were alternately present or not present throughout the session. Based on the co-production of storytelling, where voice and silence are socially constructed in conversational interactions, we understand these dominant narratives as negotiated, imposed, contested and provided (Fivush, 2010).

What shaped Niilas' story? What was going on in the storytelling act, could his narrative performance be affected by dominant narratives? If yes, who's dominant stories? Was it Niilas' or ours? What was our response to his story? The co-construction of the story told might be affected by a not present audience, whom we might think would listen to this story? Who are we as researchers talking to when we present the story of Niilas? These questions led us to four dominant narratives we found necessary to explore. These are presented in the following analysis.

80   *Rita Sørly, Vår Mathisen and Vigdis Nygaard*

The mainstream Western school of narrative

Most approaches to narrative research in academia are based in a Western school of thought that does not belong to local Indigenous epistemologies or ontologies (Caxaj, 2015). According to Zipes (2013) a narrative within the Western academy is typically defined as a bounded and structured tool or practice with particular components, mechanisms and outputs. Storytelling, the performance of narrative, is primarily understood as an expression of self-individual meaning-making (ibid.). Life stories are individually oriented, and assumptions about the world and the nature of knowledge originate from a colonial past. Caxaj (2015) underlines that the Western focus on human agency on the world may construct a dichotomy of human and nature that is contrary to Indigenous knowledge that emphasize the interconnectedness and the relational aspect of the universe. The Western understanding position humans as detached observers from the natural environment. The focus on plot and temporality may be incompatible with the Indigenous perspectives, that are both cyclical and connected to local spaces and environments (Castellano, 2008; Caxaj, Berman, Varcoe, Ray, & Restoulec, 2014). The traditional Sámi ontology takes seriously how the nature and non-humans (reindeers, for instance) influence and co-produce our world. In line with Wright et al. (2012), we understand interacting with non-humans in a Sámi reindeer context as "attending to presences, absences, silences and communication" (p. 53).

We asked Niilas' about his working day as a reindeer herder, and we were expecting a linear story, with a beginning, a middle and an end (Wright et al., 2012). Instead of telling about one working day, Niilas told us the story of the reindeer year. His storytelling is cyclical and rooted to his local spaces and environments (Castellano, 2008; Caxaj et al., 2014), describing the year from winter to next winter, when the snow comes again. He describes how the reindeer give birth, how the calves are marked, where they are in the terrain and what the weather's like during the year. Everything depends on the animals, and the reindeer herders are tightly connected to the animals' wellbeing and the surrounding nature. A Western focus on plot and temporality is not useful if we want to understand this story with Indigenous lenses. Niilas' storytelling reflect common contours of Indigenous ontologies and epistemologies, related to embodied and timeless nature of knowledge (McIsaac, 2008), knowing through multiplicity, holism and experience (Castellano, 2008), and a sense of belonging to nature (Sørly et al., 2020). Another issue that we found prominent in Niilas' story, was several pauses and passages of silence. Voice and silence are socially constructed in conversational interactions, and when Niilas is taking a break in his narrative, or is just being silent, it is like a room opens up and we all, including himself, have to listen to what is said, and what will come next. This iterative reflexivity (Caxaj, 2015) is going on throughput the interview, giving all the participants in the conversation time to reflect upon what is said, and what dominant narrative the story relates to.

Mental health research in an Arctic Indigenous context   81

The Norwegianization, assimilation policy and oppression narrative

The Norwegianization era has created a post-conflict society among the Sámi and the Norwegian population. The Sámi population experienced that their language and culture were seen as second-rate in relation to the Norwegian majority culture (Jenssen, 2006). The wounds from the discrimination are still living in the Sámi people. People have chosen different approaches toward the painful history of assimilation policy and oppression from the state. A product of the Norwegianization process was for many an enormous feeling of shame. One had been taught that one's own language and one's own culture, and then oneself, were of no value. One did not fit in Norwegian society with a Sámi background (Boine, 2011). Poverty was associated with Sámi culture and language, and this led many to distance themselves from the Sámi culture (ibid.). Shame over being Sámi led many to live with a secret identity, a double identity. They talked Sámi in small groups, among friends and family, but as soon as one came out among others they communicated in Norwegian (Boine, 2011). By looking back at history, one can see that everyday life and society itself was a greater Norwegianization catalysator than the school (Boine, 2011; Jensen, 2005; Minde, 2005). In a study by Eriksen (2018), focusing on to what extent and in what ways the Sámi people are included in national imaginary in social studies textbooks for primary school in Norway, Eriksen found that Sámi are essentialized and actively constructed as the Other through the structure and content of narratives. Externalization of the Sámi from the story of the Norwegian national day and treatment of the discriminatory Norwegianization politics, reinforce the image of Norwegian exceptionalism. In the interview with Niilas, his storytelling might be understood as a resistance narrative aimed at an invisible audience. The resistance act is a destigmatizing project, where Niilas really wants to describe what it means to be a reindeer herder. Not in a Norwegian perspective, but how he connects with the animals and nature surrounding him when he's out there. The transformative process is Niilas' expressing consciousness of the assimilation policy, and his choice of another life. King (2003, p. 10) underlines that once a story is told, it is loose in the world. You have to be careful with the stories you tell, and you have to watch out for the stories you are being told. When Niilas is telling his story, he never once mentions the Norwegianization era. Instead he performs an alternative narrative, showing us the possibilities of another way of seeing things.

The reindeer herder narrative

Reindeer herders diagnosed with a mental illness encounter a triple burden of discrimination. In addition to the diagnosis of mental illness, ethnicity and expectations of mental strength seem stigmatizing to these women and men, who are already in exposed positions because of their illness and its challenges. According to Kaiser and Salander Renberg (2012), social detachment and disruption of traditional ways of life are linked to rates of depression and alcohol abuse among Sámi reindeer herding men. Hassler (2005) underlines that Sámi reindeer herding

82   Rita Sørly, Vår Mathisen and Vigdis Nygaard

men, after a policy of cultural separation remain in a relative homogenous cultural context, while women often have a foot in both the majority and the Sámi culture. The socio-economic status of reindeer herders are lower compared to other groups, and the level of education is low, especially among men (Kaiser & Salander Renberg, 2012). Cultural separation, long term ongoing conflicts about land rights, financial stress, lack of control, discrimination and gender segregation has been described as linked to higher rates of depression and anxiety, especially among middle-aged reindeer herding men (Kaiser, Sjolander, Edin-Liljegren, Jacobsson, & Salander Renberg, 2010).

Today, reindeer herders must reconcile societal expectations that they can be good herders while simultaneously meeting the expectation that they will fulfill their roles as members of the Sámi society. As noted by Eriksen (2017), there exist a culturally rooted concealment that the Sámi, and especially Sámi women, are so strong that they can withstand everything, including violence and abuse. As a reindeer herder you are expected to take care of your family, both humans and non- humans. In Norway, several studies show that there is no significant difference between mental health among the majority population and Sámi youth (Bals, Turi, Skre & Kvernmo, 2010; Heyerdahl, Kvernmo, & Wichstrom, 2004; Kvernmo, 2004; Silviken & Kvernmo, 2007). But on the Swedish side of Sápmi young Sámi and Sámi reindeer herders are found to have poorer mental health than Swedish comparison groups (Omma, Jacobssen, & Petersen, 2012; Kaiser et al., 2010). In Sweden there is a great pressure on reindeer herders, from the surrounding communities, great predation on reindeer, interference with grazing land in the form of forestry, wind and hydropower, tourism and social infrastructure such as roads and railways (Kaiser, 2011). These challenges are well known all over Sápmi. The reindeer herders have indeed a complex position as bearers of the most important symbol of Sámi culture (Åhrén, 2009).

The story of Niilas, describing the year with the animals, is very interesting in comparison with the dominant narrative of the reindeer herder. Niilas is a Swedish reindeer herder in his mid-60s, struggling with anxiety, depression and alcohol abuse. He is need of help from SANKS for his mental distress, and he "fits" in what might be a "typical patient" within the context. Throughout the interview Niilas answered questions related to his health in the same way as he answers the question about his working day as a reindeer herder. His storytelling was presented as collective or shared experiences, intertwined in relationship with one another, the wider community, and the natural environment (Caxaj, 2015). This is very important knowledge when working with mental health in Indigenous context. The individual approach used in Western mental health services might not be suitable within a Sámi community.

The Norwegian researcher narrative

We are Norwegian researchers, working with Indigenous mental health research. We live and work in Northern Norway, and have grown up in, what is often

Mental health research in an Arctic Indigenous context   83

defined in popular terms, as an Arctic, ethnic cocktail. The popular term has its origin from the fact that people with Finnish ancestors, Sámi people and Norwegians have lived together in the area for centuries. The politics of doing Indigenous studies are well known and raises questions like "who has the right to speak, to make representations, whose voice is more authentic, and what happens to Indigenous peoples' knowledge and cultures when they study in the Western academic classrooms?"(Mackinlay, 2003). It matters how we position ourselves. When doing Indigenous studies, you are often invited into discussions related to identity and the "authority of experience" to legitimate speaking positions (ibid.). A well-known phrase is that only Indigenous people can speak for Indigenous people. This naïve Indigenous racism is described by Langton (1993) as an ancient and universal feature of racism: the assumption of the *Other*. More specifically; the assumption that all Indigenous people are alike and equally understand each other, without regard to cultural variation, history, gender, sexual preference and so on. When doing Indigenous research, we must be aware of the intersubjectivity of the participating people, that is made and remade over and over again in a process of dialogue, imagination, representation and interpretation (Langton, 1993; Mackinlay, 2003).

When gathering data for this study, we were aware of our position as "outsiders". As female, Norwegian researchers from the biggest city in Northern Norway, we presented the majority population. We realized early in the process that we needed door openers to get in touch with the people we wanted to talk to. We were, before we started the study, positioning ourselves as "outsiders". In Niilas' story you can see how he welcome us into his storytelling when one of us asks about his working day as a reindeer herder. His answer is a narrative about the reindeer year. He does not reject our question but expands it and makes it part of his narrative performance, his storytelling. As stated by Lewis (2006) story telling as research practice enables us, as researchers, to engage in stories of families, communities, and cultures. In this way we also begin to understand the transformative process of understanding oneself in relation (ibid.). In this study, we asked ourselves what contributions, if any, non-Indigenous researchers can offer toward decolonizing mental health research. In line with Krusz, Davey, Wigginton, and Hall (2020, p. 213), we found that the process of critical reflection facilitated a persistent and often shared acknowledgment of discomfort that led to developing a collective point of inquiry for continued learning. Self-awareness, mindful investigation of discomfort, and movement through nonbinary and toward nondualistic thinking are aspects that we found important to discuss through the study (ibid.).

Conclusion: Narratives as social justice and practice in an Indigenous mental health context

Based on our analysis we highlight how the notion of ongoing dominant narratives in mental health research context with Indigenous people can make us more aware of how surrounding stories affect our work. We asked Niilas about

84   Rita Sørly, Vår Mathisen and Vigdis Nygaard

his everyday life and anticipated our open question to lead us talking about mental health in an Indigenous context. Niilas' story about the reindeer year was not what we expected. When he was telling us something we immediately didn't understand, we used our inner library related to our available dominant narratives. Maybe these narratives overshadowed Niilas' story of his lifelong fight to become a reindeer herder. The unpredictable life, with hard physical work and uncertainty, with regulations from the majority society, low income, bad weather, loads and worries. In retrospect, we understand Niilas' story as a story of his mental health distress. Indigenous storytelling encourages a broader understanding of identity, community, culture and relations (Iseke, 2013), which is connected to mental health. Niilas' narrative is compelling as an alternative to a more mainstream Western approach to mental health. Indigenous storytelling enhances possibilities for achieving social intelligibility, recognition and justice (Donovan & Ustundag, 2017). Niilas' storytelling effectively covey complexities of his traumatic experiences, including his embodied experiences from childhood until today. These experiences are not always explicit present in his narrative but are visible throughout his story on the annual cycle. His story gives us a context of how we as researchers can grasp a broader understanding of Indigenous mental health. In line with Caxaj (2015), we agree that carrying out research with Indigenous communities that incorporates Indigenous storied methodologies can help develop rich, locally relevant insights that may better guide culturally responsive understandings of health experiences.

References

Ahmed, A., & Rogers, M. (2017). Polly's story: Using structural narrative analysis to understand a trans migration journey. *Qualitative Social Work*, 16(2), 224–239. doi: 10.1177/1473325016664573

Åhrén, M. (2009). *Statement by Mattias Åhrén, president of the Sámi council, on the occasion of the 6th ministerial meeting of the Arctic council in Tromsø 29*. Tromsø: Arctic Council Ministerial Meeting.

Bals, M., Turi, A. L., Skre, I., & Kvernmo, S. (2010). Internalization symptoms, perceived discrimination, and ethnic identity in indigenous Sami and non-Sami youth in Arctic Norway. *Ethnicity & Health*, 15(2), 165–179.

Blix, B. H. (2016). *Helse-og omsorgstjenester til den samiske befolkningen i Norge–en oppsummering av kunnskap*. Gjøvik: Omsorgsbibilioteket. Retrieved from: https://omsorgsforskning.brage.unit.no/omsorgsforskning-xmlui/handle/11250/2412229

Blix, B. H., Hamran, T., & Normann, H. K. (2013). Struggles of being and becoming: A dialogical narrative analysis of the life stories of Sami elderly. *Journal of aging studies*, 27(3), 264–275.

Boine, A. L. (2011). *Alt må læres.: En historisk studie av fornorskingen av samene*. Master's thesis, Norges teknisk-naturvitenskapelige universitet, Fakultet for samfunnsvitenskap og teknologiledelse, Pedagogisk institutt.

Bongo, B. A. (2012). *Samer snakker ikke om helse og sykdom. Samisk forståelseshorisont og kommunikasjon om helse og sykdom. En kvalitativ undersøkelse i samisk kultur*. PhD thesis, The Arctic University of Norway.

Castellano, M. B. (2008). Updating aboriginal traditions of knowledge. In G. J. Dei, B.-D. Hall, & G. D. Rosenberg (Eds.), *Indigenous knowledges in global contexts* (pp. 21–36). Toronto: Toronto University Press.

Caxaj, C. S. (2015). Indigenous storytelling and participatory action research: Allies toward decolonization? Reflections from the peoples' international health tribunal. *Global Qualitative Nursing Research, 2,* 1–12. doi: 10.1177/2333393615580764

Caxaj, C. S., Berman, H., Varcoe, C., Ray, S. L., & Restoulec, J. P. (2014). Gold mining on Mayan-Mam territory: Social unravelling, discord and distress in the Western highlands of Guatemala. *Social Science & Medicine, 111,* 50–57.

Dagsvold, I., Mollersen, S., & Stordahl, V. (2015). What can we talk about, in which language, in what way and with whom? Sami patients' experiences of language choice and cultural norms in mental health treatment. *International Journal of Circumpolar Health,* 74(1), 26952. doi: 10.3402/ijch.v74.26952

Dagsvold, I., Møllersen, S., & Stordahl, V. (2016). You never know who are Sami or speak Sami" Clinicians' experiences with language-appropriate care to Sami-speaking patients in outpatient mental health clinics in Northern Norway. *International Journal of Circumpolar Health,* 75(1), 32588. doi: 10.3402/ijch.v75.32588

Donovan, C., & Ustundag, E. (2017). Graphic narratives, trauma and social justice. *Studies in Social Justice, 11*(2), 221–237.

Eidsvik, E. (2016). Colonial discourse and ambivalence. Norwegian Participants on the colonial arena in SouthAfrica. In K. Loftsdóttir & L. Jensen (Eds.), *Whiteness and postcolonialism in the Nordic region* (pp. 13–29). Abingdon, UK: Routledge.

Eriksen, A. M. A. (2017). *"Breaking the silence" interpersonal violence and health among Sami and non-Sami. A population-based study in mid-and Northern Norway.* PhD Thesis, UiT The Arctic University of Norway, Tromsø, Norway.

Eriksen, K. G. (2018). Teaching about the other in primary level social studies: The Sami in Norwegian textbooks. *JSSE-Journal of Social Science Education, 17*(2), 57–67.

Fivush, R. (2010). Speaking silence: The social construction of silence in autobiographical and cultural narratives. *Memory, 18*(2), 88–98.

Gubrium, J. F. (2005). Introduction: Narrative environments and social problems. *Social Problems, 52*(4), 525–528. doi: 10.1525/sp.2005.52.4.525

Gullestad, M. (2006). *Plausible prejudice. Everyday experiences and social images of nation, culture and race.* Oslo, Norway: Universitetsforlaget.

Hassler, S. (2005). *The health condition in the Sami population of Sweden, 1961–2002: Causes of death and incidences of cancer and cardiovascular diseases.* PhD thesis, Folkhälsa och klinisk medicin. University of Umeå, Sweden.

Heyerdahl, S., Kvernmo, S., & Wichstrom, L. (2004). Self-reported behavioural/emotional problems in Norwegian adolescents from multiethnic areas. *European Child and Adolescent Psychiatry, 13*(2), 64–72.

Iseke, J. (2013). Indigenous storytelling as research. *International Review of Qualitative Research, 6*(4), 559–577.

Jensen, E. B. (2005). *Skoleverket og de tre stammers møte.* Tromsø: Eureka Forlag.

Jenssen, C. (2006). *Formidling av sjøsamisk kultur og identitet i et lokalsamfunnsmuseum i Finnmark.* Master's thesis, Universitetet i Tromsø, Norway.

Kaiser, N. (2011). *Mental health problems among the Swedish reindeer-herding Sami population: In perspective of intersectionality, organisational culture and acculturation.* PhD thesis, Umeå Universitet, Umeå, Sweden.

Kaiser, N., & Salander Renberg, E. (2012). Suicidal expressions among the Swedish reindeer-herding Sami population. *Suicidology Online, 3,* 102–113.

86 Rita Sørly, Vår Mathisen and Vigdis Nygaard

Kaiser, N., Sjolander, P., Edin-Liljegren, A., Jacobsson, L., & Salander Renberg, E. (2010). Depression and anxiety in the reindeer-herding sami population of Sweden. *International Journal of Circumpolar Health*, 69(4), 383–393.

King, T. (2003). *The truth about stories: A native narrative.* Toronto, Canada: House of Anansi.

Kirmayer, L. J. (2000). Broken narratives: Clinical encounters and the poetics of illness experience. In C. Mattingly & L. Garro (Eds.), *Narrative and the cultural construction of illness and healing* (pp. 153–180). Berkeley: University of California Press.

Klausen, R. K. (2017). *Relational insight and user involvement in the context of Norwegian community mental health care: A narrative analysis of service users' stories.* PhD Thesis, UiT The Arctic University of Norway, Tromsø, Norway.

Krusz, E., Davey, T., Wigginton, B., & Hall, N. (2020). What contributions, if any, can non-indigenous researchers offer toward decolonizing health research? *Qualitative Health Research*, 30(2), 205–216.

Kvernmo, S. (2004). Mental health of Sami youth. International Journal of Circumpolar Health, 63(3), 221–234.

Langton, M. (1993). Rum, seduction and death:'Aboriginality'and alcohol. *Oceania*, 63(3), 195–206.

Lewis, P. J. (2006). Stories I live by. *Qualitative Inquiry*, 12(5), 829–849.

Mackinlay, E. (2003). Performing race, culture, and gender in an indigenous Australian women's music and dance classroom. *Communication Education*, 52(3–4), 258–272.

Mathisen, V., & Sørly, R. (2020). Brukermedvirkning i samiske områder. Praktisering av urfolkskunnskap innen psykisk helsevern. *Tidsskrift for Forskning i Sygdom og Samfund* nr, 33, 23–46.

McIsaac, E. (2008). Oral narratives as a site of resistance: Indigenous knowledge, colonialism and Western Discourse. In Dei, G. J., Hall, B.-D. (Eds.), *Indigenous knowledge's in global contexts* (pp. 89–101). Toronto: University of Toronto Press.

Midtbøen, A. H. (2015). *Diskriminering av samer, nasjonale minoriteter og innvandrere i Norge: En kunnskapsgjennomgang.* Rapport - Institutt for samfunnsforskning (p.114).

Mikkelsen, A. K. (2013). *Natur og mennesker i det pitesamiske området.* Master's thesis, UiT The Arctic University of Norway.

Minde, H. (2005). Fornorskninga av samene – Hvorfor, hvordan og hvilke følger? I E. Boine, S. B. Johansen og S. Lund (red.), *Sámi skuvlahistorjá 1* (pp. 12–33). Kárášjohka: Davvi Girji OS.

Ministry of Labor and Social Affairs. (2000–2001). *Report no. 55 on Sámi politics.* Oslo: Arbeids- og Sosialdepartementet.

Nergård, J.-I. (2011). Når slutter en koloniprosess? I S. I Jentoft, J.-I. Nergard, & K. A. Røvik (Eds.), *Hvor går nord-Norge? Tidsbilder fra en landsdel i forandring* (pp. 119–128). Stamsund: Orkana Akademisk Forlag.

Nymo, R. (2011). *Helseomsorgssystemer i Samiske markebygder i nordre Nordland og Sør-Troms: Praksiser i hverdagslivet: "En ska ikkje gje sæ over og en ska ta tida til hjelp".* PhD thesis, Universitetet i Tromsø, Norway.

Nystad, K., Spein, A. R., & Ingstad, B. (2014). Community resilience factors among indigenous Sami adolescents: A qualitative study in Northern Norway. *Transcultural Psychiatry*, 51(5), 651–672. doi: 10.1177/1363461514532511

Omma, L., Jacobsson, L. H., & Petersen, S. (2012). The health of young Swedish Sami with special reference to mental health. *International Journal of Circumpolar Health*, 71, 18381.

Mental health research in an Arctic Indigenous context 87

Silviken, A., & Kvernmo, S. (2007). Suicide attempts among indigenous Sami adolescents and majority peers in Arctic Norway: Prevalence and associated risk factors. *Journal of Adolescence*, 30(4), 613–626.

Sørly, R., Mathisen, V., & Kvernmo, S. (2020). "We belong to nature": Communicating mental health in an indigenous context. *Qualitative Social Work*, 1–17. doi: 10.1177/1473325020932374

Statistics Norway. (2019). *Sámi statistics 2019*. Oslo, Kongsvinger: Statistisk Sentralbyrå.

Stoor, J. P. A., Berntsen, G., Hjelmeland, H., & Silviken, A. (2019). "If you do not birget [manage] then you don't belong here": a qualitative focus group study on the cultural meanings of suicide among Indigenous Sámi in Arctic Norway. *International journal of circumpolar health*, 78(1), 1–11.

Stoor, J. P., Heatta, G., & Javo, A. (2017). *Plan for suicide prevention among the Sàmi people in Norway, Sweden, and Finland*. Sami Norwegian National Advisory Unit on Mental Health and Substance Abuse (SANKS) and Saami Council. Report. Karasjok, Norway.

Turi, A. L., Bals, M., Skre, I. B., & Kvernmo, S. (2009). Health service use in indigenous Sami and non-indigenous youth in North Norway: A population-based survey. *BMC Public Health*, 9(1), 378.

Willox, A. C., Stephenson, E., Allen, J., Bourque, F., Drossos, A., Elgarøy, S., & Wexler, L. (2015). Examining relationships between climate change and mental health in the circumpolar North. *Regional Environmental Change*, 15(1), 169–182. doi: 10.1007/s10113-014-0630-z

Wright, S., Lloyd, K., Suchet-Pearson, S., Burarrwanga, L., Tofa, M., & Country, B. (2012). Telling stories in, through and with country: Engaging with indigenous and more-than-human methodologies at Bawaka, NE Australia. *Journal of Cultural Geography*, 29(1), 39–60.

Zipes, J. (2013). *Creative storytelling: Building community/changing lives*. New York: Routledge.

5 Stories of empowerment, resilience and healing

A participatory research project with two Indigenous communities in Québec

Liliana Gomez Cardona, Kristyn Brown, Mary McComber, Echo Parent-Racine, Outi Linnaranta

They say culture is medicine, culture is the treatment, culture is the suicide prevention (…) Yes, maple is medicine, yes willow is medicine, and all of the sciences are now saying 'yes it is true, this is medicine'. I'm, like, we already knew, but how do we get people to value that again is the biggest part of our work that we are trying to do here

(Nadia)

Words that we are using more here are 'healing, healing journey' (…) That might be more appropriate to say 'I know I have long way to go, but I've started on my healing journey' or 'I've started healing'. Those are words that people are starting to use more and more here

(Dana)

Introduction

Oral narrative has been central to Indigenous communities, including the Inuit and the Kanien'kehá:ka in Québec. This form of tradition has constituted a way of learning within the different spheres of life in these cultural groups. Oral narrative can be composed of sacred myths, legends, ceremonies and songs. Storytelling is an ancient practice, which despite the influence of literacy and other modern forms of knowledge transfer, remains fundamental among Inuit and Kanien'kehá:ka (Laugrand & Oosten, 2009; Petrone, 1992). Stories are produced and communicated in society, and shaped by cultural, historical and political contexts (Benham, 2007). Stories in a culture are a particularly important means of conveying premises of belief and perception. They are ways of giving meaning to the world, explaining the problematic aspects of social life, as well as providing the tools to resolve dilemmas. They can also present exemplary models of human behavior and goals to be achieved that make sense across generations. Storytelling attempts to harmonize and make the link between past and current events. In addition, stories may stimulate individual reflection and learning of different lessons. The stories are effective because they present central values and ideas in a simple and entertaining form (Geia, Hayes, & Usher, 2013; Hodge, Pasqua, Marquez, & Geishirt, 2002).

DOI: 10.4324/9781003118633-6

Research on Indigenous peoples has tended to increasingly focus on the stories and voices of members of these communities. During the last decades, different reflections on research methods and practices with Indigenous populations have aimed to correct the disparities and the unequal relations which arose in the projects carried out between researchers of Western institutions and the Indigenous individuals and groups (Baines, 2011; Kovach, 2009; Smith, 2005). In addition, these reflections have aimed to highlight Indigenous knowledge and epistemologies, and to validate the know-how produced in the Western institutions from an Indigenous point of view (Datta, 2018; Lekoko, 2007; Wright, Gabel, Ballantyne, Jack, & Wahoush, 2019). The voices, stories and narratives of Indigenous people in research can lead to a better understanding of their realities, planning safe and efficient services, improving engagement of Indigenous peoples, and obtaining better results in health programs (Baines, 2011; Sørly, Mathisen & Kvernmo, 2020; Wilson, 2008). Moreover, this approach contributes to the development of de-colonizing relationships and recognition of the ethical values of respect for persons, equity and reciprocity (NAHO, 2007; Parry, Salsberg, & Macaulay, 2009).

An empowerment approach

Empowerment is a multi-level construct that involves individuals participating and assuming control over their lives in their social and political context (Maton, 2008; Wallerstein, 1992). Empowerment is related to group-based, participatory, and developmental processes through which marginalized or oppressed individuals and groups gain greater control over their lives and environment, acquire valued resources, and reduce societal marginalization (Haswell et al., 2010; Maton, 2008). An empowerment approach aims to produce changes at the individual and community level through the participation of individuals and communities in social action processes. Through the socialization of individual and social challenges, people can strengthen a sense of community and teamwork to access resources or develop skills, therefore transforming their social conditions and believe that they have control on their surrounding world (Wallerstein, 1992). An empowerment approach explores the positive aspects of a state instead of the negative ones and seeks to identify strengths instead of listing risk factors. As a collaborative relationship, the caregiver learns about the person's background, life challenges, and culture (Zimmerman, 2000). The role of the caregiver therefore becomes one of facilitator instead of the only expert, and the patient is the participant and collaborator.

Psychosocial literature has confirmed that empowerment strategies can produce positive health impacts (Wallerstein, 1992, Wallerstein, 2006). Interventions that enhance community and individual empowerment of disadvantaged groups show better outcomes (Haswell et al., 2010; Wallerstein, 2006). Research on empowerment and empowerment strategies are particularly relevant in the context of Indigenous populations due to the impacts of disempowering histories, their need to heal from the past, and the socio-economic disadvantages and health inequalities they have experienced (Maton, 2008; Perkins & Zimmerman, 1995).

90 Liliana Gomez Cardona, Kristyn Brown, Mary McComber, et al.

The Inuit

Almost the entire Inuit nation lives north of the 55th parallel in Nunavik (Québec). Approximately 11,000 Inuit live in 14 villages spread along the Hudson Bay, Hudson Strait and Ungava Bay. Kuujjuaq is the largest community and the administrative centre. Inuktitut is the mother tongue spoken by more than 95% of the Inuit. English is the second language used by the majority of the Inuit, and French occupies the third place (Rivet & Nunavik, 2020).

The colonization, religious missions, and residential schools have had a profound impact on Inuit life and culture (Marsh, 2015; Marsh, Coholic, Cote-Meek, & Najavits, 2015). In addition, during the 1950s, the Inuit very quickly went from a semi-nomadic to a more sedentary lifestyle, changing their way of life drastically in an effort to adapt in a few short decades to the modern institutions and technological developments. This is combined with economic and political marginalization which has placed heavy burdens on Inuit communities (Fraser, Geoffroy, Chachamovich, & Kirmayer, 2015). Additionally, overcrowding is common in Nunavik residential housing (Makivik Corporation et al., 2014). According to the latest reports, suicide rates in Nunavik are 6–11 times larger than the Canadian average (Chachamovich et al., 2015; Wexler et al., 2016). The Parnasimautik Consultation Report (Makivik Corporation et al., 2014) has highlighted the lack of the region's locally accessible health care services.

With the goal of improving their living conditions, members of Inuit communities migrate to urban centers. Inuit living in urban areas are also vulnerable to mental health problems due to a number of factors: significant inequities in income, education, housing conditions, and unemployment rates (MUAHC, 2012). The results of the Montreal Urban Aboriginal Health needs revealed that more than half of the respondents reported being dissatisfied with the health services available in Montreal and perceived different obstacles such as language barriers, limited access to mental health services, and inadequate levels of cultural safety (MUAHC, 2012). There is an important need to develop effective, ecological and decolonizing approaches to enhance the mental well-being of Inuit populations (Kral, 2016).

Despite multiple adverse circumstances, the resilience of the Inuit has been recognized, especially with regard to their ability to adapt to the difficult physical environment of the Arctic (Brody, 1987). In addition, they have their own traditions of healing and resilience (Fraser et al., 2015; Marsh et al., 2015). The Inuit perspective of resilience not only includes resources internal to each individual, but also strengths that emerge from relations between individuals, collectivities, and social systems (Kirmayer & Dandeneau, 2011).

The Kanien'kehá:ka

Kanien'kehá:ka (People of the Flint), commonly known as Mohawk are Indigenous peoples in North America. They are the most populous Indigenous group in Quebec with approximately 16 400 people, spanning three main communities:

Stories of empowerment, resilience and healing 91

Kahnawà:ke (9 400), Ahkwesásne (4 900) and Kanehsatá:ke (2 100) and outside the reserves. There are also Kanien'kehá:ka communities in Ontario (Canada) and New York State (USA). Kanien'kehá:ka generally speak English; however, some speak Kanien'kéha (the Mohawk language) and French (Gouvernement du Canada, 2018).

The history of colonialism and more contemporary political issues have resulted in the exposure of Kanien'kehá:ka to challenging and even traumatic experiences such as: the reduction of land due to Jesuits cessions; the expropriation of land for the construction of modern infrastructure by the Department of Indian Affairs; the Canada's forced residential school system for Indigenous peoples (Phillips, 2000; Reid, 2004). In addition to historical factors, the Kanien'kehá:ka are vulnerable to health problems due to current environmental factors such as: significant inequities in income, education, housing conditions, unemployment rates, discrimination, as well as social marginalization (Fuller et al., 2018). All these factors have had a major impact on the health and mental well-being of Kanien'kehá:ka. During the past years, mental wellness, family wellness, psychoactive substance abuse, and addictions have been identified as important health priorities in Kahnawà:ke (Fuller et al., 2018).

Despite the difficulties experienced by these populations, Kanien'kehá:ka have shown resilience and an ability to adapt to the changing circumstances which form so much of their history. This community has responded to these challenges by gaining and maintaining control over health and community services, education, local economy, and working to revitalize culture and language. One of the main areas for action on mental health that has been identified is the connection to traditional practices and healing methods for individuals who are seeking care services (Fuller et al., 2018). Preserving language and cultural values and being united as a collective unit is an ideology that Elders feel can strengthen the community and individuals in the face of current and future challenges (Phillips, Dandeneau, & Kirmayer, 2012).

Our initial objective concerned the selection of a psychiatric measurement tool to be culturally adapted and clinically used among depressed Indigenous patients. Since our first consultations with members of these communities, we recognized that they did not tend to respond to questionnaires for measuring symptoms of mental illness. Thus, we focused on the adaptation and development of an accepted and culturally safe instrument to assess and promote well-being and empowerment. We completed a cultural adaptation of the tool and collected knowledge to support the development of a future intervention with each Indigenous community.

Our research questions concerned: (1) Which scales for measuring psychiatric symptoms are culturally relevant for Kanien'kehá:ka and Inuit or could be adapted to improve their cultural safety? (2) What are the factors of empowerment, resiliency, and healing to be taken into consideration in order to culturally adapt a tool to assess and promote mental health among Kanien'kehá:ka and Inuit? (3) What are the factors and knowledge needed to develop an intervention that improves cultural safety and healing in these Indigenous populations?

92   Liliana Gomez Cardona, Kristyn Brown, Mary McComber, et al.

A focus on narrative

For the cultural groups we have worked with, oral tradition has been the primary way to learn and teach. This approach facilitates the construction of relationships that allow the emergence of stories about lived experiences, realities, and evidence on important issues that are not always known (Benham, 2007). Privileging the voices of people studied is a methodology that is consistent with the empowerment of people because it transforms the role relationship from researcher and subject to co-participants and promotes discovering a rich content (Rappaport, 1995). In this study, we have followed an anthropological tradition by focusing on narrative as a methodological approach that was used in all stages of the project. We considered the knowledge and what the participants had to say to be crucial stories in the development of better adapted and culturally safe instruments and health services. We consider the narrative level, in a broad sense, as the source from which individuals shape their experiences. We chose the interpretative and critical medical anthropology approach, and placed narratives, stories, accounts, and histories at the center of analysis (Kirmayer, 2004; Kleinman, 1988; Scheper-Hughes & Lock, 1987).

This project has followed a *qualitative, collaborative and participatory methodology*. A qualitative methodology places the researchers on the field and consists of a set of interpretations whose aim is to capture the social construction of the world from the terms and meanings given by the people themselves (Denzin & Lincoln, 2011). Qualitative research methods, such as those we consider in this project are based on people's narratives and consistent with Indigenous perspectives of understanding and knowledge transfer (APNQL, 2014; Smith, 2005). Moreover, guides on research with Indigenous peoples have increasingly emphasized the importance of participatory and collaborative methods (APNQL, 2014; CIHR, 2018). This approach is understood to involve respectful and active relationships among partners and is based on respect, relevance, mutual responsibility, and reciprocity (Smith, 2005). We are aware of the unequal power relations that have historically dominated research between prevailing institutions and Indigenous peoples. As such, we would like to contribute to decolonizing approaches in the sense that this project should empower and benefit Indigenous communities and cultures (Baines, 2011; Battiste, Bell, & Findlay, 2002; Smith, 2005).

Our fieldwork

The first step of our fieldwork consisted of consultations with people working among Indigenous groups in Québec with the aim of determining if the research project met their needs. We started working with the first two communities that expressed their interest: the Kanien'kehá:ka of Kahnawà:ke (Kahnawa'kehró:non) and Inuit from Nunavik who live in an urban environment (Montréal). We formed an advisory group with each community and implemented focus groups to examine acceptability, relevance, and cultural adaptation of the mental health instrument (Krueger & Casey, 2014). We led: (a) Five focus groups with a Kanien'kehá:ka advisory group-KAG (4-12 people), and (b) five focus groups

Stories of empowerment, resilience and healing 93

with an Inuit advisory group-IAG (four to six people). The sample was composed of approximately 18 adults from the community and associations working with Kanien'kehá:ka and Inuit, or having significant knowledge of the issues of these communities; the majority of them self-identified as Indigenous. We contacted the participants through the directors of associations and councils that work with the communities; word of mouth was also used to recruit participants.

Each of focus groups were conducted in English lasting approximately two hours, and was recorded and transcribed. Individual interviews were also held exclusively outside of group meetings to accommodate availability of some members. Informal discussions and email exchanges were also done with co-researcher (KB) and Kanien'kehá:ka Faith Keepers to get further cultural insight. Data collection was held over a period of six months (August, 2019–February, 2020) at community service establishments in Montréal and its surroundings (Kahnawá:ke Shakotiia'takéhnhas community services, Southern Quebec Inuit Association, Ullivik centre). The focus groups were conducted using a guide with open-ended questions that concentrated on the acceptability, relevance, comprehensibility, exhaustiveness, and cultural adaptation of the scales to assess mental health. Additionally to the participants, a moderator and an assistant moderator of the research team were present at each focus group (LGC and OL) as well as a co-researcher associated with the KAG (KB). The research team members took field notes during the focus groups and held a debriefing after each meeting.

Ethical considerations

A consent form was reviewed and signed by each member of advisory committees at the beginning of the first meeting. Participants saw their identity protected throughout this study. No name has been associated with the data collected; these were associated with a participant code. The audio files were destroyed once the interviews were transcribed. A financial compensation for participation was offered to the participants, unless their activity was considered a part of their work tasks. Others decided to donate their amount collectively to a local language group for mothers and their children (Iakwahwatsiratátie Language Nest). This research has respected community protocols and the ethical framework in Indigenous contexts consisting of the principles of respect, equity, and reciprocity (Smith, 2005). We have followed the OCAP principles (Ownership, Control, Access and Possession) at all stages of the project (CIHR, 2018). We received ethical acceptance to conduct this project from the Research Ethics Board of the Douglas Mental Health University Institute (#IUSMD-19-19) and the Onkwata'karitáhtshera Health and Social Services Research Council of Kahnawà:ke. We recognize and ensure Kahnawake's Research Council ownership.

Analysis

We carried out a thematic analysis of the information gathered during the focus group, informal discussions, and emails (Braun & Clarke, 2006). This method was

94 *Liliana Gomez Cardona, Kristyn Brown, Mary McComber, et al.*

based on a systematic and methodical examination of textual information and consisted of reading the transcripts several times until identifying the common themes. The data collected in focus groups was transcribed into written form by a co-researcher and two research assistants (KB and GV). When necessary, the transcripts were back checked against the audio recordings. Interview transcripts were then organized and reviewed for pertinent data (LGC, OL, and KB) before making changes to the content of the instrument. Two co-researchers (LGC and KB) generated the initial ideas through a systematic examination of the transcribed information (e.g., reasons for the acceptance/refusal of the scales to assess mental health; reasons for cultural adaptation) (Table 5.1). We implemented an inductive approach to encourage the emergence of meaningful categories for the people themselves (e.g., focus on supportive factors versus focus on symptoms; visual and graphic elements; format; questions to be deleted/reformulated/added and reasons; culturally significant symbols and therapeutic elements to be added; use purpose of the tool) (Table 5.1).

Findings

The first step of this project consisted in determining the interest of the advisory groups in the use of three scales to measure depression: the Patient Health Questionnaire (PHQ-9), the Kessler Psychological Distress Scale (K-10) and the Center for Epidemiological Studies-Depression (CES-D-20), and three scales to measure supportive factors of mental health: the Scale of Protective Factors (SPF-24), the Self Compassion Scale-Short Form (SCS-SF) and the Growth and Empowerment Measure (GEM). These measurement scales have been selected by the research team because they have shown good psychometric properties across translations, cross-cultural validity, and measurement invariance across multiple contexts (McNamara et al., 2014).

Each of the participants examined the scales and each advisory group reviewed them independently. There was unanimity on the obstacles to accepting psychometric scales. Several participants reported that there was resistance to responding to this type of questionnaires that request a *numerical response* and were used in an *institutionalized* framework. This refusal has been witnessed by various professionals who work in psychology and social services. This is what Nadia, a member of the KAG said:

> It's not only personal safety but then it's external safety right here. Just the comment I made about filling in the SIN number, right? It becomes a community issue (…) everything is just a challenge. Soon as you are asking something government (laughter) so there's that protection, even filling out a form becomes a protective factor. So that when you're using safety, the family is asked, the social worker asks to fill out a form (…) People might be more resistant to that kind of.

According to the experience of the professionals, the reasons which motivate this resistance may derive from the mistrust that the members of the community feel

Table 5.1 Phases of the thematic analysis

	Themes		
Initial codes	*Potential themes*	*Emerging themes*	*Defined and reported themes*
Acceptability	• Reasons for the acceptance of the scales to asses mental health • Reasons for the refusal of the scales to asses mental health	• Elements that made one scale more appreciated than the other ones: focus on supportive factors *versus* western understanding of symptoms, response type, visual elements, format, institutionalized and colonialist framework	Give voice to community members on measuring mental health
Relevance	• Reasons for the relevance of the scales to asses mental health • Reasons for the relevance of each question	• Elements that made one scale more relevant than the other ones: focus, visual elements, format • Questions to be deleted and reasons	
Understandability	• Level of understandability of the scales to asses mental health • Level of understandability of each question	• Questions to be reformulated and reasons	
Completeness	• Level of exhaustiveness of the scales to asses mental health • Level of exhaustiveness of each question	• Questions to be added and reasons	
Need (or not) of cultural adaptation	• Reasons for cultural adaptation • Local cultural adaptation	• Culturally significant symbols to be included: colors, footprints, traditional activities, natural elements of the local environment • Therapeutic elements to be included: healing pathway, focus on growth and hope • Categories of questions to be included: community, family, self, body, land, spirituality • Organization of categories • Use purpose of the tool: recommendations, interaction, narrative, training	Listen to what community members have to say about improving mental health

96   *Liliana Gomez Cardona, Kristyn Brown, Mary McComber, et al.*

towards certain institutions or even towards *colonialism* which further impacts the relations between them and the western dominant groups:

> Many people have a form phobia because of the way people have been classified or objectified like report cards or whatever the case may be so they are like: 'what are you're writing that down for?' what is that for'?.
>
> (Nadia, member of the MAG)

Another reason for the rejection of these questionnaires concerned the cognitive style practiced and preferred in the local cultures. The way community members think, interpret and evaluate situations did not necessarily correspond with the scheme underlying the measurement scales. The logic of quantifying emotions was questioned by individuals in both advisory groups. Karin, member of the IAG, expressed it as follows:

> Realistically, I'm never comfortable to put numbers to rank my feelings. (...) Visual works, visual is easier (...) If people can understand the images without the statements, that makes a huge difference because even if language is an issue, I understand from this image where we are or what that means.

Traditional cultures in these two communities have tended to favor the oral transmission of knowledge, the use of symbols and images as metaphors that represent concepts and values and help to organize information about the world and the personal lives. David, an elder member of the KAG told this story:

> When we are young we are taught with symbols, hardly any words, it's all like that visual symbols. And you come from that to make sure you don't forget anything. Like the condolence cane, 8–10 hours ritual non-stop, how do they remember that just from these little symbols? Here's an artist, you work that way, and you promote visual pictures to stimulate that memory not to miss that, not to lose that (...) I use the Creation Story in all my work. It really helps them, because they are going to wonder 'What the hell just happened here?' 'Why am I going through this?' Well if they realize it's been everyone's struggle, even our ancestors struggled from the beginning, it starts to help them understand it's not just all about them.

Thus, having visual graphics and *culturally significant symbols*, instead of just sentences and numbers, was seen by the majority as being able to motivate interest and engagement of individuals. The KAG chose images of medicinal plants following the order of the seasons, and designed by a local artist. In addition, they decided to include other symbols such as the colors of their wampum belts, and the footprints of the animals that represent the three main clans in Kahnawà: ke. The IAG suggested using photos of places or practices significant to the Inuit, such as water, manual art work, tattoos, and a person's footsteps.

Stories of empowerment, resilience and healing 97

Several professionals, with years of experience, shared their discomfort with the use of symptom measurement questionnaires. As a consequence, they have wondered if alternative approaches would not be more relevant and useful. Here are the words of Dana, a member of the KAG: "give someone this tool, that's really impersonal to sit down, we were often doing that and it really throws people off to give these tools on paper and check list". Cari's words abounded in the same vein:

> Everyone got stuck in that western way and using all these tools for the last 10–15 years so they got stuck in using those assessments. A lot of them that are carrying so many clients and they don't have time to counseling, they are going from one fire to the next and they don't have the time or take the time to involve or engage for a long time with clients because there are too many (…) When the Psycho team came to us asking about tools, and they were trying to get away from this checkbox marking model, clients kind of get annoyed with that check box marking model, especially if you come straight in from intake with them (…) And, I think just because of the nature of the work or the amount of work they have, workers might be going too quickly to those checkbox assessments and this might be part of the problem.

In conclusion, the format of the psychometric scales and the way in which they have been used in the institutions are in contradiction with the vision and cultural safety of these Indigenous communities. This discourages the community members from responding to these questionnaires and using them in clinical practice.

Stories that build local Indigenous empowering frameworks

The second stage of the project involved the selection of the most appropriate instrument for measuring mental health according to the members of the advisory committees. In addition, this step consisted in determining if the chosen tool needed a cultural adaptation, and then to proceed with it. The GEM was developed to measure well-being and empowerment among Indigenous Australians (Haswell et al., 2010; Laliberté, Haswell, & Tsey, 2012). Its development was based on the knowledge gathered as part of the Family Well Being Program (FWBP) which aimed at empowering Australian Indigenous families. This instrument intended to assess individuals' own perspectives of their psychosocial well-being at a personal, family, and organizational level along with measuring the results of interventions (Berry, Crowe, Deane, Billingham, & Bhagerutty, 2012; Haswell et al., 2010). The original GEM was composed of a 14-item Emotional Empowerment Scale (EES14) followed by 12 dynamic scenarios (12S) and the Kessler Psychological Distress Scale (K6) with two supplementary questions assessing happiness and anger. The GEM was intended to be used in a variety of settings (Berry et al., 2012; Haswell et al., 2010). As part of our project, the

98   *Liliana Gomez Cardona, Kristyn Brown, Mary McComber, et al.*

12S tool was ultimately considered the most relevant and was exclusively chosen by both advisory groups (Cardona et al., 2021). The original 12S aimed to measure functional aspects of empowerment, and the extent to which the person had moved from one state to another.

The main elements that made the GEM an appealing and promising tool for advisory committee members were: the inclusion of supportive factors, the potential to facilitate interaction and storytelling, and the inclusion of cultural relevant elements. None of the groups were interested in measurement as much as the actual process of interaction about empowering, resilience, and healing factors. The KAG developed the Kanien'kehá:ka GEM (K-GEM) after a rigorous revision of the conceptual and linguistic equivalence of the GEM as well as the inclusion of identity markers, resources traditionally used for health and natural elements specific to their local environment (Cardona et al., 2021). The IAG completely changed the content and scoring of the GEM and developed an instrument called the Resilience and Empowerment Tool (RET) which contains factors of protection and resilience specific to Inuit as well as risk factors to better understand the person's context and determine the need for a security plan. The new content of the tools was developed thanks to the stories and experiences shared by the members of the committees (Table 5.2).

Both advisory groups strongly recommended that the tool support a *healing pathway*. Various of the elements of the tool have therefore been kept and/or modified so that this path of healing was underlined. For example, both groups have defined sequences of situations that ranged from the most difficult and challenging to the one where the person feels empowered and in control. According to various participants, seeing this flow of scenarios would be beneficial and could help the person to realize or become more aware that situations, thoughts, feelings and behaviours can evolve. This continuum could also stimulate focus on growth, hope, and healing possibilities instead of focusing on negative emotions. In addition, several members suggested keeping the graphics that depict footprints as a metaphor of a person walking a healing pathway. Each group have chosen culturally significant graphics such as the animal footprints that represent the main clans among the Kanien'kehá:ka and footprints of a person among the Inuit. An approach that works on a healing journey was reported as necessary among the Indigenous populations concerned. Here are the words of Nadia, member of the KAG:

> Words that we are using more here are 'healing, healing journey', so where it says 'I started to deal with', 'I started on my healing journey' that might be more appropriate to say 'I know I have long way to go, but I've started on my healing journey'. Or 'I've started healing' (…) Those are words that people are starting to use more and more here (…) Usually when people have really worked through a lot, they are going to say they are still on their healing journey (…) And if they are really in this place, they're like 'yea, I know I still have work' (…) It can be hard, so you know that you had the ability to get through it. That is the perspective here.

Table 5.2 Stories of healing, resilience and empowerment among Kanien'kehá:ka and Inuit

Stories and narratives	Kanien'kehá:ka	Inuit
Stories of Dis-empowerment	"I just look at my own parents and that's exactly what it was. There was a history of residential schools in my family. There's a lot of many factors that took away a lot of people's understanding of who they are and what does it really mean to be Indigenous". "Learned helplessness is really big in our community. It's hard for people to get off social assistance, really, it's like generations of like I am not going to be able to or it's just the way it is. This would be a good question to really help people think of that things are possible (...). So, as you read it you are getting to where you want or where you have power".	"I've seen so many people who are depressed and struggling with mental illness; a lot of them are isolated and on their own. There's a lot of silence; it's a silent killer (...) I've seen suicide attempts with my own eyes. I've seen someone on top of the house. I've seen a child running away so she can commit suicide. I've seen a lady try to commit suicide using her bra strap and when I saw it, I screamed and police came rushing (...) There's also addiction. Addiction makes the person weak". "The high rates of suicides are causing people to be in grief mode, there's no rest from it. Sometimes it feels like your entire life is one large grief process (...) we've had discussion with the community about grief, and it goes beyond just the loss of people, we're talking about loss of culture, loss of memories of childhood, loss of independence, loss of dogs". "My parents had to wear a necklace; now you know that it was a dog tag. You know; they're angry. So, if you're dealing with a kid that was brought up by an angry person. We've always been treated like dogs; they just stopped using those necklaces in the 70's I think".

(Continued)

Table 5.2 Continued

Stories and narratives	Kanien'kehá:ka	Inuit
Stories of Resilience and Healing	"When I worked in the treatment center (…) that was our big philosophy that once you engage in your culture, that is what is going to help you with your addiction".	"Word suicide prevention should stop, rather say 'celebrate life'".
	"Culture is belonging, and connection and that's healing."	"The healing journey right now is arising; I think there is hope at the end of the tunnel".
	"We knew about the cycle of seasons and that is this circle (…) Past, present, future, in terms of month to month. Ok well Harvest ceremony is coming up what happens to you at this time of the year, what are some ways you can keep yourself well during this season, what are some of the foods that you should be eating to keep yourself healthy".	"We stopped using the words 'suicide prevention' in school; instead we use 'celebrate life'. We light up the candles, we have singers and drummers; and everyone was crying. But, not just talking about suicide".
	"It's about things happen for a reason and I can manage and keep going with it (…) It gives you like the power and the resiliency to get through; it is like a learning curve (…) that's key in our culture that, bad things happen and step over it or learn from it or you get stronger from it".	"I like how in these scales, there's the positive and the negative side you can put yourself in. And, it's not just on the negatives. This is more important because, I guess, it could help with resilience here I guess you can say".
	"There is a whole teaching, legend that corresponds with the Seven Dancers. It is a famous purge today between red willow and white".	"Art therapy is key; art becomes very important especially today. Youth now are very involved in Art therapy (…) For example, in our jewelry-grieving workshop, we grieved while making necklaces and earrings".
	"When we got our clans, that young man that fatherless man says 'all you people (…) look to the birds and the animals, everything in nature it will find us to the solution to what we must do' (…) so the wisdom of the birds and the animals is what we follow because they were here before us".	"When we go out on the land and when they come back here; it's a completely different story. They say things like 'I feel better, thank you!', 'It was great, I was near the water'".
	"If you showed the Two Row Wampum, you have one going to west and one going east, because every time to move forward you have to look past, to understand where you were and where you got to go".	"Country foods are empowering, it's definitely a source of power. It indicates your link to the land (…) your relationship to your physical environment, to your own land, to your community and your culture and your behaviours (…) It's really a part of the innate culture of living (…) it's spiritual (…) it's not just lifestyle, It's spiritual its really, I don't like that term lifestyle because its bigger than that, and it's like minimizing the effect that it could have on a person and how much that could benefit somebody".
	"Spiritually protect myself with herbal medicine, cedar cleanse, red willow bath, something".	

Stories of empowerment, resilience and healing 101

The IAG has been particularly emphatic at this level by stressing the need to work in the mental health field with a framework oriented towards growth and hope:

> The healing journey right now is arising; I think there is hope at the end of the tunnel. The youth is arising by making suicide prevention awareness (…) We stopped using the words 'suicide prevention' in school; instead, we use 'celebrate life'. We light up the candles, we have singers and drummers, and everyone was crying. But, not just talking about suicide.
>
> (Emma)

Alex, another member of the IAG, commented along the same lines:

> I like how in these scales [GEM], there's the positive and the negative side you can put yourself in. And, it's not just on the negatives. An example of one focusing on negative are scales like 'on a scale of 1-5, how bad do you feel', you walk away feeling even worse. However in something like this [scenarios], yeah, I might presently identify in the negative side but you also see the graphic representation of the positive side which gives hope that things might get better; depicting a pathway to wellness. This is more important because, I guess, it could help with resilience here, I guess.

In addition, both advisory groups agreed with the necessity to include different questions which were not considered in the original version, but which were important aspects of life for community members (e.g., connection to the land, body and physical activity). By addressing these added questions, the person administering the tool would be able to better understand the person's situation and needs as well as identify their supportive factors. Moreover, each group proposed to organize the questions according to categories that correspond to spheres that influence the lives of people. Among the categories common to both groups, there was the Community. The order of categories and questions should facilitate communication between the provider and the patient therefore allowing the latter to begin answering questions with which they feel most comfortable (e.g., land attachment, community, family, self-reflection).

Lastly, the ability to facilitate *interaction* between persons concerned was also an element for which the GEM was chosen. This factor was also underlined as fundamental in any mental health program. K-GEM and RET were designed by each advisory group as being a facilitator of communication between the client and the administrator of the tool. Several participants identified the need to improve communication and patient confidence in the person providing health services. This need was seen as particularly acute among Inuit communities, where timely health resources are scarce and communication between community members and stakeholders often face significant obstacles. This is the experience narrated by Emma, member of the IAG:

> I've seen so many people who are depressed and struggling with mental illness; a lot of them are isolated and on their own. There's a lot of silence;

102 *Liliana Gomez Cardona, Kristyn Brown, Mary McComber, et al.*

it's a silent killer. When you have a mental illness going on in your life for so long, it's attached to you and there's a lot of hurt and pain (...) There would be so much anger. The anger is very powerful, I've seen that. When you come to anger management, it's almost like 'it's okay to be angry, but, how do you teach them about healthy anger management? There's a good anger and an anger that could hurt yourself and that can hurt others'. When you aren't able to identify it and talk about it, you become aggressive and it can cause suicide. Men will be more silent and aggressive.

(Emma)

As a response to these issues, and independently, both advisory groups strongly recommended that the *narrative* occupies an important role when using the tools. According to various participants, during the meeting between the client and the health provider, this latter would have the role of stimulating the client's narration so that he/she becomes aware of it, understands it, and works on it with a goal of empowerment. In both groups, this oral narrative approach was seen as relevant since it has been already known and spontaneously practiced in their traditional cultural settings. Therefore, the idea of conversation and storytelling were seen as having great potential. Here are the words of some KAG members:

NADIA: It will be a tool to learn from the client what is happening to them. So it's all about connecting.

DANA: It would be more of a dialogue where you wouldn't check off anything necessarily. I was just looking at an article using the narrative approach to assessment and treatment plans and it's the same kind of approach, and getting the person curious (...) the narrative approach is very much like that.

NADIA: The First Nations research methodology is often the narrative (...) so, it is really similar that you tell the story then you find the points in there that are uncommon and come up with whatever.

DANA: and that is definitely more of the direction that we are going. Especially with my team for sure it's all going towards more of a narrative approach to counselling (...) because the relationship should be of one collaboration, they are the expert, the community member is the expert in their lives. We are there to help them formulate that narrative, how to change that relationship of whatever is bringing them in and making the problem outside of themselves.

NADIA: and so the narrative approach, if you were to use this tool, it maybe can be we are going to talk about your relationship to safety in your life, and then they get to tell ... and you get to be with them as they are telling their life and so that process of telling the story is healing in itself.

DANA: like you say 'you were never able to say no' why don't you tell me a time when you weren't able to set a boundary? You now ... so curious, can you tell me a time when you were able to protect yourself (...) or maybe it wasn't a consistent thing but you get them to flip their story, because their story is 'I can't take care of myself, I can't protect myself' whatever. So, you get them to slowly

Stories of empowerment, resilience and healing 103

by being curious get them to change the narrative, that they can't do this, or this is my problem to 'actually you're right, I was able to do that'.

According to the majority of committee members, interaction around the tools could create a base of understanding a person's narrative and of processing the narrative towards resilience and healing. The discussion should optimally aim at increased agency in one's own life and strengthening capacities to use personal and socio-cultural resources. The tools could be used as part of a therapeutic process that will use narrative approaches towards healing and strengthening the emphasis on the cultural and social aspects of resilience.

In general, the KAG shared more traditional stories and activities that are used for healing and therapeutic purposes as well as a more active cultural revitalization process. They also stressed a need for an empowerment approach and an ongoing cultural empowerment process. In addition, they indicated more knowledge and experiences in integrating western knowledge and traditional know-how, partly due to several members have a training as psychotherapist or social work. IAG members expressed a need to move away from a stigmatizing and negative view of themselves, which has been widely conveyed by the media and groups outside and inside their communities.

Conclusions

The lack of *cultural safety* was a major issue for members of the Indigenous communities studied. They have been confronted with the psychometric and psychiatric measurement tools commonly used in social service institutions and in research. The content of the measurement tools, format, and the relational dynamics in which they are used was perceived as threatening and not reassuring by the members of the advisory groups with whom we have worked with. The obstacles to accepting psychometric measures have been caused by different socio-historical factors which may also affect other Indigenous communities in the Arctic and around the world. These factors include: the past of colonization with the imposition of western institutions and the discredit of Indigenous cultures and narratives, the unequal relations between hegemonic institutions and members of Indigenous communities, and the fragility of trust between the different sides. In addition, the differences in cognitive styles, the incomprehension between the two world views, and the lack of cultural sensitivity were all factors which obstructed the acceptance and usefulness of psychometric scales.

Recent studies have shown that cultural safety which integrates cultural awareness, cultural sensitivity, and cultural competency is a key component of quality health services for Indigenous people around the world (Brascoupé & Waters, 2009; Darroch et al., 2017). Culturally competent services can help to create an atmosphere of safety and trust (Beaton, Bombardier, Guillemin, & Ferraz, 2000; Griner & Smith, 2006; Kirmayer & Gómez-Carrillo, 2019; Kirmayer, Simpson, & Cargo, 2003). Researchers have confirmed that compromised cultural safety is one factor limiting access of Indigenous populations to effective mental health care (Boksa, Joober, &

104   *Liliana Gomez Cardona, Kristyn Brown, Mary McComber, et al.*

Kirmayer, 2015; Yaphe, Richer, & Martin, 2019). Works on cultural adaptation of mental health assessment tools has recommended that people administering the tools undergo training in cultural safety and understand the patient's definition of what safe care means (NAHO, 2007; IPAC & RCPSC, 2009). In the cultural adaptation processes we made with the two advisory groups, we paid particular attention to the cultural appropriateness and sensitivity of the tools as well as to cultural safety.

When participants discussed factors that can protect and promote the mental health and well-being of community members, elements specific to local cultures were highlighted. These factors include the metaphor of a healing journey, elements of cultural identity and symbols, resources traditionally used for health, along with questions that were significant for community members (e.g., connection to land, culture, and language). Although each group had their own traditions and socio-cultural resources, both agreed on the importance of including them to engage patients, suggest empowerment options, and stimulate communication and production of narratives. The incorporation of traditional values was also seen as being useful for therapeutic purposes. These findings confirm what health providers and researchers have concluded about the place of cultural traditions in health interventions (Kirmayer & Dandeneau, 2011; Makivik Corporation et al., 2014; Marsh et al., 2015). In a recent literature review of Indigenous mental health in Canada, Marsh and colleagues (2015) concluded that interventions should focus on strengthening cultural identity and community integration therefore increase connection among individuals and political empowerment. Spirituality has also been recognized as a key component to the Indigenous holistic view of healing. Traditional knowledge and reclaim culture and identity may improve health and empower Inuit and other Indigenous communities (Marsh et al., 2015).

As a conclusion to numerous studies and reflections on the mental health of Indigenous peoples in Canada, Kirmayer and Valaskakis (2009) have underlined how the notions of tradition and healing occupy a central place in the efforts that Indigenous continue to make to counter the consequences of injustices and suffering derived from colonization. Indigenous peoples are leading processes of healing with their own traditions and values, by repairing ruptures in the transmission of traditional knowledge and reaffirming their collective identity. When working on mental health promotion and services, the authors have recommended taking into consideration these processes as well as the place of tradition and healing in the rediscovery of identity and empowerment. Our work with members of Kanien'kehá:ka and Inuit communities has confirmed the significance of these elements in the planning of current therapeutic programs as well as engaging community members.

Furthermore, researchers have highlighted the importance of studies that encourage Indigenous individuals and groups to explore treatments that could improve health in their communities (Kirmayer & Valaskakis, 2009; Marsh et al., 2015). In our project, the common narratives told by experts and community members were decisive to have the approval of the topic, selection of mental health assessment tools, make their cultural adaptation, have recommendations on the use of tools, and plan mental health interventions. These narratives were powerful since they made visible the tensions between knowledge and practices; they

Stories of empowerment, resilience and healing   105

highlighted important questions that mobilize processes and resources that benefit professionals and institutions as well as Indigenous individuals and communities.

In addition, narrative is an interesting and relevant therapeutic approach which has powerful effects on human behavior and respects individuals and cultures. The community narratives collected spoke of personal, family, and community healing that emphasizes indigenous knowledge, wisdom and collective memory. These factors helped to facilitate acceptance of the presence of the past and what cannot be controlled while strengthening the agency. For participants, one of the main objectives of the adapted tools is to support clients to become empowered and be agents of change in their own life, family, and community. The individuals would be invited to share their story, life experiences, along with thoughts and feelings. By discovering and restoring the personal story narrative, sharing knowledge, understanding own emotions, the participants would become more confident, gain greater meaning of well-being, as well as the energy to engage in change (Laliberté et al., 2012). This dynamic will also provide individuals with a space for personal introspection (Denham, 2008; Hodge et al., 2002). Studies have shown that being able to create and tell their own life story in positive ways is a powerful resource and contributes to achieve empowerment goals (Laliberté et al., 2012; Rappaport, 1995). These abilities are highly relevant in the context of Indigenous populations where community and personal narratives have often been negatives, stereotypical, and created by others (Adelson, 1998; Benham, 2007; Williams & Mumtaz, 2008).

This project is an example of fusion of an empowerment approach and a narrative approach, in two senses. First, the narrative approach that we used in our methodology is a process that promoted the empowerment of participants. This constituted a space for sharing narratives, for individual and collective construction of solutions, and for speaking out and gaining power. Second, the narrative approach has been proposed as potentially therapeutic for patients. Giving patients a voice, listening to their stories, and stimulating the creation of new narratives are steps which aim at resilience, growth, well-being, and constitutes an empowerment process per se.

Implications

This project presents methods of a cultural adaptation and participatory process, knowledge about empowerment stories among Kanien'kehá:ka and Inuit populations as well as two tools as a product. As part of our methods, listening marginalized experiences and giving space for stories that need to be told have been contributions. Our role in collecting evidence is to welcome people's stories of suffering, but also to support in a way so that they reconstitute their individual, family, and collective projects (Das, 2008). This empowerment process can help individuals lacking valued resources to work together to gain greater control over their personal, community, and cultural strengths. In addition, we aim at validating our findings in work in mental health and psychiatry. This knowledge can be transferred to other Indigenous contexts in the Arctic and in different regions of the world. Its exploratory nature, the methods used as well as the analytical

106 Liliana Gomez Cardona, Kristyn Brown, Mary McComber, et al.

framework can continue to stimulate similar processes in different settings where colonialist relations and cultural differences between the social groups are important (Sørly, Mathisen & Kvernmo, 2020). We recommend deployment of this approach in other Indigenous populations worldwide as a promising way to increase cultural sensitivity and culturally safety of mental health tools for these peoples. The final products (K-GEM and RET) are unlikely to be used as such in other contexts but could be adapted. Initial interest for GEM was expressed in Norway, and we already started a similar project among the northern Sami to assess their opinion on the GEM and the need to make a cultural adaptation. In addition to the cultural adaptation, cultural competence is another element that stakeholders must have. In all Indigenous contexts, empowerment is a complex strategy that includes sense of community, motivation to act, strong social networks, and resource access (Laliberté et al., 2012; Wallerstein, 2006).

The multidisciplinary team together with the vision of health and wellbeing expressed by the participants contributes to a holistic approach, which is at the heart of sustainability (Mensah & Ricart Casadevall, 2019; UN Documents, 2013). This project aligns with the objectives of social sustainability and seeks to promote people's access to resources that allow them to keep themselves, their families, and communities healthy and safe. We contribute to social sustainability by respecting all people, their diversity and protecting them from discrimination and exclusion (UN Documents, 2013).

Acknowledgements

Many individuals have contributed to the development of this project. Thanks to the Onkwata'karitáhtshera Health and Social Services Research Council of Kahnawà:ke and the Southern Quebec Inuit Association (SQIA) for accepting this project and guiding the team through each step. To the members of the Advisory Committees who have offered their time and expertise, and especially Brooke Splicer, Suzy Goodleaf, Darrell Thompson, Tina Pisuktie, Stephen Puskas. We also acknowledge Melissa Haswell, Arlène Laliberté and Indigenous Australian communities, developers of GEM, for their feedback and support to expand the use of the tool to other Indigenous nations. We thank and acknowledge the artistic work of Joanne Jones. We highlight the support and advice from experts and community members, including: Pascale Annoual, the Native Friendship Center of Montreal, Gustavo Turecki, Marie-Martine Beaulieu, Francine Chapman, Dawn Lazare and Laurence Kirmayer. We thank the RUISSS McGill, the FRSQ and the CIHR for their financial support.

Funding

OL was funded by Fonds de recherche en santé du Québec (FRSQ) (grant number #252872). LGC had financial support from the Réseau universitaire intégré de santé et services sociaux (RUISSS) McGill. The principal researchers (OL and LGC) had financial support from the Canadian Institutes of Health Research (CIHR) (Application#426678 and Application#430331).

References

Adelson, N. (1998). Health beliefs and the politics of Cree well-being. *Health, 2*(1), 5–22.

Assemblée des Premières Nations Québec-Labrador-APNQL. (2014). *Protocole de recherche des premières nations au québec et au labrador.* Assemblée des Premières Nations du Québec et Labrador: 122.

Baines, D. (Ed.). (2011). *Doing anti-oppressive practice: Social justice social work* (3rd ed.). Nova Scotia, Canada: Fernwood Publishing.

Battiste, M., Bell, L., & Findlay, L. M. (2002). Decolonizing education in Canadian universities: An interdisciplinary, international, indigenous research project. *Canadian Journal of Native Education, 26,* 82–95.

Beaton, D. E., Bombardier, C., Guillemin, F., & Ferraz, M. B. (2000). Guidelines for the process of cross-cultural adaptation of self-report measures. *Spine, 25*(24), 3186–3191.

Benham, M. (2007). Chapter 20 mo'ōlelo: On culturally relevant story making from an indigenous perspective. In D. J. Clandinin (Ed.), *Handbook of narrative inquiry: Mapping a methodology* (pp. 512–534). Thousand Oaks, CA: SAGE Publications, Inc. doi: 10.4135/9781452226552.n20

Berry, S. L., Crowe, T. P., Deane, F. P., Billingham, M., & Bhagerutty, Y. (2012). Growth and empowerment for Indigenous Australians in substance abuse treatment. *International Journal of Mental Health and Addiction, 10*(6), 970–983.

Boksa, P., Joober, R., & Kirmayer, L. (2015). Mental wellness in Canada's aboriginal communities: Striving toward reconciliation. *Journal of Psychiatry & Neuroscience: JPN, 40*(6), 363–365.

Brascoupé, S., & Waters, C. (2009). Cultural safety exploring the applicability of the concept of cultural safety to aboriginal health and community wellness. *Journal of Aboriginal Health, 5*(2), 6–41.

Braun, V., & Clarke, V. (2006). Using thematic analysis in psychology. *Qualitative Research in Psychology, 3*(2), 77–101.

Brody, H. (1987). *Living arctic: Hunters of the Canadian north.* London: Faber.

CIHR, N. (2018). Canadian Institutes of Health Research, Natural Sciences and Engineering Research Council of Canada, and Social Sciences and Humanities Research Council. *Tri-Council Policy Statement: Ethical Conduct for Research Involving Humans.*

Chachamovich, E., Kirmayer, L. J., Haggarty, J. M., Cargo, M., Mccormick, R., & Turecki, G. (2015). Suicide among Inuit: Results from a large, epidemiologically representative follow-back study in Nunavut. *Canadian Journal of Psychiatry. Revue Canadienne De Psychiatrie, 60*(6), 268–275.

Darroch, F., Giles, A., Sanderson, P., Brooks-Cleator, L., Schwartz, A., Joseph, D., & Nosker, R. (2017). The United States does care about cultural safety: Examining cultural safety within indigenous health contexts in Canada and the United States. *Journal of Transcultural Nursing: Official Journal of the Transcultural Nursing Society, 28*(3): 269–277. doi: 10.1177/1043659616634170

Das, V. (2008). Lenguaje y cuerpo: Transacciones en la construccion del dolor. In F. Ortega & V. Das (Eds.), *Sujetos del dolor, agentes de dignidad.* Bogota: Ruben's Impresores Editores.

Datta, R. (2018). Traditional storytelling: An effective indigenous research methodology And its implications for environmental research. *AlterNative: An International Journal of Indigenous Peoples, 14*(1), 35–44. doi: 10.1177/1177180117741351

Denham, A. (2008). Rethinking historical trauma: Narratives of resilience. *Transcultural Psychiatry, 45*(3), 391–414.

108   *Liliana Gomez Cardona, Kristyn Brown, Mary McComber, et al.*

Denzin, N., & Lincoln, Y. (Eds.). (2011). *The SAGE handbook of qualitative research*, Thousand Oaks: Sage.

Fraser, S. L., Geoffroy, D., Chachamovich, E., & Kirmayer, L. J. (2015). Changing rates of suicide ideation and attempts among Inuit youth: A gender-based analysis of risk and protective factors. *Suicide and Life-Threatening Behavior, 45*(2), 141–156.

Fuller, C., Steensma, C., Montour, D., Diabo, V., Horne, S., Bordeau, P., ... Delaronde, C. (2018). *Onkwaná: Ta our community, Onkwata'karí: Te our health.* Onkwata'karitáhtshera, First Nations of Québec and Labrador Health and Social Services Commission.

Geia, L. K., Hayes, B., & Usher, K. (2013). Yarning/aboriginal storytelling: Towards an understanding of an indigenous perspective and its implications for research practice. *Contemporary Nurse, 46*(1), 13–7.

Cardona, L. G., Brown, K., McComber, M., Outerbridge, J., Parent-Racine, E., Phillips, A., ... Linnaranta, O. (2021). Depression or resilience? A participatory study to identify an appropriate assessment tool with Kanien'kéha (Mohawk) and Inuit in Quebec. Social psychiatry and psychiatric epidemiology, 1–12.Retrieved from https://doi.org/10.1007/s00127-021-02057-1

Gouvernement du Canada. (2018). *Profil de la population autochtone, Recensement de 2016 – Choisir à partir d'une liste.*

Griner, D., & Smith, T. (2006). Culturally adapted mental health intervention: A meta-analytic review. *Psychotherapy: Theory, Research, Practice, Training, 43*(4), 531.

Haswell, M., Kavanagh, D., Tsey, K., Reilly, L., Cadet-James, Y., Laliberte, A., ... Doran, C. (2010). Psychometric validation of the growth and empowerment measure (GEM) applied with Indigenous Australians. *Australian and New Zealand Journal of Psychiatry, 44*(9), 791–799.

Hodge, F., Pasqua, A., Marquez, C., & Geishirt, B. (2002). Utilizing traditional storytelling to promote wellness in American Indian communities. *Journal of Transcultural Nursing, 13*(1), 6–11.

Johansen, B. E., & Mann, B. A. (2000). *Encyclopedia of the Haudenosaunee (Iroquois Confederacy).* Ser. Gale virtual reference library, Westport, CT: Greenwood Press.

Kirmayer, L. (2004). The cultural diversity of healing: Meaning, metaphor and mechanism. *British Medical Bulletin, 69,* 33–48.

Kirmayer, L., & Dandeneau, S. (2011). Rethinking resilience from indigenous perspectives. *The Canadian Journal of Psychiatry, 56*(2), 84–91.

Kirmayer, L. J., & Gómez-Carrillo, A. (2019). *Culturally responsive clinical psychology and psychiatry: An ecosocial approach.* In A. Maercker, E. Heim, & L. J. Kirmayer (Eds.), *Cultural clinical psychology and PTSD* (pp. 3–21). Göttingen, Germany: Hogrefe Publishing.

Kirmayer, L., Simpson, C., & Cargo, M. (2003). Healing traditions: Culture, community and mental health promotion with Canadian aboriginal peoples. *Australasian Psychiatry, 11*(Suppl. 1), 23.

Kirmayer, L., & Valaskakis, G. (Eds.). (2009). *Healing traditions: The mental health of aboriginal peoples in Canada.* Vancouver, Canada: UBC Press.

Kleinman, A. (1988). *The illness narratives: Suffering, healing, and the human condition.* New York: Basic Books.

Kovach, M. (2009). *Indigenous methodologies: Characteristics, conversations and contexts.* Toronto, Canada: University of Toronto Press.

Kral, M. J. (2016). suicide and suicide prevention among Inuit in Canada. *Canadian Journal of Psychiatry. Revue Canadienne de Psychiatrie, 61*(11), 688–695.

Stories of empowerment, resilience and healing 109

Krueger, R., & Casey, M. (2014). *Focus groups. A practical guide for applied research.* Thousand Oaks, CA: SAGE Publications, Inc.

Laliberté, A., Haswell, M., & Tsey, K. (2012). Promoting the health of aboriginal Australians through empowerment: Eliciting the components of the family well-being empowerment and leadership programme. *Global Health Promotion, 19*(4), 29–40.

Laugrand, F., & Oosten, J. (2009). Transfer of Inuit qaujimajatuqangit in modern Inuit society. *Études/Inuit/Studies, 33*(1–2), 115–131.

Lekoko, R. N. (2007). Story-telling as a potent research paradigm for indigenous communities. *AlterNative: An International Journal of Indigenous Peoples, 3*(2), 82–95. doi: 10.1177/117718010700300206

Makivik Corporation, Kativik Regional Government, Nunavik Regional Board of Health and Social Services, Kativik School Board, Nunavik Landholding Corporations Association, Avataq Cultural Institute, and Saputiit Youth Association. (2014). *Parnasimautik, Consultation Report.*

Marsh, T. (2015). The application of two-eyed seeing decolonizing methodology in qualitative and quantitative research for the treatment of intergenerational trauma and substance use disorders. International Journal of Qualitative Methods, 14(5), 1–13. doi: 10.1177/1609406915618046

Marsh, T., Coholic, D., Cote-Meek, S., & Najavits, L. (2015). Blending aboriginal and Western healing methods to treat intergenerational trauma with substance use disorder in aboriginal peoples who live in northeastern Ontario, Canada. *Harm Reduction Journal, 12*(1), 14.

Maton, K. (2008). Empowering community settings: Agents of individual development, community betterment, and positive social change. *American Journal of Community Psychology, 41*(1–2), 4–21.

McNamara, B. J., Banks, E., Gubhaju, L., Williamson, A., Joshy, G., Raphael, B., & Eades, S. J. (2014). Measuring psychological distress in older aboriginal and Torres strait islanders Australians: A comparison of the k-10 and k-5. *Australian and New Zealand Journal of Public Health,* 38(6), 567–573.

Mensah, J., & Ricart Casadevall, S. (2019). Sustainable development: Meaning, history, principles, pillars, and implications for human action: Literature review, *Cogent Social Sciences,* 5, 1.

Montreal Urban Aboriginal Health Committee – MUAHC. (2012). *Montreal urban aboriginal health needs assessment.* Montreal: MUAHC.

National Aboriginal Health Organization – NAHO. (2007). *Considerations and templates for ethical research practices.* Ottawa, ON: First Nations Centre des Premières Nations, National Aboriginal Health Organization.

Parry, D., Salsberg, J., & Macaulay, A. (2009). *A guide to researcher and knowledge-user collaboration in health research.* Canada: Canadian Institutes of Health Research (CIHR).

Perkins, D. D., & Zimmerman, M. A. (1995). Empowerment theory, research, and application. American journal of community psychology, 23(5), 569–579.

Petrone, P. (1992). *Northern Voices: Inuit writing in English.* Toronto, Canada: University of Toronto Press.

Phillips, S. (2000). *The kahnawake mohawks and the St. Lawrence Seaway.* Montreal: McGill University.

Phillips, M., Dandeneau, S., & Kirmayer, L. (2012). *Community report: Roots of resilience: Stories of resilience, healing and transformation in Kahnawake.* Culture & Mental Health Research Unit, Report. Montreal, Canada: NAMHR.

110 *Liliana Gomez Cardona, Kristyn Brown, Mary McComber, et al.*

Rappaport, J. (1995). Empowerment meets narrative: Listening to stories and creating settings. *American Journal of Community Psychology, 23*(5), 795–807.

Reid, G. (2004). *Kahnawake: Factionalism, traditionalism, and nationalism in a mohawk community.* Lincoln: University of Nebraska.

Rivet, F., & Nunavik (2020). Dans *l'Encyclopédie Canadienne.* Retrieved from: https://www.thecanadianencyclopedia.ca/fr/article/nunavik

Scheper-Hughes, N., & Lock, M. (1987). The mindful body: A prolegomenon to future work in medical anthropology. *Medical Anthropologie Quarterly, New Series, 1*(1), 6–41.

Smith, L. (2005). *Decolonizing methodologies: Research and indigenous peoples.* London, UK: Zed Books.

Sørly, R., Mathisen, V. & Kvernmo, S. (2020). "We belong to nature": Communicating mental health in an indigenous context. *Qualitative Social Work.* doi: 10.1177/1473325020932374

The Indigenous Physicians Association of Canada and the Royal College of Physicians and Surgeons of Canada – IPAC-RCPSC. (2009). *Promoting culturally safe care for first nations, Inuit and Métis patients; a core curriculum for residents and physicians.* Winnipeg and Ottawa: IPAC-RCPSC Core Curriculum Development Working Group.

UN Documents. (2013). *Our common future: Report of the World Commission on Environment and Development.* n.d. Web. Retrieved June 27, 2013, from http://www.un-documents.net/ocf-02.htm

Wallerstein, N. (1992). Powerlessness, empowerment, and health: Implications for health promotion programs. *American Journal of Health Promotion, 6*(3), 197–205.

Wallerstein, N. (2006). *What is the evidence on effectiveness of empowerment to improve health?* Copenhagen: WHO Regional Office for Europe.

Wexler, L., McEachern, D., DiFulvio, G., Smith, C., Graham, L. F., & Dombrowski, K. (2016). Creating a community of practice to prevent suicide through multiple channels: Describing the theoretical foundations and structured learning of pc cares. *International Quarterly of Community Health Education, 36*(2), 115–122.

Williams, L., & Mumtaz, Z. (2008). Being alive well? Power-knowledge as a countervailing force to the realization of mental well-being for Canada's aboriginal young people. *International Journal of Mental Health Promotion, 10*(4), 21–31.

Wilson, D. (2008). The significance of a culturally appropriate health service for indigenous Maori women. *Contemporary Nurse: A Journal for the Australian Nursing Profession, 28*(1), 173–188.

Wonderley, A. (2009). *At the font of the marvelous: Exploring Oral narrative and mythic imagery of the Iroquois and their neighbors* (1st ed., Ser. Iroquois and their neighbors). Syracuse, NY: Syracuse University Press.

Wright, A. L., Gabel, C., Ballantyne, M., Jack, S. M., & Wahoush, O. (2019). Using two-eyed seeing in research with indigenous people: An integrative review. *International Journal of Qualitative Methods, 18*, 1–19. doi: 10.1177/1609406919869695

Yaphe, S., Richer, F., & Martin, C. (2019). Cultural safety training for health professionals working with indigenous populations in Montreal, Québec. *International Journal of Indigenous Health, 14*(1), 60–84.

Zimmerman, M. (2000). *Empowerment theory, in handbook of community psychology* (J. Rappaport & E. Seidman, Eds.). Boston, MA: Springer US.

6 Learning through lived experiences

A structural narrative analysis of one person's journey of recovery and implications for peer support services

Rita Sørly, Tony Ghaye, and Wibecke Årst

Introduction to narratives

"As we make our way through life, we have continuous experiences and dialogic interactions both with our surrounding world and with ourselves. All of these are woven together into a seamless web, where they might strike one as being overwhelming in their complexity. One way of structuring these experiences is to organize them into meaningful units. One such meaningful unit could be a story, a narrative ..." (Moen, 2006, p. 1) In Latin, the noun narrario means a narrative or a story and the verb narrare to tell or narrate (Heikkinen, 2002). A narrative is a story that tells a sequence of events that is significant for the narrator or her or his audience. Although we elaborate the point below, when narratives are looked at within the framework of sociocultural theory, we have to remember the interlinking between the individual and her or his socio-cultural context. As Wibecke tells her story, she is not isolated and independent from her context. On the contrary, it is important to remember that she is intimately connected to her social, cultural and historical context. Narratives, therefore, capture both the individual and the context.

Our starting proposition in this chapter is that we live storied lives. A second is that stories are remembered events and how these were experienced, in this case by Wibecke. We tell stories to ourselves and stories to others. Stories about ourselves and stories about other selves, some real, others imagined and sought after, or stories we wish to escape from. As a result, we do not take the position here of the 'self' as some kind of unified, fixed and singular self. We replace this with the notion of the multiple, fluid and negotiated self, which is continuously under narrative (re)construction. Hence, our presentation and analysis of Wibecke's story as one of a recovering drug addict and her quest for a more desirable and acceptable self, over time. Telling stories is one of the primary ways we "reckon with time" (Ricoeur, 1981, p. 169). We are historical beings who live in the present, under the weight of the past and the uncertainty of the future. From the structural analysis we use in this chapter, we try to portray the 'there and then', the 'here and now' and the hoped for. What Wibecke's story calls upon us to grasp is the necessity of trying to make sense of, and remember the past, in order to move ahead, attend to and grow into the future. Thus, time, memory and narrative are inextricably

DOI: 10.4324/9781003118633-7

112   *Rita Sørly, Tony Ghaye, and Wibecke Årst*

linked. Additionally, narratives and identities are intimately linked, feeding into each other, interpenetrating and overlapping. We discover more than one identity in Wibecke's story.

Additionally, in her story we find evidence of a 'self' she would rather not be living. Through a process of reflection-on-actions, Wibecke is able to re-story her life, constructing a new storyline to help her exert better control over life's possibilities, ambiguities, struggles and demons. Generally, in some of our stories, we claim ourselves as heroes. But in others we are traumatized victims, sufferers, survivors and many others. Thus, the human condition is largely a narrative condition. Storytelling is the means by which we represent our experiences to ourselves and to others. It is how we communicate and try to make sense of our lives. It is a way of giving our lives meaning and gaining a sense of perspective on things. From bedtime stories, to slices of aspects of Wibecke's life review, we listen to stories and tell stories to others. Myerhoff (2007, p. 18) called this passionate craving for story a "narrative urge."

The chapter is organized as follows. First, we describe peer recovery services. Then we briefly introduce Wibecke to position her front and centre within the text. A discussion of how structural narrative analysis, using the notion of a plot, is then articulated so as to understand the experiences of a person's attempt at recovery. Inspired by Ahmed (2013), two plots, namely the 'quest', and 'voyage and return' are outlined to gain insight into how we can interpret Wibecke's journey from being in distress and anxious, caused by addiction, to creating another life for herself and being an inspiration for others fighting for a change in their lives. The discussion gives us valuable insights into how stories can contribute to more user-oriented services and reduce stigma towards people who struggle with mental health, alcohol and/or other drug-related distress.

Peer recovery services

Peer recovery services have been implemented in mental health and substance abuse services for many years in Europe, Canada and US (Åkerblom, Agdal, & Haakseth, 2020) and can be defined as the process of giving and receiving non-professional, non-clinical assistance from individuals with similar conditions or circumstances to achieve long-term recovery from psychiatric, alcohol, and/ or other drug-related distress (Tracy & Wallace, 2016). Internationally, countries have sought to reform services aiming to maximize the potential of users to assert control over their health care decisions and throughout their trajectory of care (Ness, Kvello, Borg, Semb, & Davidson, 2017, Ness et al., 2014). A recovery orientation among systems that care for those with substance abuse distress, and often mental health distress, involves collaborating with people on personal goals, conveying hopefulness, promoting choice, and focusing on people's strengths (Chinman et al., 2017). These services can be defined as a system of giving and receiving help founded on key principles of respect, shared responsibility, and a mutual agreement on what is helpful between people in similar situations (Mead, Hilton, & Curtis, 2001).

In every person's surrounding cultural contexts, there are certain 'ways' of telling a story. The cultural context within addiction treatment in general pose challenges to rehabilitation and recovery services for many reasons. In line with Kirmayer (2012) we agree that culture influences the experience, expression, course and outcome of substance abuse distress, help-seeking and the response to health promotion, prevention or treatment interventions. Rehabilitation and recovery from drug addiction take a unique form in each society, for example based on its cultural history, politics and economy. More specifically substance abuse and tailored services reflect cultural knowledge and practice embedded in larger social contexts that define health and well-being (ibid.). Cultural worldviews, values and notions of personhood influence how people articulate their life stories.

Wibecke

Wibecke is working as a peer recovery worker, after having recovered from her own addiction (Figure 6.1). She is also a member of a collaborative, multi-disciplinary, participatory and appreciative action research group committed to generating practical knowledge and actions to improve mental health and substance abuse services in northern Norway. The first author, who is the leader of the same research group, interviewed Wibecke in a project related to stories of female entrepreneurs from the Arctic in 2018. Later, the two found out they wanted to do something more with the data and invited Professor Tony Ghaye to co- write this chapter, based on Wibecke's life story.

Figure 6.1 Wibecke having a coffee. Photo: Marie Louise Somby.

114 Rita Sørly, Tony Ghaye, and Wibecke Årst

A life story approach to structural narrative analysis

There are many approaches to life stories. They can be understood as holistic, as a whole or sections of talk, or content and form (Ahmed, 2013). We have defined Wibecke's story to be a topical life story; it focuses on her story as a former drug user and her journey of recovery. It is not a complete life history based on a comprehensive life story interview, rather a period-focused story which is on-going.

Narratives are not created in a vacuum, but rather depend upon the contexts in which they arise and develop (Klausen 2017). These contexts are in turn affected by the narratives that are created, maintained, rejected or transformed into new narratives. In this never-ending-ongoing-creation of new stories, 'truth' is shaped by the particular contexts in which the story is located, with phenomena having different meanings depending on when and where they occur (Gergen, 1999). In this way, Wibecke's story is understood as a construction of feelings, thoughts and incidents from a remembered past. For the purpose of our analysis, her story is a recorded, transcribed narrative, constructed into units for interpretation (Ahmed, 2013; Ahmed & Rogers, 2017). By narrating her story, Wibecke is examining her life and the context she lives in. In line with Featherstone, Morris, and White (2014), we take this as being of particular interest to social work practice, which is person-centered, transformative and holistic oriented. The analysis of a single narrative has both a practical and a theoretical value, as underlined by Ahmed and Rogers (2017, p. 226), the caveat being 'we are all uniquely positioned in time and space and our experiences are particular to us'. Single narratives have subjective truths of wider relevance, and Wibecke's story allow us to generalize to other recovery journeys, since she draws on wider discourses which create and shape the meanings she is constructing (ibid.).

Analyzing Wibecke's narrative

In this chapter, Wibecke's narrative is seen through the lens of a structural analysis using plot typologies inspired by Ahmed (2013, p. 2017) and Booker (2004). When Wibecke is remembering and re-constructing her story with the researcher, both are in the process of meaning-making. Recovery contexts are complex constructions, and a structural analysis of Wibecke's narrative can illuminate the relationship between meaning and action, which is useful when focusing on how recovery journeys are understood within a peer recovery worker's perspective and context. Wibecke's story demonstrates that cultural meta-narratives are not absolutes, but rather negotiated, tested, confirmed or rejected or qualified again through storytelling. Her local identity is being constructed through the narrative act, rather than 'being an inherent feature' of her experience (Ahmed, 2013). The plot of the narrative is constructed by Wibecke and holds the story together and provides an underlying structure for analysis (Ahmed, 2013). According to Riessman (1993), the plot of a narrative can be described as how narrators impose order on their experiences, and narrating experiences can be seen as organization of events in a storytelling. Multiple incidents are remembered (sometimes very selectively) made

Learning through lived experiences   115

or transformed into a story, and our plots are taken from our available repertoire that is culturally and temporally specific and linked to our social and cultural context of production (Ahmed, 2013). Inspired by Booker (2004), Ahmed (2013), and Ahmed and Rogers (2017), the 'quest' plot typology is an assimilation of the 'Seven Basic Plots' from literature, film, the Bible, ancient myths and folk tales (Ahmed & Rogers, 2017). Booker classifies the seven plots to be overcoming the monster; rags to riches; the quest; voyage and return; comedy; tragedy and rebirth. The aim of the Quest is the life-renewing goal (Ahmed, 2013; Booker, 2004, p. 2017). The five stages to the Quest are 1) The Call, where the central character feels compelled to leave; 2) The Journey, which involves a number of trials; 3) Arrival and Frustrations, where the story's main character almost reaches the goal, but there are more trials to come, 4) The Final Ordeals, where there are a number of 'tests' which the narrator must endure before reaching the goal and 5) The Goal, where the life-transforming treasure is found (Ahmed, 2013; Booker, 2004, p. 2017). A plot analysis makes it possible not only to acknowledge times where Wibecke has experienced and overcome adversity but also to gain knowledge related to her situated experience of constructing a cultural identity, advantageous for the peer recovery context she is working within. We analyze Wibecke's story in relation to the stages identified above and recognize the purpose of her narrative to be self-acceptance through constructing a drug free identity that can give other addicts inspiration to work with their own recovery. It can also engage people in decisions which affect their future, inspire social and healthcare professionals to know more – in order to do better work, and how those who come wearing "disciplines" and carrying "ologies" need to see the whole rather than the parts.

The quest – The call

The call for Wibecke was precipitated by the wish to become drug free and help others in their recovery process. She wanted to do something meaningful with her life. She started her story with telling about how she started using drugs. She was aware of her transgression of accepted cultural norms. She had the 'normal' or straight sphere where she did sports and was an active young girl. And then she had the other side of herself, being a 'rebellious' person. She had this longing for excitement:

> I grew up as a military child. I didn't come to Tromsø until I was 12. I lived one year here, one year there. All over Northern Norway, really. I didn't have any problems making friends. Sport helped a lot. I played a lot of sport... when you move somewhere new, if you have sport, you meet new people. I played volleyball for many years. At Tromsø volleyball club and...I played a lot. ...But obviously...then it started. I had a child when I was 16 with someone who did drugs. I guess I already had friends who were into that when I met him. I had a foot in both camps, in a way, I was used to that with all of the moving, and I had lots of friends from sport. Then I had this rebellious side. I started experimenting a bit when I was pretty young. I was just really curious.

116   *Rita Sørly, Tony Ghaye, and Wibecke Årst*

She belonged in two worlds and was used to changing environments and surroundings. From Wibecke's point of view, her experience and knowledge of addiction, adolescence is often a period of rootlessness, where people make some bad choices. An important message in her story, in terms of social work with children and youth, is that it is important to acknowledge and listen to young people who don't feel they belong. The constant moving in her childhood led to rootlessness, and the migration in itself might be understood as movements in between different worlds.

The journey

Wibecke was in a relationship when she was 16 years old. It was an unhealthy commitment for a young girl. Her journey across dangerous terrain encompassed a number of stages. The first stage was described as childhood and early youth, then came adolescence and young adulthood, characterized by concealment. In the stages of her young adulthood, Wibecke's survival strategy was to hide her substance abuse from her loved ones.

> For a long time the sport stopped it going too far, but when I became a mum, doing two training sessions a day and all that stuff...I didn't have time any more. And when I stopped doing sport – THEN. Then I really quickly started...if I had the weekend off, I used to hit the town. I didn't just drink, I took amphetamines and cocaine as well...those weekends were one long party. In the end that led to...I got into a relationship with someone who was many years older than me. I lived at home and got a lot of help with looking after my daughter. I had plenty of opportunities to drink and do drugs. My family didn't notice anything. You become good at hiding what you're doing. I left home when I turned 18.

For Wibecke, the dangerous terrain she was surrounded by at the time denoted the cultural and temporal context she was living in:

Things got out of control. In due course, I started taking opiates and heroin dominated my life from the age of around 19–20. That was it. That was it. I carried on using heroin until I started stopping. That's how I like to put it. Because it was hard work. I was 27 by then.

Using hard drugs became a pattern in Wibecke's life. In her narrative, her life was decided by the next fix. She describes the years of addiction as hard work, without giving any details. Her family knew by now what was going on, and she could not stop herself.

Overcoming monsters

The quest is characterized by danger, and 'the heroine' must overcome obstacles or 'monsters' in order to fulfill the quest. The term 'monster' can be used in relation to the drugs, or in relation to being made monstrous by the marginalization by other non-drug users. Wibecke knew how it felt to be marginalized by others and the stigmatization was especially hard on her as a single mother:

> There's more shame attached to being a girl and doing drugs, particularly if you're a mum. Being a mum who does drugs, there's almost nothing worse than that. Society sees it as an aggravating factor that a mother is putting drugs ahead of her child, because that's what many people think you're doing. That's because they don't understand the forces at work. I don't feel that I ever put drugs ahead of my daughter. It was just a problem that I wasn't able to handle. That's more how I see it. Of course you can say that I had a choice at one point. When I started partying at weekends…but when you're 17 or 18 you're not able to see the consequences of what you're doing. I thought that I could choose to take drugs occasionally. I didn't see the consequences of my actions. We're so bad at talking about when it turns into an addiction. It happens so quickly. It happens much faster than most people think. We all think that we're in control, don't we? The fact is it's not like that. You cross a boundary that you can't see yourself. Much earlier than you think.

Wibecke provides a perspective on drug-taking informed by her experiences of the way people judged drug-users, without understanding how addiction functions, (Gubrium & Holstein, 2009). Overcoming monsters for Wibecke meant stop using drugs:

> I wanted to stop for the sake of my daughter. She was my main motivation. And it had gone so far that I was tired of taking drugs. I felt like I couldn't go on. I wanted to be there for my daughter. It was a long process.

Constriction and release

The second stage of Wibecke's journey began when she turned 27. She wanted to quit, but was afraid to ask for help:

> I was also really afraid of the authorities who could help me. I had been arrested a few times and social services had got involved. But you get so good at fooling and tricking people and at lying and cheating. When social services got involved, I had come out of that relationship, and I was living in a nice, detached house where I was getting help from my family. It wasn't the type of place you associate with a drug addict. That made it easier for me to lie. It shouldn't have been like that, but it was.

In the quest, the journey is characterized by life-threatening constriction, followed by life-giving release (Ahmed & Rogers, 2017; Booker, 2004). Wibecke's struggle to become drug free was hard; she was often unable to resist temptations. She was torn between the desire to get high and the desire to become drug-free.

118   *Rita Sørly, Tony Ghaye, and Wibecke Årst*

Guilt and despair

The years to follow were filled with guilt and despair for Wibecke. Drugs helped Wibecke to suppress her guilt for a short moment of time, but she knew she had to fight the urge.

> In a way I understood how serious the situation had become. The first time I tried to quit I went to Portugal. I was on the waiting list of methadone-assisted rehabilitation for two years here in Tromsø. There were so many criteria you had to meet. That waiting time…

Again, Wibecke leaves the narrative 'here and now' and informs the audience of whom she is addressing her story; addiction blinds you. You cannot control it, and it haunts you:

> Obviously, it hasn't been good for my daughter, growing up with a mum who was a heroin addict. You wouldn't wish that on your worst enemy, and at least not your own child. But you don't see that when you're sick. You don't see the harm you're causing until you recover.

Taking control

The final stage of Wibecke's journey involved her becoming drug free. She does not give the process much space in her storytelling:

> I got all of my treatment in Portugal. It was expensive. I got a lot of help from my family. They spent so much money sending me down there. They also wanted it really badly, for me to go clean, for the sake of Christina. I've always been really stubborn and determined. That didn't change when I was an addict. So I went to Portugal.

The journey stage in the quest only makes up half the story, according to Booker (2004), and living drug free did not denote the end of Wibecke's quest. There were further stages where Wibecke began to change her own life to become something 'more than a former drug addict'. She reached another goal and the final stage of self- acceptance; 'arrival and frustration', and the 'final ordeals'.

Arrival and a new beginning

Wibecke became drug free, and she now lives with her daughter, who is a grown up today:

> My daughter and I live together now, and we're best friends. She has given me the opportunity to put our relationship on the right track. It has taken time. She has been by my side, and she's dared to be angry with me to my face. I admire her for that. I have a fantastic daughter.

Learning through lived experiences 119

Her daughter has forgiven her, and they have a close relationship today. Still, after becoming drug free Wibecke wanted to work and do something meaningful:

> When I started with methadone-assisted rehab, I became a team leader as part of a job training scheme run by an organization that works with addicts. I had just started taking methadone. We had received funding to run activities. The plan wasn't for me to be a team leader. I had never used a hammer in my life before! As a team leader, you were supposed to help and instruct people taking methadone. They worked four hours a day. We were given jobs by the municipality and other organizations. For example, we did up part of the User Base that we run now. We contacted businesses and asked for work. We painted city blocks and put up annexes and BBQ huts at a building supplies shop. Just imagine it: starting with nothing, and by the end of the day you've finished building a BBQ hut!

Being able to work was important for Wibecke (Figure 6.2). She was still vulnerable. She could still feel that she was stigmatized as a former drug addict. But the work activities she took part in showed her that she was useful and she could give something back to the society.

> That was incredibly important for me. And for Christina. Before that she never had an answer when people asked, "What does your mum do?". Suddenly she could say that I was working on this or on that. Being able

Figure 6.2 Wibecke at work. Photo: Marie Louise Somby.

120 *Rita Sørly, Tony Ghaye, and Wibecke Årst*

to say that I had a job did something to my own self-esteem and what I believed I was capable of. Working means participating in society and being part of a community. There are many aspects to working or studying – being useful.

Final ordeals

By now, Wibecke, was working and had found the acceptance she had been looking for. However, there were several ordeals Wibecke had to overcome before she reached her goal:

My self-confidence soon improved. I spent a year at college in the south. I got my Higher Education Entrance Qualification, and then I took a course called "Self-help in user involvement". Then I did a project management course. I focused particularly on how to run projects. That's when we had the idea of the "User Base". The town lacked a proper aftercare treatment facility for drug addicts who had either spent a long time in jail or had been through rehab. We got funding from the Directorate for Health and support from the town council to help us set up the "User Base".

She had to struggle for the rehabilitation model. Not many people believed in a rehabilitation model where peer recovery workers would help others to come out of an addiction. But Wibecke never gave up:

I am really proud. I've helped to create my own workplace, that's what it feels like. I have been allowed to do what I think is right and necessary. I've also understood how lucky I've been to be allowed to do that, because it's obviously not something you can take for granted. Now I'm absolutely sure that this is what I should be doing. I've been running the User Base for eleven years. It's no longer a project; it's a permanent peer recovery service. All of the people who work there have been through addiction and have chosen different ways to come out the other side. That's important.

The goal

The final stage of the quest is the goal, often when the hero/heroine finds a new home in a different location (Ahmed & Rogers, 2017). For Wibecke, through her recovery journey, establishing a new peer recovery-based rehabilitation model, represented the goal:

We focus on integration. It's about finding your place in society. When you've been doing drugs for many years, you become an outsider. At the beginning we spent a lot of time at the places where addicts hang out – but that wasn't the right approach. We need to go to normal cafés, to normal places. We must get people who are motivated to see normal life. Tromsø is great like

Learning through lived experiences   121

that. There's the university and the hospital, so lots of new people come here. There will always be people who are new here, and who are new at what they're doing. There's something really good about that.

Wibecke's journey has not been easy, but she achieved her life-renewing goal and arrived where she wants to be:

> It means a lot to me to run the "User Base". I know how much changing your life like this can mean. It's rewarding to help people go clean and sober. It affects families and children so much when someone close to you is an addict. I like to focus on family. We try to work a lot on that at the User Base. On getting people to be honest and open with their families. Tell your family and let them ask questions. Seeing other people manage to do this... I have the best job in the world. I wouldn't change it for anything in the world. I'm so privileged. I feel that I make a difference.

Essential themes and implications

Eliciting, appreciating and understanding Wibecke's story is an example of learning through lived experiences. More specifically, this encapsulates lived time, lived space, lived body and lived human relationships (Van Manen, 1990). Also there is learning for Wibecke through the articulation of her story and for the readers of her story, as it is a story that reflects the ways she experienced the world, across time. Her story also makes a statement that to *know* the world is profoundly to *be* in the world, in certain ways, for example, as a mother, drug user, peer support worker and so on. In this sense, and more generally, we can appreciate that knowledge is contextual and perspectival. Our position throughout this chapter holds that narratives are not and cannot be separated from the context in which they are told.

The use of structural narrative analysis in this chapter does not problem solve, as this kind of approach seeks solutions. What this analysis does is it pursues meaning. In other words, it enables us to appreciate the human significance of particular experiences and encounters, and on the basis of this, perhaps think about acting more thoughtfully or with different intentions. It brings into nearness and therefore intelligibility, that which often remains hidden, tacit and obscure. However, if we cast Wibecke as a peer support specialist, we can see her as a woman who has used her lived experiences of recovery from addiction, plus skills learned across life and from formal education, to deliver services that seek to promote mind-body recovery and even resiliency. As her story tells, she draws upon her personal knowledge and experiences to provide others with addiction, and even mental health challenges, with informal education, support and connections to other appropriate healthcare services. So what are the essential themes which emerge from the above that have relevance to the development of peer support and recovery services in an arctic context?

122 Rita Sørly, Tony Ghaye, and Wibecke Årst

Theme 1: The importance of working with user's experience

At the start of this chapter, we posed two questions, 'who's voice?' and 'who's knowledge counts? Here we argue that user's knowledge is critical if we are to develop appropriate and attuned peer recovery services. It cannot and should not be bypassed. Every user's experience is potentially an opportunity from which something can be learned (Boud & Miller, 1996). But having said this, it is important to appreciate that all individual experiences, can be distorted, self-fulfilling, unexamined, constraining as well as liberating. Simply having experiences does not imply that they are always reflected upon, understood or analyzed critically. The experiences we claim to have, are constructed *by* us as much as they happen *to* us. Therefore, to maximize the potential that user experiences offer, some form of facilitated reflective conversation, with a significant 'other', is arguably essential. In this way we are acknowledging that making meaning can be, for those involved, a constant struggle and a preparedness and ability to endure discomfort through the recognition of conflicts and the weighing up of options and the impact of the implementation of these going forward. User's lived experiences are data, or material on which to work. They are the bedrock for evidence-based peer recovery service development.

Theme 2: Acknowledging that we live storied lives

A way of looking at the world is that we live and hopefully flourish, not flounder, *in relationship.*

And we piece the many and different relationships we have into stories of experience. In other words, we can say we live storied lives. These stories of people-in-communities tell us something about what others expect of us in order to fit in, belong and thrive. For the development of peer recovery services, we are suggesting that providing opportunities for users to tell their stories is essential, if for no other reason that stories can be a way of healing. "Telling our stories and hearing the stories of others helps us know that we are not alone, that we are not the only ones to have suffered …. Telling our stories helps us acknowledge anger and shame, then move forward on our healing journey with self-compassion" (Whitney, Cocciolone, & Adams-Miller, 2019, p. 65).

Theme 3: The potential for the growth of resilience

McArthur-Blair and Cockell (2018) argue that the interplay between three elements are at the core of resilience. They are hope, despair and forgiveness. Arguably Wibecke's story contains the flavour of all three. Hope is characterized by the creation of space for power with others to generate better futures. Hope is believing that no matter what our state is at this moment, the future will open up possibilities. In Wibecke's story, we can sense the emergence of a more 'hopeful view' as she constructs a better future for herself and her daughter. Despair can be linked with user's not being able to see a clear path forward, with doubts about what really matters, or that anything matters or is possible. With the appropriate peer support, this experience of despair, paradoxically, can show those at the centre of their emerging story, what they truly believe in, what makes them strong and what they wish for themselves and others close to them. Forgiveness of self and others, if this is possible, can be the energizing force for forward movement and increased user agency. However, forgiveness is complex. It's not always possible for drug users to let go of resentment, anger and fear and simply step forward, accepting things as they are. Arguably, if forgiveness is part of the peer recovery discourse, then all involved may also have to positively embrace the will and determination needed to let go and look forward.

Theme 4: From safe to brave spaces

A final theme we wish to lift up is about the need for peer recovery services fully think through the context/s that need to be provided so that users are able to have conversations-that-matter with the inevitable discomforts involved, including pain and conflict. To facilitate these kinds of conversation much effort has been put into the creating of 'safe spaces' (Edmonson, 1999; Ghaye, 2005, 2008). Psychological safety is the shared belief by those involved in the conversation, that it's safe for inter-personal risk-taking. Recently, this notion has been expanded. For users of peer recovery services, there is still a need to build intentional spaces that attend to safety but also ones that create opportunities for courageous conversations. These have been called "brave spaces" (Ali, 2017; Arao & Clemens, 2013; Pyles, 2021).

The five main elements of these spaces, which we suggest might be useful foundational principles for the development of peer recovery services are:

- Maintaining civility between those involved when there is conflict and controversy.
- Owning one's intentions and attending to the emotional impact that one's words might have on others.
- Challenging by choice where those involved have the capability to monitor their own well-being in order to determine whether stepping into the conversation at any given moment, is right for them.
- Respecting basic personhood.
- Not attacking others so as to intentionally inflict mental or emotional harm on those involved.

Some final reflections

Arguably and generally, peer recovery services can be defined as a system of giving and receiving help, founded on key principles of respect, shared responsibility and a mutual agreement on what is helpful between people in similar situations (Mead, Hilton, & Curtis, 2001). In the North, municipalities and other administrative regions continue to strive to strengthen the integration of mental health and substance abuse services, dismantle silo thinking and develop more participatory ways

124 *Rita Sørly, Tony Ghaye, and Wibecke Årst*

of working (Åkerblom et al., 2020). Despite this commitment, there is still much progress to be made on the accreditation and certification agendas to establish national standards for training and the regulation of peer workers supporting others with their mental health and substance abuse issues (Borg, Sjåfjell, Ogundipe, & Bjørklyhaug, 2017). For example, a study by Ose and Ådnanes (2019) finds that there is a large variation between Norwegian municipalities and between city and rural areas, confirming that realizing the full potential of peer workers is at an early stage in Norway. Similar challenges have been reported in the United States and Canada, for example, for several years (Åkerblom et al., 2020).

In peer recovery, just like any other human service work, we urge all involved to continue to ask themselves and each other, 'what kind of service and therefore what kind of world are we trying to create?' Working with and from lived experiences, of the kind set out in this chapter, is only a start in answering this question. If peer recovery services are developed with the five themes in mind, that we set out above, then we are well on the way to developing something which is often called the 'capability approach' (Nussbaum, 2011). We believe this to be appropriate and significant as its premised on the idea that all people should have the opportunity to achieve their full human functioning. Key to such an approach is to create brave spaces where all involved can be allowed *to do* and *to be*.

References

Ali, D. (2017). Safe spaces and brave spaces. Historical context and recommendations for student affairs professionals. *NASPA policy and practice series*. University of Northern Iowa. NASPA.

Åkerblom, K., Agdal, R., & Haakseth, Ø (2020). *Integrering av erfaringskompetanse: hvordan opplever erfaringskonsulenter med ruserfaring sin arbeidssituasjon?* Rapport, Oslo: Senter for erfaringskompetanse.

Ahmed, A. (2013). Structural narrative analysis: Understanding experiences of lifestyle migration through two plot typologies. *Qualitative Inquiry*, *19*(3), 232–243

Ahmed, A., & Rogers, M. (2017). Polly's story: Using structural narrative analysis to understand a trans migration journey. *Qualitative Social Work*, *16*(2), 224–239.

Arao, B., & Clemens, K. (2013). From safe spaces to brave spaces: A new way to frame dialogue around diversity and social justice. In L. Landreman (Ed.), *The art of effective facilitation: Reflections from social justice educators* (pp. 135–150). Sterling, VA: Stylus.

Borg, M., Sjåfjell, T. L., Ogundipe, E., & Bjørklyhaug, K. I. (2017). *Brukeres erfaringer med hjelp og støtte 11 fra erfaringsmedarbeidere innen psykisk helse og rus*. Rapport 2017:2, Oslo: Senter for erfaringskompetanse.

Booker, C. (2004). *The seven basic plots: Why we tell stories*. Kent, Great Britain: A&C Black.

Boud, D., & Miller, N. (1996). *Working with experience – Animating learning*. London: Routledge.

Chinman, M., McInnes, D. K., Eisen, S., Ellison, M., Farkas, M., Armstrong, M., & Resnick, S. G. (2017). Establishing a research agenda for understanding the role and impact of mental health Peer specialists. *Psychiatric services* (Washington, D.C.), *68*(9), 955–957. https://doi.org/10.1176/appi.ps.201700054

Edmonson, A. (1999). Psychological safety and learning behavior in work teams. *Administrative Science Quarterly*, *44*(2), 350–383.

Featherstone, B., Morris, K., & White, S. (2014). *Re-imagining child protection: Towards humane social work with families*. Great Britain, Policy Press.

Gergen, K. J. (1999). *An invitation to social construction*. London: Sage.

Ghaye, T. (2005). *Developing the reflective healthcare team*. Oxford: Blackwell Publishing.

Ghaye, T. (2008). *Building the reflective healthcare organisation*. Oxford: Blackwell Publishing.

Gubrium, J., & Holstein, J. (2009). *Analyzing narrative reality*. Thousand Oaks, CA: SAGE Publications, Inc. doi: 10.4135/9781452234854

Heikkinen, H. (2002). Whatever is narrative research? In R. Hultmen, H. Heikkinen, & l Syrjäiä (Eds.), *Narrative research: Voices from teachers and philosophers* (pp. 13–25). Jyvfiskylü, Finland: SoPhi.

Kirmayer, L. (2012). Rethinking cultural competence. *Transcultural Psychiatry*, *49*(2), 149–164.

Klausen, R. K. (2017). *Relational insight and user involvement in the context of Norwegian community mental health care: A narrative analysis of service users' stories*. PhD Thesis, UiT The Arctic University of Norway, Tromsø, Norway.

Myerhoff, B. (2007). Stories as equipment for living. In M. Kaminsky, & M. Weiss (Eds.), *Stories as equipment for living: Last talks and tales of barbara myerhoff* (pp. 17–27). Ann Arbor, MI: University of Michigan Press.

McArthur-Blair, J., & Cockell, J. (2018). *Building resilience with appreciative inquiry*. Oakland, CA: Berrett-Koehler Publishers.

Mead, S., Hilton, D., & Curtis, L. (2001). Peer Support: A theoretical perspective. *Psychiatric Rehabilitation Journal*, *25*(2), 134–141. http://dx.doi.org/10.1037/h0095032

Moen, T. (2006). Reflections on the narrative research approach. *International Journal of Qualitative Methods*, *5*(4), 1–9.

Ness, O., Karlsson, B., Borg, M., Biong, S., Sundet, R., McCormack, B., & Kim, H. S. (2014). Towards a model for collaborative practice in community mental health care. *Scandinavian Psychologist*, *1*. Retrieved from Towards a model for collaborative practice in community mental health care (psykologisk.no)

Ness, O., Kvello, Ø, Borg, M., Semb, R., & Davidson, L. (2017). "Sorting things out together": Young adults' experiences of collaborative practices in mental health and substance use care. *American Journal of Psychiatric Rehabilitation*, *20*(2), 126–142.

Nussbaum, M. (2011). *Creating capabilities: The human development approach*. Cambridge, MA: Belknap Press.

Ose, S., & Ådnanes, M. (2019). Sintef notat. *Bruk av erfaringskompetanse i kommunene*, 1–16. Retrieved from https://www.erfaringskompetanse.no/wpcontent/uploads/2017/04/Sintefnotat.pdf

Pyles, L. (2021). *Progressive community organizing: Transformative practice in a globalizing world*. 3rd edition, Routledge, London.

Ricoeur, P. (1981). Narrative time. In W. Mitchell (Ed.), *On narrative* (pp. 165–186). Chicago, IL: University of Chicago Press.

Riessman, C. K. (1993). *Narrative analysis* (Vol. 30). CA: Sage Publications.

Tracy, K., & Wallace, S. P. (2016). Benefits of peer support groups in the treatment of addiction. *Substance abuse and rehabilitation*, *7*, 143.

Van Manen, M. (1990). *Researching lived experience*. Ontario: NY Press.

Whitney, D., Cocciolone, J., & Adams-Miller, C., et al. (2019). *Thriving women, thriving world*. Chagrin Falls, Taos Institute Publication.

7 The decline and changes in the tundra today

The nature of state systems and services as a critical factor in the condition of minority indigenous peoples in Russia

Zoia Vylka Ravna

Introduction

Historically, nation states have applied different policies of assimilation against indigenous nomadic communities around the world. These include the slaughter of bison herds in north America, collectivization during the establishment of the Russian Soviet state-run economy, and the imposition of western boarding school education in colonized territories globally. But the result has always been the same, the subjugation, assimilation, marginalization or even complete extinction of distinct nomadic and indigenous peoples and their cultures. Indigenous people's continued existence is currently estimated to be not more than 350 million all over the world, and conservative estimates suggest that more than half of the world's languages will become extinct by 2100. One indigenous language is disappearing every second week. This evidence comes from official data, published in reports (UN Permanent forum, 2018).

Then there are also scientific reports now providing data on climate change and how these are affecting the lives of indigenous people. These changes are disproportionately threatening indigenous and nomadic communities around the world. In this chapter I look at how these challenges affect nomadic Nenets reindeer herders in the Russian Arctic. This account is based on observations and interviews with nomadic Nenets people, engaged in reindeer husbandry on a professional basis throughout the year. In addition, collated research materials used as part of my recent dissertation defense at Tromso University on the intergenerational transmission of traditional indigenous knowledge are also used (Ravna, 2020). The objective of this research project was to chart and describe the main changes and challenges to nomadic Nenets culture in the context of the current Russian political, social and economic policies and climate change.

Methodology with a focus on ethnographic research

The materials presented in this chapter are collected during four field-work periods in different Nenets areas. As a visual anthropologist, I studied the pedagogical and educational methods that the Nenets nomads use for raising their children.

DOI: 10.4324/9781003118633-8

The decline and changes in the tundra today   127

I combine the results from this analysis with a statistical questionnaire-based method. At the completion of my research project, I had covered the two largest geographical areas of the Nenets lands: the Yamal-Nenets autonomous area, where most Nenets reindeer people are living today and the Nenets autonomous area, the second largest Nenets region.

At first, I collected data from reindeer herders and members of their families about indigenous knowledge and its components. Based on this data, collected during fieldwork on the Tundra, I designed and drafted a questionnaire, for girls and boys separately (14–18 years old; boarding schools of YaNAO and NAO). At this second stage, I decided that I should get data from the young Nenets from different reindeer herding communities about indigenous knowledge (IK). I then created a comparative study on the effect of their school education on IK.

To find out how young Nenets themselves value the perceptions and understanding of IK, I used a questionnaire method, because then I could cover a larger number of grades and children at the same time. I wanted to understand how this IK is transmitted to younger generations. It should be stated that the use of the questionnaire is a complementary method to my qualitative studies, based on fieldwork on the Tundra. The third task was to describe the IK of women, as it is practiced by an elder generation. Thus, I divided the process of studying and the fieldwork into four stages, by time, regions and types. When collecting data for this project, all personal data of individuals and households involved, including names, surnames and personal Ha' matyr" (reindeer earmarks) has been anonymized. Written informed consent was signed by all adults (over 16 years old in 2015).

The Nenet – A people of nomadic herders

The Nenets people today account for no more than 50,000 people (Bogojavlenskij, 2012) and approximately 16,000 of these are leading a nomadic way of life (Ravna, 2019). Their main occupation is reindeer husbandry. They move across the Arctic tundra with their herds over distances of some 1,600 km every year. Practically, it means that they are moving almost every day during the summer and approximately once a month during the winter. The Tundra Nenets refer to themselves as "Ty nu" (children of reindeer). They raise their children according to their own methods and principles. These methods are employed by the nomadic Nenets in the expectation that these children will become future reindeer herders. The nomads get their supplies, such as foods like salt, bread and sugar twice a year, when they are moving past local shops in nearby settled communities. Their children are away from their nomadic families whilst studying in boarding schools for about nine months a year.

An important part of the Nenet way of life has been the use of domesticated dogs, as companions, and as partner in herding reindeer. This is called the "laika" (hereinafter referred to as "dog"). From time immemorial, the Nenets nomads have domesticated dogs. The dog is a friend, an assistant, and a companion to talk to when alone. Nenets herders actually have a verbal "conversation" with

128   *Zoia Vylka Ravna*

their dogs on long night shifts: with its help, they drive the herds of reindeer, collecting them in a circle and guide the herd to the right place by the whistled commands and gestures of the owner. The first appearance of dogs among the Nenets is not historically recorded or documented in writing, but folklorists have recorded a fairy tale-legend, passed down through the generations by oral story telling (Medved' i zajac, 1984). The Nenets know how and why the dog came to them. They talk about it like this in their fairy tale (my short retelling):

The dog lived alone in the forest. It became boring for the dog to live alone. She began to look for a friend. After searching, the dog alternately tried to make friends with a hare, a wolf and a bear. But they were all afraid of the bigger beast: a hare afraid of the wolf and a wolf of a bear. The dog's search for a companion continued until she met a man. He took the dog home. In the evening the man went to bed. At midnight the dog barked. Instead of being scared, the man cried out:

- Dog, take it, take it!

Then the dog began to live with humans. And he still lives in partnership with them.

A good dog is expensive. Sometimes a whole reindeer is given in exchange for a puppy from a famous dog's family. But even so, the true worth of a dog usually cannot be measured until it works with the herd.

This statement is true for the Nenets of different groups and clans, be they Siberian or European, tundra or forest nomadic Nenets. The latter, by the way, to protect their dogs from blood-sucking insects, build separate tents for their dogs. And in some years the tundra Nenets of the European tundra take their dogs into their own dwellings, to protect them from wolves. Respect for the dog as a family member has been preserved both at the communal and family levels. The dog in general is a "Wenya" in the Nenets language (affectionately referred to by the diminutive noun "wenyako") (Barmič, 2015) and is similar to the North Sámi name for a dog, "Beana" and has the same root, i.e., came from one language.

Globally, the Nenets dog is called the "Samoyed Laika" (Originally bred to hunt, haul sledges, and herd reindeer, the Samoyed dog breed proved a valuable companion for northwestern Siberia's Samoyed people) and came from the old name for the Nenets themselves (Samoyed history, 2020). Where the name "Samoyed" came from is debatable, there was a lot of discussion about this in the past, but at present the version proposed by linguists is: from the word "Same Ednan" (the land of the Sami) (Golovnev, 1995). A "Samoyed" dog, snow-white in color and with a thick coat, is used as a pet and is not to be confused with working reindeer herding dogs (Figure 7.1).

The "Samoyed Laika" dog has begun to enjoy interest at the global level and has gradually become a popular breed of dog for sale on international markets. They now have their own Facebook page. The dog, previously used in the tundra, and serving for the benefit of reindeer herders, fishermen and northerners in general, has now become a popular breed among city dwellers. Thus, from a friend of

Figure 7.1 Pedavane and her friend. Photo: Zoia Ravna.

a reindeer herder, his indefatigable assistant, the dog of the Nenets people of the "reindeer herding Laika" breed has become an "expensive" purchase of several thousand rubles in foreign currency, as a "pet" for people in urban environments. The values by which a Samoyed dog can now be measured, is not based in its functional worth and abilities as a working dog for reindeer herders, but by its breed, origin and attractive appearance as a potential pet. That the significant traditional spiritual and culturally symbolic meaning of the Nenets dog is now changing, as the Nenets herders themselves recognize, to one of the breeding and rearing of a dog as agricultural livestock, as a commercialized product, which can be profitably sold as an international export.

The year of the Nenet herder

Nomads attach much of their philosophy of life to the landscape (Vy – Tundra), therefore I have provided a detailed description of the life in tundra, based on their annual migration activities. Even though the nomads have never grown and harvested their food like a settled population – farmers and pastoralists, their year is also divided into two cycles, or – as the Nenets themselves say – "Po" (Year). The first cycle is called "Syra" (Year – Winter (cycle) and the other is "Ta'" (Year – summer (cycle). This division of the year into two by the nomadic Nenets is directly derived from the cycle of seasons as experienced by them in their natural environment, from the growth of fertile vegetation in the western "spring" and "summer", to its demise in a western "autumn" and "winter", followed again by a cyclical renewal (Figure 7.2).

130   Zoia Vylka Ravna

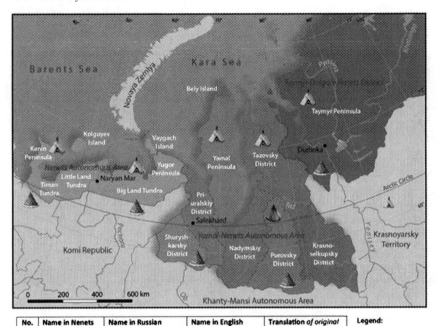

No.	Name in Nenets language	Name in Russian (ISO transliteration)	Name in English	Translation of original place name segment
	Nenets Autonomous Area [Neneckij avtonomnyj okrug]			
1	Jabta-Sale Ja	Kaninskij poluostrov	Kanin Peninsula	long, narrow cape
2	Timenskoj Ja / Tim Vy' / Timečkoy	Timanskaja tundra	Timan Tundra	From timbja (split) referring to rocks split along shistasity; word origin from legendary Sihirtå people
3	Ņudi Ja	Malozemel'skaja tundra	Little Land Tundra	little land
4	Ņarka Ja	Bol'šezemel'skaja tundra	Big Land Tundra	big land
5	Jugor	Jugorskij poluostrov	Yugor Peninsula	ambiguous origin Yugra: historical name of land and people between Pechora River and Urals
6	Holŋgov ŋo	Ostrov Kolguev	Kolguyev Island	corner, hill island
7	Vajhabc'	Ostrov Vajgač	Vaygach Island	death island
	Yamal-Nenets Autonomous Area [Jamalo-Neneckij avtonomnyj okrug]			
8	Šorvoš rajon	Šuryškarskij rajon	Shuryshkarsky District	(from Khanty lang.)
9	Pe''hevyhy rajon	Priural'skij rajon	Priuralsky District	by the Urals
10	Ņadei Ja	Nadymskij rajon	Nadymsky District	lichen land
11	Pur'rajon	Purovskij rajon	Purovsky District	mighty river
12	Ņjaryj mač'y rajon	Krasnoselkupskij rajon	Krasnoselkupsky District	(from Selkup lang.)
13	Ja'mal	Jamalskij poluostrov	Yamal Peninsula	end of the Earth
14	Sêr ŋo	Ostrov Belyj	Bely Island	white island
15	Tasu'Java''	Tazovskij rajon	Tazovsky District	flooded river
	Taymyr Dolgan-Nenets District [Tajmyrskij Dolgano-Neneckij rajon]			
16	Tajmyr Ja	Tajmyrskij Poluostrov	Taymyr Peninsula	ambiguous origin

Legend:
Regional boundary
Boundary between region and associated autonomous area
District boundary
Summer pastures — Summer chum
Summer chum in Purovsky District
Winter pastures — Winter chum

Compiled by Zoia Vylka Ravna (Norwegian Inst. for Cultural Heritage Research, NIKU) and Winfried K. Dallmann (University of Tromsø)

Figure 7.2 Map of the Nenets territories.

The Syra (Year – winter) begins with the first snow, usually includes the months from October to March and the Ta (Year – summer) starts with an ice melting (from April to September). Autumn in the Nenets language is Ngere/Ngere and spring is Nara and Aanuj/Venuj. The word Time is El'c'' (n) and a calendar in Nenets is connotation Po tolobava (Time counting). The families move with their reindeer, dwellings (tents), supplies and equipment between 300 and 500 km in the western Tundra. The longest route is taken by brigades (a common unit of several families) of an SPK (Agricultural Production Cooperative) "The path of Ilyich", which is up to 500 km. On Yamal, some of the brigades move between 1,400 and 1,800 km each year (up to 550 km in summer). My description of the economic activities during a year, including harvesting of wild plants, processing and conservation of fish products and further storage, is based on my collated 2015 (two fieldwork periods) data. The following text is about Brigade No. 5 of MOP (Municipal enterprise of reindeer herders) "Ar-Salinskij".

At the end of October, every herder should prepare to move over across the rivers, as soon as they are covered with ice. The herders that have summer pastures in the Yamal Peninsula move to the south side of the river Ob. Some of the European Nenets groups move to the other side of the Pecera River. The pastures there are the main reason for this southern migration. The Tundra-forest and the forest are rich in lichen that the animals can feed on during the winter.

The main concern for herders in the winter is to secure access to good pastures for their reindeer with a lot of accessible lichen. During wintertime there is not much other food available for them. Then, there is hunting, for instance for ptarmigan (Lagopus lagopus. An arctic grouse.); fishing and the gathering of "Chaga"-mushrooms (Inonotus obliquus). The men then work with cutting, drying and in the preparation of special types of trees for reindeer sledges, for poles for the "Ma" (tent) and other necessary equipment made from trees. Women spend the wintertime sewing new clothes for their husbands and children, as well as themselves.

October is given the name "Hor Iry" (the month of the rutting of reindeer). A mass rut begins at this time. There are often clashes between the males. Reindeer (castrated) lose their antlers in October. Other reindeer (males) are starting to look for females. The herd should not be disturbed at this time of year. Herders are only watching the herd, trying to keep animals together, waiting for the rut to end. After the rut, the camp moves to the winter pastures. Nowadays, the time for moving is regulated by the authorities. Private herds, however, may move as they wish. The difference between a "private" herd and any other type of herd is regulated by the authorities (see more in Ravna, 2020).

During the winter, people do not move often, once or twice during a month. Therefore, they sometimes refer to these periods as "holidays". At the same time, herds need to be watched, because of the risk from predators. According to respondents in different areas of the Tundra, the situation is better now. Before, there were many more predators. In previous times, the herd had to be guarded by two or three armed herders. Today, there are not so many wolves or other predators, but many more illegal poachers, who shoot and steal domesticated reindeer.

132 Zoia Vylka Ravna

That's why the informant compares these people with wolves. A young male from a completely different area, the Tajmyr, gives a similar response.

> I am a private herder. Our herd has about two thousand reindeer already… We manage to grow the herd. First, the wolves are gone [extinct]. Secondly, we learned how to treat diseases. We are buying first-aid kits, for veterinary treatment. Thirdly, probably, we learn how to think.
>
> (Young Nenet herder)

At the end of winter, the reindeer herders usually count their animals. For Brigade No. 5, this is usually done at "Naby Si'vy" (the meadow surrounded by forests). When the count is completed, the intensive move to the north begins.

> In the middle of March, we count our animals [reindeer]. We do this, according to the circumstances, when we manage to collect them all. We do it in a certain order, we pass the herd through corrals… Usually we do it in March 25-26. Last year, however, due to ice, we started on March 10th.
>
> (Herder, Brigade No. 5)

Late March and the beginning of April are known as the Month of False Calving, because the very first calves are born at this time (the main calving season starts in May). This is also a time when Brigade No. 5 must cross the river Ob. Sometimes the brigade moves up to 60–70 km each day. They are in a hurry because of the melting snow and ice on the river, which if it was completely melted, would prevent them from crossing the river. May (the Month of the Ordinary Calving) and/or the Month of Singing Water is the most hectic month for reindeer herders and their families. Calves are born every day and it is necessary to keep mothers – female reindeer close to each of the new-born calves. In June, the last calves of the year are born. Usually, the herd is split into two parts: the calves and their mothers, while the second part consists of other reindeer. Young people are trained to help with the calving at this time of the year. One of the women told me how:

> I lived in the Tundra for a long time. I worked as a herder sometimes. During calving in spring, the different parts of the herd are separated. I finished my 7th grade in school that summer. The family was big. Mom was sick all the time. Then, the father told us [me and my sisters] that some of you will continue to study, and some will need to help mom. I was a very active energetic girl, so I stayed. In the spring, when the male reindeer were separated from the main herd, we need two herders to watch the herd. One - at the head of the herd, and then usually an experienced herder is watching the calving. I have always been there, at the head of the herd. After one or two days, I was moved to watch the male reindeer part of the herd… because it was necessary.
>
> (Woman, Brigade No. 5)

The decline and changes in the tundra today   133

Since each female reindeer remembers where it was born, she will return to the same places, year after year, to give birth herself, to her own calves. The reindeer herders know this, and therefore they are all in a hurry to get to these places in time. The calving sites require a very specific set of natural conditions. The reindeer mothers are trying to find open spots on the ground. There should not be too many trees, preferably small hills, where the snow melts first. The reindeer herders try to help female reindeer by protecting them against predators, such as polar fox, wolf, owl, buzzard and eagle. Also, there are often blizzards at this time of the year.

Spring fishing now begins. Women must pack all the family's winter things and store them for half a year. The methods used for the storing of winter covers for tents, winter clothes and shoes represent the accumulated experience of generations of nomads. Since the route is always the same, the Nenets leave winter equipment in cargo sledges, which are left in open, windy places, usually on the top of the hill. This place should be reached between 10th and 15th of June. It is a time, when people change winter shoes and clothes to summer covers, clothes and shoes. They are waiting for nice weather, when it is dry and sunny. All the equipment made from reindeer hides should be dry, before it is stored for approximately five months. Brigade No. 5 usually store the winter sledges near Ugly Po'se. Women and men pack and tie the sledges and leave them until the autumn. Then, on the way back, usually between the 10th to 20th October on the way to winter pasture, when the nights become colder and the first snow can already cover the earth, the brigade will come back to this place again. Then the summer sledges will be changed to winter sledges.

Stored winter clothes, shoes and tent covers will be taken out for usage in the wintertime. The summer things will be packed for the next year. Usually, children's sledges, toys, clothes and other equipment, like fishing nets will be also packed for storage here, because the school helicopter takes the children to the settlement. Other Nenets people never touch these sledges, because it is their custom. Neither do predators destroy it, because it is too far north, as the reindeer herders explained to me. By contrast, the southern brigades may sometimes have their sledges ruined, turned upside down or destroyed by larger animals, like bears.

The main principle for such a logistical solution is to avoid carrying "everything at the same time". The summer sledges are lighter in weight, but they can be easily broken in winter. Since the reindeer are used as transport animals both in summer and winter, and for both cargo and passenger sledges, their construction and weight are of great importance. During the winter, brigade No. 5 travels about 20–30 km a day during one movement (Yamal, informant, 2015). Of the 88 sledges, approximately half are used as "winter" sledges (they are built heavier, longer and higher). Other sledges can be used for the whole year, usually these are passenger sledges.

There is an ecological limit on the pastureland, and everyone from the nomadic community is aware of this limitation. It is the only land they have. Their culture and life depend on these pastures, in which productivity is so low that reindeer would not survive if they don't find a "Naarèj" (lichen grazing places) in winter, late autumn and early spring. The process by which pastures are ecologically damaged or destroyed is explained by reindeer herders as follows:

134   Zoia Vylka Ravna

This is a multi-step process. At first, the reindeer tread down and thin the [fertile] soil. Then, due to global warming, the temperature rises and contributes to an even more destructive environmental factor - the permafrost layer thaws. Furthermore, the permafrost does not penetrate as deep into the ground, and the sand masses come out, and rise. The protective layer again becomes smaller and waterlogging begins. And again - moss is being supplanted. Sandstones spread faster due to the wind.

(Herder, Brigade 5)

Nowadays, reindeer herders also consider the "refuse" left behind after a camp is dismantled as a problem, for several reasons. The "Madyrma" (campsite) after the "Mâ-Tent" can be seen only by the discolored circle on the surface and garbage, which is usually cleaned up and collected in a nearby slope or pit. In order to get an understanding of the influence of these slopes or pits on reindeer herders, it is important to recognize their way of seeing nature and at the same time to use the scientific biological knowledge of processes of decomposing of different types of garbage in high latitudes. This is referred to the increasing use of single use plastics/baby's diapers, etc.

The reindeer herders in Soviet times, when there were not so many private reindeer herders had control over their pastures, because each brigade had a route and the campsites (not a tent) were always built in the same place, to within a few square km. Now, due to the changes, there is almost no control over the private enterprises the campsites are chosen at random, according to the whims of each reindeer herder:

Now, there is a Madyrma on all the hills here.

(Herder, Brigade 5)

The consequences of these new deregulated private campsites are heaps of garbage which does not decompose. Due to changes in habits, like the use of diapers, plastic toys, bags and different objects made from artificial materials, littering has now become a problem in previously clean Tundra areas. This pollution is spread by the nomads, not caused by the industrial development in this area. As a consequence, indigenous knowledge is having to adapt and apply itself to changing conditions:

The old people were moving; they were trying to not "destroy the land". They were not leaving any garbage behind. Today there are children's diapers. Earlier all the surfaces on the Tundra was cleaned. Now, when we arrived at our campsite, there is garbage everywhere. A. is trying to clean everything up, including the boxes. Old tin cans are usually buried.

(Herder, Brigade No. 5)

Another problem on Yamal (not in the western Nenets territories), connected to the increasing number, but smaller sized herding communities are structural changes: reindeer herding has become more and more focused on meat production; therefore, the number of animals is now at a critical level of carrying capacity (approximately 750,000).

> There is less and less lichen for the reindeer.
>
> (Herder, Brigade 5)

The economy of each individual family is often vulnerable because it is based solely on the number of reindeer owned and the subsequent financial income produced by that reindeer herd (Figure 7.3). Too many reindeer have problems getting enough food. Then, many reindeer starve. Another reason for the death of reindeer is natural disasters. For a number of reasons, the death of reindeer is not something unusual, it is in fact now becoming more common because of disasters in recent years: death from hunger in 2008 and 2013–2014, death from anthrax in 2016, death of calves in the spring of 2017 due to ice.

> The catastrophic year was the winter of 2013-2014. The first year's calves were all dead. From the total number, 10% survived, the year calves all died. Less than half of the adult ox population survived, because the stock has been exhausted. The transport reindeer, usually oxen, are constantly exhausted, and the animals are heavily emaciated by spring. Almost all female reindeer survive.
>
> (Herder, Brigade 5)

Figure 7.3 The caravan of reindeer http://lelang.ru/english/films/forrest-gamp-na-anglijskom-yazyke-s-subtitrami/appears in the following order: Nerdena (in front), Muzandana (leading), Pudana (the last). (Interview 17). Photo: Zoia Ravna.

136 *Zoia Vylka Ravna*

The brigade at that time had about 120 reindeer. This informant had only 30 left from 60. Some of his reindeer were mixed with other brigades or private herds. He had to go to Salemal by the river Ob to collect his reindeer. Some of the nomadic herders become involuntarily settled. The herders talked about their losses without emotion, but I could see that they were sad.

> 2015 – the second year after the terrible 2013, when 1/3 of the total livestock fell (half of the unrealized production), if you include unborn calves. The year started hard. Despite all the efforts of the reindeer herders, we came to Ûribej too late. Since the herd was so weakened. We waited for a long time, about three weeks, because the rivers thawed earlier [than usual]. Spring took us surprisingly early. We usually cross over the ice. In 2015, everything was already melted.
>
> (Herder, Brigade 5)

Some of the changes are critical. For instance, they are facing more frequent, unseasonal and unusual climate changes. The reason for abnormally rapid melting of snow and ice, the reindeer herders explained to me, are many sunny days, plus high temperatures. All of it influenced the ability of the herd and people to cross rivers. Therefore, at the beginning of my field work, the whole human community of Brigade No. 5 was stranded on the southern coast whilst herders and the whole herd, including the transport ox, had crossed to the other side. Because of this, the son of one of my informants was left to stay in the village. He was lucky to get work as an electrician. However, he was not envied by the other nomads:

> It is impossible to predict [these changes]. The old men in the 1970s survived a total loss of reindeer. All the reindeer died. People were left without reindeer. They sat down in the villages. Became carpenters, etc. A few were left in reindeer husbandry and managed to rebuild the herd. These were able to restore the herd and [help to return to Tundra].
>
> (Herder, Brigade 5)

In the Summer, the brigade moves almost every day. Their journey terminates on the northwest side of the Yamal Peninsula by the Kara Sea. Out on the Yamal Peninsula, the reindeer find relief from annoying mosquitoes and other insects and can graze peacefully. By the coast, the animals have access to good and lush pasture with green grass, leaves and other green food. Later, on the way back, reindeer will start to search for mushrooms at the end of the summer. The whole peninsula is rich in fish both in rivers and its countless lakes.

Fish is the biggest and most important part of the nomadic Nenets's everyday menu in the summer. There are many types of fish. Among them are Arctic char (Salvelinus alpinus), Arctic cisco (Coregonus autumnalis), Sig-pyzhyan (C. lavaretus pidschian), Muksun (C. muksun), Brod whitefish (C. nasus), Pelyad (C. peled) and Nelma (Stenymus thymnus) (Bogdanov & Melnichenko, 2016). The fish are eaten boiled, raw or fried over a fire. Reindeer herders use fishing nets which they set at the end of large lakes. One or two experienced men usually go with the adolescents to fish, just after the brigade stops to build a new camp. While the women and the oldest children set up the summer tent called "Tany

Ma", collect firewood and drinking water, the men often return with a supply of fresh fish. The fish are usually divided equally between all those living in the brigade. Reindeer meat is rare at this time of the year. Only on special occasions can you slaughter for food during the summer. The workday often starts at night. Unsurprisingly, nomadic people do not follow the same daily rhythm as settled populations. There is a proverb saying that there are not reindeer for the Nenets, but Nenets for reindeer Nenets obeys the rhythm of the reindeer's life.

> He gets up at 4 am in the winter and in the summer. As soon as the birds twitter, he gets up. I remember – we sleep, very well, about 4 in the morning. Father, standing on a sledge, claps on the walls of the tent: "Still sleeping?" We get out, quickly. You cannot hesitate, especially in the summer. The gadfly will destroy the reindeer; they will lose weight and their skins will become bad, that's all.
> (Herder, Brigade 5)

Summer is also time for gathering eggs, hunting goose, ducks and other types of birds. According to Nenets custom, only one or two eggs can be picked from one nest. None of the other eggs should be touched. Late in the summer, Marangga (cloudberries Rubus chamaemorus), Lamtuj (blueberries Vaccinium myrtillus) and at the end of August, Enzedej/End'ej (lingonberries Vaccinium vitis-idaea) and Harë ngodâ (cranberries Vaccinium oxycoccos) are ripe. Then women and children go to pick the berries (Figure 7.4).

Figure 7.4 Women are walking back to the camp with firewood they have gathered. Photo: Zoia Vylka Ravna.

138   *Zoia Vylka Ravna*

August Pilû irij (Botfly Hypoderma tarandi) is also the month for the slaughter of that year's calves which provide hides from which the Nenets sew new clothes and shoes. The men select a number of calves, slaughter them, and cut the meat while the women dry their hides and prepare them for further treatment. At this time, girls learn the basics of reindeer skin preparation, as well as preparing "Pena" (the hides from reindeer feet) used for sewing shoes and bags. Children also help by placing hides over the sledges, in order to get them dry. Boys learn how to repair fishing and hunting equipment, how to make and throw "Tynzâ" (lasso), slaughter and cut the meat as well as how to find fishing spots. In addition, the elderly generally spends a lot of time telling the youth about traditions, special signs such as weather, landmarks and conditions to be thoroughly familiar with in these areas, as well as stories associated with certain or special places. As for the women, many summer evenings are dedicated to sorting, arranging, packing, and making new clothing. The men at the same time prepare and arrange winter equipment, like making new lassos, repairing sledges, or fixing the harnesses they use for transportation.

In the summers, when the "Ngovta Ngysy" (joint grazing) happens, usually at end of June, or the beginning of July, the reindeer herders join together. As they say, "the gnats gather reindeer" (Interview 17). The main reason for joint grazing is that in summer it is easier to watch and protect larger herds than smaller ones. But there is also a need for more herders at this time.

> Depending on the livestock, if he for example has 500 heads of reindeer, then he needs to change the pastures much more often. In other words, having many reindeer is good, having few is bad. The one who has fewer reindeer is more mobile. At the same time, you have more control over a smaller herd. The one who has a lot of reindeer can share these. It is more profitable to have more people [herders].

> (Herder, Brigade 5)

In September during the "Veba'ha"amva irij" (The month of Fall of leaf), also called "Seljbja irij" (the month of ossification of reindeer antlers), the brigades and their reindeer start slowly to move southward towards their winter pastures. For all nomads this phase is also a very stressful period in terms of emotions. Children have to leave their families for a long time. They are usually transported by helicopters at the end of the summer to villages and cities to study for 9 months until the next holidays.

Changes threatening sustainability on the tundra

These communities are undergoing changes, and these are caused by both internal and by external influences. According to the elders, the changes that are now occurring can be categorized as follows (without dividing them into human or non-human causes):

- Fewer girls and young women will continue to live on the Tundra.
- Decreasing number of elders in the Tundra (the needs of old people cannot be taken care of due to a shortage of female workers).

The decline and changes in the tundra today   139

- Increasing number of people in the nomadic community, compared to the late 1990s (on the Siberian side of the Ural Mountains).
- Increasing usage of modern artificial materials that do not decompose (for instance, diapers, canned food and plastic packaging.

Then, there are other problems, not necessarily directly influenced by the school-system; but the ability to solve these problems is dependent on the competent possession of IK:

- Unstable weather and unusual or unexpected seasonal changes (temperature variations from high to low, especially in winters).
- Changes in the structure of pastures: sands are increasing, some places have increasing wetland areas, in other places lakes are drying up.

In the territory of the European Nenets, in addition to the mentioned changes, the lack of girls in reindeer husbandry has become a critical problem. A lot of women were displaced in the Soviet years. My respondents also categorize this as one of the inside influences. Because it is an internal wish of parents to provide the necessary resources to educate their children and to let children, especially girls continue their education. One of these reasons is also explained by a respondent:

> Why the girls today do not want [to live in the Tundra]? I think it is because they went through the school system. Passed through boarding schools. The living conditions are much more favourable, there is an accomplishment there. Nice, warm toilet, shower rooms. Of course, now that they have this, they do not want to live on the Tundra. Other interests have emerged. Those who study in Nar'an-Mar want to stay in Nar'an-Mar. Some study outside the area, in Arkhangelsk, in Moscow, in St. Petersburg. Of course, it is more interesting to live there, life there is more fun, more diverse, fuller. There are places to spend your free time… to have fun.
>
> (Nenet woman)

Another important change that is more common now in the territory of the European Nenets, is the displacement of elders. Due to the official policy, pensioners should leave the Tundra and move to the village. However, since there are already so few women to take care of the old and the disabled on the tundra, it is becoming an impossible task:

> I used to visit a man, from Amb-to [Long lake]. He was an elder, placed in Indom (from Russian: invalidnyj dom: the disabled house). So, he wanted so much to go back to the Tundra. When I came to visit him, I used to give him a cell phone. I dialed the number to his children, and they talked. And he said all the time: take me, take me! He spoke in the dialect [of the Nenets language], I hardly understood him. …Once, they didn't take him

140   *Zoia Vylka Ravna*

there for the summer, and he was so worried. So, when I came the next time, he talked to me as if they had already planned to go next summer. He says they'll come to take me! I need a bag. For my daughters-in-law, please buy the shawls. He then collected this bag. But they [his children] did not take him, and he was so disappointed... And the next summer I told his children: take him! He wants it so much, at least for a while! They finally brought him home the next summer, but the weather was so hot there and he died. From a stroke, or from something else. But at least, he was there! At home [in the Tundra]!

(Nenet woman)

This shows that changes affected the people and the herds in the past too. Reasons may have been different, but we live in a changing world. According to herders, you need approximately 10 years for the pastures to recover and about 5 years to restore the reindeer herd.

If there were good years, then you need 5 years to restore the livestock. It is necessary that it is chilly in summers. It all depends on nature. Old people say that there are usually three bad years in a row.

(Herder, Brigade 5)

At the same time, these numbers only apply if there are no additional impacts. On one occasion, on the winter or forest pastures, as they are also called, the Yamal reindeer herders were on the Hènska side (winter pastures): Once there was a major forest fire, and the pastures here couldn't be used for 20 years.

(Herder, Brigade 5)

The Yamal Peninsula has also been under the pressure from the oil and gas industry for about 50 years. In the years 2000–2010 many infrastructural facilities were constructed there, and most of them are built on pastureland. These pastures were used by generations of the reindeer people of Yamal. Among the industrial constructions is a railroad known as the "Obskaja – Bovanenkovo – Karskaja"-line. It runs from the river Ob, the gas extraction and production facility "Bovanenkovo", to the last station, situated by the Kara Sea. The main purpose of this railroad is to deliver shift workers and cargo for the Bovanenkovskoe and Harasavèjskoe oil and gas condensate fields. The settlement of Bovanenkovo together with the Bovanenkovskoe field used to be summer pastures for the Nenets and it is situated on the route to the Kara Sea. The reindeer herds move there every year in the middle of July.

Bovanenkovo is now a huge settlement, almost a town, with many shift workers there around the clock. The railroad has transported people and goods back and forth to Bovanenkovo since it opened in 2010. Brigade No. 5 still use the same route to the Kara Sea, however. One of the reindeer herders told me about their annual difficulties crossing the railroad and the Bovanenkovo settlement. Since

The decline and changes in the tundra today   141

the railroad was built, the pastures are exhausted, because every family and every brigade now use the same route.

> We don't have Synej anymore (Synej nada - a good place, with a lot of lichen, at the same time without much biological diversity. Reindeer eat a lot, but they do not really grow in body-mass and fatness; like they should. Important in terms of resting area). The problem is that the pastures have been exhausted by the time we arrive.
>
> (Herder, Brigade 5)

Since everyone is moving the same way, there is ongoing conflict over the pastures.

Conclusion

As we have seen, there are many different changes of various kinds affecting nomadic Nenets life today. These kinds of changes are also affecting reindeer herders all over the northern hemisphere. At the same time, in response to my questions about the future of reindeer herding, people in Yamal, all agree that nomadic Nenets reindeer husbandry should be preserved. However, the Nenets reindeer herders themselves emphasized that it can only be developed and adapted to meet these changes, if the herders themselves are properly consulted, included in policy development and decision making and actively involved in making the necessary changes:

> The Nenets reindeer husbandry is preserved because we are constantly with the animals. The shift method is unacceptable for us. Passivity in reindeer herding is unacceptable.
>
> (Herder, Brigade 5)

In conclusion, and in summary, the Nenets reindeer husbandry of today face a number of threats and challenges. First of all, they face the consequences of global warming. In the late autumn the usual temperatures would be about 40–45°C below zero, now such temperatures are rare. Ice on pastures occurs more often than before. Sometimes, there is too much snow on the winter side (southern bank) of the Ob River. Rising temperatures in the Arctic can lead to more humidity and snow fall.

Second, they face territorial encroachments on their pastures in the form of gas pipelines, infrastructure, construction of numerous industrial facilities. Loss of "Nedarma" (a dry, hilly place) and good grazing land as well as. The winter pastures are now in use during the summertime, which is unfavorable. As a result, critical pastures are subject to environmental depletion in the form of overgrazing, as the number of reindeer exceeds the grazing capacity of remaining pastures.

Finally, the Nenets are facing social disruptions that threaten their traditional way of life. Recruitment and retention in reindeer husbandry are now an urgent problem. At the same time, due to a long period of displacement of women, the problem is also found in the loss of the Nenets language. Displacement of elders causes an additional obstacle in the inter-generational transmission of indigenous

142 Zoia Vylka Ravna

knowledge and skills. When I asked them about the future of reindeer husbandry, they all agreed that it will be difficult, due to the changes in the Yamal area:

> In 10 years, there will be chaos here. The more civilization comes, the less land we have. The more we lose. About 50% of the land on the Yamal Peninsula is no longer suitable for reindeer herding. And more and more this land will be lost.
>
> (Herder, Brigade 5)

According to the reindeer people themselves, these changes are disproportionately threatening indigenous and nomadic communities around the world. In this chapter I have tried to give an overview of these challenges, as they affect nomadic Nenets reindeer herders in the Russian Arctic. The future of this tiny threatened community, which still survives and retains a unique culture, should be a matter of international concern. If the Nenet culture and way of life is eradicated, this represents an irreversible loss to our global human and cultural diversity, which itself has been a necessary basis for the progress of human civilization to this day. These issues need to be addressed by decision makers and leadership at an international level.

References

Barmič, M. J. (Ed.). (2015). *Russko-neneckij slovar' [the nenets-Russian dictionary]*. Sankt-Peterburg: Almaz-Graf.

Bogojavlenskij, D. D. (2012). *Dannye vserossijskoj perepisi 2010* [Data of the All- Russian Census of 2010]. Retrieved from http://raipon.info/peoples/data-census- 2010/data-census-2010.php

Bogdanov, V. D., & Melnichenko, I. P. (2016). Harakteristika ihtiofauny polu-ostrova Âmal (Âmalo-Neneckij avtonomnyj okrug) [Characteristics of the ichthyofauna of the Yamal Peninsula (the Yamal-Nenets autonomous area)]. *Fauna Urala i Sibiri, 1*, 105–113. Retrieved from https://cyberleninka.ru/article/n/harakteristika-ihtiofauny-poluostrova-yamal- yamalo-nenetskiy-avtonomnyy-okrug

Golovnev, A. V. (1995). *Govorasie kul'tury. Tradicii samodijcev i ugrov [Talking cultures. Traditions of the samoyeds and ugric peoples]*. Ekaterinburg: UrO RAN.

Ravna, Z. V. (2019). "Catching a child": Giving birth under nomadic conditions. The methods of pre- and postnatal care of the Nenets mothers and babies. *International Journal of Circumpolar Health, 78*(1), 1–14. doi: 10.1080/22423982.2019.1586275

Ravna, Z. V. (2020). The inter-generational transmission of indigenous knowledge by Nenets women: Viewed in the context of the State Educational System of Russia. Dissertation for the degree of Philosophiae Doctor, University of Tromso, Norway.

Samoyed history. (2020). *The Samoyed Club of America*. Retrieved from https://www.samoyedclubofamerica.org/the-samoyed/in-depth/breed-origin-and-history/

The UN Permanent forum on indigenous issues. Together we achieve. The UN Department of Public Information. (2018). Retrieved from https://www.un.org/development/desa/indigenouspeoples/wpcontent/uploads/sites/19/2018/04/Indigenous-Languages.pdf

Tonkov, V. (1984). *Medved' i zajac tèvasi. Neneckie skazki [The bear and the hare tevasi. Nenets fairy tales]*. Moscow: "Malysh" Publishing House.

8 Overcoming isolation in the Arctic during COVID-19 times through new ways of co-writing research

Rita Sørly, Bård Kårtveit, Vigdis Nygaard, Anne Katrine Normann, Ludmila Ivanova, Svetlana Britvina & Larissa Riabova

Introduction

In our project team, we are seven researchers with different backgrounds – we are social and political scientists, economists and researchers working with environment, anthropology and mental health. As researchers, we write papers, reports and journal articles, individually and in co-operation with other researchers. Until now, we have not written work together based in what is called autoethnography. The very word autoethnography points to the range from the personal to the cultural. Auto involves introspection and observation of the writer, her or his reflections, thoughts and feelings. Ethno involves culture, and the focus is on the cultural context and its practices. Graphics is the very projection of the systematic examination of narratives, experiences and observations to personal insight and scientific knowledge (Brinkmann, 2017).

Autoethnography has its origins in debates in the 1980s about how and whether it was possible to write about culture as a statement of experiences. Related to methodology, it is about the relationship between the experienced and observed reality, field notes and ethnographic text. Within the tradition of autoethnography, different approaches have developed that emphasize different aspects of the autoethnographic method and spelling (Olson, 2015). The author writes that autoethnography is an examination of changes in oneself that can be related to major social, political and cultural events. Furthermore, some authors suggest that the main idea of autoethnography is that personal narratives can address central theoretical debates in sociology (Aure, 2019; Laslett, 1999) and, we can add, in other social disciplines.

Autoethnography is both a research method and a distinct way of writing based on the Greek word "grapho" – to write. Thus, autoethnography is more than a representation of one's own experiences. The goal is to create a text that can represent a dialogical approach to culture *and* experiences (Karlsson & Sørly, 2021). Seikkula (2008) writes that dialogue is talking together, not individually or only to oneself, but together. If we go to the historical roots of the word, we find that it is composed of the Greek "dia", which means "through" and "logos" which means "word", "speech" or "reason". A dialogue is thus an activity which is carried out through words, and which is sensible, at least according to the original meaning of the word. And it may

DOI: 10.4324/9781003118633-9

144   *Rita Sørly, Bård Kårtveit, Vigdis Nygaard, et al.*

well include many people (Svare, 2019). The dialogue presupposes that I allow myself to be moved by the other's expression and allow these to create impressions in me which in turn create expressions that create impressions in the other. This continues in an infinite spiral (Seikkula, 2008). This is described by Seikkula (ibid.) as the polyphony of dialogue, understood as meaning that the basic features of dialogue are complex, polyphonic and diverse. It is not just about exchanging expressions and impressions with each other. It is about communication, about response and thinking and talking together (Karlsson & Sørly, 2021). In this chapter, we suggest that collective autoethnography can be both a way to overcome isolation and a novel method to gain and share scientific knowledge in times of a pandemic. In our context, such an approach can be referred to as poly ethnography – where seven writers design their texts inviting each other to respond in the form of texts.

In the following, we will give a brief introduction of our research project, before we describe poly ethnography as a method. Next, each of us will provide our stories related to our professional and personal experiences of isolation during the pandemic. The stories are presented as individual snapshots. In line with Richardson (2003), we agree that the more different voices are honored within qualitative research, the stronger and more interesting, that research community will be. We relate our stories to the concept of co- researching, as a relational and dynamic process, underlining the importance of stories as movements of spatial, temporal, affective, sensory and cognitive experiences (Turunen, Čeginskas, Kaasik-Krogerus, Lähdesmäki, & Mäkinen, 2020). To reflect on stories as capable of changing individual isolation experiences together is a movement away from isolation, towards a common research community across borders. In our reflections, we also relate our stories of overcoming COVID-19 isolation as family members, researchers and citizens to sustainability issues in the Arctic regions.

The Norwegian- Russian social work research project

The Norwegian-Russian three-year long research project *"Adapting to a changing society. The case of civil society in the Murmansk region – VOLRUSS"*, funded by the Norwegian Research Council, was planned to start up in the beginning of 2020. The project's primary objective was to gain an understanding of how non-governmental organizations operating in the border region Russia-Norway adapt to changing legal, political and social circumstances and how they approach local communities' socio-economic and public health needs. We would also gain insight into Russian NGOs cooperation with Norwegian NGOs. The Norwegian and Russian project researchers wanted to study this in the context of the tightening grip on political expressions in Russia, and the growing diplomatic tension between Russia and Western nations. Our ambition was to generate insights of direct relevance to policy makers as well as the public in Russia and Norway, thereby offering research expertise to policy formulation at municipal, regional and national levels in both countries, in aspects of social affairs, foreign policy and security. By studying citizen involvement, we anticipated documenting best practices and knowledge gaps. For the global research community, the interdisciplinary nature

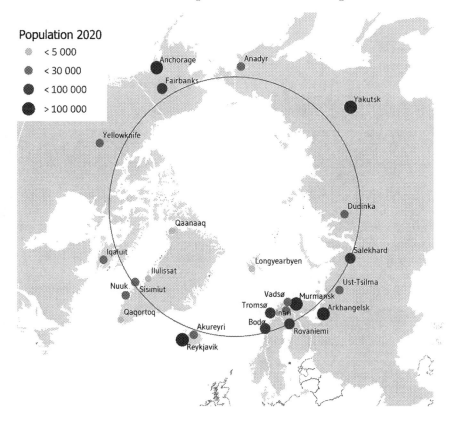

Figure 8.1 The Arctic. Source: Arctic centre, University of Lapland.

of our research would add to knowledge in social sciences, including contributing to theory development of NGOs, international collaboration and inequal resource access, contextualized in political and economic changes.

Some of the VOLRUSS researchers had previously collaborated on Norwegian-Russian projects, but we had not met as a project group. The Norwegian researchers planned to go to Murmansk in March 2020, to kick off the research project in the first physical project meeting with the Russian researchers. Instead, our plans – and our everyday lives – were turned upside down within a few days, with the arrival of Covid-19. This chapter tells our different stories about how we adjusted to abrupt changes in daily lives, and or communities and how we strive to retain sustainability in our personal relations, and in our efforts to pursue a joint research project while remaining separated by borders and pandemic restrictions.

The poly ethnographic method

The process of bringing different disciplinary perspectives into a coherent approach led us to search for new methods in the VOLRUSS project. In recent years, there

146 *Rita Sørly, Bård Kårtveit, Vigdis Nygaard, et al.*

has been a shift from traditional ethnography to more collaborative team ethnography (Spiller et al., 2015). Collaborative ethnography enables researchers to focus on connections and associations rather than single units (Turunen et al., 2020). Rather than producing "thick descriptions" of cultural practices, collaborative ethnography engages with complex experiences and cultural phenomena. This resonates with our experiences so far in the project, motivating us to do collaborative ethnography. We were further encouraged by theories on language and communication by Russian philosopher and literary theorist Bakhtin. Bakhtin's contribution to the field concerning polyphonic dialogues is easily transferable to our context. Ethnography as a method can be said to be polyphonic in nature; it is a context where many voices and discourses cross each other simultaneously to produce knowledge about personal narratives and social life (Tanggaard, 2009). No utterances can be regarded as independent units; they exist in the world within a contextual meaning, and the understanding of a speech is always dialogic (Bakhtin, 2010). Language is social, and the living language consists of combinations of different social languages (Tanggaard, 2009) in which certain narratives are more dominant or authoritarian than other narratives. Bakhtin defines language as heteroglossic, complex and a combination of different social languages or narratives (Bakhtin, Holquist, & Emerson, 1981). Inspired by Bakhtin, we have defined our method as a poly ethnographic approach.

Seven researchers, seven stories

In the following, we present our seven stories. The stories all interrelate and intertwine with each other.

Larissa's story: When a wild card plays

At the end of 2018, I happened to be a part of a future-scenario research workshop. We were thirty researchers creating future narratives for our home area, the Murmansk region. One of the steps was to indicate "wild cards" – low-probability high-impact events that, if occurred, would severely affect people and the places where they live. Only one person in our group indicated a wild card as a "global pandemic". A year later, this card played. In early March 2020, it became clear that we were facing something unexpected and unknown that covered all aspects of our lives with a huge cloud of uncertainty.

As the COVID-19 pandemic unravelled, it brought me fear for my loved ones, especially for my parents. My father in his 80s was working as a doctor and returned every evening home to my mother, who was thus also at risk. There was anxiety for our children, one going to school and another living in Europe where transmission cases rapidly grew, and for my husband, who in his job had regular contact with many people. And there were worries about friends, especially those who did not take the pandemic seriously, and for other people around and far away.

At times it felt as if a war had started, with non-stop news on TV reporting about the numbers of cases and deaths, governmental efforts, mobilized resources

Overcoming isolation in the Arctic during COVID-19 147

and doctors and volunteers joining the battle against the pandemic. The lockdown began at the end of March, and new rules like mask and gloves wearing and social distancing were introduced by the government. Life changed, and it was no longer possible to do many things that we took for granted before: go to the office, travel to other parts of the world or have lunch with friends and colleagues in a cafe, as we often did.

An escape from the ills of isolation was promised by professional life. After the turn to remote work, Zoom meetings were a channel of collective communication, and in this way together with our Norwegian colleagues we started a new cross-border project on NGOs in the Murmansk region (Figure 8.2). Performing the project was a challenge because we could not do what we used to do as social scientists – go on fieldwork, meet people and conduct interviews to get the data.

The pandemic moved the project's focus to those NGOs and new volunteer structures that were fighting COVID-19. Instead of face-to-face interviews, we followed regional, local and social media and made phone interviews when possible. For example, I did phone interviews with a young local journalist, who was an activist informing the elderly on how to get volunteer help. In early April 2020, the volunteer centre was established in our town within the national action "We are Together" initiated by coalition of public and political organizations – All-Russia People's Front (ONF). 17 similar centres were organized across the Murmansk region thanks to the joint efforts of ONF and regional and local authorities. I

Figure 8.2 Meeting on Zoom. Photo: Vigdis Nygaard.

148   *Rita Sørly, Bård Kårtveit, Vigdis Nygaard, et al.*

knew some of the volunteers in person – a woman at the local administration leading the new centre, my former student, who later received the President's award for selfless volunteer work, the owner of a pizzeria who used his own car to bring food and medicines to the elderly and some others.

Phone talks with friends were giving some relief from isolation, and the family trips to the nearby forests or to the lake would bring back the feeling of peace. In the wisdom of nature life seemed normal again. The pandemic made me realize that living in an Arctic town, where nature is so close that you can walk to the woods in 20 minutes, is a gift. Throughout the pandemic months, we were discovering beautiful spots around the hometown regaining our sense of freedom.

I also realized that at that particular time the social scientist in me was hardly able to apply a critical approach when analyzing the work of new volunteer centres. I could not see myself coldly looking for the errors in the actions of people who do important work for the community, putting their health and even lives in danger. Fortunately, I had not much so far to be critical about. Based on the mobilization approach, the response to the situation was quick, and it seems to be quite effective under the emergency circumstances.

Now we are in the second and seemingly a worse wave of the pandemic. I hope that with more experiences and information, I will be able to focus on gaps, or, rather, lessons of the pandemic for NGOs and voluntary movements in my town and region – I see it as my task as a social researcher. But for now, I am only proud of these people and grateful to them for making the game of the wild card of the pandemic less wild for everyone in our town

Vigdis' story: Coping with COVID-19 from a Northern Norwegian small town

Looking back at 9 months that changed much in most people's daily life, I want to focus on all the things that I was fortunate to be able to complete because I am lucky to live in a small Northern town. Living far away from big cities and COVID-19 hotspots took me through the first months of the pandemic with only minor adaptions. Governmental decision to close schools and businesses seemed at that time as an overreaction as we had a very small number of infected persons in our region, and it was under control. Some of our municipalities tried to limit people from the south, as well as migrant workers, to enter the Northern regions, introducing travel quarantine. This gave our medical service time to build up capacity for testing and treatment.

I was fortunate, and still am, able to go to my office every day, as I have a small number of colleagues, spacious office premises, and not dependent on using public transport. My walking distance from home is only 20 minutes, and the stroll is good for clearing the head. I was able to continue working with my research projects, but now with zero travels. This gave me something to think about, as most projects could easily go on in the new mood of Teams and Zoom meetings, interviews, webinars instead of live presentations of research results. Our cooperation project with Russian researchers was an exception as everything had to

Overcoming isolation in the Arctic during COVID-19 149

be reorganized due to the restrictions in travels. Our new way of communicating through zoom gave us a channel for discussing project related and personal experiences with the pandemic. From my safe office I could follow the alarming development of increasing COVID-19 numbers just across the closed border and worried about my dear research colleagues, some I have known for 25 years. Through their experience of being confined at home offices and observing the alarming situation in their home city, I got an opportunity to reflect on how this pandemic takes different routes and how the role of governmental, regional and local authorities dealing with the pandemic differs in our two countries. Do we trust our authorities, and how do we as citizens react on their restrictions and solutions?

Summer came, and the governmental restrictions were lifted here in Norway. My teenager went back to school for a few weeks before the holidays started, businesses resumed and we were able to go on holiday, this time only within Norway. I made several hiking trips in my own region and managed to go south to celebrate my mother's 80th birthday with the rest of the family. I even succeeded to convince my teenagers that their presence was needed in these trouble times. We knew little when we could see our old family members in the risk group the next time. My mom was taken care of by other family members, but did she fully understand the need of taking precautions when moving around in the shopping mall? She kept saying "I have not heard about anyone with the virus here, I have not noticed it at all". From the media I knew that her neighbourhood has high numbers of infected persons.

Autumn came and the second COVID-19 wave hit Norway, this time not only affecting the bigger cities but also smaller communities in the North. In our small town, it first became evident to us when our regional hospital in the neighbouring city experienced infections among employees and patients. By the end of October 2020, our local infection rate increased, involving a new group of young people. Private parties were the place for transmitting the virus, and now the municipal authorities had to take tough actions towards social distancing. This coincided with the governmental pledge of two weeks of "low key activity", very close to lock down. By doing this we hope to stabilize the situation for the Christmas festivities our Prime minister said. In my northern small town upper secondary school were again closed. Now my worries switched to my teenager, back to home school and not able to meet friends. I can't stop thinking about our youth that lose out on important formative years of education and social contact, need to develop new friendships, find themselves. Hold on, keep distance!

Svetlana's story: Welcome to the pandemic era? Bearing the new reality

Now that the widely predicted but still unexpected the second wave of COVID-19 has arrived, we have to admit that we are living in a different world, so welcome to the pandemic era. Looking back to the beginning of spring 2020, I am trying to understand how quickly this new reality has become a norm? or has it not?

150   *Rita Sørly, Bård Kårtveit, Vigdis Nygaard, et al.*

The new 2020 has started quite well, we had a lot of snow and good expectations (however, as every New year). By February 2020, some mentions of the new viral infection appeared, which seemed to be more serious than the usual flu. But it used to happen before, therefore I did not feel anything special. I was looking forward for the new project with the Norwegian colleagues, began as usual some practical arrangements for my summer. But not this time! As it said – if you want to make the God laugh, tell him about your plans. The news became more alarming, but still everything was happening somewhere, "not in my backyard". As a first bothering call the project kick-off seminar was cancelled and we had first project online meeting. And yet – it was a turning point, from that day (when the Russian project team was sharing the same room) until today (March 2021) I have not meet in person with one member of our team. In a week the first case was detected in our city. And this was the first change in the daily routines – instead of looking at the weather forecast, I began my mornings with studying pandemic statistics in my city, region, Russia and world.

The word "quarantine" started being heard more often, but quarantine was not officially introduced in Russia. On March 25, 2020, President V. Putin announced the "non-working days" – a new term in our everyday life – they were extended twice more and in general amounted to a month and a half. Some other terms easily entered our vocabulary and became habitant such as "isolation", "self-isolation" and "observation. Then changes came to our daily life, changing its quality. The ski resort (the main attraction of our cities for the winter season) stopped working on March 26, 2020. In early April 2020, at the entrance to the city a gate appeared, allowing only officially registered residents of Kirovsk and Apatity to enter the city. We were instructed to leave home as little as possible; masks and gloves became mandatory attributes. Swimming pools and public sport facilities were closed. Additional vacations were announced for school pupils, then classes were transferred to a remote mode, and from May 12, 2020 (half a month earlier than usual) the summer holidays started.

During the first 2 months, I really followed recommendations and one more new term – «COVID dissident» – did not come to me. From our first Zoom meeting, we decided to shift the project attention to the Russian COVID-19 volunteers. Considering NGOs as the familiar and trustable source of information I conducted brief phone interviews with representatives of four NGOs. The main idea was to find out; have NGOs been asked by the local authorities to disseminate reliable information and/or offered help. Our research revealed that along with the old NGO structures such as the Red Cross new volunteer centres appeared through the organized in the whole country subdivisions of the All-Russia People's Front and the connections of regional and local authorities with this political institute. At the same time, NGOs were not contacted by regional and municipal authorities neither for help nor with an offer of assistance.

Thus, after two months from the beginning of the pandemic, everything seemed to be as usual: I worked, although from home, I communicated with my colleagues, although via phone and Zoom, I was shopping, although once a week, wearing a mask and gloves (but even before the pandemic I did not shop more often). And nevertheless, I felt locked up and it was not a nice thing to feel. The "locked up" feeling intensified by the spring end as for me summer has always been associated with travelling – for many years. I used to leave home in May and coming back in September. In addition, when I got sick (not COVID-19), I fully felt that the healthcare system was so busy with the pandemic that it had no time for other patients. By the end of May, 2020, despite my living in the same city, there was a somewhat strange feeling that it was a somehow different place. I believe it was my personal crisis in experiencing a pandemic. From the mid of June, 2020 after summer arrived, I started getting better.

Does this mean that this new reality became the "norm" for me? I do not know. Am I accustomed to the fact that I cannot work the way I would like, go where I would like to, hug my dear people (even if they are in the same city as me)? Of course not. Am I willing to accept this new reality, given my sense of responsibility and the value of life? It seems that, yes. Do I hope that this new reality will someday end? Oh, yes, of course. Do I believe that this new reality will really end? I'm afraid, no …

Bård's story: Striving for normalcy

In mid-March, 2020, my Norwegian colleagues and I were planning a trip to meet our Russian colleagues in Murmansk. In late February, Denmark, Norway and Sweden had all recorded their first Corona cases. Even as the virus was getting closer, it still felt like a distant treat. In early March, 2020, however, as the number of confirmed COVID cases in Norway started rising, it became clear that this would affect our lives more profoundly than we imagined just weeks earlier. On March 11, 2020, my Norwegian colleagues and I assessed the situation and decided we had no choice but to cancel the trip. The following day, Norway was shut down. All schools and kindergartens were closed, and people were told to work from home if possible. The following weeks were chaotic. Everything was shut down. I was stuck at home in Oslo, with two restless kids in the house, and nowhere to hide and get some work done. I heard of friends and neighbours who were let go from their jobs, and everything that had seemed stable and solid a week earlier were on shaky grounds.

On March 18, 2020, the project team met for a Zoom-chat and talked about how to proceed with our project. We decided that the pandemic itself and people's adaptations to it would have to be a central part of it. Through the following months, we received updates from our Russian colleagues on the COVID situation in Murmansk. These updates served as a reminder of the relative ease of COVID restrictions in Norway. In Murmansk, society was locked down, schools, kindergartens and non-essential businesses were shut down. At home, once schools were reopened in late April, 2020, we could return to some kind of normalcy, though with some restrictions on social interaction still in place. While schools were closed, and people were stuck at home with their whole families, hiking and other outdoor activities became an important part of their everyday coping strategies. The timing of the lockdown coincided with the start of spring, and a period blessed with nice weather and rising temperatures.

152   *Rita Sørly, Bård Kårtveit, Vigdis Nygaard, et al.*

During the summer, infection rates were low, and social restrictions as well as norms of social distancing gradually loosened. After the summer, the pandemic returned in full force. Rules of social distancing have been upheld, and restrictions on travel, on businesses, on cafes, restaurants and on all kinds of public events have changed almost weekly. This time, the restrictions are much harder to adjust to. People are COVID fatigued, and restrictions on the use of public transportation, home visits and all indoor socializing are more difficult to uphold when it gets darker and colder each day, than during a breezy spring. Overall, the pandemic eliminated all the good things about living in a city – cafés, entertainment, social diversity and having good friends and neighbours nearby – and highlighted the downsides – cramped apartments, big crowds everywhere and being surrounded by urban landscapes rather than nature. For me, the end of 2020 is about coping with a partial lockdown, while trying to create a more or less normal everyday life for my kids. This involves celebrating Christmas at home – without visiting old and frail family members – and preparing for a winter in partial lockdown. News of a vaccine on the horizon will make it easier to hunker down for a few more months.

Ludmila's story: Life experiences during the pandemic

In January the new year of 2020 seemed full of nice expectations. I had a long list of planned travels for the whole year. Number one in the list was the first meeting of the Russian-Norwegian research team in Murmansk to start up the VOLRUSS project. However, the project start coincided with the restrictions introduced due to the pandemic, and we did not meet. My list of cancelled trips is still there, on the desk in my office. The situation developed fast, bringing new strange life (work at home, no meetings, closed public places, only quick shopping for foodstuffs in masks and rubber gloves, with long lists of items to be bought at once in order to limit visits to shops). Comprehension of the situation lagged behind the mechanical actions.

My 89-year-old mother got several phone calls from organizations helping vulnerable population groups. By the Victory Day on May 9, 2020, volunteers brought her a big set of foodstuffs from her former employer.

Gradually, we got used to the constrained life. We luckily had a good summer, with, of course, much of light here in the North. It was giving hopes for coming back to normal. Telephone became the basic communication means, lots of telephone talks every day, exchange of funny stories, pictures and videos. Also E-mail, Skype, mastering Zoom. Every day at 11 a.m. information on the number of infected is updated. I check it even before checking E-mail. It is a new habit already. Also, we have got other new habits: making sure that a mask is available before going outdoors, keeping distance from other people. Strange, but time goes surprisingly fast, lots of work. All days are the same. Meanwhile winter is coming, and it is getting darker. And stress continues, first of all because of the uncertainty and unpredictability of the future. Will it ever stop? Shall we be the same people as we used to? Difficult to answer.

Anne Katrine's story: Finding the professional and private silver lining during isolation

On March 12, 2020, we were instructed to work from home, and schools nationwide were shut down. This was the day after Denmark implemented such strict protective measures, which was head-spinning. Surreal. My employer regularly informed COVID-19 protective measures, how to adjust, why and that whatever travel plans we had both professionally and privately had to be cancelled. The staff was told not to feel overwhelmed should our efficiency temporarily drop, and the company management went out if its way to be supportive.

While my employer's responsible take on the situation maintained my spirits, it was challenged on a private basis. My child's school and teachers did a tremendous job in setting up digital routines but school days became notably shorter, sports and culture activities were on hold and social interaction was to be kept at a minimum. In practice, after 13.00, I balanced keeping my child busy, while trying to deliver at work. Forced to pause contact with my elderly mother, the situation took an emotional toll on the three generations of us. A quote from my child during the first wave: "The worst thing with this stupid corona is that I cannot hug my own grandmother".

During the first pandemic wave, days got brighter while we had to face the longest and hardest winter in 25 years in Tromsø. During the second wave in the fall of 2020, days got darker towards winter. In between waves, we have seen authorities fluctuating between imposing strict regulations, and then being too lenient and optimistic, hesitant to implement mandatory measures, instead counting on people's and businesses' responsible actions. Only to be let down by many groups of people, and business, for example, a national landmark cruise operator, that somehow decided it was acceptable to let a crew member, sick with COVID-19, take a taxi to a local hospital, without notifying the taxi driver. Which was just one of several peculiarities deliberated upon by the cruise operator management. So, we got the second wave. With tougher protective measures, that to an increasing degree were being enforced when not complied with.

In between COVID-19 waves, VOLRUSS has been adjusted. Zoom replaced physical meetings, and the pandemic forced us to think differently. Field work no longer an option, we had to rethink and innovate our methodological approach.

There are silver linings to the situation. A general experience is the rather quick adjustment to use digital meeting platforms. It has forced us to think on our feet on how to rearrange a well-planned project such as VOLRUSS. This was possible partly because the researchers in Norway and Russia knew each other quite well from other projects. On a personal level, it has made me appreciate working relations even more, including the social interaction at work. It has made me appreciate how crisis management is real and important, and how important it is to be aware and prepared.

Rita's story: The smell of summer in Murmansk

This year has been an *annus horribilis*, to use the Latin phrase. The world got hit by a pandemic, and nobody could imagine the consequences this would bring to all of us. My professional life as a researcher became more complicated, working from home, our house filled with impatient and restless teenagers. As days went by, I started appreciating their loud voices and music more and more. Everything else felt so quiet. Cafes, schools, restaurants. All so quiet. No life in the streets. Quiet. Like I was standing by the sea, close to my childhood house, and all sounds from the outside was turned off. I could not listen to the news; I could not understand what was going on. As time went, I started walking long walks. I looked at neighbour houses, I looked at strangers – they had the same look in their eyes as I had in mine.

The citizens of my hometown gradually gained hope again as summer was getting close. The first wave of the pandemic calmed down, they said on Norwegian television. The grass was getting greener. Birds were singing in trees. The pandemic had forced us all to stop for a moment in time. Every one of us had to decide what to do with the moment we had been given from an unexpected disaster.

I thought of my Russian colleges in Apatity. I wondered how their summer looked. Do they have the same insects over there, the bees and the flies? Do flowers smell the same on the other side of the border? I have a Russian colleague and friend here in Tromsø. She is a very good storyteller, and I love her stories. She once told me that Russian fairytales are much more exciting than Scandinavian fairytales. She says it's because in Russia they like to emphasize that life isn't simple; it is complicated and filled with both good and bad intentions. One story is never just *one* story. It is filled with many stories, many experiences. Doing the morally right thing is complicated, my friend Tatiana says, also in everyday life. We need to remember that. I agree with my friend. She told me the Russian version of Pinocchio, Burationo. She said; *you Scandinavians, you want everything to be so straight and simple, but the world is messy, chaotic and unpredictable*. It is. She is right. We don't know how long this second wave will last, and when we will be able to experience the smell of summer in Murmansk.

Reflections: Sharing stories, sharing knowledge – Practicing active reflexivity

These stories offer glimpses of how each of us experienced the abrupt changes brought about by the pandemic, to our personal lives, our communities and to our common project. Our stories contain different spatial, temporal, affective, sensory and cognitive experiences. Our stories can be said to be in continuous flux, processual and intertwined: they include elements of (1) suddenness and surprise, (2) experiences of the unexpected, (3) social action and interaction and (4) affect, emotion and empathy (Turunen et al., 2020). We all share similar experiences and challenges coping with the unpredictable in our common Arctic region. Performing autoethnography together is a dynamic and dialogical exercise, transgressing and exceeding traditional expectations of academic papers (Sørly, Karlsson, & Grant, 2019). When we started writing our stories, we had no idea that our experiences would be so similar. In that sense, we agree with Malkki (2008), that ethnographic research always contains an element of surprise. When we investigated our stories, we came to perceive their importance for understanding something new about stories of isolation; we were all moving our personal experiences towards a common research community, and in this way produce and share knowledge about the COVID-19 pandemic as a new social phenomenon.

We also reflected on the dissimilar actions of responsibility by authorities at local, regional and national levels in our two countries. All the stories move from suddenness and surprise to experiences of the unexpected. The social action and interaction are the writing process, which leads to affect, emotion and empathy. As we all sought to establish a common ground, through our stories, we realized that these experiences and the insights they brought, may change the way we look upon stories and knowledge. We have provided reflections about the ways in which suggested approaches and practices of co-writing help to reduce mental stress and doubts about the ability to conduct research during the crisis (buffering effect), maintain mental health and research interest despite the crisis (bolstering effect) and strengthens one's psychological resources and research capacities (building effect).

Our stories of overcoming COVID-19 isolation as family members, researchers and citizens expose and help us to understand issues of sustainability at several levels. At a personal level, in a time of isolation, sustainability means overcoming stress, depression and a sense of lost freedom, and developing a balanced healthy consciousness which can function in harmony with family members and other people. We shared our experiences of striving for sustainability at this level through communication with families, friends and nature, and by focusing on things that we can complete.

We found that at the level of a research project, when it is threatened by a pandemic, sustainability means maintaining working relationships with fellow researchers, continuing research work in feasibly possible ways and developing, in a creative manner, novel ways of doing research both across newly emerged geographical borders and across new ones that have emerged as a result of the pandemic.

The insights as articulated through our poly ethnographic exercise and the reflexive act of telling stories show that sustainability at this level could emerge from interpersonal working connections, involvement in a common group and research community.

Sustainability at a societal level means that we need to enable the proper functioning of social-economic structures by making them work in balance with people's needs. Within our project, we look for better understanding of how in the Russian–Norwegian Arctic local communities' socio-economic and public health needs are approached under changing legal, political, and social circumstances. We hope that our research results, including insights from this paper, will help to navigate a way towards positive societal outcomes in terms of developing a coordinated policy response widely involving non-governmental structures. Such policies at local, regional and national levels, with more focus on the balance of centralized versus decentralized approaches to societal management, can help to mitigate negative effects of the pandemic crisis and strengthen protection of the most vulnerable social groups beyond this crisis, paving the way for greater sustainability in our common Arctic region.

156 *Rita Sørly, Bård Kårtveit, Vigdis Nygaard, et al.*

References

Aure, M. (2019). Hit by a stroke: An autoethnographic Analysis of intergenerational care across geographical distances. In P. Naskali, J. Harbison & S. Begum (Eds.), New challenges to ageing in the rural North. International perspectives on aging, vol 22 (pp. 147–157). Cham: Springer. https://doi.org/10.1007/978-3-030-20603-1_9.

Bakhtin, M. M. (2010). *Speech genres and other late essays.* Austin: University of Texas Press.

Bakhtin, M. M., Holquist, M., & Emerson, C. (1981). *The dialogic imagination: Four essays.* Austin: University of Texas Press.

Brinkmann, S. (2017). Philosophies of qualitative research. New York, NY: Oxford University Press.

Karlsson, B., & Sørly, R. (2021). Medvirkningens etikk og refleksivitet. In R. Sørly, B. Karlsson, & T. Sjåfjell (Eds.), *Medvirkning i psykisk helse- og rusarbeid* (pp. 62–75). Oslo: Universitetsforlaget.

Laslett, B. (1999). Personal narratives as sociology. *Contemporary Sociology, 28*(4), 391–401.

Malkki, L. H. (2008). Tradition and improvisation in ethnographic field research. In A. Cerwonka and L. H. Malkki (Eds.) Improvising Theory (pp. 162–188). Chicago, IL: University of Chicago Press.

Olson, M. (2015). An auto-ethnographic study of "open dialogue": The illumination of snow. *Family process, 54*(4), 716–729.

Richardson, L. (2003). Writing: A method of inquiry. *Turning points in qualitative research: Tying knots in a handkerchief, 2,* 379.

Seikkula, J. (2008). Inner and outer voices in the present moment of family and network therapy. *Journal of Family Therapy, 30*(4), 478–491.

Spiller, K., Ball, K., Daniel, E., Dibb, S., Meadows, M., & Canhoto, A. (2015). Carnivalesque collaborations: Reflections on 'doing'multi-disciplinary research. *Qualitative Research, 15*(5), 551–567.

Svare, H. (2019). *Kunsten å skape dialog.* [The art of making Dialogue]. Available: https://psykologisk.no/2014/08/kunsten-a-skape-dialog/ [Accessed November 6 2020].

Sørly, R., Karlsson, B., & Grant, A. (2019). My Mother's skull is burning: A story of stories. *Qualitative Inquiry, 25*(9-10), 1011–1021.

Tanggaard, L. (2009). The research interview as a dialogical context for the production of social life and personal narratives. *Qualitative inquiry, 15*(9), 1498–1515.

Turunen, J., Čeginskas, V. L., Kaasik-Krogerus, S., Lähdesmäki, T., & Mäkinen, K. (2020). Poly-space : Creating new concepts through reflexive team ethnography. In T. Lähdesmäki, E. Koskinen-Koivisto, V. L. Čeginskas, & A.-K. Koistinen (Eds.), Challenges and Solutions in Ethnographic Research : Ethnography with a Twist (pp. 3–20). London: Routledge. https://doi.org/10.4324/9780429355608-1

9 Green colonialism

The story of wind power in Sápmi

Bård Kårtveit

Introduction

> Sápmi is not a candybag where dáža (Norwegians) can simply grab the resources they want!
>
> -Sámi politician during debate on the "green transition" in the Sámi Parliament, March 10, 2021.

Norway's national wealth relies heavily on extraction of oil and gas, which is exported mainly to the European Union and to the UK (Norwegian Petroleum, 2021). As Norway's oil reserves becomes an increasingly untenable, and finite source of income, a growing number of voices are calling for a green transition to reliance on clean, renewable sources of energy, such as hydro and wind power. While Norway has utilized hydro power for more than a hundred years, wind power been hailed in the last two decades as a new source of energy with great potential for expansion.

The call for a green transition is a part of a growing focus on sustainability in public policy. The term encompasses an environmental, economic and a social dimension, but in public usage, these terms are weighted against each other in different ways, allowing for the term to be used in support of widely different agendas (Gad, Jacobsen, & Strandsbjerg, 2018).

This is evident in disputes over wind power plants in Norway, which has grown in scope and intensity in the last few years (Gulbrandsen, Indreberg & Jevnaker, 2021, p. 1). Since the summer of 2019, there has been a nation-wide mobilization against the establishment of wind farms in wilderness areas throughout the country. In Arctic and mid-Norway, the building of wind power plants has been met with fierce resistance, especially from Sámi reindeer herders, who argue that their livelihood and way of life is threatened by the installment of wind turbines. New wind power plants are often justified with reference to sustainable development. At an international level, this refers to climate change mitigation. At a local level, this will refer to income from corporate and property taxes and possible employment opportunities in wind farm-hosting communities.

DOI: 10.4324/9781003118633-10

158 Bård Kårtveit

In conflicts over the use of land and natural resources, collective narratives can play an important part in justifying – or mobilizing resistance to particular land-use plans.

Political narratives

This article will look at local resistance towards wind power production in predominantly Sámi communities in Arctic Norway, with a special focus on the process around Davvi – a large-scale wind power project in the interior of Finnmark that has yet to be licensed by Norwegian Authorities. The Sámi is an Indigenous people with great internal linguistic and cultural diversity who populate areas that today are under Swedish, Norwegian, Russian and Finnish sovereignty. In each country, the Saami population has struggled to advance certain rights, while at the same time trying to challenge the continuity of colonial relationships and legacies (Lehtola, 2015). In doing so, they have applied different political narratives to make sense of the challenges they face, and their relations with the nations states in which they live.

Here I lean on Molly Andrews who define political narratives as *"stories people tell about how the world works, how they explain the engines of political change, and the role they see themselves, and those whom they regard as being part of their group, as playing in this ongoing struggle"* (Andrews, 2007, p. 8). In later writings she adds that *"the meaning of 'political narrative' is not limited to stories which are told or untold, lived, dreamed or imagined by individuals. Rather, it can also refer to a larger cluster of national stories, within which individuals position themselves, explicitly or otherwise"* (Andrews, 2014, p. 355)

These narratives are not just stories people tell themselves, but stories through which they position themselves in matters of dispute, and in relation to others. *"Through the use of political narratives, we tell our-selves and others who we are. These are the hardships we have endured; these are the principles for which we stand; these are rewards that we as a people have procured. Our group identity claims rest upon our stories"* (Andrews, 2014, p. 358).

In Norway, as well as in Sweden, Sámi leaders and activists have invoked the notion of green colonialism as a way of describing the intrusion of wind power plants in Sápmi (Fjellheim, 2020; Retter, 2021). At this juncture, I will argue that green colonialism serves as a political narrative, one that connects the particular struggles facing Sámi communities today with those of earlier times, and within a broader struggle for Sámi indigenous rights and ways of life. This paper will explore how different aspects of Sámi encounters with the wind power industry, and with Norwegian state authorities fit within a narrative of green colonialism, how this serves as a challenge to national and international discourses on sustainability and green transitions.

In different sites of dispute, a narrative of green colonialism offers a clear response to claims about wind power as a path to sustainable development. This is very much the case with reference to the Davvi-project.

In this paper, I will look at Sámi opposition to the Davvi Wind Farm, with a focus on the following Questions:

> What are the key components of a narrative of green colonialism, and how does this inform Sámi opposition to the Davvi-project?
> In what ways does a narrative of green colonialism offer a response to "pro-wind"- invocations of sustainability?

By looking at the narratives invoked, we can get a sense of kind of what kind of motives and modes of action are ascribed to agents of wind power production, and what Sámi activists view as the endgame in their struggle against particular wind power plants in Sápmi. This article is based on publicly available documentation from the various stakeholders involved, and from Norwegian authorities, monitoring of media coverage and online debates about wind power and other extractive industries operating in Sápmi, as well as debates on social media forums focusing on Sámi reindeer herding, indigenous rights, environmentalism and industrial development in the Arctic. In 2020, I attended two public conferences in Alta, one on economic developments in Sápmi and one on the incursion of the wind power industry in Sápmi. At these conferences, I listened to presentations and the discussions that followed, and talked to members of different Sámi organizations, political parties, herders, environmentalists and others who represented a broad range of opposition to wind power projects in different parts of Sápmi. In the aftermath of the last conference, I contacted individuals who had engaged with the Davvi wind power project in particular and conducted extensive interviews with two Sámi activists mobilizing against Davvi, one representative of a local herding district, one Sámi nature conservationists, and one prominent politician in the Sámi Parliament. Those who were interviewed for the project were given information letters explaining the purpose of the project, and a letter of content which was signed prior to the interviews taking place. Each of the interviews took 1–2 hours, and they were all digitally recorded. The Sámi activists and the politician were interviewed twice.

The story of wind power in Norway

Before diving further into the Davvi-project, we should add a few words about the wind power industry in Norway. As in the rest of Europe, wind power has been hailed as a vital part of a green transition away from carbon emitting energy production towards clean energy. Norwegian authorities started facilitating the construction of wind farms in the late 1990s. In Norway, the introduction of wind power can be separated into three phases:

> The start-up phase, 1998–2008. Norwegian authorities start facilitating the construction of wind farms, with a focus on technology development, support for embryonic technology, and the establishment of a regulatory systems for the construction of wind farms.

160   *Bård Kårtveit*

The red-carpet phase, 2008–2018. Norwegian authorities commit to international goals on climate change mitigation and renewable energy production, identifying wind power production as central to this commitment. Through state subsidies and smooth licensing processes, efforts are made to attract private wind energy investments on Norwegian soil. As a result, several licenses for wind farms along the whole Norwegian coastline are granted.

The blowback phase, 2018–present. A national strategy document on wind power is released by the Norwegian Water Resource and Energy Directorate (NVE), faces massive popular resistance, and is withdrawn after a few months of turbulence. The licensing process for wind farms is revised, and wind farms under construction are met with growing popular protests throughout the country

(Vasstrøm & Lysgård, 2020).

Norwegian authorities have referred to the need for climate change mitigation, secure and stable access to energy and a green transition in their efforts to sell wind farm construction in Norway. The main normative case for wind power in Norway is that the country has a lot of uninhabited land and that wind power production can help the country dramatically reduce its carbon emissions, power emerging green industries in Norway and provide the European market with clean energy as well (Olje og energidepartementet, 2020). Commercial actors who wish to build wind farms also emphasize employment opportunities and investments in local industries as a means of gaining local support. Wind power has been hailed as a new industrial adventure for Norway – both on land, and off-shore, once the technology allows for it. Wind power enthusiast have argued that wind power – in combination with hydropower - may fulfil all of Norway's national energy needs and allow Norway to become a net exporter of green energy to continental Europe. Following state initiatives to power off-shore oil platforms with land-based electricity, the pressure to expand Norway's capacity for the production of renewable energy – including wind power – is likely to grow in strength.

As of March, 2021, 1164 wind turbines had been installed in 53 wind power plants throughout Norway. These turbines offer a total production of 13,65 TWh (NVE, 2021), and more power plant are being built. Permits have been granted for the building of 32 new wind power plants, while applications for another 17 are currently being processed (Ibid). A pattern has emerged whereby small, often local companies initiate the licensing process for wind power projects, obtain the rights to build wind power parks and then sell those rights to big, transnational investment funds (Hovland, 2020).

Opponents against wind farm projects tend to argue that these projects are permitted in spite of local opposition, thatwind turbines kill both plants and animals, damage the biological diversity of their surroundings and have a devastating effect on reindeer herding, in addition to ruining dramatic and visually stunning landscapes (Omholt, 2020).

Green colonialism   161

In the last few years, several large-scale wind power projects, such as Haramsøy and Tysvær, on the West Coast of Norway have mobilized fierce local opposition (Staupe-Delgado & Coombes, 2020). The construction of vast industrial installments in spectacular mountain landscapes offend Norwegians affection for, and conceptions of wild, pure and unspoiled nature, and of wilderness areas where one can retreat and recharge (Brattbakken 2014, p. 26–27; Omholt, 2020, p. 43–45).

When wind power plants are built on ancestral Sámi land, this adds an indigenous dimension, and brings the issue of environmental justice to the center (Normann, 2020). This has been the case with Fosen and Øyfjellet, two areas in mid-Norway where the building of wind power parks have attracted national attention and fueled broad popular resistance. These areas are of crucial importance to local reindeer herding districts, and it is widely agreed that the installment of turbines in these areas will have a devastating effect on local reindeer herding practices (Fjellheim, Carl, & Normann, 2020).

At Øyfjellet, the building of a large wind power plant stretching over vast wilderness areas will deprive local reindeer herders of vital winter pastures for their reindeer, making them dependent on feeding to make it through the winter (Fjellheim, 2020). In April 2020, wind energy company Eolus Vind broke ground for Øyfjellet wind plant. Oyfjellet wind project is owned by Aquila Capital, a German company. Before building the wind farm, they have already made a lucrative deal to supply power produced by the wind plant to a nearby aluminium smelter (Fjellheim, Carl, & Normann, 2020). According to the project website, the developers seek to "promote growth, green industry and green employment through long-term investment in renewable energy"(Øyfjellet, 2021). At Fosen, recognition of the devastating effect wind farms at Fosen will have on local reindeer herding, a regional court has sentenced Fosen Vind to pay local herders 90 million NOK in compensation for their loss of vital winter pastures. In response to this verdict, the Norwegian government attorney has decided to support the wind power company, legally and financially, in their efforts to appeal the compensation claim.

At Øyfjellet, the construction of a wind power plant started in the spring of 2020, while an appeal from a local herding district was still being processed in the court system. After taking the wind power company to court, local herders were been saddled with paying the wind power company's legal expenses of 1.7 million Norwegian Kroner. When finalized, the wind power plant at Øyfjellet is feared to have a crippling impact on reindeer husbandry in the region (Valio, Eira & Granefjell, 2019). In both these cases, Norwegian state authorities are widely perceived as siding with the wind power companies against Sámi reindeer herders.

The wind industry has also turned its attention to Finnmark, the most northern and sparsely populated part of Troms and Finnmark, the only fully Arctic county in Norway. Finnmark is roughly the size of Denmark but has a population of roughly 75 000 people. A few smaller Wind farms have been built in mountain areas near the northern coast, primarily by regional energy companies in close dialogue with local authorities.

Davvi Wind Farm

Grenselandet AS, a company headquartered in Harstad, and owned by one Finish and two Norwegian energy companies, has introduced plans to build Davvi Wind Farm, the largest wind power plant in Northern Europe in the interior of Finnmark, in a large wildlife area just north of the mountain of Rásttigáisá. According to their website, the projects objective is "to realize some of the potential for clean energy production in one of Europe's most promising areas for wind power". Further on, they stress that "wind power is central to the task of developing sustainable energy sources for the future" and that "The climate crisis has highlighted the need to reduce our consumption of fossil fuels, such as oil, coal and gas". Wind power is presented as the obvious and necessary answer to this challenge.

The pure scale of the plans for Davvi Wind Farm are quite staggering (Figure 9.1). The plans involve the building of up to 231 turbines at the height 116 meters. With blades the length of 58 meters, the full construction of each turbine will tower 175 meter above the ground (Grenselandet AS, 2019, pp. 24–25). These will be spread out across an area covering, 775,000 m^2 – centred around Vuonjalrášša just north of Rásttigáisá, a mountain considered sacred within the Sámi community. For installation, use and maintenance of the turbines, the wind farm will require the building of 120 km. of road through wilderness areas that contain no other human infrastructure (Eira, Blom, & Eira, 2017).

As of today, the area in which the wind park will be placed constitutes the second largest wildlife area in Norway, is home to a diverse fauna and animal life and cultural remains from human settlements dating back thousands of years (Henriksen, 2008). Most dramatically, areas around the planned site of the wind farm are used as fall and winter pasture for District 13, one of the largest herding districts in Finnmark. If the wind park is built, herders fear that

Figure 9.1 Imagined view of Davvi Wind Farm as seen from Rásttigáisá.

Source: Kjetil Mork, Multiconsult Norge AS

reindeer from District 13 will lose vital pastures, be forced into neighbouring districts, mix with other herds, graze on pastures with limited carrying capacity and overturning the delicate ecological balance that the division of pastures is based upon (Eira, Blom, & Eira, 2017, pp. 57–59). The construction of Davvi Wind Park also depends on the installment of a new 420 kW power grid which is now set to be built across the plains between the Western and Eastern part of Finnmark.

If built, Davvi will affect a large area that is used by herders, hunters and fishermen, outfield harvesters, hikers and others from five different municipalities, Karasjok, Tana, Lebesby and Porsanger in Norway, and Utsjok, a predominantly Sámi municipality across the border in Finland. However, according to the most recent plans (Olsen, 2020), the turbines will all be built on land belonging to Lebesby, a sparsely populated municipality, whose population is concentrated mainly along the coast a considerable distance further north, and largely out of sight from the planned wind farm. As such, as the sole host of the wind farm, Lebesby municipality may have a decisive say in the licensing process and stand to reap great benefits in the form of a hefty property tax of at least 43 million NOK a year (Mork et al., 2019, 5). At the same time, three of the four neighbouring municipalities have population centres closer to the planned industrial zone and, as such, will be affected by the planned wind farm in more significant ways. As part of the process of obtaining a building permit from the Norwegian Water Resource and Energy Directorate (NVE), Grenselandet AS has ordered several environmental impact assessment (EIA) reports from different scientific and consulting specialists to fulfil the obligations of EIA studies. These reports assess the potential damage to the area's natural environment to be "somewhat negative" (Rannestad, Ryvarden, & Flydal, 2019, pp. 6–7), the loss of valuable natural resources, the noise and pollution caused by the building of the wind farm, including connecting roads, to be limited (Mork, Flatlandsmo, Undem, & emet-Jon, 2019, pp. 3–6). These findings are disputed by those who oppose the Davvi project, who argue that the loss of natural diversity, and the effects in the area at large are far more dramatic. Furthermore, consultants hired by one of the local herding districts have concluded that a wind farm in this area will have a devastating effect on local reindeer herding (Eira, Blom, & Eira, 2017, p. 58). Grenselandet filed for a permission to build in December 2019. As of May 2021, the Norwegian government is working on new procedures for the system through which applications for new wind power projects are evaluated. Until a new system is in place, all new wind power projects are put on hold.

Wind power companies such as Grenselandet AS present a largely uniform story: Wind power production can replace oil as a source of energy and income and enable Norway to rely on clean, renewable energy alone. Wind power production is a vital part of a green transition that will help mitigate devastating climate changes. When establishing wind farms, this is done with sensitivity to local concerns, in dialogue with local and indigenous communities, often bringing much needed income and job opportunities to these same communities.

164   *Bård Kårtveit*

A political narrative of green colonialism

Among opponents of different wind farm projects, there are different stories about their effects, and about the methods used by wind farm developers, but one dominant narrative has come to frame the opposition to wind power within the Sámi community: a narrative of green colonialism. This concept reflects a broader experience within the Sámi community. In the current context, green colonialism incapsulates the different stories and points of contention highlighted by opponents of wind power plants in Sápmi.

A narrative of green colonialism has been most powerfully invoked by Aili Keskitalo, the newly retired President of the Sámi Parliament in Norway. In a number of public statements, she has used the term to describe the process whereby wind power companies are permitted to build on land Sámi herding land, at the cost of Sámi reindeer herders. In an interview with the International Journal *Skylark*, she offers a historical backdrop for its usage:

> It makes me so sad to see all these plans for building wind power plants on our homeland. The government tells us "oh, but you have to provide the solutions for climate change". But we already gave land because of energy production. Many wind power plants have already been built or are planned to be built upon Sámi reindeer herding areas. And we have earlier been forced to give up land to hydroelectric power plants. In fact, one of the greatest political conflicts between the Norwegian government and the Sámi people was because of the Alta Dam. We have already given up land to save Norway's energy needs so it has to stop, it cannot go on forever. We will be eradicated... It's a bitter fact that it's done in the name of the environment, but I have no other word for it than green colonialism because it is colonialism. It's the same thing over again. It's the same thing they did before and now they're doing it again but they're changing the rhetoric. They say it's because the world needs green power but we have no more land to give and I do not believe the wind power industry is as green as it's claimed
>
> (Keskitalo quoted in Skylark, 2020).

Within the framing of green colonialism, the building of wind power plants on herding land is placed in a long line of land grabs sanctioned by Norwegian authorities, justified with reference to modernization and economic development. She references the conflict around the Alta Dam, a controversial hydro power project that involved the flooding of a nature reserve of great importance to the Sámi community. The Dam project mobilized a powerful alliance of environmentalists and Sámi activists, who staged mass protests at the site itself, including protesters chaining themselves to installations, as well as in the capital in front of the National Assembly. The protests win international attention and broad national support, but failed to stop the project; the Alta Dam was built.

Nonetheless, the Alta Dam controversy became a turning point in the Sámi struggle for cultural recognition and indigenous rights. While the protesters failed to stop the project, the Alta Dam protests remain a powerful symbol of Sámi self-assertion, of the fight for indigenous right and an example of fruitful alliance-building between indigenous Sámi activists and environmentalists.

By referencing the Alta Dam, Keskitalo places the building of wind power plants on herding land within a long line of territorial violations for the sake of resource extraction on Sámi land.

The concept of green colonialism har struck a chord among Sámi and non-Sámi opponents to wind power plants. In the case of the Davvi project, a narrative of green colonialism encapsulates the different themes of local resistance to the project.

Among these themes are environmental justice, asymmetrical power relations, destruction of indigenous livelihoods, environmental destruction, the desecration of sacred places and a Sámi cultural heritage and the link between the Davvi project and earlier extractions of Sámi land and resources.

Environmental injustice

The concept of environmental justice is high on the agenda within the Sámi communities of Norway, Sweden and Finland. It refers to the notion of an equitable sharing of environmental burdens and benefits through fair treatment and substantial treatment of the people involved. A focus on environmental justice has grown out of processes that has led to an uneven distribution of costs and benefits from the extraction of resources, especially in the global south, and often at the cost of indigenous communities (Schlosberg, 2004, 2013). This has been the experience within the Sámi communities as well.

With the building of wind power plants, Sámi communities are asked to accept a high price for the sake of climate change mitigation. To most Sámi activist, this claim feels deeply unjust.

> We want to take care of the climate as well. But we are already suffering a double burden. We have already had to give up a lot of land for the building of hydro power plants, electric cables and other wind power plants. In addition, we are already feeling the effects of climate change on our plains. Finding good pastures throughout the year is getting harder. And we're not the ones who have caused this! And yet now, the wind power people are coming here, telling us we have to contribute and give up our land to saving the climate". We have already given up too much!
>
> (- Sámi Activist, Lebesby.)

This is the argument Sámi activists get most riled up about. In their view, Non-Sámi Norwegians simply don't have the moral authority to demand more painful sacrificed from the Sámi in the name of climate change mitigation, especially considering their own management of natural resources and the environment. For the most part, they believe wind power developers are driven more by greed than by climate-based motivations. Furthermore, many of them question the

166 *Bård Kårtveit*

value of building wind power plants in wilderness areas as a climate change mitigating effort.

Indigenous rights, informed consent and the trappings of "dialogue"

Norway was the first country in the world to ratify the International Labour Organization's (ILO) convention 169 in 1990. ILO 169 provides indigenous groups with the right to Free, Prior and Informed Consent (FPIC). This allows them to give or withhold consent to a project that may affect them or their territories (Hanna & Vanclay, 2013).

There are disagreements over the extent of influence Sámi communities should have regarding final decisions on projects they oppose within their own core areas. But at the very least, they are to be involved in the decision-making process.

In Norway, this is achieved through formal consultations, and through "dialogue" between reindeer herders and developers. According to Sámi activists, these consultations are often a sham, a process by which reindeer herders enter with no chance of influencing the project itself. The concept of a "dialogue" serves to conceal the vast asymmetry in power and resources between industrial developers and local Sámi herders and to create an impression that they have been included in the decision-making process.

> It's a theatre. A farce. The leaders of the company have been making "coffee-chat visits", stopping by stores in various places, swinging by for a few hours before heading on. It's all been very sudden, and poorly advertised, so that no one who are engaged could have the time to prepare, or make it there in time to engage them. I don't know why they do this. I guess it just to be able to say they've engaged with and listened to the locals. They've also tries to engage in "consultations" with the reindeer herders, but they've been skeptical. What's the use? Consultations are just a formality, a meeting where developers can present their plans, and where the herders can accept or object, it doesn't make a different. But if you've showed up, they can say they've engaged in a dialogue.
>
> (- Local activist in Tana)

Others refer to direct consultations between herders and developers as a "dialogue trap". As explained by a prominent member of the Sámi parliament, this can take different form.

> If they (reindeer herders) agree to meet with wind power developers, and are presented with the plans, they can make their objections, but those will be ignored. And once you've met with them, the developers can say that they've engaged in a dialogue with you and tried but failed to reach a shared understanding.
>
> (- Prominent member of the Sámi Parliament)

Green colonialism   167

If you meet with developer, the contents of those meetings can also be misrepresented by the developers involved. The same Sámi MP refers to a case in which members of a herding districts were presented with plans to build wind turbines on one out of two mountains these herders used for winter pasture. When objecting that turbines of any of those mountains would be devastating to them, they were told that there would be turbines on one of them, and that it would be in their own interest to tell which of the two mountains was of most vital importance to them. After identifying which mountain was most essential to them, the developers obtained a license to build turbines on the other mountain, arguing that the herders had now accepted this. A forced choice between two unacceptable scenarios was then framed as an acceptance of the developer's plans.

Based on such experiences, herders and other stakeholders in Finnmark are skeptical of engaging in anything that can be presented as a dialogue with the Davvi project developers. Most problematic, the concept of dialogue serve to paper over the vast asymmetry in relations between local stakeholder and developers in terms of power and resources at their disposal. The concept of dialogue indicates a meeting taking place on a level playing field. In general, Sámi activists engaging with industrial agents in their home areas rarely find themselves operating on a level playing field.

Destruction of indigenous livelihoods

The most well-known point of objection to the Davvi Wind Farm-project related to its impact on reindeer husbandry. The area in which they wish to build the wind farm is winter pasture, spring and calving land for District 13 and contain vital migratory routes for neighbouring districts.

Reindeer husbandry is a traditional source of livelihood and a way of life within the Sámi community. Reindeer husbandry employs more than 3000 people in Norway today, 2200 of these live in Finnmark. From a total of 250 000 reindeer in Norway, 185000 are in Finnmark (Landbruks og matdepartementet, 2019). As practiced within most herding districts, reindeer husbandry in Norway is characterized by semi-nomadic pastoralism – the animals move between different areas, as pasture is made available in different areas throughout the season. Most herding districts have their winter pastures in the interior and their spring/summer pastures in coastal areas. In some areas, this demands an intricate system of coordination between neighbouring herding districts.

Reindeer husbandry involves a careful management of reindeer herds within the constraints set by pastures and grazing conditions throughout the year. The primary condition for sustainable reindeer husbandry is access to pastures throughout the year. In Norway, there is no overview of how much pasture land has been lost to industrial projects, cabins, road construction and electric cables. Around 40% of Norway's land mass is used as pasture for reindeer. Most of these areas are arid areas unsuitable for agriculture. Reindeer husbandry employs around 3000 people in Norway today, 2200 of these live in Finnmark. From a total of 250 000 reindeer in Norway, 185000 are in Finnmark.

168   *Bård Kårtveit*

Wind power plants can block access to vital pastures, or disrupt the migration of reindeer, especially in the winter, when they are often weakened and at risk, especially pregnant mothers and newborn calves. Research has shown that the Saami's semi-domesticated reindeer avoid grazing in areas where they can see or hear wind turbines (Strand et al., 2017). The scale of this avoidance effect has been disputed, but recent studies indicate that reindeer avoid grazing within a radius of at least ten kilometers from wind turbines, far more than earlier estimated (Colman, Eftestøl, Tsegaye, Flydal, K., & Rannestad, 2020). Based on a report commissioned by herding district 13, the Davvi Wind Farm will have devastating consequences for reindeer herding in the area. Once completed, the wind farm, in combination with other territorial incursions, will have damaged 62% of District 13s herding land. The District will be forced to drastically reduce its herds, and large portion of its herders would have to find employment elsewhere. A lack of available winter pastures and migratory paths will also create difficulties for neighboring districts. The loss of jobs within reindeer herding and related fields will be significant (Protect Sápmi 2017, pp. 58–59). According to representatives for the district, Grenselandet AS, offered the district 133 million NOK (approximately 14 million Euro) for consenting to the Davvi-project, as compensation for the loss of herding land. Their rejection of the offer reflects their belief that this project cannot be reconciled with their own adaptation and way of life as reindeer herders in this region (Herding District 13, 2019).

From the perspective of reindeer herders, the Davvi project represents a form of colonial landgrab that has a long history in Sápmi, as in other areas settled by indigenous people. In pursuit of a valuable resource, external actors seek to deprive herders of vital winter pastures, a fundamental basis for their own indigenous way of live. The fact that the resource being pursued is wind energy rather that oil or minerals is of little help to the herders. If anything, this makes it worse, since wind power plants claim far more land than any other form of resource extraction.

Desecration of holy places

The area targeted for the building of Davvi Wind Farm is filled with areas regarded as sacred according to local Sámi traditions. The areas around Rásttigáisá mountain and south towards Levanjok by the Tana River are particularly rich in natural resources. The river is one of the most salmon-rich rivers in the world, and on the plains towards and around Rásttigáisá there used to be plenty of wild reindeer. In addition, the plains were rich in berries and other edibles. Early Sámi settlements, dating back more than 2000 years, lived of this combination of river salmon, wild reindeer and edibles that grew in the plains. As such, these areas became natural centers of settlement in the interior. Early Sámi settlers may have bestowed holiness to these areas due to their abundance in natural resources. With time, some of these areas became sites of animal sacrifice, a central ritual in traditional Sámi religion (Äikäs, 2015). The sites of such sacrifices and other rituals would be ascribed with a living essence of their own – one that ought to be respected and revered (Äikäs & Spangen, 2016). The areas between the Tana River and Vuonjalrášša as well as broader parts of the Laksefjord plains are filled with places regarded as holy, and the mountain of Rásttigáisá is regarded as the holiest mountain in traditional Sámi religion. In this region, these religious traditions are still kept alive in some quarters, and the notion of Rásttigáisá as a holy mountain holds broader resonance within the nearby Sámi communities. According to local activists, this has been dismissed as irrelevant by the wind farm developer.

> I tried to tell them about how the mountain, and the entire area is sacred to us, and what that means. They really couldn't care less. They don't even pretend to.
> -Local wind farm opponent, Karasjok.

The position of Rásttigáisá as a sacred mountain among the Sámi has gained little traction with local and regional authorities, according to another activists who feels ambivalent about raising the issue (Figure 9.2). There is some hesitation about raising and elaborating on the significance of this area in traditional Sámi religion with Norwegian authorities, especially considering how Sámi religion and religious practices has historically been treated. As one local activist put it:

> We shouldn't have to explain why or in what way this area is sacred to us. It should be enough to state that it is!

The wind farm developers disregard for the sacredness of the area at hand fits well into the story of a colonial endeavor. This resonates with a broader picture of

Figure 9.2 View to Rásttigáisá (1066 m above sea level), regarded by many Sámi as a sacred mountain.
Source: Frank M. Ingilæ.

170   *Bård Kårtveit*

the wind power industry as a largely external force that is encroaching on Sámi land, demonstrating only contempt for their way of life, their traditions and their cultural practices.

Environmental destruction

Finally, the Davvi project is seen as representing a destruction of natural wildlife areas on a scale not seen in Norway before. The area in question constitutes the second largest contiguous wildlife area in Norway. Though large parts of the area consist of barren rock, it also contains a distinctive fauna and animal life, with some species that are barely found elsewhere. In this area, the erection of 231 wind turbines at the height of 116 meters will require the carving out of large mountain areas, the removal of any vegetation in the areas where the turbines will be installed and the building of more than 100 kilometres of roads suitable for heavy trucks, to facilitate the transportation and erection of turbines. The scale of destruction to be brought down on an almost untouched natural reserve is difficult to imagine. In order to make this relatable, Sámi activists turn to their most familiar point of reference, the Alta Dam. Based on currently available plans for the Davvi Wind Farm, they argue that the project will cause the destruction of wildlife areas at the scale of 22 Alta Dams.

Given the scale of this environmental destruction, opponents of the Davvi project also question its "green" credentials. Increasingly, they dispute its positive effects in terms of climate change mitigation, as well. In the words of one environmental activist:

> It is one thing to erect massive turbines in already industrialized areas in Denmark or Germany. It is quite another to transport those turbines by road to Arctic Norway, and build new roads and industrial infrastructure in order to erect turbines in vulnerable wildlife areas.
>
> - Nature conservationist – Porsanger.

The objection here is twofold. On the one hand, it is argued that the process of transporting turbines and equipment from continental Europe to the Northernmost tip of Norway, as well as building a wind farm in rugged wildlife terrain will require the release of more carbon emissions than the clean energy produced by the wind farm can ever make up for. And even if it did, this wind power production can never make up for the environmental destruction caused by the building of the wind farm. While climate change mitigation is on top of the international agenda, and a central part of the 2030 International Sustainability Goals, so is the protection of global biodiversity.

Green colonialism as a mobilizing narrative

These various issues of environmental injustice, the threat to indigenous ways of life, the deception of dialogue, the desecration of holy places and environmental

Green colonialism 171

destruction, all add up to a broader picture of a colonial project. A narrative of green colonialism also places these wind power plans within a historical trajectory of step-by-step encroachment on Sámi land.

A framework that places this project in a historical context could have a debilitating effect on local resistance. Many earlier projects involving the extraction of resources from Sápmi have been fiercely resisted among local Sámi, only to be pushed through in the end. The Alta Dam is the most famous one. Since then, however, several mineral extraction projects, power grids, roads, cabins, military installations, and most recently, wind farms have been built in Sápmi, against the will of Sámi communities, and at the cost of reindeer herders. Invoking this story of lost battles may invite defeatism rather than a fighting spirit. In this case, however, it appears to have a mobilizing effect. When rallying support for the battle against Davvi, activists invoke the enduring protests against the Alta Dam as a source of inspiration and an example to emulate. Present-day images from Fosen and Øyfjellet, two areas where turbines are currently being built on herding land, offer new reminders of the urgency of fighting against this new project.

The notion of green colonialism invokes an image of an enduring but righteous battle, one that has to be fought, and that will be won, eventually.

The colonial framing also invokes determination and sense of moral urgency to this battle. One activist from Karasjok, describes the stakes involved with reference to history of colonial dispossession.

> We have accepted a lot. The Alta Dam was built. Nussir is being built. Smaller wind power plants are installed many places. But this. this is the last straw. We can only accept so much from the colonial masters. If they go through with this, if they allow the developers to start building this wind farm, a lot of people who will simply not accept this, and we'll be forced to take drastic measures.

While some express despair at the very thought of this wind farm being built, others are driven by optimism, and a firm conviction that this is a battle they will win. One central activist from Tana pointed to several reasons for cautious optimism.

> There's a strong sense of local unity, and a shared understanding that this is something we don't want. This is different from other industrial disputes I've been involved in: The really massive opposition towards Davvi in all parts of our community, among all kinds of people. There are very few who are positive about this (Davvi). And I find that very inspiring. It gives me the energy to keep fighting. To know that you are firmly supported by a large part of the local population.
>
> – Seasoned Sámi activist based in Tana.

Within the local Sámi communities, this resistance has been strong since the plans for the Davvi project first got out. In 2017, during the first meeting between

172 Bård Kårtveit

local herder and a concerned citizens based around Sirma the municipality of Tana, many locals wore their *Gákti*, the traditional Sámi attire – inside out – a dramatic show of protest and discontent according to Sámi tradition. Since then, local Sámi resistance to Davvi has not subsided.

The value of good allies

Another source of optimism is that they're not alone in this battle. In recent years, they have won the support of several nation-wide environmentalist organizations in their struggles against wind power plants in reindeer herding areas. After seeing the environmental destruction caused by wind power industry in Fosen and at Øyfjellet, environmentalist organizations are mobilizing national support for their fights against the Davvi Wind Project in particular. The fight against Davvi has been picked up by Motvind – a new organization that fights against wind power plants in Norway altogether, the Norwegian Society for the conservation of nature (Naturvernforbundet), World Wildlife Foundation (WWF 2020) and Nature and Youth. These and other movements have organized conferences focusing specifically on wind power projects in Sápmi, with a strong focus on the Davvi-project. This means a lot to Sámi activists. One of the lasting lessons from the Alta Dam protest – where Sámi activists joined forces with environmentalist groups – was the value of broad alliances (Nilsen, 2020). Since then, the alliances between indigenous movements and environmentalists have proven powerful, not just in Norway but in other contexts where indigenous groups find their ancestral lands encroached on by industrial developers (Cappelli 2018; Pickerill, 2018; Toohey, 2012).

While placing themselves within an enduring battle against colonial dispossession, they feel that they are at a turning point that after losing some painful battles against the wind power industry in other parts of Sápmi, this is a battle they will win.

Conflicting notions of sustainability

When looking at the different points of objection to the Davvi project, and the process around it, it is easy to see how this can be experienced as a colonial project. However, something that also comes to the forefront in this conflict, and in other conflicts over industrial projects in Sápmi, is a tension between conflicting notions of sustainability. Across the Arctic, a discourse of sustainability is highly present in any efforts to pursue industrial projects, or government-run development programmes. Aspirations of resource extraction, economic development, innovation and social planning are defined in terms of sustainability. But so are local and Indigenous efforts to maintain a community or a particular way of life (Gad et al., 2018, p. 3). Throughout the region of Finnmark, everyone will support an overarching goal of having sustainable societies, but there are different conception of what are the core elements of a society that ought to be sustained, as well as how this can be best achieved. In Sámi communities, we find this tension in questions over how to preserve traditional industries and how to approach new economic opportunities.

Writing about Nussir AS, a controversial mining project in Kvalsund, Finnmark, Angell, Nygaard and Selle describe a rift within Sámi communities between a traditionalist and a modernist approach to industrial and economic development (Angell, Nygaard, & Selle 2020; Falch & Selle, 2018,). In crude terms, a traditionalist approach puts a premium on preserving traditional Sámi forms of adaptation such as reindeer herding, small-scale fjord fisheries and farming and protecting these from new industries keen on utilizing some of the same land and resources. By contrast, the modernist approach starts with the premise that Sámi communities cannot rely on traditional industries alone, but most be innovative and willing to embrace new economic opportunities, including partnering with large-scale industrial actors in order to survive and prosper (Angell, Nygaard & Selle, 2020, p. 49–50). This tension is also found in non-Sámi communities in Northern Norway, as well as in indigenous communities in other parts of the world (Falch & Selle, 2018).

These positions may be seen as representing different notions of sustainability as well. Within an ideal-type traditionalist perspective, traditional industries, especially reindeer herding and small-scale fisheries represent fundamentally sustainable forms of adaptations, a harvesting of natural resources adjusted to the ecological constraints of the area. These forms of adaptations also constitute core elements of a Sámi cultural heritage – things that define local Sámi communities. From this perspective, traditional industries, and reindeer herding in particular, must be preserved in order to sustain local Sámi communities and a Sámi cultural heritage.

From a modernist perspective, the sustainability of local Sámi communities may depend more on their capacity to offer work and economic opportunities for its members and attract or keep a sufficient number of young people from leaving – than its capacity to preserve traditional industries with limited or no growth potential. From this perspective, Sámi communities in Finnmark, with limited economic opportunities and a steady population decline, must adapt, innovate and embrace new economic opportunities in order to sustain themselves. This tension between traditionalist and modernist perspective is very much present in Sámi politics as well, with vocal advocates of both perspectives.

In this context, advocates of Davvi Wind Farm may present themselves as representatives of a "modernist" approach, fighting conservative forces bent on resisting new developments. Grenselandet AS, the company behind Davvi tries to appeal to this perspective within the Sámi community as well. In their application for a permit to build Davvi, they offer to set aside a sum of roughly 10 million NOK a year (approximately 1 million Euros), for a Sápmi innovation fund, to support Sámi start-up enterprises and innovation projects with job-creating potential in the heartland of Sápmi (Grenselandet AS, 2019, p. 4).

However, opponents of the Davvi project, both reindeer herders and non-herders, firmly reject this juxtaposition. While eager to preserve their livelihoods and way of life, herders stress their own willingness to adapt to changing circumstances, embrace new technologies, combine herding with other forms of work and engage with an ever more complex government bureaucracy, and an

174   *Bård Kårtveit*

international marked economy. Young Sámi activists who are not involved in reindeer herding are acutely aware of the need for more economic opportunities to stall the depletion of young, resourceful people from the region.

However, they have little faith that a massive wind power plant represents any opportunity for local communities. On the contrary, Davvi is seen as a threat to jobs, livelihoods and a way of life in reindeer herding, a threat to a quality of life defined by one's close proximity to the Arctic wilderness, a wilderness area that may, under the right circumstances, attract new residents to their local communities, as well as tourists to the region. If the Davvi Wind Farm is built, all of this will be lost. To them, Davvi does not represent an opportunity. It represents a reckless gamble with the future of the area, and with their own way of live. Their idea of a sustainable future for the Laksefjord Plains and for the local communities surrounding the area simply cannot be reconciled with the building of a large wind farm.

Conclusion

Forty years have passed since the main protests against the Alta Dam project. Back then, the Alta Dam was built against the will of local Sámi activists and herders, as well as passionate environmentalists, who were met with arguments about the growing need for power in Finnmark, and the promise of good local jobs at Alta hydropower plant (Nilsen, 2020).

Today's opponents against wind power plants in Sápmi face many of the same promises and arguments, and their responses to this are informed by four decades of territorial encroachments on Sámi herding land, and extraction of natural resources in Sápmi. Few of these encroachments have brought new jobs and opportunities to local Sámi communities.

The story of green colonialism serves as a political narrative among Sámi activists in that it helps describe "how the world works", what kind of forces they are up against, and what kind of role they see for themselves in ongoing struggles against industrial encroachments in Sápmi. Among those who work to prevent the realization of a Davvi Wind Farm, a narrative of green colonialism also offers firm responses to climate-based appeals, as well as promises of local jobs and economic opportunities. Among Sámi herders and activists, a narrative of green colonialism places wind power initiatives in Sápmi in a historical context, it serves to mobilize local resistance, and connect it with indigenous struggles in other parts of the world. Finally, it provides Sámi activists with a faith that this battle can be won. As the licensing process is tightening, and public opinion sours on wind farms in the Norwegian wilderness – their optimism may be justified.

References

Äikäs, T., & Spangen, M. (2016). New users and changing traditions – (Re) Defining sámi offering sites. *European Journal of Archeology*, 19(1), 95–112. doi: 10.1179/1461957115Y.0000000009

Green colonialism 175

Äikäs, T. (2015) From Boulders to Fells: Sacred Places in the Sami Ritual Landscape. Translated by S. Silvonen. Monographs of the Archeological Society of Finland No. 5.

Andrews, M. (2007). Shaping history: Narratives of political change. Cambridge: Cambridge University Press.

Andrews, M. (2014) Narrating moments of political change. In P. Nesbitt-Larking, C. Kinnvall, T. Capelos, H. Dekker (Eds) *The Palgrave Handbook of Global Political Psychology. Palgrave Studies in Political Psychology Series.* London: Palgrave Macmillan. https://doi.org/10.1007/978-1-137-29118-9_20

Angell, E., Nygaard, V., & Selle, P. (2020) Industrial development in the North – Sámi interests squeezed between globalization and transition. *Acta Borealia, 2020, 37*:1-2, 43–62. doi: 10.1080/08003831.2020.1751995 https://doi.org/10.1080/08003831.2020. 1751995

Brattbakken, B. (2014) *Hvilke konsekvenser har utbygging av vindkraft for folks utøvelse av friluftsliv?* Masteroppgave i Idrettsvitenskap, Seksjon for kroppsøving og pedagogikk. Norges Idrettshøgskole.

Cappelli, M. L. (2018). Standing with standing rock: Affective alignment and artful resistance at the native nations rise March. *SAGE Open, 1–13.* doi: 10.1177/215824401878570.

Colman, J. E., Eftestøl, S., Tsegaye, D., Flydal, K., & Rannestad, O. T. (2020). Sluttrapport. Rákkočearru vindparks effekter på reinens arealbruk og den lokale reindriften. Oslo: Institutt for Biovitenskap, Universitetet i Oslo.

Eira, A.O., Blom, A., Eira, I. H. (2017) Reindriftsfaglig utreding i forhold til Davvi Vindkraftverk. Desember 2017. Protect Sápmi.

Falch, T., & Selle, P. (2018). *Sametinget. Institusjonalisering av en ny samepolitikk.* Oslo: Gyldendal Akademisk.

Fjellheim, E. (2020). Decolonial perspectives on south Saami history, indigeneity and rights. In A. Breidlid, & R. Krøvel (Eds.), *Indigenous knowledges and the sustainable development agenda.* New York, NY: Routledge.

Fjellheim, E. M., Carl, F., & Normann, S. (2020). Green colonialism is ruining Indigenous lives in Norway. *Al Jazeera.* Retrieved from: https://www.aljazeera.com/indepth/opinion/colonialism-ruining-indigenous-lives-norway-200703135059280.html

Gad, U. P., Jacobsen, M., & Strandsbjerg, J., (2018). Introduction: Sustainability as a political concept in the arctic. *The politics of sustainability in the arctic: Reconfiguring identity, space, and time.* (Eds) Ulrik Pram Gad, Jeppe Strandsbjerg. London: Routledge.

Gulbrandsen, L. H., Indreberg, T. H. and Jevnaker, T (2021) Is political steering gone with the wind? administrative power and wind energy licencing practices in Norway. *Energy Research & Social Science, 74,* 101963.

Grenselandet, AS. (2019). *Konsesjonssssøknad Davvi Vindkraftverk, Lebesby og Tana kommuner.* 01.11.2019. Retrieved from: http://webfileservice.nve.no/API/PublishedFiles/Download/201700703/3077960

Grenselandet, AS. (2019). *Davvi Vindkraftverk, Tana/Lebesby. Informasjonsbrosjyre, Oktober 2019.* Retrieved from: https://webfileservice.nve.no/API/PublishedFiles/Download/201700703/3077965

Hanna, P., & Vanclay, F. (2013). Human rights, indigenous peoples and the concept of free, prior and informed consent. *Impact Assessment and Project Appraisal, 31*(2), 146–157.

Henriksen, J. E (2008) Rapport 2. Leavvajoga ja Rástigáissá sámi kulturmuittut, 14. – 16. juni ja 04. – 10. september 2008. UiT. The Arctic University Museum of Norway. https://motvind.org/wp-content/uploads/2020/03/Kulturminneregistrering_rapport_2_ J%C3%B8rn_Erik_Henriksen.pdf

176   Bård Kårtveit

Herding District 13(2019). *Høringsuttalelse til NVEs forslag til nasjonal ramme for vindkraft.* Reinbeitedistrikt 13 – Lagesdouttar. 13.09.2019.

Hovland, M. H. (2020, May 16). Vindkraft i Norge [Wind power in Norway]. E24. Retrieved from: https://e24.no/olje-ogenergi/i/8mya6A/bygger-vindkraft-i-nord-odal-med-norske-pensjonspenger-dette-har-jeg-ventet-paa-i-flere-aar/

Landbruks og matdepartementet (2019). Reindrift. https://www.regjeringen.no/no/tema/mat-fiske-og-landbruk/reindrift/reindrift/id2339774/

Lehtola, V. P. (2015). Sámi histories, colonialism, and Finland. *Arctic Anthropology, 52*(2), 22-36.

Mork, K., Flatlandsmo, I., Undem, L. S. I.ár, & emet-Jon, L. (2019). *Konsekvensutredning: Davvi vindkraftverk med tilhørende nettilknytning. Fagområder: Naturressurser, annen arealbruk, støy, forurensning og verdiskapning.* Multiconsult. Retrieved from: https://webfile-service.nve.no/API/PublishedFiles/Download/201700703/3077969

Motvind (2019). *Hvor stort areal blir berørt av vindkraftverk?* Temarapport 1-2019

Motvind (2019). *Vindkraftverk på bekostning av Sámisk reindrift?* Temarapport 2-2019

Nilsen, A. (2020). *Alta-kampen. Miljøkampens største folkereisning.* Haldde Forlag AS.

Normann, S. (2020). Green colonialism in a nordic context: Exploring Southern saami representations of wind energy development. *Journal of Community Psychology,* Special Issue, 1–18. Wiley Publications.

Norwegian Petroleum (2021). *Exports for oil and gas.* Retrieved from: https://www.norsk-petroleum.no/en/production-and-exports/exports-of-oil-and-gas/

Norwegian Water Resource and Energy Directorate - NVE (2021). *Ny kraft: Endelige tillatelser og utbygging. Fjerde kvartal* 2020.(Quarterly report on government processing of wind power Projects) Retrieved from: 29.03.2020: https://webfileservice.nve.no/API/PublishedFiles/Download/b61a5621-9aad-44b7-8e8a-e322bcbe9dbb/201202014/3420898

Olje-og energidepartementet (2020). Meld. St. 28 (2019-2020) *Vindkraft på land. Endringer i konsesjonsbehandlingen (Government White paper on wind power).*

Olsen, B. W. (2020, October 19). Bekrefter at Davvi trekkes ut av Tana. *Sagat.* 19.10.2020. Retrieved from: https://www.sagat.no/nyheter/bekreftet-at-davvi-trekkes-ut-av-tana/ 19.24279

Omholt, M. B. (2020). *Public opposition to wind power projects in Norway.* Master thesis in Energy, environment and society, University of Stavanger.

Øyfjellet Wind Park (2021). *About us.* Retrieved from: https://oyfjelletvind.no/en/about-us/

Pickerill, J. (2018). Black and green: The future of indigenous–environmentalist relations in Australia. *Environmental Politics, 27*(6), 1122–1145. doi: 10.1080/09644016.2018.1466464.

Rannestad, O. T., Ryvarden, L., & Flydal, K. (2019). *Konsekvenser for naturmangfold ved utbygging av davvi vindpark i finnmark.* Naturrestaurering, Rapport nr: 2019-02-04.

Retter, G. B. (2021). Vi kaller det for grønn kolonisering. *Morgenbladet,* 24–27, January, 15–21, 2021.

Schlosberg, D. (2004). Reconceiving environmental justice: Global movements and political theories. *Environmental Politics, 13*(3), 517–540.

Schlosberg, D. (2013). Theorising environmental justice: The expanding sphere of a discourse. *Environmental Politics, 22*(1), 37–55.

Staupe-Delgado, R., & Coombes, P. R. (2020). Life in anticipation of wind power development: Three cases from coastal Norway, *Sustainability* 12(24), 10666. https://doi.org/10.3390/su122410666

Green colonialism 177

Strand, O., Colman, J. E., Eftestøl, S., Sandström, P., Skarin, A., & Thomassen, J. (2017). *Vindkraft og reinsdyr. En kunnskapssyntese.* NINA-rapport 1305.

Toohey, D. (2012). Indigenous peoples, environmental groups, networks and the political economy of rainforest destruction in Brazil. *International Journal of Peace Studies, 17*(1), 73–97. Retrieved from: http://www.jstor.org/stable/41853029

The Skylark (2020). *Could a renewable energy lead to the eradication of an Indigenous Arctic community?* 03.09.2020. Retrieved from: https://theskylark.org/2020/09/03/without-us-having-a-possibility-to-give-or-withhold-consent-attempts-at-dialogue-are-pointless/

Valio, T., Eira, A. J., & Granefjell, S. O. (2019). *Inngrepskartlegging og reindriftsfaglig utredning i forhold til Øyfjellet vindkraftverk.* Protect Sápmi. Retrieved from: http://protectSápmi.com/assets/Dokumenter/Ojfjellet-Vindpark/Utredning-endelig-juni-2019.pdf

Vasstrøm, M. H. Lysgård, K. (2020). Bevegelser i norsk vindkraftpolitikk – Drivkrefter, motkrefter og fremtidige utfordringer. Policynotat Windplan

WWF Verdens Naturvern & NOF Norsk Ornitologisk Forening (2020). *Davvi vindkraftverk må stanses.* Letter to the Parliamentary comittee on Energy and Environment. 20.11.2020. Retrieved from: https://www.wwf.no/assets/attachments/20201120_Davvi-vindkraftpark_WWF-NOF.pdf

10 Transforming Arctic municipalities

The winding road to low-emission communities

Nils Aarsæther and Hege Westskog

Introduction

This chapter addresses tensions at the local level, related to the implementation of measures aimed at a dramatic reduction in climate gas emissions. How do small, periphery municipalities in the Arctic respond to the demand for radical reduction in greenhouse gas emissions? Is it realistic to expect bold, transformative policies to be worked out and implemented in municipalities firmly entrenched in high-emission life styles and production modes? Under which circumstances can a low-emission policy shift prevail at the local level? These are important questions in today's political debate and answering them should be informed by studies that encompass community life, municipal planning and decision-making, as well as central government's climate policy obligations.

In today's Norway, many coastal municipalities in the Arctic have experienced a second wave of modernization – during the last decades they have attained an advanced, state supported public service system, and a profound transformation has taken place in economic sectors. Local communities formerly based on income from fisheries, agriculture and manufacturing industries have turned into places dominated by municipal sector employment, fish farming productions, and (nature-based) tourism. Both the expansion of public services and the growth in the fish farming and tourism sectors have, with a few exceptions, been developed to create welfare, jobs, and profits, often by neglecting the environmental impacts of the new practices. And today, it is fair to say that most local people, even in the extreme periphery, experience overall well-being, privately in the form of ownership of large houses, car (and skidoo) transportation, by-road access to regional centres, and (at least until March 2020) affordable flight tickets to destinations overseas.

But in recent years, with the new focus on climate policy, in particular highlighted by the Paris 2015 agreement, municipalities are expected to plan for a radical reduction in (fossil) energy use and greenhouse gas emissions within their territories. In this respect, the municipality's own operations are targeted, but so are also the emission levels of local businesses, from transportation, and from daily life-styles. Obviously, adapting to new, and potentially transformative practices will pose a problem to the municipal level decision-makers, because the

DOI: 10.4324/9781003118633-11

expectations (and demands) from central government may easily be adverse to the wishes (and demands) from the local citizenry. A majority of local people will normally vote for parties and candidates that offer better welfare services, better infrastructure, and jobs. This rather pessimistic view may be countered by the potential of creating local jobs by innovative, green-economy business development, as well as changes in life styles that combine liveability and reduced emissions.

In the periphery, securing employment is a dominant issue. The rationalization within primary occupations and manufacturing industries has reduced the demand for labour, and this loss must be matched by a supply of novel employment, lest further population decline occurs. Studying the municipal responses to the central government's climate policy urges, regulations, and incentives is important, especially in contexts where lifestyles and jobs are heavily based on practices that, in a climate perspective, no longer can be defended. As will be shown in this chapter, the responses at the local level differ between municipalities, and they have the character of being incremental rather than transformative. An analysis of the predicaments of local level climate policies will not in itself contribute to a more effective effort to reach the low-emissions society. But our findings may help both central level and local level decision-makers in the quest for policy-making that bridges the gap between citizens and representatives and also between municipalities and central authorities. At the end of the chapter, some suggestions for action are presented, with a hope that our modest social science endeavour will somehow matter.

Two Arctic municipalities: The case study approach

To answer the initial research questions, we have chosen a case study approach, studying how climate policy measures are discussed, planned for and implemented at the local level. Two neighbouring municipalities in Northern Norway have been selected, the municipalities of Skjervøy and Lyngen, both with about 3,000 inhabitants. Each of them has a municipal council with 19 directly elected members, and the councillors elect their (full-time salaried) mayor by four years terms. To serve the councils, the administration is led by the municipal director. The municipality is responsible for primary education, children's day care, services to the elderly, primary health services, the culture school, library & sports facilities, technical infrastructure and business development. To govern the service system and overall activities, budget and planning officers are part of the municipal director's staff.

The research forming the basis for this account is the TRANSFORM project, funded by the Norwegian Research Council (2017–2021), identifying and analyzing transformative municipal efforts to move from high-emissions to low-emissions local communities in Norway. In the TRANSFORM project, case studies have been carried out in 13 Norwegian municipalities, with Skjervøy and Lyngen as the two Northernmost units. When collecting data from these municipalities, we have followed the ethical guidelines for research set by the Norwegian Center

180 *Nils Aarsæther and Hege Westskog*

for Research, anonymized interview data, ensured secured storage of data and obtained consent from all interviewees for recording.

The idea behind the TRANSFORM project is that as time is running out for states and other actors to halt the planet's temperature rise, incremental, slow moves will not suffice to reach the goals in time, consequently it is time to consider transformational policy measures.

On the basis of the Paris 2015 agreement, the Norwegian state has called for transformative action to fulfil the ambitions of reaching the low-emissions society by 2050, but the central level authorities are faced with a decentralized decision-making system, leaving local level discretion with the 356 municipalities. The Paris agreement aims can hardly be reached unless municipalities initiate or comply with radical policies aimed at reaching a low-emissions society. The national level may pass legislation to make the municipalities move in the low-emissions direction, both by a separate Climate Law (enacted 2018) but also by the Planning & building act (2008). However, in the Norwegian (and Nordic) tradition of local self-government, the municipalities are free to choose the means, based on the specific local circumstances, including the utilization of local knowledge, in their climate policies.

Obviously, policies aimed at local community transformation, and not merely adjustments and incremental moves, may easily provoke resistance at the local level. This may be the case even if the need for fundamental changes in lifestyles and productions are widely acknowledged. On the other hand, the prospects of further temperature rise and its consequences may elicit action both in the form of political mobilization, and willingness to make radical shifts in life styles, consumption and productions. In the 356 municipal councils, one may thus expect different outcomes of the debates between the defenders of established life styles and green activists, when radical climate policy issues enter the agenda. The need for more knowledge in this field is obvious, both on the agents for change and the typical obstacles in the quest for low-emission policy moves at the municipal level.

Climate policies come from the top

Theoretically, the TRANSFORM project is based on a rather traditional policy implementation approach. Climate policies are definitely top-down-based, starting with natural science observations and analyses, then informing national levels and not least, international organizations, about the alarming status and trajectories of the planet, if the present (fossil fuel based) life and production modes were to be continued into the future. International agreements are made up, and the national governments all over the world complied with them and made laws, regulations, and incentive systems to their lower-level authorities, and to citizens and businesses. In 2009, the central government of Norway issued planning prescriptions for municipal climate and energy policies, and by 2016 an arrangement of economic incentives was implemented to spur the process of creating climate strategies and specific actions (Amundsen, Hovelsrud, Aall, Karlsson, &

Westskog, 2018). At the municipal level, officers and professionals receive the climate policy prescriptions, laws, and incentive systems from the national level, and they are expected to inform the political leadership of the need to initiate and implement climate plans, and to apply for government funding for specific projects aimed at reducing local climate gas emissions.

This way of "doing politics" however is very far from the expectations that local people and their elected representatives have to municipal action. For almost two centuries, people in Norway have been used to do politics the other way round: By forming municipal councils that could help solving problems experienced by local people, and by the help from the state, addressing these by setting up educational, caring/health, and infrastructure facilities in the first place, and in addition, supporting the productive (and employment-enhancing) activities of local farmers, fishermen and industrial entrepreneurs.

Typical of the Nordic municipal system then is the cooperation between the central government level and the local level. What comes from above then is traditionally something that has at the start been fought for at the local level. This policy "chain" is normally characterized as bottom-up mode policymaking. The contrast to climate (and environmental) policies is obvious: These policies emanate from international research and follow a top-down script. And in the Norwegian tradition, top-down policies are very often contested at the local level.

"The local level" and "the municipality" tend to be portrayed as an entity that has "a voice", constituting a platform for common action (ibid.). This may be the case, but in the overwhelming number of instances, local communities are made up by actors and groups with different ways of life, perspectives, and interests. In the case of transformative climate policies, there will be adherents as well as opponents at the community level. In the case of radical climate policies to counter global warming, however it is too simplistic to assume that there will be a unanimous opposition to measures and demands imposed by the central government. Today, local people are fully aware of the gravity of the environmental predicament, even if the consequences are yet to be experienced. However, as climate policies are best characterized as politics made in the top-down mode, local scepticism to directives from central government will occur, and sometimes form a dominant stance, also among elected councillors.

Institutional analysis – and narratives: A combined approach

Tensions related to the demand for, and introduction of climate policies at the local level may be studied and analyzed in several ways. In the TRANSFORM project, an institutional approach was chosen at the outset, focusing on the municipality's planning and decision-making in climate related policies. By studying documents from local planning and decision-making, and by interviewing municipal political and administrative leaders, the aim was to determine the transformative elements in the municipal responses to the central government's demand for radical climate policies. This institutional approach was supplemented by community

182 Nils Aarsæther and Hege Westskog

level studies, interviewing leaders of key businesses and people representing local voluntary organizations. During the field work in the two municipalities, however the researchers became aware of formulations, words, behaviour, and attitudes that could not easily fit into the institutional policy analysis. Many of the actors interviewed or engaged in informal talks signalled an understanding of themselves and of their community that might rather be analyzed in the form of storytelling and narratives.

Our research design, however, falls short of systematically collecting and recording narratives. Following Kaplan (1993), a narrative should have a beginning, a middle, and an end, exposing a plot. Narrative analyses are examining the stories of everyday life and often include observations of communities and their people to reveal local experienced patterns of social life (Gubrium & Holstein, 1999). What we recorded were only fragments in the form of utterances and observations of daily life in the two municipalities. To trigger story-telling responses, we started each interview by asking the respondent to reflect upon what "transformation" (in Norwegian: "omstilling") in the local community meant to her/him. The results, as recorded in the interview material, were rather meagre, and the coupling of "climate measures" and "(societal) transformations" that we probed for in the follow-up questions did not elicit any rich response. Climate policies and measures tended to be conceived of as separate "things", to be added to the municipal repertoire, so to speak, rather than being perceived as a process penetrating community life or the municipality in total, expressed by one informant as follows:

"Transforming to a low emission society means that we need to have new buildings. We must tear down the old ones and start over. In Lenangen this was done. Here we built a new school. Then the probability of achieving climate targets is increased" (Informant, Lyngen).

Hence, our modest epistemological attempt at combining institutional analysis and a narrative approach in this respect did not pay off.

Consider the story-line: "Some years ago, this community performed exactly as a low-emission society, harvesting from the nearby waters and the land. Today, in the face of the climate crisis we want to regain our low-emission status, by combining local knowledge of the past with novel technologies". This was a storyline we as researchers hoped for, but never heard. There is an ironic twist to the quest for climate measures in the two Arctic municipalities studied: One hundred years ago, the municipalities in question, like many other municipalities along the coastline, could be described exactly as low-emission communities. Households were organized as work units, with a subsistence agricultural activity, based on local terrestrial resources, and cash earnings from small scale fisheries, harvesting fish stocks in nearby waters (Paine, 1965). People in these municipalities then has, over less than four generations, experienced a transition from low-emission mode living and production, to today's lifestyles and production systems much based on fossil energy and its inherent high levels. The transition from low to high emission practices however was accompanied by the transition from poverty to overall well-being. Perhaps this is the reason why stories of the type we wanted are seldom told: Reflecting upon a rather recent past, most people may feel that the low-emission society is definitely not the promised land. On the contrary, the low-emission society might remind people of the poverty endured by their ancestors. A study explicitly designed to collect and analyze stories of identities and community transformation might expose narrative richness, but from our research it is doubtful if such stories would include elements of climate relevant transformation. Our overall impression is that decades of progress and modernization, in the form of better roads, private cars, out-reaching welfare, and industrial productions is experienced as both welcome and natural to many people living in Arctic regions.

In the (national level) TRANSFORM study, the research team found that the municipalities selected performed in very different ways. Three out of thirteen cases could be characterized as "front runners" in climate policy, these municipalities operated systematically to transform their respective organizations and their local communities from fossil fuel-based to low-emission local communities. Some of the remaining ten municipalities studied were characterized as "midfield" performers, but a majority of the municipalities in the study displayed very modest transformative ambitions and measures, and among these were Skjervøy and Lyngen. To determine the categorization of frontrunners, midfielders, and the "modest ones", we studied the climate policy motivated measures planned for or deployed. The measures were assessed on a nominal scale ranging from transformative (=3), via developmental (=2), and incremental (=1) to irrelevant, or negative (=0). The assessment was made on the basis of the depth, scope and time dimension for each policy measure mentioned in the interviews, or found in planning documents (Westskog et al., 2021, forthcoming).

In the present study then, the aim is to explain and understand why Lyngen and Skjervøy are among the municipalities in which the pursuit of *transformative* climate action has not gained ground. In May 2017, the research team conducted a series of individual and group interviews in the two municipalities. We talked to a series of local level actors supposed to have an impact on local level climate policies. In addition, we spoke informally with local people and (over a short period) observed local daily-life practices by occasional home visits, visiting industrial sites, observing street life, shops and café activities. At the time we did our interviewing, the Norwegian economy was running high, with a soaring fishery/fish farming export sector and a tourism sector that had extended the market to include also Asian middle-class customers. Both Skjervøy and Lyngen had their share of the booming sectors: Skjervøy, as a coastal municipality had its emphasis on fisheries/fish farming, and the period of expansion the largest industries relied heavily on incoming workers from Eastern Europe. Lyngen, a fjord municipality experienced growth in nature-based winter tourism. In addition, Lyngen had developed a diversified industrial sector, ranging from marine products to the manufacturing of plastic-based building products, and even a whisky distillery.

184 Nils Aarsæther and Hege Westskog

Identifying actor groups

In any municipality, there will be different actor groups involved in decision-making processes. In the TRANSFORM project, we selected persons for interviews according to their status as: (1) Municipal administrative officers and (2) municipal political leaders, surrounded by (3) local business leaders, (4) leaders of local environmental organizations. In addition, by staying some days in each municipality, we hoped to get an impression of how local people, as voters and in their daily-life practices acted and spoke of environmental challenges. In developing climate policies, we expected the key groups to be administrative officers, the political leaders, and environmental organizations/political parties. The argument for this selection is that we expect the administrators (within the municipal organization) and the green lobby (in the community) will be the first to pick up signals, prescriptions and incentive arrangements from central government (with the help from regional authorities). But, and this is important, there is no packet or specific arrangement for the municipality to adopt: The municipality must by itself identify what it thinks is the most effective means to reach the overall climate policy goals. In this respect, the incentive arrangement of the central government ("Klimasats", 2016–) could provide funding for municipal initiatives. This is the point in which the "green lobby" has its window of opportunity, because the elected political leadership has not been entrusted by the voters to prioritize climate policies, most likely they have gained their positions by offering the voters the prospect of new schools, roads and stimulating job opportunities in their respective communities. In the case of climate policies, there will be almost no pressure from the local community, but the politicians may me be informed or pressed by the local green lobby to adopt or develop climate policies, especially if funded by central government money.

Ideally, then a municipality will be expected to implement transformative climate measures if

- The local administrators are competent "brokers" between national level prescriptions and local politicians/public opinion.
- A local environmental "lobby" is present and works in an entrepreneurial mode.
- The political leaders are persuaded (or pressed) to prioritize climate action.
- Local business leaders are aware of their climate footprints and willing/able to comply with climate measures.
- The local culture and daily life practices resonate with climate and environmental concerns.

Administrators

In the interviews, the responses from the administrators in both municipalities centred on incremental moves, especially related to heating practices in municipal buildings, to construction methods, and to improve waste processing and water supply. In Skjervøy for instance they had a strong focus on energy performance

Transforming Arctic municipalities 185

in municipal buildings and mentioned this as a central part of their climate and energy plan:

> In our climate and energy plan, energy savings in municipal buildings were pointed to as a key measure to implement. We started a huge project on energy savings where we insulated our buildings, drilled to get geothermal heat and made overall technical improvements. As a results the energy use in our buildings is drastically reduced.
>
> (Informant, Skjervøy)

Political leaders

The mayors and other political leaders we talked to showed moderate interest in climate policy issues, but when asked about changes at the level of the community, municipal leaders in Skjervøy pointed to the climate measures deployed in the business sector.

Green lobbies

We observed "green lobbies" in both Skjervøy and Lyngen. From national political programmes, we regard three parties as belonging to the green lobby: The greens, the green liberals, and the left socialist party. In Lyngen the greens had one representative (out of 19) in the municipal council, and the corresponding number in Skjervøy was 2 (left socialists) out of 19. Only in Lyngen was there a spokesperson for the Nature Conservation Association, and she told us that they had to take on a defensive position, against further motorization of nature-based tourism, including pressure to use helicopters to offer peak experiences (literally speaking). In Skjervøy, however, the municipality had organized an "environment committee"; this committee, we were told operated more as a watchdog than exerting pressure for transformative action.

Businesses

In Lyngen, most business leaders we interviewed were sympathetic to the environmental and climate concerns, but the dominance of plastics industries and airborne (mountain) tourism seemed to represent hindrances to profound changes. As a contrast, the two large companies in Skjervøy, both in fish farming, were in a process of transition as to energy types: From diesel-powered engines in feeding operations and on the small vessels, these were in the process of being replaced by machinery powered by electrical cables or batteries. However, these industries relied on imported soya-based foodstuff, and the products were brought to the market by long-distance, diesel-powered trucks. We also noticed that these industries were supporting construction of family flats and houses for incoming workers from Eastern Europe. A more stable work force would be an advantage to the firm, and this would also benefit the climate by far less airborne commuting.

186   Nils Aarsæther and Hege Westskog

Completely outside of the municipal sphere then, these industries had taken on a role of climate policy frontrunners in the Skjervøy community.

Local people

In both Skjervøy and Lyngen, people leave a solid footprint in the form of what may be characterized as an excessive car use, by 2017 almost exclusively powered by fossil fuels.

> Private car use is in extreme in Skjervøy. There is a culture for using cars and parking fees are out of question. There are no more than 5-6 electric cars here, and people have them as their car number two. They have these cars because it is economically beneficial and not because of environmental concerns.
>
> (Informant, Skjervøy)

In Lyngen, with houses scattered along the coastline, and almost completely without public transportation, the use of private cars seemed to be part of the local culture. Also housing standards were high, indicating high consumption levels – including the freedom of travelling to far away destinations by air. For many people, even the replacement of a fossil powered car with an electric powered car would be regarded as a loss in comfort (heating, we were told, is "far better in fossil-powered cars", and the winter is long and cold). In the month of May, we observed several instances of vehicles, parked but with their engines running, while the owner was inside a shop.

Given the composition and propensities and the power of the groups discussed above, the prospects for transformative climate action are assessed as very limited in Lyngen and Skjervøy. Some (but not all) business leaders could be characterized as frontrunners in their electrification policies, but limited to their own industries. Community leadership in matters of transformative climate policies we found lacking, but on the other hand, we detected projects of climate policy relevance in both municipalities. In the following sections, short accounts of these projects and their contexts will illustrate the potential for entering a stage of "transformative" climate policies.

Lyngen: Place development for compact living

In Lyngen, the TRANSFORM team organized a group interview with local administrative leaders, followed by a series of interviews with business leaders, political leaders and the leader of an environmentalist organization. In addition to the interviews, the municipality's "planning strategy" of 2016 was analyzed. The planning strategy is meant to identify challenges and to prioritize planning for solutions for these challenges in a four years-perspective. The planning strategy had been worked out with maximum participation from the elected politicians, with committee and council meetings turned into workshops to elicit perspectives and suggestions from the elected politicians. Obviously, these exemplary rounds of participation did not lead to a focus on climate and environmental concerns. The impression from the interviews were partly measures of an incremental type, or defensive strategies to counter further degradation of nature, e.g., by turning down helicopter-based mountain tourism. But in the interviews with the municipal director, we learned that the municipality had embarked on a large effort of "urbanizing" and developing the municipal centre, called the "Lyngenløftet" – "lifting Lyngen". This project, intended to make a compact municipal centre by integrate dwellings and shops/restaurants at the seafront, and to develop an activity park in the immediate hinterland, alongside with a small shopping centre, public services and tourism facilities - all within walking and bicycling distances. The development project had so far resulted in an "environmental street" connecting the seafront with the service and shopping centre, and a rent-an-electric-bike station located in the seafront area. One on our informants in Lyngen explained the purpose of the "Lyngenløftet" in the following way:

> The idea with Lyngenløftet is that people could use their village and do it by walking or biking.... The work with Lyngenløftet has brought leading expertise here to think about development of our center and to make it attractive for cycling and walking.
>
> (Informant, Lyngen)

The design of the Lyngenløftet facilities was commissioned from an architectural firm in Bergen. This initiative had come about as a result of talks between business leaders and political leaders in the municipality, and sufficient funding had been mobilized to organize a 5-years development project. In the context of Lyngen's traditional settlement patterns, the place development project may be assessed as a transformative move, aiming at assembling living and working space for a growing number of service providers and administrative employees. The construction of the compact seafront flats and the seaside promenade had so far not materialized, but physical plans had been made, and the municipal actors were proud of their initiative.

Today, less than 800 of the municipality's 3,000 inhabitants are living in the municipal centre, much due to the attractiveness of living along the fjord stretches - settlements typical of Northern Norway. During our stay in Lyngen, we observed no activity in the electric bike renting facility, no activity in the activity park, and very few pedestrians using the "environmental street". Outside the small café and shopping centre at the end of the street however we observed a large number of cars being parked outside. Some car owners obviously had a preference for not using the fee-free car parking lot, but instead placed their cars close to the café, and a couple of them with the engines running while the owner went shopping or coffee-drinking inside (Figure 10.1). "Yes, we have a car culture here", one of the interviewed actors remarked. The results of the Lyngenløftet so far seem to be limited to a compact urban-inspired plan, with design qualities and a park competently remade by the use of landscape architecture, but so far with

Figure 10.1 Parking in front of the main grocery store in Lyngen.

negligible effects on climate gas emissions. Excessive car use and dubious car parking practices seem not to be challenged by this project, but prospects for a new lifestyle are laid out for future inhabitants. At the time of our fieldwork, we did not detect a new storyline of seafront-compact living in the municipal centre of Lyngen, inspired with the Lyngenløftet project. Nevertheless, by 2020, there are signs that this story is spinning in the background, for a series of new (commercial as well as public services) projects seem to pop up in the municipal centre, or with the centre as basecamp for uphill and fjord experiences.

Skjervøy: Fighting plastics pollution – And fish farming goes electric

As in Lyngen, the utilization of local resources in Skjervøy (shrimps and cod-based industries) went into troubles about the turn of the century, and has been replaced by two large-scale fish farming (salmon) operations. Contrary to Lyngen the settlement structure of Skjervøy is definitely more centralized, with about 2,500 of the municipality's 3,000 inhabitants living in the municipal centre (Figure 10.2). The centre is a typical fishery harbour, with industries serving the fishing fleet, today dominated by a large fish farming business, employing about 200 workers. Another large fish farming business, locally owned, with about 70 employees, is located on the Arnøya island (served by ferry connection).

The TRANSFORM team started interviewing in the municipal administrative headquarters, meeting the mayor, the municipal director, planners, technical and educational leaders. Skjervøy municipality, we were told, had been a frontrunner by using electric cars, in particular for home-based services to the elderly. But the first-generation electric cars did not function satisfactorily in the

Figure 10.2 Skjervøy.

Arctic winter climate, and the municipality has since replaced the electric-powered cars with fossil fuel powered vehicles. The main municipal focus today was on replacing oil-based heating in schools and other institutions with (hydro) electricity. The efforts of the municipality seemed to be rather modest, but with one conspicuous exception: The municipality has a long coastline, and when the story of the whale dying by eating plastic waste went on TV, Skjervøy as a coastal municipality took immediate action. The environmental committee organized an offensive against plastic waste: It was to be located, assembled and dispatched for re-circulation, not only along the beaches, but along the roads as well as in the urban centre. The cleaning up of Skjervøy was organized by the *dugnad* principle, with the responsibility for streets as well as beach stretches divided between voluntary organizations, political party groups, community groups and municipal staff. Travelling in the centre and in the villages, we noticed an overall cleanliness, together with several heaps and bags with plastic waste, waiting to be collected.

As in Lyngen, the "car culture" seemed to dominate daily life in Skjervøy. One conspicuous example must be mentioned: The research team took a coffee break, sitting outside of a village shop in the sun; then a large truck turned up to park outside the shop, and the driver went inside without turning off the engine. When the driver returned from the shop he was asked if he found it reasonable to let us have our coffee break in the exhaust fumes. He gave a short answer: "Yes", and then drove off.

Interviews with leaders of the two large salmon farming and processing plants however made quite a different impression. Both firms had observed the signals of the need to reduce climate gas emissions and were in the process of a total replacement of diesel-powered machinery with hydro-electric energy. The

190   *Nils Aarsæther and Hege Westskog*

process of electrification was not limited to landside operations, it included the machinery for distributing food, and the powering of small vessels in the operations. And one of the firms had targeted the large truck "fleet" transporting the products to the European market, in an attempt to reduce emissions from transportation. Compared to the measures deployed by the leading firm, the municipality's endeavours were very moderate and incremental: Heating practices and energy saving in municipal buildings were the measures highlighted by municipal leaders.

Discussion

In both Lyngen and Skjervøy, the overall character of the climate measures is incremental. "*In Norway today there is a long way from word to action*", as one of our informants in Lyngen expressed. One of the main obstacles fronted by informants is the lack of political courage. "Politicians must dare to take action even when facing negative economic effects from climate measures". Further, informants also underline that the municipalities' room of manoeuvre is limited: "The larger structures need to be changed". Without this people do not understand why they should contribute, and "in the end everyone needs to have an income". Hence, the lack of willingness to take action both from the political level and the local community prevents radical changes, according to these informants. The main dilemma here is like the hen and the egg – who will take the first step to trigger action – the political level to initiate changes affecting local life styles or the local community demanding changes from politicians? And with both strategies, the economic consequences for the municipality – and for local people – will guide (or limit) the possibilities for changes. However, some indications of possible pathways to a low-emission community emerge from our studies:

The municipalities cover a broad range of services and activities, and each department observes climate/environmental regulations and strives in an incremental mode to use less energy for heating, etc. In such a setting, the key to enhance radical climate policies, we think, lies in initiating specific *projects*. Projects in themselves mark a break with everyday routines, they may lead to an innovation and to the mobilization of local people, voluntary organizations, businesses, and it may vitalize the municipal service system. We located two projects initiated by the municipalities, both of them with an outreaching character: The plastic waste offensive in Skjervøy, and the *Lyngenløftet* place development project in Lyngen.

The plastics waste offensive in Skjervøy, we were told, mobilized almost everyone in the Skjervøy municipality. An environment-oriented project that succeeds in overall mobilization is of great importance, especially in a community that live on in the "car culture". The environmental relevance of the project is obvious, and directed towards marine animals, saving them from plastic waste. In a marine community like Skjervøy, the importance of this offensive is undisputed. As a bi-product, clean beaches, roads and streets are certainly widely appreciated. On the other hand, a plastic waste handling project neither question the production and uses of plastics, nor the extraction of non-renewable resources. Focus on plastic waste easily becomes a focus on individual mismanagement rather than the role of plastics in aggravating the climate situation. However the broad mobilization appeal is an important aspect of this project, including the "schmoozing" effect of dugnad participation. Successful transformation projects, to be effective, must have an immediate popular attractivity linked to it, it is hard to mobilize people if they are invited to join by sacrifice something for the benefit of coming generations. Ideally, people should be willing to do so, but this is so far not the situation.

The *Lyngenløftet* project – urbanizing the seafront centre of Lyngen municipality differs from the plastic waste project in many ways. It is a project with a long-time span (starting in 2016), it is led by an alliance of investors and municipal leaders, it has obtained funding from several external sources, it is directed towards both residents and incoming tourists, and it is directly challenging ways of life among the residents of Lyngen, by introducing a rural version of a compact city concept. The environmental/climate policy dimension is not the strongest one (the electric bike rent operation is running at a very low level), but this dimension is explicitly highlighted in the presentation of the project.

Finally, although not having the status of municipal project, the electrification and business/community initiatives of the leading fish farming operation in Skjervøy must be mentioned. A thorough electrification strategy, and alternative ways of fuelling long distance trucks – will make the fish farming operations independent of fossil fuels, which is exemplary in a climate perspective. Also the housing strategy of the firms, providing family houses and flats to stimulate permanent residence for workers coming from abroad, is a positive move on behalf of the global climate situation.

Conclusion

The municipalities of Skjervøy and Lyngen can, in a comparative national perspective be characterized as slow movers in a global process of rapid action to curb temperature rise. But our combined approach of studying institutions and stories (in the form of project accounts) show that important steps are being taken for the benefit of the climate, in these Arctic municipalities – partly by leading businesses alone, partly by public-private partnerships, partly by broader networks of cooperation, involving citizens, voluntary organizations, and external agencies. A multitude of incremental measures and potential "transformers" are in operation, too slow perhaps to reach the Paris 2015 goals by 2050, but nevertheless well under way.

Returning to the three questions posed at the beginning of this chapter, we may conclude that: (1) the small Arctic municipalities studied respond to the demands from the state in an incremental way, in these municipalities we find no traces of encompassing transformative strategies at the municipal level. (2) The car culture entrenchment and the overall emphasis put on creating new

192 Nils Aarsæther and Hege Westskog

employment opportunities make it unlikely, at least in the short run, to expect community level support for transformative strategies. (3) The way out then seems to be entrepreneurial or crisis-driven project making, not necessarily with an explicit transformative ambition on behalf of the climate, but at least with a built-in transformative potential.

References

Amundsen, H., Hovelsrud, G. K., Aall, C., Karlsson, M., & Westskog, H. (2018). Local governments as drivers for societal transformation: Towards the 1.5 c ambition. *Current Opinion in Environmental Sustainability*, *31*, 23–29.

Gubrium, J. F., & Holstein, J. A. (1999). At the border of narrative and ethnography. *Journal of Contemporary Ethnography*, *28*(5), 561–573.

Kaplan, T. J. (1993). Reading Policy narratives: Beginnings, middles, and ends. In F. Fischer & J. Forester (Eds.), *The argumentative turn in policy analysis and planning* (pp. 167–185). Durham, UK: Duke University.

Paine, R. (1965). *Coast Lapp society (2)*. Oslo, Norway: Universitetsforlaget.

Westskog, H., Aarsæther, N., Hovelsrud, G., Amundsen, H., West, J. J., & Dale, R. F. (2021, forthcoming). The transformative potential of local level planning and climate policies. Case studies from Norwegian municipalities. Article submitted for journal publication.

11 The quest for fresh vegetables

Stories about the future of Arctic farming

Doris Friedrich

Introduction

> What if I told you I can grow food in a place where there's no sun three months of the year? Would you believe it?
>
> (Polar Permaculture, 2018)

In recent years, the number of farms seems to be on the rise in various parts of the Arctic. Many reasons might contribute to this trend, including the warming climate in some regions. The potential benefits are numerous and the hope is that a better, more affordable supply of vegetables in Arctic communities will help battle public health issues, improve food security, decrease the economy's dependence on oil, lead to a more sustainable system of food production and a reduction of greenhouse gas emissions.

Many Arctic communities suffer from food insecurity, which can be defined as the "inadequate availability and access to healthy food of sufficient nutritional quality" (Lamalice et al., 2018, p. 327). A large part of people's diets stems from store-bought food imported from more southern regions, which is often expensive, of inferior quality and/or unavailable. The high costs of imports, poorly developed infrastructure and inadequate storage aggravate the problems. Due to these difficulties, which are particularly straining in the case of fresh, perishable foods, supermarkets in isolated Arctic communities tend to limit the amount of fresh foods offered and instead rely on non-perishable, highly processed foods of low nutritional value (Chen & Natcher, 2019).

Despite something akin to an agricultural boom in the Arctic over the last years (Nobel, 2013), there is little scientific literature on vegetable farming and gardening in the Arctic (Chen & Natcher, 2019; Loring & Gerlach, 2010; Naumov, Sidorova, & Goncharov, 2020; Skinner, Hanning, Metatawabin, & Tsuji, 2014). However, in the last years, a multitude of news articles have described different initiatives and developments related to the cultivation of vegetables in the Arctic (see, e.g., Friedrich, 2018; Hoag, 2016; Nobel, 2013).

DOI: 10.4324/9781003118633-12

Development and challenges

The histories of farming in various Arctic regions differ widely. In the Arctic regions of European countries, agriculture developed already in the pre-industrial era, while in Alaska, Canada and the Arctic parts of Siberia and the Russian Far East, the boom of the oil and gas and mining industries a few decades ago entailed a concomitant development of agriculture (Naumov et al., 2020). However, one thing that most Arctic Indigenous communities had to deal with is the disruption of their way of life and with it their possibilities to meet their nutritional needs (Lamalice et al., 2018).

Today, the importance of agriculture is also very varied in distinct Arctic countries and regions. In the European Arctic, Iceland has the biggest share of agricultural land (18.2%), contributing to 5.1% of the GDP, while Norway has the lowest with only 2.6% of its total land area contributing to 2.1% of the country's GDP. However, the two countries differ less drastically in the share of agricultural employment: While 3.1% of Iceland's total employment is in agriculture, it is 2.04% in Norway. In northern Canada, Saskatchewan and Alberta are by far the provinces with the highest share of agricultural surface with 36.1% and 28.9%, respectively (8.4% and 1.4% contribution to Gross Regional Product (GRP)), while in Russia, Krasnoyarsk Krai leads by a great deal with 19.8% of surface dedicated to agriculture and 3.9% contribution to GRP (Naumov et al., 2020). Naumov et al. (2020) conclude from their study on models of agricultural development in the Arctic that the Canadian provinces and Alaska demonstrate the highest productivity of agricultural labour, followed by northern European countries. From 2000 to 2016, the surface area in Arctic regions used for the cultivation of grain and potatoes significantly dropped, with the exception of wheat in Sweden and Finland. Recently, urban agriculture started to develop in the circumpolar north, based on technologies such as vertical greenhouses and hydroponics. In Norway, the Gulf Stream enables farming further north in Norway than in other regions of the same latitude. Currently, around 90% of Norway's agriculture is destined as livestock feed, including cereal crops. The remaining 10% are made up of 8% cereal crops for food, 1% potatoes and 1% vegetables. However, thanks to climate change, farmers could soon be able to diversify the types of crops they cultivate (Bardalen, 2016b; Gewin, 2016).

Nevertheless, growing conditions in the Arctic are far from easy. Some of the inherent environmental difficulties of vegetable farming in the Arctic and subarctic include short growing seasons and the high variability and unpredictability of frosts (Loring & Gerlach, 2010). The lack of adequate soil is an often-cited challenge and shipping it from southern regions, as is the practice in some areas, is very costly (Nobel, 2013) and not environmentally friendly. In some cases, liming and fertilizing the local soil would make it useable for cultivating crops (Lamalice et al., 2018). In general, materials that need to be imported are expensive and considerably raise the costs of farming at high latitudes (Naumov et al., 2020; Nobel, 2013). Man-made contamination and pollution also play a role: Joan Nymand Larsen, professor at the University of Akureyri's School of Humanities

The quest for fresh vegetables   195

and Social Sciences (Hoag, 2016), points to the challenges to farming stemming from mining in southern Greenland, worrying farmers about the radioactive or chemical contamination of the soil. Likewise, traditional food sources are at risk of environmental contamination (Skinner et al., 2014).

Alaska, US – Growing potential

The history of agriculture in Alaska extends back some centuries. Loring and Gerlach (2010) took a closer look at the history of what they call "outpost gardening" in interior Alaska. They point to different forms of crop cultivation by Alaska Native communities over the last few hundred years, such as family, community and school gardens. Haida and Tlingit peoples in southeastern Alaska were already known in the eighteenth century to grow potatoes, other vegetables and cereal grains both for food and trade in coastal gardens. By contrast, the gardens of Interior Alaska received little attention. In the pioneer era, the Department of Agriculture pursued the industrial-agricultural development of Alaska, mainly through experiment stations. Meanwhile, the so-called "outpost agriculture", informal gardens to increase the local economic diversity and food security, became a "prevalent and successful strategy" (Loring & Gerlach, 2010, p. 184). They helped to fill gaps that were due to the natural variability of wild game and the unpredictable supply from the south.

At the turn of the twentieth century, state educational agent Sheldon Jackson and high-latitude farming specialist Charles Christian Georgeson spurred a movement to populate Alaska with aspiring farmers from the lower 48. The US Census in 1929 revealed 500 farms in the state. However, the building of railway lines reduced the prices of imported good, with which higher priced Alaskan goods could not compete. Together with the difficult growing conditions, this led many farmers to abandon their ambitions (Loring & Gerlach, 2010).

This development of agriculture in Alaska, introduced to stave off a perceived famine in Native communities and to "educate" (read: civilize) the Natives, parallels the introduction of reindeer herding, which was also introduced by Sheldon Jackson, but considered a failure and relatively quickly abandoned again (see Friedrich, in press; Loring & Gerlach, 2010). As with reindeer herding (Friedrich, in press), gardening was adapted and integrated into local cultures and subsistence strategies reflecting "local knowledge, awareness, and responsiveness to these ecosystem patterns" (Loring & Gerlach, 2010, p. 191). While neither potatoes, turnips and rutabagas are native to Alaska, they are now integral parts of recipes considered traditionally Athabascan and used in the potlatch ceremony.

In 1941, Alaska Native Service garden programmes were formally revamped as "program of Native Education", whose goal was not only to improve food security but also to meet educational "needs" (Loring & Gerlach, 2010). Agriculture was believed an effective "mechanism of economic development and civil progress" (Loring & Gerlach, 2010, p. 190).

The participation and crop yields of the gardens varied widely from year to year. For instance, gardens in Venetie in the Yukon-Koyukuk Census Area produced

196   *Doris Friedrich*

at high level from 1961 to 1967 but were abandoned in the 1970s. Loring and Gerlach (2010) argue that this variability was due to the communities' experimentation with techniques and timing, which was not on the administrators' radar, and that diversity was valued over economic growth. Communities in the Yukon Circle developed strategies for managing the gardening work to fit timewise with the spring trapping season, the summer fishing season and the fall hunting season. In addition to the yearly cycles, the strategies followed multiyear and multidecadal ecological and climatic cycles. As a result, in some years, gardening conflicted with subsistence activities due to differences in weather and animal populations. However, the lack of a visible progressive transition towards agriculture as primary subsistence activity disappointed officials, which saw it as "failed development". This was blamed squarely on the Natives, who were labelled lazy or lacking in ambition (Loring & Gerlach, 2010). Loring and Gerlach (2010, p. 190) attribute the apparent failure of the gardens to the administrators' approach of "overinnovation, where top-down prescriptions for development are made, often by those with a colonialist mind-set, which are negligent to local social and cultural structures". Instead of recognizing flexibility and diversity as traditional strategies of Alaskan Indigenous peoples, Indigenous communities were viewed as stereotypical hunter-gatherers.

So the "story" administrators recounted was that of a failure to establish industrialized agriculture in Alaska, because the Indigenous peoples were not interested in it, despite being on the brink of famine (as – wrongly – perceived by the administrators). Therefore, the gardens of Alaskan Natives are generally not considered customary or traditional. As one respondent quoted in Loring and Gerlach's (2010, p. 192) article argued: "Using a motorboat (...) doesn't make us less traditional, but digging for potatoes when we could be fishing, to some people, does". One concern is that the cultivation of vegetables could be at the expense of other subsistence activities, as authorities might use it to justify stricter hunting or fishing regulations. This has implications for Arctic communities looking to vegetable farming as "innovative responses to rapid ecological, climatic, and socioeconomic change" (Loring & Gerlach, 2010, p. 183).

The same holds true in other Arctic regions, where plants, with the exception of seaweed, berries and some herbs, are not considered part of the traditional Indigenous diet.

Nevertheless, some question this. Lone Sorensen, who is originally from Denmark and founded the local food advocacy group "Northern Roots" in Yellowknife, NWT (Canada) challenges the general belief that it's impossible to grow plants that far north. In the 1930s, some gardens in Alaska and northern Canada already supplied potatoes and greens to the mineworkers. This changed after the Second World War, when fuel became cheaper and allowed an increased reliance on imported goods (Nobel, 2013).

However, the way in which gardening and farming techniques were adapted and integrated into Indigenous cultures was a part of the story routinely omitted by both administrators and in the academic literature.

The quest for fresh vegetables   197

Nowadays, many Alaskans start to recognize the state's potential in vegetable farming. When Governor Walker said in a speech in 2017 that the state is producing only 4% of its food consumption compared to 50% in 1959, he attributed this partly to Alaskans having lost their vision and become too dependent on oil. This reliance on oil at the expense of other industries is in spite of the number of farms in Alaska, in total more than 750, some of them producing more than 500,000 USD worth annually. This means that most of the 2 billion USD spent annually on food is invested in out-of-state producers (Phu, 2016).

Nevertheless, despite the downward trend of the last decades, the number of projects aiming at supplying people in Alaska with fresh vegetables, including farmers markets, is now increasing. In 2010, Loring and Gerlach suggest that gardening practices have entered a phase of revival, as some schools develop new gardening curricula and the Cooperative Extension service of the US Department of Agriculture, which focuses on the "well-being of families, communities and agriculture enterprises" (USDA, n.d.), supports more than 40 rural gardening initiatives.

"Arctic Greens", a subsidiary of the local Native association Kikiktagruk Inupiat Corp. (KIC) in Kotzebue, is one of the companies that were founded in the last years. Based on a system of high-tech containers developed by the Anchorage-based company Vertical Harvest Hydroponics, their goal is to reach at least 30 communities in Alaska and northern Canada.

The company delivered their first vegetables to supermarkets in 2016. Alaska Natural Organics, another company further south in Anchorage, grows the vegetables year-round, hydroponically – in water – using LED lights in an old dairy warehouse (Alaska Natural Organics, n.d.).

Calypso Farm, located in Ester, Alaska, at 64° North, relies on a different concept. Founded in 2000 and successful since, it grows the vegetables in fields outside, which might be possible because of the area's microclimate in the subarctic region.

The story of Calypso Farm, Alaska

"By the 5th year that we were established and doing really well, many people started telling us that initially they thought we were completely crazy and that it would never work. But no one told us when we started. When we started, everybody was so supportive. And they were really happy that they've been proven wrong, because it has been successful. And it's a change in mind-set of what a farm is" (S. Willsrud, personal communication, November 25, 2020).

Talking to Susan Willsrud, co-director and farm manager of Calypso Farm (Figure 11.1), she highlighted that changing people's misconceptions about what a farm should look like and how successful it can be in Alaska is at the heart of her and her husband's vision. The goal of their "educational farm" is to bring gardening and farming closer to the people. When I interviewed her, Willsrud explained: "Our mission is to encourage local small-scale agriculture through

Figure 11.1 View of one of Calypso Farm's fields, 2020. Photo: Calypso Farm.

hands-on education for people of all ages. We also train farmers and home gardeners. The base of our educational programmes is the farm" (personal communication, November 25, 2020).

Founded in 2000, Calypso Farm, whose three acres seem relatively small compared to farms in other US states, is set within the boreal forest on a south-facing slope. From the end of May until the beginning of October, Willsrud and her colleagues grow vegetables, herbs, cut flowers and tend to chickens, sheep and dairy goats. While Willsrud grew up in California, her husband and co-director of the farm, Tom Zimmer, grew up on the US East Coast and in England. Initially, sceptical about Alaska's farming potential, they decided to give it a try. Willsrud remembers:

I went to graduate school at the University of Alaska Fairbanks. We had community here and we liked Alaska. It seemed crazy to establish an education farm someplace like this. So we left, thinking that we'd look further south. After leaving, we just really missed Alaska! The place, the people … We came back feeling

The quest for fresh vegetables   199

it's worth a try. Even though our season is short, it's very good growing. (personal communication, November 25, 2020)

Similar to the diversity and flexibility in Alaskan Natives' diets, Calypso Farm counts on a broad range of income sources. In terms of edible plants, Calypso Farm grows around 30 different types of vegetables, as well as apples and berries. This includes everything that doesn't require very hot summers, such as broccoli, cabbage, cauliflower, lettuce, peas, beets, carrots and radishes. In contrast to other farms at high latitudes, the greenhouses are primarily used to grow plant starts in the spring and tomatoes and peppers in the summer.

Community-driven

Risking mirroring the history of educational farming described above, Willsrud is careful to distance herself and the farm from colonial practices and to make sure to provide only the community-desired support for Indigenous-led programmes:

> There is a really long history of white people in the state trying to help or you know, work in village communities. And it's a long failed history. So we have been hesitant to be a part of that. But over the years, many different people, also Native people, wanted to talk about agriculture. So right now, we're trying to play a support role and provide some funding to support Indigenous-led efforts, to train one another across different Native cultures.
> (personal communication, November 25, 2020)

Willsrud corroborates Loring and Gerlach's (2010) argument that vegetables have become an important part of Alaskan Native diets and points to Alaska's history of small-scale farming and home gardening: "There is a long history of agriculture in village communities all around the state. Probably 50–70 years ago or longer even, there were more home gardeners than there are now. This is partly because of food supply: It was harder to get stuff up here". According to her, the last years have seen a renewed attention to gardening after several decades of dwindling interest:

> A lot of Indigenous people picked up gardening and grew beautiful gardens. In terms of the older Indigenous food tradition, they tend to be centred around fishing and hunting in different communities, and then agriculture as supplementary aspect. 50 years ago, this was definitely a more established tradition. And then now, there is a new generation of Indigenous people in Alaska that are combining their food sources with gardening.
> (personal communication, November 25, 2020)

Meeting the needs and wants of the community has been at the centre of Calypso Farm: "Each year, we're evolving, adapting, responding to what people in the community want". Correspondingly, Willsrud describes the reaction of the community to Calypso Farm and especially its community-based nature education as "amazing": "We have so many people in the community who volunteer and

200 *Doris Friedrich*

contribute to the work that we do, participate in the programs, come to our events. It's been overwhelming outpouring of support over all these years. And that just keeps continuing. It's really encouraging".

One of the farm's projects is the school gardens, which have a big impact on the community, getting "kids involved in the gardens in the summer in a really meaningful way" (S. Willsrud, personal communication, November 25, 2020). However, they are more difficult to manage, due to the competing priorities of the schools and the quick turnaround of the staff among other reasons.

Common preconceptions

The project, as well as its success, has surprised many people. Common images people have regarding farming are big industrial farms with extensive fields. However, this doesn't fit the reality of farming in Alaska, which is what Calypso Farm has set out to communicate, reaching out to people about their vision for the farm, changing conceptions in the process. Talking about the school gardens, Willsrud enthuses: "It's exciting to introduce all these kids every year to something that looks like a farm, but also looks accessible. It's not a bunch of big machinery. It's people with tools growing food, which is why we originally did the school gardens: We wanted to bring farming even closer to home for kids" (personal communication, November 25, 2020).

While they have been up against the preconception of people from outside of Alaska that Alaska consists of snow and darkness year-round, they have also had to overcome Alaskans' ideas of farming and gardening, in particular the idea that the state is unsuitable for cultivating crops. However, the renewed interest in gardening is witness to the changing ideas in Alaska: "A growing number of home gardeners realizes how easy it is to grow food here, but even Alaskans have that misperception that it's not possible to grow our own food", says Willsrud (personal communication, November 25, 2020).

Encouraging home gardening and small-scale farming

Calypso Farm caters to home gardeners by selling plants at the beginning of the season and offering a variety of workshops. In 2019, close to 200 customers bought seed starts for their home gardens. In 2020, the big plant sale was changed into a pre-order and pickup due to the COVID-19 pandemic. This enabled hundreds of customers to pre-order plants. The age of home gardeners as well as their experience varies widely. Some are long-time gardeners, excited to learn more and connect, others are first-time gardeners. However, all of them live in the region.

Another target group is farmers, who participate in Calypso Farm's farmer training programmes. While the aspiring farmers tend to be from diverse backgrounds, many of them are between 25 and 35 years old. Their common goal is to make a living from small-scale farming. The programmes have not only attracted avid learners from the state of Alaska but also from other countries, including – somewhat surprisingly – Ghana.

Great potential

Willsrud sees a great potential for vegetable farming in Alaska and other Arctic regions (Figure 11.2). She points to the 24 hours of sunlight in the summer: "Half the year, we're just soaking in sun. People don't picture that". While the soil needs building up through the addition of organic matter like compost, it is a great substrate: "In this area, we have all of that wind-blown glacial silt. There are not many nutrients in the soil. We built tons and tons of compost to build the soil up. And it's just incredibly productive". In combination with the sunlight, this is a starting point with an enormous growing potential, as the historical developments of gardening in Alaska shows.

Willsrud observed a flourishing interest in growing food over the last years, in particular in the Fairbanks area, gauging by the participation in the farm's gardening programmes as well as the sales of plants in the spring: "We're in the early

Figure 11.2 Addie Willsrud harvesting beets during the 2020 season. Photo: Calypso Farm.

202   Doris Friedrich

stages supporting Indigenous folks in training and I've been hearing the same thing from them. There seems to be a renewed interest in village communities and more and more people here are gardening". In particular, the global outbreak of COVID-19 has renewed people's focus on food security: "I think the pandemic was a spark. A lot of people are feeling nervous and wanted to grow their own food last spring. We'll see how much this carries into this coming spring. I hope it does" (S. Willsrud, personal communication, November 25, 2020).

Svalbard, Norway – The northernmost greenhouse

Twenty-four hours of daylight allow the cultivation of potatoes and other vegetables despite the north's short and cold growing season, according to Bioforsk (n.d.) (now NIBIO), the Norwegian Institute for Agricultural and Environmental Research, which is specialized on northern growing conditions and food products.

Reports estimate the potential contribution of Norway's marine, forestry and agricultural sectors to the bioeconomy, which in 2016 stood at €33 billion and represented approximately 6% of the economy, up to €110 billion by 2050 (Gewin, 2016). As in Alaska, some see a green turn to more vegetable farming or a "bioeconomy" as a promising step towards a sustainable future based on renewable resources instead of fossil fuels (Gewin, 2016; Ministry of Climate and Environment, 2018).

In 2016, agriculture accounted for 8% of the greenhouse gases emitted by Norway. As a response, the Norwegian Farmers' Union vowed to make Norway's agriculture climate-neutral by 2030 (Bardalen, 2016b; Gewin, 2016; Usland, Gimming, Martin Karlsvik, Thorine Lundstein, & Hansdatter Kismul, 2015). Norway's vision is that "By 2050: Norway will be world-leading in climate-smart food production" (Ministry of Climate and Environment, 2018, p. 55). To achieve this goal, a new study on the regional and structural dimensions by Mittenzwei (2020) suggests regionally concentrating agriculture, extensifying animal production and switching from animal to crop production. The last recommendation, however, counters the argument that while consuming less meat is beneficial for the climate, increasing Norway's domestic production of meat in order to reduce imports can cut down transportation-related emissions (Gewin, 2016).

The Norwegian archipelago of Svalbard is halfway between the north of Norway's mainland and the North Pole and can only be reached by airplane or ship. In the past, some communities on Svalbard experimented with farming, however, all on a small scale. The two Russian settlements Pyramiden and Barentsburg harboured greenhouses and some livestock. While the settlement of Pyamiden was closed in 1998, the greenhouse in Barentsburg is still active and grows onions, tomatoes and peppers to help bolster the food security of the community, which is completely isolated during winter (Umbreit, 2005).

Reaching Longyearbyen, Svalbard's administrative centre, takes three hours by plane from Oslo or two days by ship on the shortest sea route from Tromsø on the Norwegian mainland. This affects the quality and nutritional value of the imported vegetables, in particular leafy greens. What is more, around 30% of the fresh food is lost during transport (Urban Farm, 2020). This is one of the reasons

The quest for fresh vegetables 203

why Benjamin Vidmar, a foodie and chef from Florida, established the world's northernmost greenhouse there: Polar Permaculture.

The story of Benjamin Vidmar and polar permaculture

When Vidmar moved to Longyearbyen in order to work as a chef at the Radisson Blu hotel (Weinstein, 2019), he didn't anticipate that he would later, in 2015, establish a greenhouse and start revamping Longyearbyen's entire food system. However, he realized that there was ample room for improvement in the food system, as all of the food has to be imported and waste is either shipped back to mainland Norway, or in the case of organic waste and sewage, dumped into the ocean. "People come here for the nature, but we're not actually, you know, so ecologically minded here. Polar Permaculture is trying to change that and make this place more sustainable", Vidmar explains in an interview with NBC (Polar Permaculture, 2017).

The philosophy behind "Polar Permaculture" can be summarized as follows, as Vidmar explains on the organization's Facebook site: "We want to help connect people back to the nature and connect people back to the food and help people be better here on the island, to live here more sustainably" (Polar Permaculture, n.d.c). Another crucial reason for establishing the organization Polar Permaculture was to make locally grown, fresh food available to the community of Longyearbyen. As such, the organization has set lofty goals: By 2021, it wants to produce 10% of the local greens, by 2030 even half of the greens consumed in the community (Polar Permaculture, n.d.d).

Despite believing that it's one of the most challenging place for growing vegetables, Vidmar says: "I have been living here since 2007 and I could not think of any other place to establish it but here" (personal communication, November 17, 2020). He further explains: "I had initially wanted to do a permaculture project in Florida, where I presently spend a month each year, but something told me to do it here in Longyearbyen. There was a massive need for it (...), so I believe the place chose me to complete this mission, to help make this place more sustainable" (as cited in Sant, 2020). "It's our home (...). We wanna make it better. We wanna make it better here for everybody", he adds (Polar Permaculture, 2017). For him, locally growing vegetables improves many aspects of the community's well-being: "The more we grow locally, the better our community will be" (personal communication, November 17, 2020).

Polar Permaculture is set within a geodesic dome of around 50 m²: Permaculture principles unite with ecological design to form a resource-efficient circular economy, "where resources are cycled instead of listed as waste", as Vidmar explains (as cited in Friedrich, 2018). The idea behind "permaculture is basically looking to nature and seeing how nature's been doing things for a long time. And then we try to mimic that and design systems based around that" (Polar Permaculture, 2017). The geodesic dome uses passive solar energy from the end of May until the end of September (Urban Farm 2021, n.d.). During wintertime, LED lighting is necessary for plant growth (Weinstein, 2019). In 2017, after only two years

204   *Doris Friedrich*

of operations, the company turnover reached NOK 800,000, breaking even (B. Vidmar, personal communication, February 1, 2018).

Being a professionally trained chef, Vidmar had to do a lot of researching and experimenting: "We've just been experimenting and seeing what's possible, because we're not farmers, we're not biologists, we're not horticulturalists. We're just people who love food. And it was just basically for us to have the freshest food possible" (Polar Permaculture, 2017).

Broad range of benefits

The benefits of growing food on Svalbard relate mostly to the diversity and quality of the produce that can be offered, including its freshness, taste and nutrients. Added food security is another benefit: "It's very vulnerable here. If we don't get food shipped up, it can be a big problem. If you can have some food grown in town, you reduce the risk of not having food" (Polar Permaculture, 2017). One aspect that is often not mentioned is how problematic it is for customers in Svalbard to return produce that is not of satisfying quality to the seller. Vidmar sheds light on Longyearbyen's dependence: "We pay the most probably for the produce. They send like the worst stuff here, because we can't really send it back. Somebody doesn't want it? Ugh, send it to Svalbard" (Polar Permaculture, 2017). The local production also offers environmental advantages, including fewer CO_2 emissions and the enhancement of the local value chain through a circular economy, which encompasses the composting of organic waste instead of dumping it into the fjords (Polar Permaculture, 2017).

Unexpected difficulties

While the location is very remote and the logistics expectedly challenging, Svalbard's strict agricultural law creates unexpected difficulties for farming. Vidmar states: "I never realized how much politics would play into this project" (personal communication, November 17, 2020). One of the major hurdles was the Government approval of worms, which are crucial to jumpstart the organic compost Vidmar uses as fertilizer. After a wait of one and a half years, the permission to import the worms finally arrived. Then, however, the Food Safety Authority in Tromsø, mainland Norway, became sceptical of the quail eggs, a popular product of Polar Permaculture's own quails. Despite successful rigorous sanitary testing, the quails eventually had to be put down (Weinstein, 2019).

"It's been an uphill battle, because we had to deal with the politics, we had to deal with the logistics, there was no laws really for agriculture and now they have to make new rules, new laws, so I guess we kind of threw ourselves into the politics. We just wanna grow food", Vidmar announces (Polar Permaculture, 2017). This has an impact that goes beyond Polar Permaculture, as it might pave the way for similar projects in the future, as Vidmar acknowledges: "So with our permaculture project, we are rewriting all of the history books, looking to change the laws and grow food here once again" (as cited in Sant, 2020).

A bright outlook

Vidmar and his organization look towards a bright future. Realizing his ideas in Svalbard rather than someplace else does have advantages: "Working here in Svalbard, we are at the cutting edge of possibilities, and want to develop systems that can be used in other parts of the world", Vidmar elates (as cited in Friedrich, 2018). This might be in form of a Polar Permaculture kit for other remote regions, so that they can get a quick start on growing their own vegetables while reducing the CO_2 emissions and the waste that are inherent in transporting fresh foods over long distances (Weinstein, 2019).

His plans for the future and current main preoccupation are scaling up the company: "We applied to have a 2500 square meter place and we would like to have large-scale composting" (Polar Permaculture, 2017). In addition, Polar Permaculture hopes to be able to convert waste into biogas, which could then be used to heat the greenhouse (Sant, 2020).

Vidmar has one advice for people interested in growing food in the Arctic and other places with climates that hardly seem suitable for crop cultivation: "Never give up on your dreams! If we can do this here, then it can be done just about anywhere", he asserted in a personal communication with me (November 17, 2020). His dream is to go around the world and help others set up similar projects, "to inspire people around the world with advice and encouragement to do exactly the same thing" (Polar Permaculture, 2018). So far, the initiative has been very well received, as Vidmar confirmed "There are presently many contacts from around the Arctic curious about what we are doing here in the 'northernmost' town" (as cited in Friedrich, 2018).

Canada – Fighting against food insecurity

Northern Canada's history of gardening and growing vegetables resembles that of Alaska. Similar to other Arctic communities, profound energetic and nutritional transitions took place in isolated communities over the past four centuries due to the changes brought upon by colonialism (Martin, 2003; Myers, Fast, Berkes, & Berkes, 2005). The arrival of European whalers in the 17th century led to the commercialization of many wildlife species, which resulted in the depletion of important resources for the Inuit over the eighteenth and nineteenth centuries. The forced settlements and associated building of infrastructure, as well as the slaughtering of sled dogs (Laugrand & Oosten, 2002), substantially altered the human-environment relations of Canada's indigenous population. Air traffic facilitated the transport of food items. The fuel-dependent vehicles that replaced sled dogs rendered access to country foods hunted or collected on the land more expensive. Both of these developments thus intensified the "westernization" of Indigenous diets. Nowadays, for instance in Nunavik, a territory situated in the northernmost part of the Canadian province of Québec, 80% of nutritional intake is store-bought. Low-quality, high-sugar, high-fat foods accounted for 36% of the region's energy intake in 2004 (Blanchet & Rochette, 2008). The First

206 Doris Friedrich

Nations Regional Health Survey recognizes a link between colonial structures and food insecurity. It shows that adults, who were not affected by Residential Schools, are less likely to suffer from severe food insecurity than those who were either directly or intergenerationally affected (FNIGC, 2018).

Food insecurity is significant in northern Canada, and even more so among indigenous peoples (De Schutter, 2012; FNIGC, 2012, 2018; Tarasuk, Mitchell, & Dachner, 2016) and in particular the Inuit, who experience the highest food insecurity of all indigenous peoples in developed countries (Rosol et al., 2011). This leads to numerous health-related problems, including delayed development in children, increased rates of anaemia and what seems counterintuitive at first, obesity and diabetes (Chen & Natcher, 2019). However, these can be explained by the low quality and inadequate nutritional content of the foods available and consumed.

In response to a United Nations Report on the Right to Food (De Schutter, 2012), Canada's government established programmes focusing on northern agriculture, among others Growing Forward I and II, as well as investments in northern agricultural training (Chen & Natcher, 2019). Recently, the Indigenous Agriculture and Food Systems Initiative was introduced. Its aim is to support Indigenous communities and entrepreneurs to start agricultural or agri-food businesses or build their capacity to participate in this sector (AAFC, 2020).

In the context of Nunavik, Lamalice et al. (2018) note the interconnectedness and complexity of the food, water and energy systems. If not properly planned, these three systems can be in competition. Efforts to increase food production often result in the degradation of land and ecosystems, as well as increasing greenhouse gas emissions. They conclude that the local production of produce could remediate some of the issues associated with the import of fresh food, if the interrelations of these systems are factored in and carefully planned.

In their inventory of community gardens and greenhouses across northern Canada, Chen and Natcher (2019) identified 36 community gardens and 17 greenhouses. Of these initiatives, 36 are located in the Northwest Territories, 10 in the Yukon, three in Nunavut, two in Labrador and two in Nunavik (Figure 11.3). A majority of them (64%) are situated in communities with fewer than 1,000 residents. In addition to vegetables, these projects stimulate other forms of food production, in particular livestock such as poultry, which also provides fertilizer for the gardens.

The story of "Arviat Goes Green" and its contribution to indigenous well-being

"When we began sharing produce and ideas/recipes about how to use it, we got lots of positive responses such as 'I never knew that lettuce actually had a taste' or 'I used to throw away vegetable greens, but you can do so many different things with them", Shirley Tagalik shares her experience with people's response to the local produce grown in Arviat, which is situated at 61° North in Nunavut, Canada

Figure 11.3 Research in the greenhouse centred on what fertilizer could best enhance locally inert soil and which plants were most productive. Each bed contained a different soil mixture, but the same type of plants. Photo: Aqqiumavvik society.

(personal communication, November 17, 2020). Tagalik is a community educator and one of the directors of the community organization "Aqqiumavvik Society", the Arviat Wellness Society, which offers programmes aiming at increasing food security.

Health as catalyst

For Arviat, the push to start growing vegetables came from finding out about the community's children's poor eating habits. In a personal communication (November 12, 2020), Tagalik recounts:

A key catalyst for this work came about in 2012 when we conducted a research project called Inusiqsiarniq. This project created a nutrition profile for our children aged 6–12. Results indicated that our children consume only 3 servings of vegetables in a week and 2 servings of fruit. The bulk of the nutritional intake is in the form of highly processed carbs and sugar-high drinks. We decide to focus on two areas of nutritional promotion – improving access to nutrient-rich country foods and "eating green".

As one way to address this concern, the community started looking at the local potential for producing food, such as a community greenhouse. In addition, knowledge about the potential benefits of climate change, such as warmer and longer growing seasons, combined with local observations of a "significant

Figure 11.4 Plants were tended daily by a team of youth researchers. They also monitored aspects of heat, humidity and soil moisture. Photo: Aqqiumavvik society.

change in the quantity and diversity of plants" encouraged the community on this path (Tagalik, personal communication, November 12, 2020). Seeking alternative ways to supply fruits and vegetables in a more environmentally friendly way, Aqqiumavvik started out with research and collaborated with "local youth and visiting researchers to experiment with different growing methods and conditions to find ways of utilizing the summer growing periods (Figure 11.4). Elders also shared Inuit knowledge of local plants and their uses" (Aqqiumavvik, n.d.a).

Their project "Arviat Goes Green" entails various activities, including

1. Research with Elders: Assessing the quantity, growing conditions and sites of locally harvestable edible plants that could be used to augment family diets
2. Use of local edible plants: Using locally harvested and increasingly abundant plants and berries
3. Composting: Introducing organic composting to the community
4. Growboxes (systems for raising plants): Utilizing the increased growing season to introduce home growing options for families through the "Adopt a Growbox" programme
5. Greenhouse: Establishing a research greenhouse to determine optimal plants for food production and the effectiveness of various kinds of soil fertilizers
6. Outreach: Providing an overview of the «Arviat Goes Green» initiative accessible to community members (based on personal communication with Tagalik, November 12, 2020; and Arviat Goes Green, n.d.)

Sustainable knowledge

One of the initiative's many takeaway was the knowledge and connection to the land that people gained. The project showed participants the use of local plants and mushrooms becoming more abundant thanks to climate change, such as purple saxifrage, fireweed, Arctic Willow and sorrel. Berry picking workshops, which were popular events, disseminate ways to use and preserve berries. Tagalik is positive that people continue to use the knowledge and skills they learned: "I see many families continuing to gather land plants in the late summer and fall" (personal communication, November 17, 2020).

The growboxes were another popular programme and a good example of an activity that can bring a range of added benefits that can be sustained over time. "Adopting a Growbox" allowed families to look after a growbox already planted with a variety of vegetables and to start growing at home with their children. In addition to this full "starter kit", they received a lot of information and support: "growing workshops, at home support by regular student visits to monitor growth, information on how to use the plants for family meals and the possibility of attending our Community Kitchen project to expand their skills". Tagalik adds: "When we closed the research greenhouse there were many families wanting to keep the growboxes for themselves and keep planting". According to her, the success of the project can also be measured by the hamlet's decision to build two commercial hydroponic greenhouses in partnership with GreenIglu, a non-profit using dome greenhouse technology, "in the belief that there is sufficient interest in using fresh produce that these would be viable enterprises" (S. Tagalik, personal communication, November 17, 2020). And so far, they are. (Figure 11.5)

Figure 11.5 Growth in each bed was monitored, measured and logged to help determine the most effective soil combinations and the types of seeds that resulted in the biggest yield. Photo: Aqqiumavvik society.

210 Doris Friedrich

In addition, the initiative had a positive impact of the food security and consumption of healthy food in the community. Tagalik reports: "We did see strong uptake of both the use of country food in meal preparations and also regular participants in our community kitchen cooking program. (…) We definitely see kids eating more country food".

Sustainability and climate change

The Arctic is warming twice as fast as the global average (Hassol & Corell, 2006). Climate change affects the procurement of some country foods, for example, by altering the growing conditions and range of wild plants. Wild game might change their migration routes (Seebacher & Post, 2015) and some transportation modes become more dangerous, such as travelling on ice to hunt seals (Berkes & Jolly, 2002; Ford, 2009).

However, changing climatic conditions can also potentially be challenging for the cultivation of crops, as extreme weather events become more frequent, and some regions might experience droughts, floods and unpredictable rainfall (see e.g. Bardalen, 2016a; Hansen et al., 2014; Nobel, 2013). What is more, the warmer temperatures allow animals considered as pests and diseases to expand further north, however, arguably slowly thanks to low winter temperatures (Bardalen, 2016a). This would have the advantage of requiring fewer pesticides (Gewin, 2016). Asked about whether she has noticed environmental changes over the last 20 years, since Calypso Farm was founded, Willsrud answered:

It's hard to see those types of changes, but the thing that's been most noticeable to me is the extremes. It's not necessarily warmer summers or longer seasons, although there is a trend towards that. But the thing that's most noticeable is the unpredictability. In the past 10 years, we've had our hottest summer, our coldest summer, our wettest summer and our driest summer.

This unpredictability, which sometimes results in changes of six weeks in the growing season, requires a great deal of flexibility from farmers: "You have to be really flexible and ready for anything" (Willsrud, personal communication, November 25, 2020). For this reason, Willsrud generally considers climate change a disadvantage: "It's easy certain summers. The last five years maybe, we had more rain, which has been an advantage, because we're dealing with an environment, where we can have really dry summers. So it would be easy to say that climate change is benefitting farming. And it *might* play out that way in the longer term. But the unpredictability makes farmers really vulnerable". She tells the story of friends, who experienced very hot summers when they started farming. This led them to focus their production and investments on different kinds of peppers. Willsrud cautions: "And that was it. There hasn't been another hot summer quite like that. So they ended up going out of business" (personal communication, November 25, 2020).

Some initiatives to grow vegetables in the Arctic stem partly from responses to the threats presented by climate change. Tagalik ties this to the flexibility and adaptability of her community: "Arviammiut [people of Arviat] are

The quest for fresh vegetables 211

experiencing climate change impacts now and community members want to make sure that we are responding well to our new circumstances". As a consequence, the community has researched the repercussions of climate change – both positive and negative:

Arviat has been actively investigating the potential impacts of climate change for the past six years. One of the big laws or *maligarjuaq* of Inuit is to continually plan and prepare for the future. (…) Since the distant future is constantly unsure, Inuit put heavy reliance on *pilimmaksarniq* or ensuring that everyone develops the skills and knowledge that will help them to be successful regardless of changing circumstances. (S. Tagalik, personal communication, November 12, 2020)

These skills should ensure that youth can "successfully address climate change through innovative and adaptive planning" (Tagalik, personal communication, November 12, 2020).

While environmental changes thus might negatively affect food security in Arctic communities, it also makes the climate in some areas more conducible to crop cultivation. Higher temperatures might enable the growth of vegetable varieties previously unsuited to the northern climate. A warmer climate might also allow several harvests during the summer time because of the long hours of summer sunlight (Friedrich, 2018; Gewin, 2016). What is more, it is getting easier to grow vegetables right outside in the ground instead of insulating the growing patches from the permafrost soil.

Tagalik explains: "We observed that climate change is presenting us with a new opportunity for growing food as a result of warming temperatures, more abundant plant life and increasing soil option as permafrost melts". All these changes make it easier for individual families to start growing vegetables: "Climate changes support growing conditions which make local production of plants viable for families. There are local plants, which have significant nutrient potential and can be used as local foods, particularly in salads. We had positive youth and family responses to growing foods locally" (Tagalik, personal communication, November 12, 2020).

The cultivation of vegetables is not only a way to mitigate the effects of climate and other environmental changes affecting food security and other aspects (Chen & Natcher, 2019). It might also be beneficial for the climate, depending on a variety of factors, such as the import of materials and the energy required. As agriculture and other forms of land-use are major contributors to greenhouse gas emissions, a "green shift" in food production is one way to reduce them (Bardalen, 2016a). While many Arctic communities are likely not major contributors to climate change and their diet does not contribute much to their carbon footprint (Lamalice et al., 2018), growing vegetables in the Arctic and the sub-arctic instead of strenuously importing them from southern regions nevertheless lowers their contribution to climate change (Lamalice et al., 2018).

Bardalen (2016a) also sees a great potential for food production in the Arctic in a world undergoing difficult climatic changes, as the region will be less impacted by water scarcity, but rising temperatures will benefit crop cultivation. He estimates northern regions' potential growth in the next 30 years at 20% or more.

212 Doris Friedrich

For Willsrud, small-scale farms, which are prevalent in the Arctic, have a lot of advantages over bigger farms when it comes to sustainability and being climate friendly:

Small-scale operations, where people are making a living and are able to sell *directly* to their community, feels like path forward, especially for Alaska. Because any kind of transportation, any kind of import or export from here is thousands of miles of travel and fossil fuel use. In terms of sustainability and climate change, these small farms have the ability to be a lot more resilient, because on a practical level, it's easier to be more diversified, it's easier to minimize the use of fossil fuel. (Willsrud, personal communication, November 25, 2020)

Due to the smaller size of farms in the Arctic and their environmental benefits, Willsrud suggests that Arctic farms can be a good example:

In Alaska, small-scale farming is an accepted reality, so I feel that we can be a model for other places, where little farms have to fight for their legitimacy in the midst of a bunch of big farms. That feels like a healthier future to me, if a community can feed itself by numerous small-scale farms.
(personal communication, November 25, 2020).

Many initiatives cite environmental reasons as a motive for growing their own food (e.g. Skinner et al., 2014). Iqaluit's Piruqsiavut greenhouse for instance is a local answer to climate change (George, 2008). In a personal communication (November 17, 2020), Vidmar, the manager of Polar Permaculture, points to the environmental impact of Longyearbyen: "Our town has one of the highest CO_2 outputs per capita and we want to change this by producing more local food". Besides reducing greenhouse gas emissions, the local production of food also has the potential to positively affect other environmental issues, such as resource management and pollution (e.g. Skinner et al., 2014).

All in all, many of the initiatives report positive environmental repercussions in the community besides those directly associated with the project. Often, the success of the initiatives elicit very positive responses and encourage other local residents to take up gardening and managing resources more carefully, including composting and recycling. Vidmar outlines the repercussions of Polar Permaculture's local vegetable production on the inspired community: "Now the town wants to become a circular economy in regards to energy production, food production, and waste management" (personal communication, November 17, 2020). In Arviat, produce from the greenhouse was offered to the summer camp and the community kitchen. Tagalik and her team further held workshops and produced videos to help promote "going green". As a result, there were lines of people wanting to taste and use the vegetables in their home recipes during the weekly harvest giveaways. To inform people about additional ways to act environmentally friendly, Aqqiumavvik has published a Community Climate Change Manual (Aqqiumavvik, n.d.b). As Tagalik recounts: "Although Aqqiumavvik has stepped away from actively operating a local greenhouse, we feel that we successfully planted the seeds for these endeavours in the community and have seen improvements in local levels of consumption and use of fruits and vegetables" (personal communication, November 12, 2020).

Discussion and conclusion

This contribution introduced three Arctic states and regions and three initiatives that set as their goal to grow vegetables in Arctic and sub-Arctic climates and thereby improve their community's food security, lessen their impact on the environment, as well as alleviate the negative effects of climate change and use its positive changes to their advantage.

In Ester, Alaska, Susan Willsrud and her team founded Calypso Farm as an educational farm. While the farm covers its costs through the produce they grow and sell, their focus is on outreach and providing training for home gardeners and small-scale farmers.

In Svalbard, Norway, Benjamin Vidmar established the world's northernmost greenhouse. In addition to growing vegetables, he inspired his community Longyearbyen to think about its environmental impact and to attempt to reduce its environmental footprint (or foodprint) through a circular economy.

In Nunavut, Canada, Shirley Tagalik and her team from Aqqiumavvik have conducted extensive research on the local youth's eating habits and climate change, climate change's effects on the potential use of local wild plants and mushrooms and on the possibilities for growing vegetables. Through their workshops, their research greenhouse and the "Adopt a Growbox" project, they have managed to arouse local families' interest and enthusiasm for growing their own food and healthy eating habits.

Climate change affects Arctic communities' possibilities to procure country foods and also intensifies the unpredictability due to changing seasons and extreme weather events, which is a drawback for farmers. Nevertheless, the warmer climate is a boon for growing vegetables, as is the smaller need for pesticides and other chemicals. Importantly, local crop cultivation lowers communities' environmental impact. Reducing food imports and the associated use of fossil fuel contributes to lower greenhouse gas emissions and less waste. In combination with environmentally friendly measures such as a circular economy, recycling and composting, communities can become even more sustainable. Economically, growing food in the north can also be sustainable, if the majority of the materials used are local.

Calypso Farm, Arviat Goes Green and Polar Permaculture are modern pioneers in northern farming, using new technologies and applying techniques recollected from previous generations to meet the challenges of the present that manifest both locally and globally. These projects further point to the interdependence of the local and the global. Local initiatives are an important foundation for global change, for instance in the direction of environmental sustainability and the fight against climate change. Vegetable farming in the Arctic has the potential to actively contribute to achieving several of the United Nation's Sustainable Development Goals, such as "zero hunger", "sustainable cities and communities", "responsible consumption and production" and "climate action" (United Nations, n.d.).

214 *Doris Friedrich*

Hoag (2016) concludes that there is a need for investment and direction in the form of research identifying the plant species most promising and the best soils and sites for crop cultivation in the Arctic. Likewise, Bardalen (2016a), of the Norwegian Institute of Bioeconomy Research, argues that Arctic food production can help alleviate the challenges stemming from climate change. However, the right support and investment is needed. He further emphasizes the importance of highlighting the special qualities of the products and of "telling consumers the stories behind these out-of-the-ordinary foods".

More research is also needed on the demographics of those who participate and benefit from community gardens and greenhouses, as there is the danger that those most in need of reliable food supply might be excluded from those projects due to monetary and time constraints (Chen & Natcher, 2019).

To sum up, the projects introduced in this contribution show that a variety of techniques and technologies can enable vegetable farming in places that seem unsuitable at first sight. What is paramount to succeed is a good knowledge of the local growing conditions, ideally supported through research, and persistence in the face of potential initial failures.

References

AAFC (Agriculture and Agri-Food Canada). (2020). *Indigenous agriculture and food systems initiative*. Retrieved from https://www.agr.gc.ca/eng/agricultural-programs-and-services/indigenous-agriculture-and-food-systems-initiative/?id=1542835055742

Alaska Natural Organics. (n.d.). (2020). About *Facebook*. Retrieved December 5, 2020, from https://www.facebook.com/alaskanaturalorganics/about/

Aqqiumavvik. (n.d.a). *Arviat Goes Green*. Retrieved December 5, 2020, from https://www.aqqiumavvik.com/youth-media-team

Aqqiumavvik. (n.d.b) (2020). *Community climate change manual*. Retrieved December 5, 2020, from https://b4be1162-391a-4a89-9354-530c0ff9b928.filesusr.com/ugd/1f7032_829bfba6a0454e23848d246190d3f07f.pdf

Arviat Goes Green, (n.d.). (2020). *About Facebook*. Retrieved December 5, 2020, from https://www.facebook.com/Arviat-Goes-Green-359227010893368/about/?ref=page_internal

Bardalen, A. (2016a). Arctic agriculture: Producing more food in the North. *Arctic Deeply*. Retrieved from https://deeply.thenewhumanitarian.org/arctic/community/2016/11/02/arctic-agriculture-producing-more-food-in-the-north

Bardalen, A. (2016b). Nordic Agriculture facing climate change – The Norwegian Approach. Retrieved from https://www.slideshare.net/mmmviestinta/nordic-agriculture-facing-climate-change-the-norwegian-approach

Berkes, F., & Jolly, D. (2002). Adapting to climate change: Social-ecological resilience in a Canadian Western Arctic community. *Conservation Ecology*, 5(2), 18.

Bioforsk. (n.d.).(2020) *Arctic Agriculture*. Retrieved December 5, 2020 from http://www.bioforsk.no

Blanchet, C., & Rochette, L. (2008). *Nutrition and food consumption among the inuit of nunavik. Nunavik inuit health survey 2004, qanuippitaa? How are we?* Quebec: Institut national de santé publique du Québec (INSPQ), Nunavik Regional Board of Health and Social Services (NRBHSS

The quest for fresh vegetables 215

Chen, A., & Natcher, D. (2019). Greening Canada's arctic food system: Local food procurement strategies for combating food insecurity. *Canadian Food Studies/La Revue canadienne des études sur l'alimentation*, 6(1), 140–154. doi: 10.15353/cfs-rcea.v6i1.301.

De Schutter, O. (2012). *Report of the special rapporteur on the right to food*. Olivier De Schutter: Mission to Canada, United Nations General Assembly, 1–21.

FNIGC (First Nations Information Governance Centre). (2012). *First nations regional health survey (RHS) 2008/10: National report on adults, youth and children living in first nations communities*. Ottawa, Canada: FNIGC. Retrieved from https://fnigc.inlibro.net/cgi-bin/koha/opac-retrieve-file.pl?id=ccd66b67e9debb2c92f4a54703e1d050

FNIGC (First Nations Information Governance Centre). (2018). *National report of the first nations regional health survey phase 3: Volume one*. Ottawa, Canada: FNIGC. Retrieved from https://fnigc.ca/sites/default/files/docs/fnigc_rhs_phase_3_national_report_vol_1_rev_july_2018_0.pdf

Ford, J. D. (2009). Vulnerability of inuit food systems to food insecurity as a consequence of climate change: A case study from igloolik, Nunavut. *Regional Environmental Change*, 9(2), 83–100. doi: 10.1007/s10113-008-0060-x.

Friedrich, D. (2018, January 3). Vegetable farms 'Mushrooming' across the Arctic. *High North News*. Retrieved from https://www.highnorthnews.com/en/vegetable-farms-mushrooming-across-arctic

Friedrich, D. (forthcoming) Caribou people versus reindeer enthusiasts and the implications for human-environment relations. *Austrian Studies in Social Anthropology*. Retrieved from Friedrich-Ende.pdf (univie.ac.at)

George, J. (2008, September 4). Ignoring earlier failures, 'pioneering: Gardeners vow to bring green revolution to Iqaluit. *Nunatsiaq News*. Retrieved from https://nunatsiaq.com/stories/article/Ignoring_earlier_failures_pioneering_gardeners_vow_to_bring_green_revolutio/

Gewin, V. (2016, November 1). Arctic agriculture: Norway's ambitious green shift. *Arctic Deeply*. Retrieved from https://deeply.thenewhumanitarian.org/arctic/articles/2016/11/01/arctic-agriculture-norways-ambitious-green-shift

Hansen, B. B., Isaksen, K., Benestad, R. E., Kohler, J., Pedersen, ÅØ, & Varpe, Ø (2014). Warmer and wetter winters: Characteristics and implications of an extreme weather event in the high arctic. *Environmental Research Letters*, 9(11), 114021. doi: 10.1088/1748-9326/9/11/114021.

Hassol, S. J., & Corell, R. W. (2006). Arctic climate impact assessment. In H. J. Schellnhuber, W. Cramer, N. Nakicenovic, T. Wigley, & G. Yohe (Eds.), *Avoiding dangerous climate change* (pp. 205–213). New York, NY: Cambridge University Press.

Hoag, H. (2016, October 31). Arctic agriculture: Farming opportunities on the horizon. *Arctic Deeply*. Retrieved from https://deeply.thenewhumanitarian.org/arctic/articles/2016/10/31/arctic-agriculture-farming-opportunities-on-the-horizon

Lamalice, A., Haillot, D., Lamontagne, M. A., Herrmann, T. M., Gibout, S., & Courchesne, F. (2018). Building food security in the Canadian Arctic through the development of sustainable community greenhouses and gardening. *Écoscience*, 25(4), 325–341.

Laugrand, F., & Oosten, J. (2002). Canicide and healing. The position of the dog in the inuit cultures of the Canadian Arctic. *Anthropos*, 97(1), 89–105.

Loring, P. A., & Gerlach, S. C. (2010). Outpost gardening in interior Alaska: Food system innovation and the Alaska native gardens of the 1930s through the 1970s. *Ethnohistory*, 57(2), 183–199.

Martin, T. (2003). *De la banquise au congélateur: mondialisation et culture au nunavik*. Saint-Nicolas, Canada: Les Presses de l'Université Laval.

216 *Doris Friedrich*

Ministry of Climate and Environment. (2018). *Better growth, lower emissions – the Norwegian Government's strategy for green competitiveness.* Retrieved from https://www.regjeringen.no/contentassets/4a98ed15ec264d0e938863448ebf7ba8/t-1562e.pdf

Mittenzwei, K. (2020). Greenhouse gas emissions in Norwegian agriculture: The regional and structural dimension. *Sustainability, 12*(6), 2506.

Myers, H., Fast, H., Berkes, M. K., & Berkes, F. (2005). Feeding the family in times of change. In F. Berkes, R. Huebert, H. Fast, M. Manseau, & A. Diduck (Eds.), *Breaking ice: Renewable resource and ocean management in the Canadian North* (pp. 23–46). Calgary, Canada: University of Calgary Press. doi: 10.2307/j.ctv6gqvp5.9

Naumov, A., Sidorova, D., & Goncharov, R. (2020). Farming on arctic margins: Models of agricultural development in Northern regions of Russia, Europe and North America. *Regional Science Policy & Practice*, 1–13. doi: 10.1111/rsp3.12273

Nobel, J. (2013, October 18). Farming in the Arctic: It can be done. *Modern Farmer.* Retrieved from https://modernfarmer.com/2013/10/arctic-farming/

Phu, L. (2016, September 9). Alaska grows only 4% of its food. Can we do better? *Alaska Journal of Commerce.* Retrieved from https://www.alaskajournal.com/2016-09-09/alaska-grows-only-4-its-food-can-we-do-better

Polar Permaculture. (2017). How to garden in the Arctic. *Youtube.* Retrieved December 5, 2020, from https://www.youtube.com/watch?v=EJE69B5ZZwE&ab_channel=PolarPermaculture

Polar Permaculture. (2018, May 8). We are now on Patreon ... *Facebook.* Retrieved from https://www.facebook.com/watch/?v=1036354779862786

Polar Permaculture. (n.d.a). *Benefit for Longyearbyen.* Retrieved December 5, 2020, from https://www.polarpermaculture.com/benefits-to-longyearbyen

Polar Permaculture. (n.d.b). *Polar Permaculture Solutions, AS is growing food near the north pole!* Retrieved December 5, 2020, from https://www.polarpermaculture.com/

Polar Permaculture. (n.d.c). (2020a). Polar Permaculture. *Facebook.* Retrieved December 5, 2020, from https://www.facebook.com/polarpermaculture

Polar Permaculture. (n.d.d).(2020b). *What is Polar Permaculture?* Retrieved December 5, 2020, from https://www.polarpermaculture.com/pps

Rosol, R., Huet, C., Wood, M., Lennie, C., Osborne, G., & Egeland, G. M. (2011). Prevalence of affirmative responses to questions of food insecurity: International polar year inuit health survey, 2007–2008. *International Journal of Circumpolar Health, 70*(5), 488–497.

Sant, P. (2020). Circular economy: The project polar permaculture. *WhatsOrb.* Retrieved from https://www.whatsorb.com/agri-gardening/fresh-food-doomsday-seed-vault-polar-permaculture

Seebacher, F., & Post, E. (2015). Climate change impacts on animal migration. *Climate Change Responses, 2*(1), 5.

Skinner, K., Hanning, R., Metatawabin, J., & Tsuji, L. J. (2014). Implementation of a community greenhouse in a remote, sub-arctic first nations community in Ontario, Canada: A descriptive case study. *Rural and Remote Health, 14*(2), 2545.

Tarasuk, V., Mitchell, A., & Dachner, N. (2016). *Household food insecurity in Canada, 2014.* Toronto, Canada: Research to identify policy options to reduce food insecurity (PROOF). Retrieved from https://proof.utoronto.ca/wp-content/uploads/2016/04/Household-Food-Insecurity-in-Canada-2014.pdf

Umbreit, A. (2005). [1991]. *Spitsbergen: Svalbard, Franz josef, jan Mayen,* 3rd edition. Bucks, England, and Guilford, USA: Bradt Travel Guides.

The quest for fresh vegetables   217

United Nations. (n.d.). *The 17 goals*. Retrieved March 25, 2021, from https://sdgs.un.org/goals

Urban Farm. (2020). *Polar Permaculture Solutions, AS (Longyearbyen, Norway)*. Retrieved December 5, 2020, from https://drive.google.com/drive/folders/1LdOJdqtuHFap90ySqEc2lY4nRA3PP2Ax

Urban Farm 2021. (n.d.). *Longyearbyen – Polar permaculture dome*. Retrieved December 5, 2020, from https://site.unibo.it/urban-farm/en/cities-and-locations-2020/longyearbyen-polar-permaculture-dome

USDA. (n.d.). *Co-op Research and Extension Services*. Retrieved December 5, 2020, from https://www.usda.gov/topics/rural/cooperative-research-and-extension-services

Usland, B., Gimming, B., Martin Karlsvik, I., Thorine Lundstein, A., & Hansdatter Kismul, A. (2015). *Klimasmart og bærekraftig matproduksjon - Rapport fra arbeidsgruppa*. Retrieved from https://www.bondelaget.no/getfile.php/13692000-1426757036/MMA/Dokumenter/Klimasmart%20og%20b%C3%A6rekraftig%20matproduksjon%20...pdf

Weinstein, V. (2019). Meet the Arctic farmer supplying fresh, sustainable greens to remote regions. *Here Magazine*. Retrieved from https://www.heremagazine.com/articles/arctic-farming-norway

12 Greening discourses of the Nordic Arctic region

The region as vulnerable, late bloomer or the arena of possibilities?

Trond Nilsen and Jukka Teräs

Regional innovation processes driven by discourses on greening of the North

There is an increasing need to better understanding of societal processes in the overall Northern context due to the complex challenges in the social, economic and environmental processes in the Northern region. In this context, green transition in the Nordic Arctic innovation system is a highly complex task due to the fact that extractive industries and natural resource-based economies dominate the composition of the Nordic Arctic economy. We interpret green transition as the *megatrend* that is currently penetrating through the global community. By adding document studies and qualitative interviews on firm level innovative characteristics of the Norwegian, Swedish, and Finnish parts of the Nordic Arctic, this chapter will discuss three dominant discourses of the Nordic Arctic in the context of economic sustainability and green transition. By doing this, we seek to enhance our understanding of important ongoing transformations within the Nordic Arctic region.

The literature on regional renewal and development has highlighted the outcomes of development processes as a material phenomenon. However, in this chapter, we seek to balance such a view. We consider regional development as a *relational phenomenon* constituted by discursive conditions. Discourses are not expressed directly and are not reducible to grammatical or other linguistic elements. Neumann (2001) argued that they set the preconditions for the narrative topic and trigger expectations. Our understanding of social phenomena influences how we talk about them and consequently how we behave. Thus, it is relevant to study the content of discourses as they are the context for the creation of meaning and argument. The framing of various dimensions of regional development and how they unfold in spatial contexts in Nordic Arctic can provide lessons about the role of articulation in rural development.

Furthermore, it is relevant to understand how these processes develop and why different actors attribute different meanings to them. For instance, we need to know whether such rhetoric (tactics) may be profitable for governments, MNCs and local business actors on different spatial scales. In this context, it is pertinent to study how the industry actors frame their activities and relationship

DOI: 10.4324/9781003118633-13

Greening discourses of the Nordic Arctic region   219

with green regional development as an *opportunity or threat* to the renewal of peripheral regions. In public opinion, positive or negative expectations of new industry initiatives are often a result of discourses established by powerful actors with legitimacy to the general public. Hence, this chapter investigates how three different discourses of the Nordic Arctic societies encompassing different regions and countries, influence on the innovative capability for industry firms and business actors within the region. The research question is formulated as follows: *How can the three discourses; the vulnerable North, the North as a late bloomer or the region as possibility, influence on green innovative capability in the region?*

The rest of the chapter is structured as follows. First, we introduce the theoretical framework to analyze the three different discourses in connection to regional development and regional renewal. This section is followed by a short description of the methods used to gather this data. The empirical section contains a brief description of the three discourses, while the discussion reflects on to what degree and how the different discourses opens or close the innovative capability within the region. Finally, we conclude by addressing the research question and suggest further research suggestions on this topic.

Discourses in social sciences

This section introduces the theoretical approach of the paper by highlighting theories of discourses as well as regional development, with particular attention to the role of rural regions and innovation.

The literature on discourse theory contains many different approaches in the social science literature. We concentrate on two main categories of theories in the social sciences. We draw a distinction between discourse theory in general and critical discourse analysis, based on post-structural epistemologies. Those in the first category, discourse theory, view the entire social world as a discursive construction (Neumann, 2001). The second category, critical discourse analysis, has grown out of the work of Fairclough (1995) and Laclau and Mouffe (2001). While Foucault claimed that discourse was a fundamental structure and constitutes the basis for all social practice, the second category (critical discourse analysis) emphasizes changing paradigms of meaning, knowledge and political claim making. Neumann (2001) and Laclau and Mouffe (2001) stressed the practices of "articulation" of claims and saw them as efforts to "fix meaning" in political struggles. Our discourse approach draws less on Foucault and more on Laclau and Mouffe, Neumann and Fairclough. Yet to capture the voices of regional renewal and politics, we find it useful to supplement their concept of articulation with that of discourses.

Rose (2001, p. 138) defined discourse as "the process used to produce the meaning of a topic that inherently structures the perceptions and practices of the participants, although without their necessarily being conscious of being controlled". In this context, discourses become the specific perceptions or modes of explanations promoted by an actor or group of actors concerned with a certain topic (Rose, 2001).

220 Trond Nilsen and Jukka Teräs

Theories of regional development and innovation in dispersed regions

The evolutionary turn in theories of innovation and regional growth represents historical dimensions as formative for regional structures (Grabher, 2009). Experienced competencies developed over time by entities in certain localities regulate present formations as well as paths in the future (Kogler, 2015). This suggests that history matters in shaping places and its economic and social scenery. Involved in such thinking, the notion of path dependent regional industrial development is of great interest to researchers within the field. Path dependent regional development focuses on the "negative and positive lock-in effects that pushes a technology, an industry, or a regional economy along one path rather than another" (Narula, 2002). In such, path dependence means that regional industries may enter into path extension through mainly incremental innovations in present industries and technical paths.

The evolutionary approach in economic geography have added theoretical contributions that supplement these notions of path dependent developments that focus on continuity and lock-in, by alternative paths where dynamics occurs. Changes may follow from different elements of re-organization of industries in a region (MacKinnon, Cumbers, Pike, Birch, & McMaster, 2009). Path renewal occurs when local businesses shift into different activities. The content of regional firms like knowledge bases shape to some extent the degree of renewal that is observed. Typical, path renewal is often developed within the industry as a regional industry transform and broadens the industrial structure into new or related areas of activities.

While peripheral regions have other characteristics and differ from core areas when it comes to development of knowledge bases, one should be aware of approaching the same explanatory models in order to understand innovation and growth processes in such different regions (Eder, 2019; Isaksen & Trippl, 2017; Nilsen, 2017). While core areas draw on a great amount of analytical knowledge and combine with synthetic knowledge bases, studies of new industrial paths in less-favoured regions point to the role of exogenous development impulses such as arrival of innovative firms from outside and other forms of inflow of external knowledge (Isaksen & Trippl, 2014). Key sources of new path creation, it is argued, are extra-regional arrangements like new technologies, industries, firms or institutions (Martin & Sunley, 2006).

Scholars argue that emerging new paths do not grow out of what neo-classical market economists reflect as situations without any social intervention of active actors (Grillitsch & Sotaratuta, 2020; Simmie, 2012; Sanches, 1992). Consequently, they argue for bringing in pioneering individuals, universities and/or public agencies and governments (op.cit, 769). A comparative study of two sectors in ICT and software industry in peripheral areas in Austria and Norway shows that exogenous development impulses in form of the inflow of new analytical and synthetic knowledge through the inward transplantation from outside initiated new paths (Isaksen & Trippl, 2014). They found that policy-makers and other key actors have played a pivotal role in creating and sustaining new industrial activities in the periphery. Sanches (1992) argues that the main type of new path development in peripheral regions is efforts by regional or national governments to attract external investments. Still, conceptualizations of regional path development have given no attention to the role of state (MacKinnon et al, 2009). Research on regional path development tends to neglect the role of policy interventions in new path creation (Dawley, 2014; MacKinnon et al, 2009; Martin 2012; Morgan, 2013; Sanches, 1992; Simmie, 2012).

Interviews and text analysis as information sources to understand discourses in the Arctic

We have used interviews and text analysis to assess how greening of industries have been represented in an Arctic context. First, we have conducted 26 interviews with representatives of staff in MNCs (Equinor, Vår Energi, LKAB) complemented with interviews with representatives of a range of SMEs and company associations as Port of Tromsø, Remiks, Maritime Forum North, local energy companies as well as Nordic Arctic regions in Norway, Sweden, and Finland. The interviews were carried out with a semi-structured interview guide as a background, and each interview lasted between 30 and 45 minutes. The interviewees answered questions on specific efforts in greening such as renewable energy, how the internal set-up of organizational structure could facilitate renewable energy strategies, and in what way climate change is dependent upon energy companies' efforts to invest in new technology. The aim of this is to increase our understanding of how ideas of greening have been represented within the firm. In addition, we wanted to supplement the qualitative interviews by analysis of texts. The text analysis was categorized according to three actor groups in order to sort out the different actors. The first group of documents had the aim of highlighting the relevance of international bodies of renewable energy such as institutions, and supranational bodies such as the EU and energy associations. This group of documents was followed by documents related to national government in Norway and provided the context and institutional frames for the specific case, highlighting regulations and subsidies related to greening. The third group of documents comprised internal company reports mainly from the following MNCs: Equinor, Vår Energi, LKAB, and Northvolt. These documents provided important information in order to contextualize their operations, i.e., the the annual summaries of the companies in their Sustainability Reports series. These documents provided additional information and were analyzed to validate the information collected from the interviews.

The vulnerable North

The first discourse is the *vulnerable North* where the region is a passive receiver of exogenous factors that impact negatively on the region either based on economic vulnerability and "thinness" of the innovation system, social processes or climate change. This has been studied especially from the viewpoint of social and environmental sustainability where the Nordic Arctic region goes through (often

222 Trond Nilsen and Jukka Teräs

negative) changes due to climate change. The aim of environmental sustainability is reflected at the international and national level mainly through policy documents. The "Paris Agreement", include a temperature limit of 2°C and even more of practical relevance, it also include long-term emission goals for nations involved. EU holds another hegemonic position in the discourse. The Directive from EU on renewable energy from 2008, points forward to a commitment to increase the share of renewable energy to over 22% in 2010. In addition, the Climate Settlement, implemented in 2008 with broad political consent in Norway, points to the aim at becoming carbon neutral in 2030. We experience this discourse especially within questions of wind-power in the region, where a number of initiatives are promoted by the regional industry actors and companies, while being reduced to environmental problems, due to the vulnerability of the region.

Another example from this discourse is representations of the negotiated nature in the region between traditional land-use and nature- based business activities. The dominating actors are Saami Parliament and the Reindeer Management administrative body. Consequently, the dominating representations are mainly negative towards an active and progressive development of industry activity, i.e., wind-power or dam extension (interview data). The most prominent example of neglecting wind production is the reindeer herders as they actively oppose this development by arguing for their rights to land preservation and business activity. Reindeer herding is the cultural and business fundament of the Saami people. The wind companies, both from the region and MNCs, plan to invest on land already used by the Saami reindeer herders and for other harvesting activities. The position of the Saami people in the region is strong as institutionally embedded within a contextual frame of seeking to ensure land user rights. This implies that the licensing process of windmill parks, regulated by the Energy Law, gives the Saami people's representative parliament a possibility to be heard through consultations with NVE. The indigenous dimension folds out as a counterpart to the notion of Finnmark as a vast and untouched land available for new industrial development. Traditional Sámi livelihood with reindeer herding occupies practically all land of the region as the annual trekking of 146,000 reindeers follows a pattern using the inland for winter pasture, and the coast for summer pastures (interview data). Territories used in autumn and spring are particularly important for breeding and calving. This is the period when the reindeers are most vulnerable to external interference. A third example is the diverging representations (conflict) between interest of oil development and fisheries in the North. While increased oil and gas activity has proven to increase regional development paths in a positive matter for some regions in the North (Nilsen, 2019), the conflicts between the fisheries organization and oil companies can be traced back to a discourse of the vulnerable region of the North. The discourse contains mainly dominating actors within pro-interests of sustaining small and specialized industries along a dispersed region, where small-scale fisheries is the main source of employment. They claim that the very foundation of the regions' employment and settlement can be threatened by economic diversification from other sectors. The argument is that small communities have vulnerable and path-dependent structures which have led to strong dependency towards one sector, and that new sectors can intrude and even destroy the fundament of settlements in these communities.

Overall, the vulnerable discourse main contribution is that new economic growth trajectories challenge the North. Industry initiatives are obstructed in the process due to a fear of undermining existing (and traditional) industries in the region. Hence, this discourse reduces the green innovative capability for firms in the region as the discourse points at continuation instead of change towards new regional trajectories.

The North as a late bloomer

The second discourse points at the *North as a late-comer* in economic development highly dependent on subsidiaries from central part of Norway or Europe. The discourse is composed of how lacking regional density and agglomeration produce a specific outcome where the notion of the late-comer becomes the output. The main content within this discourse is territorial and focuses on peripheral communities, long distances, small firms, harsh climates and thin innovation systems. Few innovative firms within traditional sectors with low levels of innovative capabilities make the transformation to green transition a difficult case for the firms and thus challenge the economic sustainability in the Nordic North region.

Our interviews indicate that the Nordic Arctic as a whole is not at the forefront of green transition. One way of exemplifying is through the implementation of sustainability goals, e.g., SDG thinking, and we observe that the region is rather a late comer in this respect – not too many SMEs in the Nordic Arctic have really adopted the SDG concept yet. Having said that, there is a gradual transition towards greener thinking and greener processes going on, e.g., in the maritime sector, an important sector for the Arctic. However, maritime innovations at some scales have been launched elsewhere. We note that innovations have been introduced in battery technology in the western part of Norway (Sotarauta & Suvinen, 2019). The introduction of a ferry on battery technology increased the greening of the sector and reduced the emissions from the maritime traffic. The novelty, as argued by Sjøtun, lies in the combination of existing technology used in its construction, including the infrastructure underpinning Ampere. In order to provide Ampere with electricity, charging towers were built on both sides of the fjord. The diffusion of this technology has only to a rather limited degree reached the Nordic Arctic part of the coast and hence, the sector is lagging behind in the respect of battery technology in the Arctic. This is also confirmed by the data from a research project focusing on green transition in the Arctic. Traditional SMEs are not at the technology forefront when it comes to developing new solutions based on greening of new sectors. Hence, the SMEs are followers, and not pioneers in this development.

When it comes to bigger companies and the different MNCs in the region, they are more likely to introduce green solutions within the region that has already been introduced, and that have been developed elsewhere. As Nilsen (2017) points at, the company Equinor, one of the biggest MNCs in Europe, has taken

224 Trond Nilsen and Jukka Teräs

strategic decisions regarding what kind of technology trajectories the company seeks to follow. Introducing offshore wind is one of the major strategic decisions. However, none or very few of these technologies or solutions have been anchored within the Arctic region or build upon knowledge from the region. Still we see experiences of industries in the Arctic region that have been developing green solutions and have been pro-active in order to achieve greening of their activities. Within this discourse, however, we believe that a greener global trend forces the Arctic SMEs to change towards a more sustainable trajectory in such a respect. The firms within the Arctic context are path dependent when it comes to green transitions, meaning that previously experiences increases the probability follow the same path of decisions and strategies in the discussion of the future activities.

The main contribution of the late comer discourse is that new economic growth trajectories are based on previously experiences in the region and point in a direction where the region lacks relevant knowledge and skills in order to take a lead position within the transition towards greening of the economy. Industry initiatives have been taken elsewhere and successfully adopted to existing industries and are either not anchored within the Arctic region or developed without knowledge from the region. Hence, this discourse prolongs and extends the existing path of Arctic firms being hindered by lacking innovative capability. The discourse points at continuation instead of change towards new regional trajectories.

The region of possibilities

The last discourse demonstrates another trajectory for the region as they are pointing in another and more optimistic direction. Hence, the third discourse is the *region of possibilities* where endogenous economic growth and rich natural resources present in the area is the most important ingredients. Foreign direct investments (FDI) increase the number of entry firms in the North, increased learning occurs, shared new technologies are distributed and the overall innovation capability increases in the region. Green transition is at the forefront of firm behaviour and the established technological systems is being step-by-step replaced by a greener system of production within important sectors for the region. Examples of green transition in the Arctic regions in Sweden and Finland, with large industrial companies and MNCs often showing the way, are presented to illustrate the current trend and activities towards a greener Arctic industry.

Sustainable development is high on the agenda for both Norrbotten and Västerbotten in Sweden. Large-scale and capital-intensive industrial projects have recently placed North Sweden in the global spotlight with regards to sustainable and climate-neutral investments in emerging and fossil fuel replacing technologies (Teräs, Koivurova, Eikelund, & Salenius, 2021, forthcoming). In 2020, the mining conglomerate LKAB announced an extensive investment into the development and scaled-up implementation of a fossil-free steel production. Centred in Norrbotten and estimated at close to EUR 40 billion over two decades, the industrial investment counts among the largest in Sweden's history (LKAB, 2020). Northvolt investments in battery technology in Västerbotten represent another

Greening discourses of the Nordic Arctic region   225

important green transition investment in North Sweden. Northvolt was founded in 2017 with the mission to build the world's most sustainable batteries. Northvolt employs more than 700 people at its facilities in Sweden, Germany and Poland, and the production in Skellefteå alone will employ over 3,000 people by the time of full production capacity (www.northvolt.com). Building the factory in Northern Sweden enables access to fossil-free and inexpensive energy sources. Skellefteå is part of a raw material and mining cluster and has a long history of process manufacturing and recycling, and because the factory will be powered by 100% renewable hydro power, the manufacturing process will produce close to zero carbon dioxide emissions (Teräs, Salenius, Fagerlund, & Stanionyte, 2018). The battery factory initiative is situated amidst a growing regional competence network with relevant industrial capacity, cheap and clean energy production and well-functioning public administration. The Swedish government announced in 2020 that a national coordinator ("samordnare") will be nominated to promote the coordination of issues (competences, infrastructure, housing, climate) related to large-scale investments in Norrbotten and Västerbotten (Regeringskansliet, 2020).

The industrial circular economy has been developing in the Finnish Lapland for decades, with the famous principle of waste of one actor being a resource for another actor. The Kemi-Tornio region, close to the Swedish border, with a concentration of process industry companies, has a long tradition of utilizing the potential of industrial circular economy collaboration in a context of a concentration of Arctic process industry. The systematic development of an Arctic industrial circular economy cluster took off in 2012–2014 including, e.g., the mapping of industrial by-product flows conducted in 2013–2014. The Industrial Circular Economy Centre was established in 2017, including establishment and coordination of the network of Finnish eco-industrial parks. In 2020, the Ministry of Economic Affairs and Employment in Finland selected the Industrial Circular Economy Centre as the flagship project to create the National Knowledge Platform for Industrial Circular economy in Finland, including network building with Nordic industrial circular economy actors. Lapland's expertise in industrial circular economy demonstrates the potential of a well-established regional specialization to be empowered and scaled up through the empowerment of locally led initiatives and efforts.

Overall, the main contribution of the "Region of possibilities" discourse is that new economic growth trajectories open up new developments in the North in a constructive way. Industry initiatives are supported in the process due to a belief that green transition is possible. Hence, this discourse increases the innovative capability for firms in the region as the discourse points at renewal instead of continuation towards new regional trajectories.

Contested discourses of the Arctic

The premise for this chapter is that territorial dimensions matter for the greening of MNC and MNE in the Arctic. We have launched three different discourses of dimensions of greening in the region that influence differently on the

226 Trond Nilsen and Jukka Teräs

way green transition grows forward in the region, and whether the industries are influenced by the discourses in their greening activities. However, the premise that territorial dimensions per se influence on renewal is contested. While there is much evidence that territorial dynamics is a mechanism that influences on regional renewal (i.e., Boschma & Frenken, 2006), a study of green innovation in California, Chapple, Kroll, Lester, and Montero (2011) showed that green innovation varies widely between different sectors, meaning that there is heterogeneity between firms and sectors within the same region (see also Faber & Hoppe, 2013; Makkonen & Inkinen, 2018; Oltra & Saint Jean, 2009). This implies that the sectorial belonging is of greater importance in the greening activities of firms compared to what kind of territorial belonging firms have. In an Arctic context, such a perspective can be of high relevance due to the lacking density within the region, often combined with low levels of competence and high regional specialization.

The discourses point in different directions when referring to the role green transition has for the region. The first discourse seems to have strong connections to path-dependence and lock-in for green industries like wind power. The potential of greening of electricity production is hindered by decisions taken at the national policy level based on indigenous people rights and the interests of institutions like the Sàmi Parliament. The role of regional interests that are pro-greening and argue for energy transitions by the use of renewable energy in order to secure a solid electricity feed into the grid, meet resistance when they seek renewal based on the regions willingness to secure preservation of traditional nature-based activities, like reindeer herding and securing Sámi interests. Two conflicting interests encounter in this discourse and our examples highlight that dominant positions within the discourse hinder the role of green transition based on energy transition in the region. Hence, the first discourse hinders the innovation capability of firms within renewable energy.

However, the discourses relate to each other in different ways in the Arctic region. Preserving nature and holding on to existing nature-based business seem to be a rather hegemonic interest within the region as underlined in the first discourse. The second discourse implies that the region as a whole is a late comer in green development which has been underlined by the lacking knowledge on technology renewal related to greening of the sectors. We note that maritime industries have taken big green steps in the western part of Norway, and this sector is now facing a possible "technology shift", implying that new energy carriers and technologies (e.g., battery, biogas/diesel, hydrogen, hybrid solutions) may replace conventional fossil energies (Sjøtun, 2020; Sotarauta & Suvinen, 2019; Steen, Bach, Bjørgum, Hansen, & Kenzhegaliyeva, 2019). These developments have grown forward without the participation from key actors in the Northern Arctic region. Similarly, technologies of green transition like carbon storage and capture (CCS) have the potential to be a game-changer within the petroleum industries. The technology development within these areas usually takes place outside the Nordic Arctic region (Njøs, Sjøtun, Jakobsen, & Fløysand, 2020). Hence, we would argue that within the two major sectors in Norway, petroleum

Greening discourses of the Nordic Arctic region 227

and maritime sector and in relation to battery technology, the key actors in the Nordic Arctic region are lagging behind and are following instead of leading the green development. The discourse of the late comer in green transition means that firms in the region have a strong competence bias compared to regions in the south-west, where necessary competence mostly is located outside the region in the cases of maritime and petroleum sector.

When investigating other sectors like waste management and within services in general SMEs, we find a different pattern where firms in the region take a more pro-active role. The example of Port of Tromsø effort to develop an "Energy hub" is promising where they seek to develop onshore power supply, LNG-supply systems to supply ships and other initiatives as well. Another promising example is Remiks in Tromsø in the field of waste management where they develop measures in order to reduce the environmental impact of waste in the region. In addition, we find that Remiks seeks initiatives to create an agglomeration of firms that cut across the whole region in collaboration of waste management. This could be supported by the growing body of literature on socio-technical transitions that argues that greening of industrial activities in regions should be approached by investigating their multi-scalarity (Coenen, Moodyson, & Martin, 2015; Martin, 2020).

The discourse of the region as opportunity points in a different direction. Here the opportunities of proactive greening are at the centre. Increased value creation, more jobs and a greener environment seem to be at the core of this discourse (interview data). Actors within large-scale industries, such as LKAB, Equinor, Vår Energi among others, seek new business models and solutions based on their existing industrial activities. The Northvolth initiative of battery technology is a good example of what is possible inside the Nordic Arctic region based on building competence by utilizing exogenous and endogenous competence bases in the region. Another example is the industrial circular economy in Arctic conditions as pointed at from the lens of Finland which now is gaining momentum in the light of increased focus on greening of industries. Re-structuring the production by utilizing waste as an input into the production process is at the core of the business model.

The MNCs inside large industries seem to be eager to take a leading role inside green transition in the region, according to our study. One dimension that needs to be taken into consideration in this respect, however, is the role of legitimacy and possible "greenwashing". Two of the companies being most active in the greening debate in Norway are the two major oil companies. These companies have the necessary technology, competence, networks and capital to take an active part in the green transition inside and outside the region. However, they are at the same time increasingly contributing to pollution in the Norwegian part of the Northern Arctic region, and hence have a social responsibility to find solutions based on the aspect of legitimacy within the institutional system. The motivation that pushes the companies in a green direction could be questioned. However, the consequences of greening will inevitably promote a more sustainable future for firms and people living in that region.

228 Trond Nilsen and Jukka Teräs

Values and growth dilemmas

The identified discourses in the regional context of the Arctic can all be seen as "perspectives on" sustainability. However, pulling the discourses together highlights how the discourses relate to each other and particularly demonstrate the contrast, dilemmas and value conflicts between the discourses. The first discourse contains institutions (i.e., norms) which highlight the role of traditional way of living in the region based on utilizing nature as a way of doing business for different actors. The role of conflicting interests is particularly evident in wind-power agencies interests and how they relate to traditional reindeer-herding interests in the region. The role of greening industry activities is neglected and interests of traditional sectors with historical traditions in the region are lifted up. The value conflicts become relevant between industry growth based on green energy on the one hand, and preserving indigenous interests on the other. Even though we find examples of different outputs in this respect, our examples from this discourse demonstrate that values of greening of industry production is downplayed in the first discourse, and values of preserving nature-based industry traditions is the dominating interest. Hence, the second discourse, the North as a late bloomer, highlights mostly how the regions position within green transition take a path-dependent role. Important technology and development processes are taking part outside the region, and challenge values of endogenous capacity and capabilities of adapting to radical changes in a rural and sparsely populated region. Increased learning and connections to other regions and other institutions outside the region is key in this respect. The dilemma here, from the regional point of view, is that decisions already taken in an early period of time strengthen already strong milieus in different regions. Hence, these decisions taken by strong companies outside the region prolongs the notion of "the late bloomer" path in the region. The tendency of path-dependence is strengthened, and the greening trend can make the region even more locked-in to existing paths with severe challenges of breaking out of dominating trajectories.

Conclusion

This chapter has demonstrated that the discourses of greening in the Northern Arctic region are being contested. We have identified three different discourses of greening in the region and discussed to what extent the discourses influence firm innovative capability. The chapter which is based on interviews and document studies demonstrates that the discourses in different dimensions influence on green transition and possibilities of innovation capability. The first discourse of the vulnerable north obstructs green transition within the energy sector with particular focus on renewable wind power. The conflicts between traditional and nature-based industries in the region challenge renewal inside wind industry and hence the ability of local firms to take part in new supply chains and to explore new market opportunities. Second, the discourse of the region as a late bloomer influences the innovative capability in the region to much lesser degree. The third discourse highlights that necessary competence to take part in the green transition within particularly maritime and petroleum sector requires competence, technology and skills that mainly are developed outside the region. This fact implies that local firms do not have access to arenas where new competence is developed inside these two important sectors for the region. Hence, the late comer discourse influences the continuation path of regional innovative capability. The discourse of possibilities points in a different direction. The discourse contains opportunities, job creation and value creation based on greening activities. The main actors inside this discourse of greening are MNCs which to a large degree argue that greening increases the innovative capability in the region. They utilize exogenous networks, capital and technology and seek to contribute to green transition in the region.

We argue that regional competence, networks, capital and technology are not sufficient to actively take part within the new megatrend of green transition. Firms that seek central positions in the development need to take into account how regional industries develop in connection to external networks and competencies outside the region. Thus, bringing in a multi-scalar perspective in the understanding of greening of the industries in the Arctic is at the core of our understanding of green transition.

However, a few considerations need to be taken into account in discussing the path forward for green transition in the region. The first consideration is related to the development of the existing raw material prices. A continuation of high prices on raw material could be a barrier towards greening since already existing strategies in the region pay off economically. We know that success inside one path or technology can be an obstacle towards diversification towards new trajectories. Another consideration is whether companies important for the economic development in the region have access to new and prospective areas of resources. A third factor is how the greening strategies develop as a whole based on technology and pricing in the years to come. Forth, the companies' priorities on green strategies are important based on existing business models and how diversification towards new strategies will be balanced in this respect.

References

Boschma, R., & Frenken, K. (2006). Why is economic geography not an evolutionary science? Towards an evolutionary economic geography. *Journal of Economic Geography*, 6, 273–302.

Chapple, K., Kroll, C., Lester, T. W., & Montero, S. (2011). Innovation in the green economy: An extension of the regional innovation system model? *Economic Development Quarterly*, 25, 5–25.

Coenen, L., Moodyson, J., & Martin, H. (2015). Path renewal in old industrial regions: Possibilities and limitations for regional innovation policy. *Regional Studies*, 49(5), 850–865.

Dawley, S. (2014). Creating new paths? Offshore wind, policy activism, and peripheral region development. *Economic Geography*, 90(1), 91–112. doi: 10.1111/ecge.12028

230 Trond Nilsen and Jukka Teräs

Eder, J. (2019). Innovation in the periphery: A critical survey and research agenda. *International Regional Science Review*, 42, 119–146.

Faber, A., & Hoppe, T. (2013). Co-constructing a sustainable built environment in the Netherlands: Dynamics and opportunities in an environmental sectoral innovation system. *Energy Policy*, 52, 628–638.

Fairclough, N. (1995). *Critical discourse analysis: The critical study of language*. New York, NY: Longman Publishing.

Grabher, G. (2009). Yet another turn? The evolutionary project in economic geography. *Economic Geography*, 85(2), 119–127.

Grillitsch, M., & Sotarauta, M. (2020). Trinity of change agency, regional development paths and opportunity spaces. Progress in human geography, 44(4), 704–723.

Isaksen, A., & Trippl, M. (2014). "New Path Development in the Periphery," Papers in Innovation Studies 2014/31, Lund University, CIRCLE - Centre for Innovation Research. Retrieved from New Path Development in the Periphery (repec.org).

Isaksen, A., & Trippl, M. (2017). Exogenously led and policy-supported new path development in peripheral regions: Analytical and synthetic routes. *Economic Geography*, 93, 1–22.

Kogler, D. (2015). Editorial: Evolutionary economic geography – Theoretical and empirical progress. *Regional Studies*, 49(5), 705–711.

Laclau, E., & Mouffe, C. (2001). *Hegemony and socialist strategy: Towards a radical democratic politics*. London: Verso Trade.

LKAB. (2020). *Historic Transformation Plan for LKAB. LKAB Press Release 23 November 2020*. Retrieved December 1, 2020, from https://www.lkab.com/en/news-room/press-releases/historictransformation-plan-for-lkab-the-biggest-thing-we-in-sweden-can-do-for-the-climate/

MacKinnon, D., Cumbers, A., Pike, A., Birch, K., & McMaster, R. (2009). Evolution in economic geography: institutions, political economy, and adaptation. *Economic geography*, 85(2), 129–150. doi:10.1111/j.1944-8287.2009.01017.x

Martin, R. (2012). (Re) placing path dependence: A response to the debate. *International Journal of Urban and Regional Research*, 36, 179–192. doi: 10.1111/j.1468-2427.2011.01091.x

Martin, H. (2020). The scope of regional innovation policy to realize transformative change – A case study of the chemicals industry in Western Sweden. *European Planning Studies*, 28(12), 2409–2427.

Martin, R., & Sunley, P. (2006). Path dependence and regional economic evolution. Journal of economic geography, 6(4), 395–437.

Makkonen, T., & Inkinen, T. (2018). Sectoral and technological systems of environmental innovation: The case of marine scrubber systems. *Journal of Cleaner Production*, 200, 110–121.

Morgan, K. (2013). Path dependence and the state: The politics of novelty in old industrial regions. In P. Cooke (Ed.), *Re-framing regional development: Evolution, innovation, transition* (pp. 318–340). New York, NY: Routledge.

Narula, R. (2002). Innovation systems and "inertia" in R&D location: Norwegian Firms and the role of systemic lock-in. *Research Policy*, 31(5), 795–816.

Neumann, I. B. (2001). *Mening, materialitet og makt. en innføring i diskursanalyse*. Bergen: Fagbokforlaget.

Nilsen, T. (2017). Firm-driven path creation in arctic. *Local Economy*, 32(2), 77–94.

Nilsen, T. (2019). Global production networks and strategic coupling in value chains entering peripheral regions. *The Extractive Industries and Society*, 6(3), 815–822.

Njøs, R., Sjøtun, S., Jakobsen, S.-E., & Fløysand, A. (2020). Expanding analyses of path creation: Interconnections between territory and technology. *Economic Geography, 96*, 266–288.

Oltra, V., & Saint Jean, M. (2009). Sectoral systems of environmental innovation: An application to the French automotive industry. *Technological Forecasting and Social Change, 76*, 567–583.

Regeringskansliet (2020). Retrieved from https://www.regeringen.se/pressmeddelanden/2020/12/regeringen-tillsattersamordnare-for-samhallsomstallning-vid-storre-foretagsetableringar-och-foretagsexpansioner-i-norrbotten-och-vasterbotten/

Rose, G. (2001). *Visual methodologies: An introduction to the interpretation of visual material.* London: Sage Publications.

Sanches, A. M. (1992). Regional innovation and small high technology firms in peripheral regions. *Small Business Economics, 4*, 153–168.

Simmie, J. (2012). Path dependence and new technological path creation in the Danish wind power industry. *European Planning Studies, 20*(5), 753–772. doi: 10.1080/09654313.2012.667924

Sotarauta, M., & Suvinen, N. (2019). Place leadership and the challenge of transformation: Policy platforms and innovation ecosystems in promotion of green growth. *European Planning Studies.* doi: 10.1080/09654313.2019.16340

Sjøtun, S. (2020). *"Engineering" the green transformation of the maritime industry in Western Norway.* Norway: University of Bergen.

Steen, M., Bach, H., Bjørgum, Ø, Hansen, T., & Kenzhegaliyeva, A. (2019). *Greening the fleet: A technological innovation system (TIS) analysis of hydrogen, battery electric, liquefied biogas, and biodiesel in the maritime sector.* Report SINTEF 2019.

Teräs, J., Koivurova, T., Eikelund, S., & Salenius, V. (2021, forthcoming). *Arctic smart specialisation strategies for sustainable development.* A report to the EU JRC S3 Seville Platform.

Teräs, J., Salenius, V., Fagerlund, L., & Stanionyte, L. (2018). *Smart specialisation in sparsely populated European arctic regions,* EUR29503 EN, Publications Office of the European Union, Luxembourg, 2018, ISBN 978-92-79-98266-8.

Reflections
What can we create together?

Tony Ghaye, Loughborough University in London, England
Rita Sørly, The Arctic University of Norway/NORCE
Bård Kårtveit, NORCE

Introduction

Stories not only capture and recount what has happened, they can actually shape the life we choose to move towards and the world we wish to create. Arguably, this book of different kinds of Arctic-related stories contributes to our appreciation of what a vibrant, flourishing, dignified and truly humane future, or otherwise, we might imagine for the region. If we focus only on eco-anxious (problem) stories, we will learn a lot about our eco-anxieties, but little about a socially just, economically viable, livable Arctic inhabited by future generations in peace and harmony and where everyone can thrive and flourish. Of course, there are many ways to human flourishing. It has something to do with (1) happiness and life satisfaction, (2)physical and mental wellbeing, (3) life that has meaning and purpose, (4) individual and community character and virtues and (5) positive social relationships. To thrive and flourish, we should not forget to focus on what we want more of in the region, and not only on what we want less of. So much thinking, resources and money are committed to trying to solve what's going wrong in the Arctic. What might happen if we spent more time, energy and imagination focusing more on what's right, how to amplify this and on having conversations about what we care about most?

Features of the old, dominant and established stories are those that speak about separation, mastery over nature, individual consumerism, colonization, subjugation, scarcity, struggle and ecological destruction. The challenge is how we can change the story to one which features such things as harmony with nature, collective co-creation, abundance and ecological balance (Hendersson & Wamsler, 2020). If we wish to change the storyline, we need to change the questions we ask. Change these and we have a chance of changing the conversation. In turn, this gives us the opportunity to change the action. This question-conversation-action sequence underscores a fundamental idea about change in the Arctic. If you want to change behaviour related to an Arctic issue, we need to begin by changing the ways we talk about it. We need to change the conversation!

So what do the stories in this book tell us? Certainly that change is a form of action and not all action brings about improvement. There are, of course, many kinds of action. As an editorial team, we have sensed that the stories in this book may incentivize readers to think further about five kinds of Arctic-related

DOI: 10.4324/9781003118633-14

What can we create together? 233

action (or more specifically *inter*-actions) going forward. We suggest these might be *inter*-actions to do with:

Belonging – Through our association with places and spaces where we feel safe, among friends and connected to our roots. It's understanding that these things are intimately linked with identity and that they feed into each other, inter-penetrating and overlapping. Randall (2001) reminds us that to be a person is to be a story. *"The story of my life does not exist apart from our identity, as something we just happen to possess. It is our identity, the basis of our being in the world"* (p 57).

Bolstering – Through the development of sustainably literate local–global citizens who collectively use this literacy to build a better Arctic history.

Buffering – Against those people and processes that turn hopefulness into hopelessness through the development of collective people-planet resilience. *"Without the ability to be anticipatory and see how the future might unfold from the present, it is difficult to hold onto hope"* (McArthur-Blair & Cocknell, 2018, p. 31).

Bridging – Across traditional geo-political and socio-economic boundaries as both local and global issues become increasingly inseparable due to a whirlwind of volatility, uncertainty, ambiguity and general chaos caused by the COVID-19 pandemic. Greater complexity is one driver behind the need for bridging *inter*-actions, as well as the impact of globalization, with the whole world more connected, inter-dependent and competitive. Bridging *inter*-actions are compromised when people are locked into mindsets, traditions and positions which make the consideration of possibility a worthwhile activity. These people can have tendencies to discard possibilities out of hand, and/or vilify others in order to sustain and universalize their own preferences for a particular way of understanding human lives (Atkinson et al., 2003). This is what Bourdieu (1998) called *symbolic violence*. It involves convincing some groups that what matters to them is inferior, less worthy and even irrelevant and therefore they are also inferior (Smith & Sparkes, 2006).

Building – Appreciations that the processes that safeguard the lives and livelihoods of everyone, everywhere in the Arctic matter, and that feeling that one matters is a basic human right.

If we wish to inhabit a region where human co-operation and creative resourcefulness are top of everyone's "to do" list, then we need to focus on these things and prioritize them. So, another key generative question emerges which is, *what do we want the region to look like tomorrow and how can we best create it?* This is enormously complicated as it's not just about the whats and the hows, but also the values that guide them. By whom, for whom and what for are part of this action agenda. What may be appropriate actions now, may be very different for the future we are hoping to create. The expectations of what might "help" could be very different as we determine how to live and work together, facing previously little understood and even unknown challenges, moving "frontiers'" and wicked problems caused by inter-twined, cross-cultural, bio-physical, technical, social and economic changes in the region.

But there is also another element to bear in mind, one that complements this "to do" list and that is the "to be" list! We suggest this is both a personal and community issue. *Who is it we wish to be in the Arctic region?* In a subtle but significant

234 *Tony Ghaye, Rita Sørly, and Bård Kårtveit*

way this "to be" issue shifts our thinking and attention from stories "about" the Arctic to those that speak "from" it. It shifts our attention from a preoccupation with being story analysts to the role and significance of storytellers. We suggest the challenge for all Arctic communities and those "interested parties" from outside the Arctic Circle, is not only about having a vision, or even a dream, (important though these are) of what they wish the region to become. The real challenge is to discover enabling and empowering ways to engage with all Arctic citizens that can bring this new possibility into being. In this way, we constantly remind ourselves that we need not see the Arctic as a problem to be solved, but a possibility to be lived into. Of course, for some, to choose possibility, means they may have to confront cynicism. If we find ourselves in a local or global community of problems to be solved, those who best articulate the problems and who can come up with the "best" solutions, tend to dominate the conversations and therefore the developing storyline. So, to create a new and better Arctic story, we first need to come to terms with the current one!

This possibility to be lived into is more than just a collection of individual longings, desires and wishes. It can be thought of as a "communal local-with-global" possibility which gets its power to act from the question, *what can we create together?* This possibility, *"emerges from the social space we create when we are together. It is shaped by the nature of the culture within which we operate but is not controlled by it......it lies at the intersection of possibility and accountability. Possibility without accountability results in wishful thinking. Accountability without possibility creates despair, for even if we know we are creating the world we exist in, we cannot imagine it being any different from the past that got us here"* (Block, 2008, p. 71). What would it take for us to let go of the tight grip some have over the notion of local and global communities of problems and re-see them as communities of possibility?

And in conclusion we ask, with regard to change and sustainability in the region, *what might usefully be regarded as the Arctic's future positive north star?* One answer to this is to take notice of what's right, good and just, not only what's wrong, bad and unjust. Another answer is that to put a flourishing Arctic future first, we must try to put our differences aside. This of course is not an easy thing to ask of people. It begins by appreciating not what stands between us, but what stands before us.

References

Atkinson et al. (2003). *Key themes in qualitative research. Continuities and Changes*. Oxford: AltaMira Press

Block, P. (2008). *Community: The structure of belonging*. San Francisco, CA: Berrett-Koehler.

Bourdieu, P., (1998). *Practical reason*. Palo Alto, CA: Stanford University Press

Hendersson, H., & Wamsler, C. (2020). New stories for a more conscious, sustainable society: Claiming authorship of the climate story. *Climatic Change*, 158, 345–359.

McArthur-Blair, J., & Cocknell, J. (2018). *Building resilience with appreciative inquiry*. Oakland, CA: Berret-Koehler.

Smith, B., & Sparkes, A. (2006). Narrative inquiry in psychology: Exploring the tensions within. *Qualitative Research in Psychology*, 3(3), 169–192.

Index

Note: Page numbers in *italics* indicate figures and **bold** indicate tables in the text.

12 dynamic scenarios (12S) 97–98
14-item Emotional Empowerment Scale (EES14) 97
Aarsæther, N. 12
administrators 184–185
Ådnanes, M. 124
Agreement (2018) 25–26
agriculture 195; in Alaska 195–196; arid areas 167; concomitant development of 194; greenhouse gases 202, 211; importance of 194; income of local communities 178; of Norway 194, 202; outpost 195; in pre-industrial era 194; small-scale 197; urban 194; *see also* fresh vegetables
Ahkwesásne 91
Ahmed, A. 76, 112, 114–115
Alaska 195–197; agriculture in 195–196; Calypso Farm 13; fresh vegetables 195–199; quest 195–197, 198–200
Alta Dam 164–165, 170
analysis: encroachment 46; institutional 181–183; interviews and text 221; participatory research project 93–94; structural narrative 111–124; thematic **95**
Andrews, M. 65, 158
apocalyptic narratives 20
approach: capability 124; case study 179–180; empowerment 89; life story 114
Aquila Capital 161
Arctic *145*; amplification 21; 'braided,' river 6; changes in 3; climate paradox 11; environmental challenges 9; extractive paradox 11; flourishing 36–37; identity, space and places in 5; industrial extraction of resources 11; international industries in 11; local communities in

11; militarization of 32; as a region of myths and resources 10; revitalization and decolonization of 57–69; as a rich region 10; sustainability scholarship in 34; of sustainable development 32
Arctic 5 25
Arctic art 65–66
Arctic Circle 19, 22, 23
"Arctic Greens" 197
Arctic LNG 2 22
Arctic municipalities 178–192; case study approach 179–180; climate policies 180–181; fighting plastics pollution 188–190; identifying actor groups 184–186; institutional analysis 181–183; Lyngen 186–188; place development for compact living 186–188; Skjervøy 188–190
Arctic Ocean 26, 58
Arctic peoples: cares 18; challenges 18; introduction 16–18
Årst, W. 12, 111–122
art *see specific art*
art-based action research (ABAR) 63–65, 66
art-based creative tourism 67
"Arviat Goes Green" 206–208
attachment theory 18
autoethnography 143; *see also* collective autoethnography

backfire effect 29
Bakhtin, M. M. 146
Baldacchino, G. 66
Bardalen, A. 214
Barrett, F. J. 17
Barry, J. 52

236   *Index*

Berkman, P. A. 25
Bongo, B. A. 75
Booker, C. 114–115, 118
Bowlby, J. 18
brave spaces 29–30
Britvina, S. 12, 149–151
Brown, K. 12
Bushe, G. 4
businesses 185–186

Calypso Farm, Alaska 13, 197–199, *198*
Canada 12, 25, 32, 205–206
Canadian Institutes of Health Research (CIHR) 106
capability approach 124
Cardona, L. G. 12
care 75
CareBongo, B. A. 75
Carvill, A. 32
Caxaj, C. S. 77, 80, 84
Center for Epidemiological Studies-Depression (CES-D-20) 94
Central Arctic Ocean (CAO) 25–26
Central Arctic Ocean Fisheries Agreement 26
Chambers, R. 8
Chapple, K. 226
Chen, A. 206
Christianity 59, 62
climate change 3, 9, 11, 20, 22, 29–30, 36, 41, 44, 51, 221–222; affects Arctic communities 213; Arctic environmental challenges 9; biophysical collapse due to 20; flourishing Arctic 36; fresh vegetables 210–213; ice layer 22; mitigation 11, 157, 160, 163, 165–166, 170; negative effects of 213; potential benefits of 207; potential impacts of 211, 213; repercussions of 211; scientific reports 126; secondary impacts of 44; sustainability and 210–213; unseasonal and unusual 136
climate goal (2030) of Norway 11
Climate Law 180
climate paradox 11
climate policies 180–181
Cockell, J. 122
collaborative ethnography 146
collective autoethnography 144
collective communication 147
colonial expansion 42
colonialism 41; *see also* green colonialism
colonization 43–44
commodify, human tendency 27

community: art 65; based art education 67; leadership 186; *see also* specific communities
conflicts 20, 21–22, 158
Constitutional Amendment 45
conversations-that-matter: about sustainability issues 25; characteristics of 16–37; role of doubt in sustainability 26–28; *see also* sustainability conversations
Coombe, D. 18
Cooperrider, D. L. 17, 37
COVID-19 36, 146–152; COVID dissident 150; hotspots 148; life experiences during 152; as new social phenomenon 155; from Northern Norwegian small town 148–149; professional and private silver lining during isolation 153; protective measures 153; second wave of 149–150; striving for normalcy 151–152
culturally significant symbols 96
cultural safety 90–91, 97, 103–104

Dandeneau, S. 104
Daniels, J. 66
Dasgupta Review 19–20
Davey, T. 83
Davvi Wind Farm 158–159, *162*, 162–163, 173–174
decolonization 45–46
deficit-based (problem) questions 32
Denmark/Greenland 25
Denmark–Norway border 43
Denning, S. 1
development: of agriculture 194; Arctic change 8; for compact living 186–188; fresh vegetables 194–195; quest 194–195; regional 220–221; sustainability 8; sustainable 5, 20, 32
dialogue 143–144
dialogue trap 166
dilemmas 20, 21–22, 74, 88, 190, 228
disturbances 46–51
dominant narratives 72–73, 79–83
doubt 26–28, *28*
doubting narratives 28
drunken forests 32

economic transformations 19, 30
Einstein, A. 17
empowerment 89
encompasses 157
encroachments 41, 44, 46–51, 141, 171, 174
English 90, 91

environmental destruction 170
environmental impact assessment (EIA) 163
environmental justice 165–166
Eolus Vind 161
Equinor (oil company) 11, 221, 223, 227
Eriksen, A. M. A. 82
Eriksen, K. G. 81
ES&G sustainability 6
essential themes and implications 121–123; importance of working with user's experience 122; potential for growth of resilience 122–123; from safe to brave spaces 123; storied lives 122
ethnography 64, 143–144, 146, 154; *see also* traditional ethnography
extractive paradox 11

Fairclough, N. 219
Family Well Being Program (FWBP) 97
farming *see* fresh vegetables
Featherstone, B. 114
Fellman, J. 58
Fennoscandia 41–44
Ferrari, B. 17
Finland 42
Finnish settlers 59
Finnmark Act 45
First Nations culture, Canada 32
fish farming 188–190
Fivush, R. 72
flexibility 41–53; colonization and control 43–44; decolonization 45–46; encroachments 44; land-use, encroachments and disturbances 46–51; modernization 44; overview 41–42; personal engagement with reindeer husbandry 46; Sámi Reindeer Husbandry (SRH) 42–43
flourishing Arctic 36–37
Fonds de recherche en santé du Québec (FRSQ) 106
food insecurity 205–206
foreign direct investments (FDI) 224
Forest Sámi 58–59
Free, Prior and Informed Consent (FPIC) 166
freezing 27
fresh vegetables: Alaska 195–199; benefits of growing food 204; bright outlook 205; Calypso Farm 197–199, 198; climate change 210–213; common preconceptions 200; community-driven 199–200; development and challenges 194–195;

food insecurity 205–206; great potential 201–202; health as catalyst 207–208; home gardening 200; indigenous well-being 206–207; northernmost greenhouse 202–203; polar permaculture 203–204; quest for 193–214; small-scale farming 200; sustainability 210–213; sustainable knowledge 209–210; unexpected difficulties 204
Friedrich, D. 13
future 24–26

gardening *see* fresh vegetables
Gazprom 22
Generation Z 18
generativity 4–5
Georgeson, C. C. 195
geostationary orbit 30
Gerlach, S. C. 195–197, 199
Ghaye, T. 12–13, 35, 113
Gielas: cause–impact–effect chains in **49**; MySheep GPS plot **50**; natural infrastructure of collecting and migration zones 48; summer to winter 49
globalization 19, 30
global–local interdependence 19–21
Goldsworthy, S. 18
good allies 172
Grant, A. 7
grassroots 7
green colonialism 44, 157–174; conflicting notions of sustainability 172–174; Davvi Wind Farm 162–163; environmental destruction 170; environmental injustice 165–166; holy places desecration 168–170; indigenous livelihoods destruction 167–168; Indigenous rights 166–167; informed consent 166–167; as a mobilizing narrative 170–172; overview 157–158; political narratives 158–159, 164–165; trappings of "dialogue" 166–167; value of good allies 172; wind power in Norway 159–161
green lobbies 185
green transition 13
Grenselandet AS 163, 173
Gross Regional Product (GRP) 194
Growth and Empowerment Measure (GEM) 94, 97–98, 101
Gulf of Ob 22

Haida 195
Hall, N. 83

238   Index

Haramsøy 160
Hassler, S. 81
healing pathway 98
health as catalyst 207–208
Hendersson, H. 9
Hoag, H. 214
holy places desecration 168–170
home gardening 200
Hudson Bay 90
Hudson Strait 90
Huhmarniemi, M. 12, 66, 67

Indigenous communities 10; *see also*
    non-indigenous communities
indigenous knowledge (IK) 65, 127
indigenous livelihoods destruction
    167–168
Indigenous peoples 89; Arctic 26; Arctic
    environmental challenges 9; in Canada
    104; health services for 103; knowledge
    and cultures 83; land and water as
    52; natural resources as 45; in North
    America 90; relations of 59; research
    on 89; residential school system for
    91; rights 74; in Russia 126–142;
    see also Sámi communities; specific
    communities
Indigenous racism 83
indigenous rights 166–167
indigenous well-being 206–207
institutional analysis 181–183
International Covenant on Civil and
    Political Rights (ICCPR) 45
International Labour Organization's (ILO)
    166
Inuit advisory group (IAG) 93, 96, 98, 101
Inuit communities 90, **99–100**
Inuktitut 90
"isolation" 150
Ivanova, L. 12

Jackson, S. 195
Jokela, T. 12, 57, 58, 60, 62–66

Kahnawà:ke 91
Kaiser, N. 81
Kanehsatá:ke 91
Kanien'kehá:ka 90–91, **99–100**
Kanien'kehá:ka advisory group (KAG) 92,
    96–97, 102–103
Kanien'kehá:ka Faith Keepers 93
Kanien'kehá:ka GEM (K-GEM) 98, 101
Kaplan, T. J. 182

Karl, Duke (Karl IX) 58–59
Kårtveit, B. 12–13, 151–152
Kemi-Lapland church 58
Keskitalo, A. 52, 164
Kessler Psychological Distress Scale 94, 97
Kidder, R. M. 33
Kikiktagruk Inupiat Corp. (KIC) 197
King, T. 81
Kirkkokuusikko 57, 58, 60, 62, 65–66
Kirmayer, L. 1, 104, 113
Kohlrieser, G. 18
Kola Peninsula 41, 42
Kroll, C. 226
Krusz, E. 83
Kuujjuaq 90
Kvaløya 43

Laclau, E. 219
Lacy, S. 65
Lamalice, A. 206
land-use 46–51
Langton, M. 83
languages 16–17; defined 146; *see also*
    English; *specific languages*
Lapp Codicil 43
Larissa, R. 146–148
leaders of local environmental organiza-
    tions 184
Leinaweaver, J. 9
Lester, T. W. 226
Lewis, P. J. 83
Linnaranta, O. 12
Lippard, L. 65
listening principles 17
lobbying 7
local business leaders 184
Longyear river, Svalbard 6
Loring, P. A. 195–197, 199
Ludmila, I. 152
Lyngen 179, 183, 185–188
Lyngenløftet 187–188, 190, 191

Malkki, L. H. 154
Marsh, T. 104
Mathisen, V. 12
mattering 22–23, 24
McArthur-Blair, J. 122
McComber, M., 12
mental health issues 32
mental health research: in Arctic
    Indigenous context 72–84; *see also* Sámi
    communities
Messenius, J. 58

Index 239

Minde, H. 74
Mittenzwei, K. 202
mobilizing 7
modernization 44
Mondros, J. 7
Montero, S. 226
Montreal Urban Aboriginal Health
Committee (MUAHC) 90
moral imagination 19
Morris, K. 114
Mouffe, C. 219
municipal administrative officers 184
municipal political leaders 184
Myerhoff, B. 112

Napoleonic Wars 43
narratives 1; apocalyptic 20; dominant
72–73; doubting 28; institutional
analysis and 181–183; oral 88, 102;
political 158–159, 164–165; practice in
an Indigenous mental health context
83–84; progress 20; as social justice
83–84; tradition 59; urge 112
Natcher, D. 206
National Expectations 46
nationalism 43
natural gas 11
Nature and Youth 172
Nature Conservation Association 185
Naumov, A. 194
Nenets 126–128; dog 127–128; fish 136;
"laika" 127; lands 127; language 131;
Nenets autonomous area 127; nomadic
herders 127–129; territories 130; Yamal-
Nenets autonomous area 127; year of
129–138
Nenets lands 127
neo-colonialism 41
Neumann, I. B. 218–219
Ngere/Ngere 131
Niilas: assimilation policy 81; dominant
narratives 79; Norwegianization 81;
Norwegian researcher narrative 82–83;
oppression narrative 81; reindeer herder
narrative 81–82; story of reindeer year
77–78; Western school of narrative 80
Nilsen, T. 13, 223
Niva, P. 57
non-indigenous communities 10
"non-working days" 150
Nordic Arctic region 218–229; contested
discourses of 225–227; discourses in
social sciences 219; innovation in

dispersed regions 220–221; interviews
and text analysis 221; North as a late
bloomer 223–224; possibilities 224–225;
regional innovation processes 218–219;
theories of regional development
220–221; values and growth dilemmas
228; vulnerable North 221–223
Nordic municipal system 181
Normann, A. K. 153
Normann, S. 12
northern knowledge systems 65
northernmost greenhouse 202–203
Norway 11, 25, 41–42, 45, 77, 157; agriculture of 194; hydro power 157; low-emissions local communities in 179; national
wealth relies 157; nationwide mobili-
zation 157; oil reserves 157; reindeer
husbandry employs 167; wind power
plants in 157, 159–161
Norwegian Center for Research Data 75
Norwegianization 74, 81
Norwegian Research Council 179
Norwegian researcher narrative 82–83
Norwegian- Russian social work research
project 144–145
Norwegian society 72
Norwegian Swedish reindeer pasture
convention 43
Norwegian Water Resource and Energy
Directorate (NVE) 160, 163
noun narrario 111
Novatek 22
Novogratz, J. 19
Nunavik (Québec) 90
Nussir AS 173
Nygaard, V. 12, 148–149
Nymo, R. 75

"observation" 150
OCAP principles (Ownership, Control,
Access and Possession) 93
open-mindedness 28–29
oral narrative 88, 102
Ose, S. 124
outpost agriculture 195
Øyfjellet 161, 171

Päiviö 59–60, 62
paradoxes see climate paradox; extractive
paradox
Parent-Racine, E. 12
Paris 2015 agreement 178, 180, 222
Parish of Kittilä and Metsähallitus 57

240   Index

Parnasimautik Consultation Report 90
participatory and appreciative action-based research (PAAR) 35
participatory research project 88–106; analysis 93–94; collaborative methods 92; empowerment approach 89; ethical considerations 93; fieldwork 92–93; findings 94–97; focus on narrative 92; Indigenous empowering frameworks 97–103; Inuit 90; Kanien'kehá:ka 90–91; overview 88–89; participatory methodology 92; qualitative methodology 92; thematic analysis **95**
Patient Health Questionnaire (PHQ-9) 94
peer recovery services 112–113
personal engagement with reindeer husbandry 46
place-conscious art education 67–68
place-specific public art 65–66
Plan and Building Act (PBA) 45, 180
planning strategy 186
plasticity 41
plastics pollution 188–190
plundering 20
polar permaculture 203–204
political leaders 185
political narratives 158–159, 164–165
political transformations 19, 30
politicians 8
poly ethnography 144, 145–146
Porter, L. 52
positivity 29
practicing active reflexivity 154–155
preachers 8
precautionary principle 25
prediction 25
principle of accompaniment 34
progress narratives 20
prosecutors 8
psycho-cultural transformation 9
public art 65
Putin, V. 150

"quarantine" 150
Québec 88, 90, 92–93, 106, 205
quest: Alaska 195–197, 198–200; arrival and a new beginning 118–120; the call 115–116; challenges 194–195; common preconceptions 200; constriction 117; control 118; development 194–195; final ordeals 120; for fresh vegetables 193–214; the goal 120–121; guilt and despair 118; home gardening 200; the journey 116; overcoming monsters 116–117; release 117; small-scale farming 200
questions 30–33

Rásttigáisá 162, 168, 169, *169*
Ravna, Z. V. 12
reflectiveness 34
reindeer herder narrative 81–82
Reindeer Husbandry Act 45
reindeer pasture districts (RPD) 42, 44, 46, 51
remote work 147
Réseau universitaire intégré de santé et services sociaux (RUISSS) 106
Resilience and Empowerment Tool (RET) 98, 101
respect 33
responsibility virus 24–25
revitalization and decolonization through art 66–67
Riabova, L. 12
Richardson, L. 144
Riessman, C. K. 114
Ringvassøya 43
Riseth, J. Å. 12
Rogers, M. 76, 114–115
Rose, G. 219
Rukeyser, M. 1
Russia 25

Salander Renberg, E. 81
Saltdal Museum 62
Sámi communities 10, 41, 43–45, 58–60, 72, 73–74; in Arctic Norway 158; context of 75–76; current situation 74–75; data and methods 75; decolonization process 74; environmental justice 165–166; harsh assimilation policy 74; health services for 74–75; language of 73–74; linguistic and cultural oppression 74; mental health 74–75; narrative of green colonialism 164; Norwegianization 74; participants 76; population 73; storytelling 77
Sámi Norwegian National Advisory Unit on Mental Health and Substance Use (SANKS) 76, 77, 82
Sámi Parliament 45
Sámi Reindeer Herders Association (NRL) 45
Sámi Reindeer Husbandry (SRH) 41, 42–43, 44, 51–52
Sámi Rights Commission (SRC) 45

Index 241

Samoyed Laika 128–129
Sanches, A. M. 221
Sápmi 42–43, 44, 82, 159
Scale of Protective Factors (SPF-24) 94
Schefferus, J. 62
secure base, defined 18–19
Seikkula, J. 143–144
seizing 27
Self Compassion Scale-Short Form (SCS-SF) 94
"self-isolation" 150
semi-nomadic pastoralism 167
Senja 43
separating art 66
Serotetto, Eiko 22
sharing knowledge 154–155
sharing stories 154–155
Skjervøy 179, 183, 185–186, 188–190, 189
Skookum Jim (Keish) 33–34
Skylark 164
small-scale farming 200
socio-psychological mind 17
Somby, M. L. 35, 113, 119
Sørly, R. 12–13, 35, 153–154
Srivastva, S. 17
state systems and services nature 126–142; changes 138–141; methodology with ethnographic research 126–127; Nenets 127–138
stereotypical sustainability 10
stories: about 72; in a culture 88; of empowerment, resilience and healing 88–106; importance of 1; local Indigenous empowering frameworks by 97–103; making 1; mutual understanding from 9; telling 1
stories transmitted through art 57–69; art-based action research (ABAR) 63–65; historical knowledge 58–59; memorial 62–63; northern knowledge, via place-specific public art 65–66; place-conscious art education, resources 67–68; revitalization and decolonization 66–67; story of a Church in a forest 57–58; visually crafted language 60–62, 61; voices 59–60
Story of Kirkkokuusikko, The 12, 59–60, 62, 63, 64–68
storytelling 77, 88, 112
strengthening 19
structural narrative analysis 111–124; essential themes and implications 121–123; life story approach to 114; overview

111–112; peer recovery services 112–113; Wibecke 113, 113, 114–115
subjective wellbeing (SWB) 34–35
Sullivan, G. 5
sustainability: change agent 10; characterization of stories 10; conversations-that-matter about 25–28; ES&G 6; as flourishing 17, 33, 37; fresh vegetables 210–213; global–local interdependence 19–21; governing values of 27; growing realization within 10; as human-centred concept and process 20; issues 9, 17, 19; as political concept 5; popularization of 5; in public policy 157; relationships with mattering 24; role of doubt in 26–28; scholarship 34; social and cultural aspects of 67; stereotypical 10; stories 10; as surviving 17, 37
sustainability conversations 32; characterization 33; human tendency to commodify 27; learn from failure 25; mattering 23; open-mindedness 28–29; optimistic comments 29; places 30; principle of accompaniment 34; reflectiveness in 34; role of doubt in 26–28, 28; spaces 31
sustainable Arctic region 5
sustainable development 5, 20
Sustainable Development Goals, United Nation 20, 21
sustainable future 5
sustainable knowledge 209–210
Svalbard, Norway 202–203
Sweden 42, 77, 82, 158
Sweden–Finland border 43
"Syra" 129

Tana River 168–169, 171
Teräs, J. 13
Tlingit peoples 195
toxic positivity 29
traditional ethnography 146
TRANSFORM project 179–180, 181, 184
Troms County 45–46
Tromso University 126
tundra see Nenets; state systems and services nature
Tundra Nenets 127; see also Nenets
Tuominen, M. 57–58
Tysvær 160

Ungava Bay 90
UN Indigenous Declaration 74
United States 25

242 *Index*

University of Lapland 64
UN-report Our Common Future (1987) 5

Vidmar, B. 203–204
Vodden, R. 66
VUCA (volatile, uncertain, chaotic and ambiguous) 5
vulnerable North 221–223
Vuonjalrášša 168–169
Vylegzhanin, A. N. 25

Wamsler, C. 9
warrior cries 23–24
Western academy 80
Western school of narrative 80
Westskog, H. 12

White, S. 114
Wigginton, B. 83
Willsrud, A. 201, *201*
Wilson, S. 7
wind power 11, 12, 157–174, 222, 228; plants in Norway 157, 159–161
World Wildlife Foundation (WWF) 172
Wright, S. 80

Yamal LNG 22
Young, O. R. 25

Zimmer, T. 198
Zipes, J. 80
Zoom meetings 147, *147*

Printed in the United States
by Baker & Taylor Publisher Services